LINGVA
LATINA

A Companion to
Familia Romana

Second Edition

Based on Hans Ørberg's *Latine Disco*, with Vocabulary and Grammar

LINGVA LATINA

A Companion to
Familia Romana

Second Edition

based on Hans Ørberg's *Latine Disco*, with Vocabulary and Grammar

Jeanne Marie Neumann

Davidson College

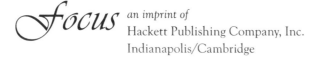

an imprint of
Hackett Publishing Company, Inc.
Indianapolis/Cambridge

Dedication

Jon et Conor, filiis iucundissimis medullitusque amatis.

A Focus book

Focus an imprint of
Hackett Publishing Company

Copyright © 2016 by Hackett Publishing Company, Inc.

All rights reserved
Printed in the United States of America

21 20 19 18   2 3 4 5 6 7

For further information, please address
        Hackett Publishing Company, Inc.
        P.O. Box 44937
        Indianapolis, Indiana 46244-0937
        www.hackettpublishing.com

Cover design by Brian Rak
Interior design by Elizabeth L. Wilson
Composition by Integrated Composition Systems, Inc.

Library of Congress Cataloging-in-Publication Data

Names: Neumann, Jeanne Marie, author. | Oerberg, Hans H. (Hans Henning),
    1920–2010. Latine disco. | Oerberg, Hans H. (Hans Henning), 1920–2010.
    Lingua Latina per se illustrata. Pars I, Familia Romana.
Title: Lingua latina : a companion to Familia romana : based on Hans Oerberg's
Latine disco, with vocabulary and grammar / Jeanne Marie Neumann.
Description: Second edition. | Indianapolis ; Cambridge : Hackett Publishing
Company, Inc., 2016. | "A Focus book."
Identifiers: LCCN 2016002499 | ISBN 9781585108091 (pbk.)
Subjects: LCSH: Latin language—Grammar. | Latin language—Textbooks.
Classification: LCC PA2087.5 .N48 2016 | DDC 478.2421—dc23
LC record available at http://lccn.loc.gov/2016002499

The paper used in this publication meets the minimum requirements of American
National Standard for Information Sciences—Permanence of Paper for Printed
Library Materials, ANSI Z39.48–1984.

∞

Contents

Preface   vii
For the Instructor   xi
  Familia Romana: Suggestions for the Classroom   xi
  Lingua Latina *as a Two-Semester Course*   xi
To the Student   xv

   I. Imperium Rōmānum   1
   II. Familia Rōmāna   9
   III. Puer Improbus   18
   IV. Dominus et Servī   27
   V. Vīlla et Hortus   35
   VI. Via Latīna   42
   VII. Puella et Rosa   50
   VIII. Taberna Rōmāna   58
   IX. Pāstor et Ovēs   69
   X. Bēstiae et Hominēs   78
   XI. Corpus Hūmānum   89
   XII. Mīles Rōmānus   96
   XIII. Annus et Mēnsēs   108
   XIV. Novus Diēs   120
   XV. Magister et Discipulī   128
   XVI. Tempestās   138
   XVII. Numerī Difficiles   147
   XVIII. Litterae Latīnae   155
   XIX. Marītus et Uxor   165

XX. Parentēs   175

XXI. Pugna Discipulōrum   183

XXII. Cave Canem   195

XXIII. Epistula Magistrī   206

XXIV. Puer Aegrōtus   217

XXV. Thēseus et Mīnōtaurus   227

XXVI. Daedalus et Icarus   237

XXVII. Rēs Rūsticae   246

XXVIII. Pericula Maris   258

XXIX. Nāvigāre Necesse Est   268

XXX. Convīvium   279

XXXI. Inter Pōcula   288

XXXII. Classis Rōmāna   296

XXXIII. Exercitus Rōmānus   307

XXXIV. De Arte Poēticā   320

XXXV. Ars Grammatica   330

Grammatica Latina   333
Vocabulary by Chapter   369
Latin–English Vocabulary   383
Grammatical Terms   398
Index   400

Preface

Ørberg's Lingua Latina Per Se Illustrata series, conceived as a completely acquisition-based approach to learning Latin, offers an unparalleled resource for Latin learning, enabling the motivated student to acquire skill *in* reading Latin *by* reading Latin. Lingua Latina guides readers through an expanding world of Latin syntax while they enjoy a delightful story of a Roman family of the early imperial period. The reading mirrors "real" Latin in the way it unfolds the periodic structure and idiomatic features of the language, introducing early critical features: students meet the relative pronoun in Cap. 3, the passive voice in Cap. 6; by the time they get the full verbal paradigm of the present tense in Caps. 15–17, they have mastered the concept and workings of active and passive voice. Length of readings, number of vocabulary words and complexity of sentence structure increase as the chapters build on each other, all in support of a narrative that engages students from middle school through college (and beyond).

Lingua Latina Per Se Illustrata offers a smooth and efficient path to acquisition of the language and immerses the student from the first in a true experience of Latin. Instead of reading discrete, even random, sentences chosen to illustrate the grammatical principles under consideration, Lingua Latina offers considerable practice in both grammar and a rich vocabulary in an engaging context of well-written Latin. The impetus of this book, therefore, arose not from any flaw in Ørberg's method, but rather from the differing needs of students and classrooms.

Different students learn differently; learning environments also differ: *Alii aliis viis Romam perveniunt.* At my own institution, students signing up for Latin commit to a two-term introductory experience, followed by a term of reading ancient texts. Reading *Familia Romana* in a two-semester course in introductory Latin, meeting three times a week for two 13- or 14-week semesters, becomes a Herculean task. Lingua Latina, however, and its results proved too good to abandon. There seems to me no better guide than Lingua Latina for students who want to learn Latin *through Latin*. Students clamored for us to keep the text, but make it suit their needs. We use the *Companion* to strike a balance between a purely inductive method and the study of grammatical rules and paradigms. But it can also serve as an ancillary guide for the natural (inductive) method of language acquisition. Lingua Latina can be used to teach students Latin as early as age eight, yet the story engages adult readers as well. Although introductory language courses at the college level do not always have the same luxury of gradual acquisition, the Ørberg text can be highly effective for university students. This book, therefore, is designed for different audiences: university students, instructors of home-scholars, and independent learners whose learning style appreciates such a guide: it is for all students of Ørberg's Lingua Latina Per Se Illustrata (LLPSI) who want a touchstone to assess their understanding of the text and the language.

Home-schooling parents and instructors of students learning outside of the traditional classroom, especially those with little or no Latin training, can use this book as a companion to Lingua Latina for their own preparation. The instructor will be the best judge of where and when it is a useful guide. For the most part, students should gradually learn the whole of Latin grammar by working out grammatical rules from their own observation as they begin to read actual Latin in the text, while their instructors can feel more confident in their grasp of the material and can use the added examples from *Familia Romana* to review and reinforce concepts or answer questions their charges present. The goal is to confirm the Latin and the structures that are learned in the inductive method, facilitating the process of language acquisition.

As is clear from the very useful listserve for LLPSI (https://groups.google .com/forum/#!forum/llpsi), instructors at elementary and high schools lead their charges through the text at the pace appropriate to their students and the learning environment. Explanations of morphology and syntax appear according to their introduction in the course of the chapter: Section I, II, or III, making the *Companion* practical regardless of the pace of an individual course.

How does this book fit into the Lingua Latina series? What does it replace? This book replaces the *Latine Disco*, the *Grammatica Latina*, and the *Latin–English Vocabulary*. It does not replace the *Exercitia*.

What are the primary features of this book? The book provides a running **grammatical commentary** on the narrative of Lingua Latina. It differs from the *Latine Disco* in scope and aim. *Latine Disco* provides clear and concise information that students need in order to acquire an understanding of Latin at their own pace. This book builds from Ørberg's original *Latine Disco*; the presentation and formatting have been altered and more explication and examples are offered. To the degree possible, the **commentary corresponds to the reading sections** within each chapter, enabling students to view just the grammar for each section. Important and challenging structures are illustrated with several **examples** from the story. As the grammatical concepts build, they are collected and reviewed in **periodic *recensiones***, facilitating an overview of the language and enabling students to know where to look for the places in the story where, e.g., they learned about accusative and infinitive construction. Beginning with **Res Grammaticae Novae**, a synopsis, in categories, of the material covered in the chapter, further facilitates an overview. The end of each chapter presents vocabulary divided by parts of speech; a full vocabulary can be found at the back of the book. In addition, **vocabulary review** is enhanced by an appendix listing the vocabulary according to chapter but without meanings; students can quiz themselves on their grasp of vocabulary outside the context of the story. Since Ørberg's own mastery of the language shows through in his ability to write lucid, idiomatic Latin, student attention, where appropriate, is directed to *points of style* that highlight the way the language works syntactically or idiomatically. Finally, this edition includes a grammatical index.

Changes to the Second Edition

In addition to some revisions to the text, this edition includes a section on cultural context tied to the narrative content of the chapter.

Jeanne M. Neumann
Davidson College

Acknowledgments

Editio Princeps:
Amicis qui me librum hunc scribentem adiuverunt maximas gratias et ago et habeo, praecipue Jarrett Welsh, Keyne Cheshire, Megan Drinkwater, Michael Johnson, Kevin Muse, Gina Soter. Discipulis apud Collegium Davidsoniense linguam Latinam discentibus gratias quoque ago, praecipue William E. Begley et India Watkins. Nam illi et menda typographica notaverunt et consilium quo liber melior et clarior fieret praebuerunt.

Editio Altera:
In hac editione paranda multi et collegae et discipuli mihi adiumento erant. Multum Jarret Welsh, Keyne Cheshire, William Begley, India Watkins, Darian Totten debeo. Patrick Owen menda typographica benigne notavit et locos minus perspicuos monstravit.

For the Instructor

Teaching Latin via the method Winston Churchill was subjected to (*My Early Life: 1874–1904*, p. 10–11) is pretty easy. Take this paradigm. Memorize it. Spit it back. Repeat. Teaching via LLPSI offers more of a challenge and infinitely more rewards for the instructor and (more importantly) for the students. The instructor's approach to LLPSI will vary according to the age of the students and, critically, the amount of time that one can devote to the project. At the college level (for the approach at Davidson, see below), the pace is brisk, the course an invigorating challenge. But *Familia Romana* does not have to be digested in a two-term course and taking more time allows the instructor to engage in more activities with the text.

No matter the time frame, the active use of Latin with students lies at the foundation of the successful implementation of LLPSI. Using Latin actively in the classroom can be a challenging experience for those of us who have learned Latin as a passive language. Before guiding others through the text, the instructor can learn a great deal about talking about Latin in Latin by becoming familiar with the Grammatica Latina sections at the end of each chapter and by studying the selections from Dōnātus's *Ars Minor* in the final chapter of *Familia Romana*.

Familia Romana: Suggestions for the Classroom

1. Read Latin aloud.
2. Use questions (in Latin, in English) to determine if students are understanding the text.
3. Encourage students to respond in Latin to questions: *Pensum C.*

Lingua Latina as a Two-Semester Course

What follows is a brief explanation of how we have adapted *Familia Romana* to our introductory sequence at Davidson College. The constraints of two semesters propel the course forward quickly, with usually two class days devoted to each chapter. This pace makes "catch-up" cramming difficult, if not impossible. Therefore, the relative weight of each facet of evaluation reflects the philosophy of the course:

DAILY USE OF A LANGUAGE IS THE ONLY WAY TO MASTERY.

Daily work carries the greatest weight in the course (i.e., quizzes, homework, tests, and class preparation and participation), while the final exam accounts for a much smaller portion of the grade. Students should expect to spend one hour each day working on Latin skills: that means seven hours a week of work outside of class. We encourage students to break up this work into small, frequent encounters with the Latin throughout their day: 20 minutes three times a day is far more effective than an hour once a day.

The pace of the course and presentation of the material both complicate and energize the instructor's presentation. The text can be used as a basis for asking questions in Latin. When students answer in Latin, they strengthen their grasp of the vocabulary and the syntax, and their ability to stay in the target language. Longer, more difficult sentences can be paraphrased in Latin to facilitate understanding or broken down into smaller components. While the bulk of our classes are conducted in English, moving back and forth frequently between the two languages will help the students' Latin get strong enough to read the ever lengthening stories and ever more complex sentences.

There follow two different sets of instructions for a course that aims to read *Familia Romana* in two terms of three meetings a week. These are offered as examples of the approaches of two instructors at Davidson and represent the general guidelines offered to students. The approaches are quite different: the first has the students read the chapter before any instruction, either verbal or from the *Companion*, while the second introduces all major grammatical concepts before the students read the text.

There are many roads to Rome and other ways of using the *Companion* as a pedagogical aid. We offer our experience as examples. The Lingua Latina pages at Hackett Publishing provide a wealth of further materials, including flash cards and audio files. Instructors will find a large circle of support and ideas at the Google Groups (https://groups.google.com/forum/#!forum/llpsi).

One Approach

Assignment for Day One (the first of two class days spent on a given chapter):

- Study the *marginalia* in *Familia Romana* (*marginalia*: the material written in the margins of the Lingua Latina text).
- Read the entire chapter in Latin; each chapter is divided into three sections, marked by Roman numerals in the inside margins of the text. In Cap. II, for example, Section II begins with the words, "*Estne Medus filius Iulii?*" (p. 14). Each new section practices a different grammatical principle.

- Try not to translate each sentence into English but to understand the sentences in Latin (a challenge which grows easier with time). If you find a sentence hard, re-read it. Mark it with a *pencil* check mark in the margin and return to it after reading the whole assignment (and after you have had a break).
- Study the *Grammatica Latina* at the end of each chapter in *Familia Romana*. Pay attention to the phrasing of the grammatical explanations: this section of the book will teach you how to talk about Latin grammar in Latin.
- Only then, after reading the chapter, the marginalia, and the GRAMMATICA LATINA, review the pages in the *Companion*.
- If you cannot grasp the meaning of a vocabulary word from context, look it up in the Latin-English vocabulary at the end of the chapter or the back of this book. Vocabulary words recur frequently. If you need to look up a word more than once, or find the next day you cannot remember what it means, memorize the word by making a flash card. Carry the flash cards around with you and review frequently. (There are also web-based flash card systems you can use.) DO NOT WRITE ENGLISH IN YOUR BOOK! Your eye will go to the familiar language, inhibiting your ability to read the Latin.
- Complete homework as assigned.

After the second day:

- Re-read the entire chapter, paying close attention to the forms and grammatical principles, and making sure you have a firm understanding of both the grammar and meaning of the chapter. At this reading, it should be much easier not to translate in your head from Latin to English.
- Review the marginalia and the vocabulary. In the margins of each chapter of *Familia Romana* is a list of new vocabulary. Make sure you understand those words out of context. If you don't remember, find the word in the text *before* looking it up.
- Complete homework as assigned.
- Look ahead briefly to discover the emphasis of the next chapter.

A Second Approach

Day 1:

- Introduce the chapter (vocabulary and all major grammatical concepts) before students see anything.
- Homework: read *Companion* and *Familia Romana* narrative; study for quiz.

Day 2:

- Quiz on new vocabulary.
- Questions about the reading? (Have them marked by line number with notes.)
- Warm-up with *Pensum A*.
- "Conversational" Latin: Ask questions about the reading and their lives. Have students illustrate a scene or act it out. Have them pantomime verbs. Follow with other activities in Latin.
- Homework: carefully chosen *Exercitia*.

Both approaches are intense, but students enjoy and profit from the course.

To the Student

You will learn far more Latin more quickly, and in a more interesting way, if you first work with the book and the readings and the (very important) marginalia (that is, the words and images in the columns next to the reading), then refer to this book to help you organize what it is you have encountered. By this method, the book helps you confirm what you have already learned.

The value of the marginalia and the images in the *Familia Romana* text cannot be overemphasized! The marginalia mark out new things you will learn, and help you to understand the Latin quickly and visually. The illustrations will be valuable clues to what the Latin itself is saying.

Try *not* to translate into English as you read. Instead, keep images in your mind and work as much as you can in Latin. Only by increasing your stamina for reading and thinking within the Latin language will you gain proficiency in understanding. *Do not write English in your book! Do not write out translations of the text as you read*: make yourself confront the text anew each time you read it. Only then will you become familiar with the language.

A note on translations: You will find that translations accompany only a few of the illustrative sentences in this book. These translations demonstrate how a particular construction works in the English language in order to help you understand how Latin works, not to encourage translation into English. Remember, the goal is Latin!

The more actively you engage, the more you will learn. Quiz yourself by going back into earlier chapters and randomly picking a word. Do you know what that word means without reading it in context? If not, reread the surrounding sentences and see whether context prods your memory. If not, look the word up. Do you recognize its case (if appropriate)? Could you reconstruct the nominative from that case? If the word is a verb, recount to yourself all you know about it (the amount you will know will depend on how far into the course you have proceeded). Try to write short synopses of the reading in Latin. Read out loud. Send a classmate a text or email in Latin! The more you engage different senses, the faster you will learn and the more you will retain.

Before you start

Orthography

Latin was written (orthography) as it sounded. Therefore, the spelling of Latin changed with natural variations of pronunciation that occurred over time and place. So, for example, Cicero would have written *equos* for "the horse," while Caesar Augustus would have written *ecus*; we find this same word in our Latin texts as *equus* because editors of Latin texts generally adopt the spelling of the first century AD, when variations in orthography had leveled out. We still find variation in the treatment of the semi-vowels *u/v* and *i/j*, however (on these semi-vowels, see below under pronunciation).

Latin Pronunciation

Latin was spoken through many countries over many hundreds of years. When you think how much pronunciation varies in different regions of our own country during our own time, the very thought of how to "correctly" pronounce Latin becomes daunting. We actually know quite a bit about how upper-class educated Romans living in Rome during a relatively short time span spoke Latin because Roman writers themselves have given us various hints. This pronunciation is called the "Restored Pronunciation." Even though the Restored Pronunciation may be the way Horace recited his *Odes*, for example, or Vergil his *Aeneid*, we should not feel constrained to try to duplicate it. In our own language, English, we don't feel we need to research how Shakespeare might have spoken in order to read *Hamlet*. Elizabethan actors might be amazed at our renditions, but we aren't talking to them. Our goal is to be faithful to the principles of the language and to be understood by others. But—you may object that we can't really appreciate the beauty of a Latin poem unless we hear it as the Romans did. If that were true, we would need more than sounds to appreciate Latin literature—we would need the full spectrum of cultural values that comprise aesthetic appreciation.

The other traditional method of pronunciation is called the "Ecclesiastical Pronunciation." If you listen to Latin liturgical hymns, you will hear the subtle differences: *caelum* (sky, heaven), for example, is pronounced "kai-lum" in the restored pronunciation but "che-lum" in the ecclesiastical pronunciation. Ecclesiastical Latin retains the mellifluous beauty of Italian. An audio recording of Caps. I–XXXI of *Familia Romana* is available from Hackett Publishing Co. in the Restored Pronunciation; an audio recording of the whole of *Familia Romana* is available from the same publisher in Ecclesiastical Pronunciation.

So, how to pronounce Latin? If we are faithful to a few principles, we can read with confidence and feeling, and understand and be understood by others. In order to utter Latin well, we must understand the quantities of vowels and syllables, know where to put the accent and how to enunciate. Thus, while the guide below will suggest pronunciations that mirror some of the things we know about ancient pronunciation, if you pay attention to quantities, accent, and enunciation, you will be understood whether you pronounce *c* hard (i.e., like "k") as the Romans did or soft, as Ecclesiastical Latin.

But first, let's look at the alphabet.

The Alphabet

The Latin alphabet can be most simply divided into vowels and consonants. That broad division has subdivisions as well. The Latin alphabet has twenty-three letters; it lacks the English *w*; *y* and *z* were Greek imports, as were *ch, ph, th.*

Vowels

- Latin has both single vowels and diphthongs (two vowels that form one sound).
- Vowels can be either "long" or "short." A long vowel is pronounced for twice the length of time. Compare the "a" in "father" and the first vowel in "aha." We hold the "a" sound twice as long in "father." Long vowels in this book are marked by a bar over the vowel called a "macron" (i.e., *ā, ē, ī, ō, ū*). The Latin vowels are:
- a
  - ▷ short: *a* as the first *a* in "aha": *amat*
  - ▷ long: *ā* as in "father": *ālā, pānis*
- e
  - ▷ short: *e* as in "let": *et, bene*
  - ▷ long: *ē* as in "prey": *mē*
- i
  - ▷ short: *i* as in "fit": *in, nimis*[1]
  - ▷ long: *ī* as *ee* in "feet": *hīc, līberī*
- o
  - ▷ short: *o* as in "hot": *post, modo*
  - ▷ long: *ō* as in bone: *pōnō*
- u
  - ▷ short: *u* as in "full": *num, sumus*
  - ▷ long: *ū* as in "fool": *ūna, tū*
- y (represents the Greek *upsilon*)
  - ▷ short: y as French u in "lune": Syria
  - ▷ long: ȳ as French u in "pur": Lȳdia

---

1. The sound as in *fit, hit* does not occur in the modern Romance languages, suggesting that short *i* had more of an *ee* sound, but held for a shorter time.

- Diphthongs, being two vowels together, take twice as long to pronounce as single short vowels and so are considered long. They are:
- *ae* as *ie* in "die": *Graecia, laetus, paene*
- *oe* as *oi* in "boil": *foedus, poena*
- *au* as *ou* in "loud": *aut, nauta*
- *eu* as *e+u* combined into one syllable (ĕhoo): *Eurōpa, heu, heus, neu, seu.* (But the endings *-us, -um, -unt* form separate syllables after *e*: *de|us, me|us, e|um, e|unt, aure|us*.)
- *ui* in *cui, huic, cuius, huius* as *u+i* combined into one syllable

Semi-vowels (glides)

Latin has two letters called "glides," which represent either a vowel or a consonant sound depending on the letters around them. These letters are represented in our book as *i* and *u/v*:

- *i*: The father of our family is Iulius, the same as the English Julius. The "j" and "i" of his name represent the same letter in Latin, which was always represented by *i* by the Romans. <u>Sound</u>: Before a consonant, *i* represents the vowel sound "i" and before a vowel, the consonant sound "y."
- *u/v*: The word for slave shows you the other glide in Latin. The word for slave is *servus*, in the plural, it's *servi*. The *v* and *u* are actually the same letter and work the same way as "i" and "j." In some Latin texts, you will find *servus* written as *seruus*; this text distinguishes *u* and *v*. <u>Sound</u>: Before a consonant, *u* represents the vowel sound "u" and before a vowel, the consonant sound "w."

Consonants

Most consonants are the same as, or very similar to, English.

- *b* as in English: *bibit, ab*
- *bs* and *bt* as *ps* and *pt*: *absunt, obtulit, urbs*
- *c* is always hard as in "cat" (= k, without aspiration): *canis, centum, circus, nec*
  - ▷ *ch*, as *k* with aspiration: *pulcher*
- *d* as in English: *dē, dedit, ad*
- *f* as in English: *forum, flūmen*
- *g* as in English: "get" (never as in "gem"): *gallus, gemma, agit*
- *gn* as *ngn* in "willingness": *signum, pugna, magnus*
- *h* as in English (tending to disappear): *hīc, homō, nihil*
- *l* as in English: *lūna, gladius, male, vel*

- *m* as in English: *mē, domus, tam*
  - ▷ In the unstressed endings *-am, -em, -um*, it tended to disappear.
- *n* as in English: *nōn, ūnus*; before *c, g, q* as in "i**n**k": *incola, longus, quīnque*
- Before *s*, it tended to disappear: *mēnsa, īnsula*
- *p* as in English (without aspiration): *pēs, populus, prope*
- *ph* as English *p* with aspiration: *amphitheātrum* (see above under *ch*)
- *qu* as English *qu* in "quick": *quis, aqua, equus*
- *r* rolled or trilled: *rēs, ōra, arbor, cūr*
- *s* as in English "gas" (never voiced as in "has"): *sē, rōsa, is*
- *t* as in English (without aspiration): *tē, ita, et*
- *t* is always hard (not like *t* in na*t*ion)
- *th* as English *t* with aspiration: *amphitheātrum* (see above under *ch*)
- *v* as English *w*: *vōs, vīvus*
- *x* as in English (= *ks*): *ex, saxum*
- *z* as English *z* in "zone": *zōna*

Thus, very generally, the sound of Latin consonants can be compared to those of English:

- Like English: *d, f, l, m*, and *n* (initial and medial)[2], *p, qu, z*
- Like English + variations (see above): *bs, bt, gn*
- Always a hard sound: *c, g, s, t, x*
- Softer than English: *h*, final *m, n*
- Different: *r* (trilled) *v* (like *w*)

Now we return to our guidelines for pronunciation of quantities, accentuation, and enunciation. In Cap. XVIII, your text gives you an excellent lesson in the concepts below, in Latin.

1. **Syllables**:
   a. A word has as many syllables as it has vowels and/or diphthongs:
      i. *Est, nōn, sunt*
      ii. *Rō ma, Nī lus, quo que*
      iii. *Flu vi us, op pi dum, īn su la*
      iv. *Brun di si um, Hi spā ni a*[3]
   b. Note that in the examples above:
      i. A consonant goes with the following vowel: *Rō ma*
      ii. Two consonants are divided: *op pi dum*

---

2. I.e., beginning a word (initial) and in the middle of a word (medial).

3. If a combination of letters could be used to begin a word (like the *sp* in *hi spa ni a*), those letters are kept together and go with the following vowel.

    c. Some consonants stay together:
- ~ *ch, ph, th, qu*
- ~ *l* or *r* preceded by *b, d, g, p, t, c,* and *f*

2. **Vowel quantity:**
   a. A long vowel takes twice the time to pronounce as a short vowel.

3. **Syllable quantity**:
   a. A syllable is either:
      i. open (ends in a vowel)
      ii. closed (ends in a consonant)
   b. Long/Heavy syllables:
      i. Closed syllables
      ii. Open syllables with long vowel/diphthong
   c. Short/Light syllables:
      i. Open syllables with a short vowel

4. **Accent:**
   a. The last three syllables of a Latin word determine accent.
   b. These syllables are called:
      i. ultima (for *syllaba ultima*: the last syllable)
      ii. penult (for *syllaba paene ultima*: almost the last syllable)
      iii. antepenult (for *ante paene ultimam syllabam*: "before the almost the last")
   c. The accent, or stress, of a Latin word depends on the length of the second to last, or penultimate, syllable.
   d. The penult (penultimate) syllable is accented when long/heavy (closed or has long vowel or diphthong).
   e. Otherwise, the accent moves to the antepenult.
   f. Examples:

   Rṓma in Ítáliā est. Itália in Euŕṓpā est. Grǽcia in Euŕṓpā est. Itália et Grǽcia in Euŕṓpā sunt. Hispánia et Itália et Grǽcia in Euŕṓpā sunt.

5. **Enunciation:** this last principle sounds easy, but most people who feel nervous about saying a word correctly try to say it as fast as possible. Some tips:
   ▷ Speak slowly and say what you see.
   ▷ Doubled consonants (two consonants in a row) are both pronounced.
   ▷ Long vowels take twice the time to pronounce as short vowels.

Parts of Speech with Examples

[The chapter in brackets gives the first introduction of the part of speech.]

Noun (substantive) [Cap. I]:

    1. names a person, place or thing

    2. properties:

        a. gender: masculine, feminine, or neuter (neither masculine or feminine)

        b. number: singular or plural

        c. case: different endings depending on the role of the word in the sentence

        Exempla Latīna:

            Rōma

            fluvius

            oppidum

Adjective [Cap. 1]:

    1. qualifies a noun

    2. sometimes stands on its own as a substantive

    3. has (like nouns) gender, number, and case

    4. has (unlike nouns) all three genders (can stand in agreement with any noun)

    5. matches (agrees) with its noun in gender, number, and case

        Exempla Latīna:

            magnus (fluvius)

            parva (īnsula)

            parvum (oppidum)

Pronoun [Cap. II]:

    1. points to, or stands for, a noun without naming it, e.g., "he," "whom," "they"

    2. has (like nouns) gender, number, and case

        Exempla Latīna:

            quis   *cuius*

            quae   *quid*

Verb [Cap. I]:

    1. shows action, state of being

    2. properties:

        a. person: 1st (I/we), 2nd (you), 3rd (he, she, it/they)

        b. number: singular, plural

        c. tense: time frame of the verb:

        i. present (continuing action in the present)[4]

        ii. imperfect (continuing action in the past)

        iii. future (projected action)

        iv. perfect (completed action)

        v. pluperfect (action completed before another completed action)

        vi. future perfect (action to be completed before a projected action)

    d. voice:

        i. active (subject is the agent of the verb)

        ii. passive (subject is the recipient of the action of the verb)

    e. mood: expresses the speaker's attitude to the verb

        i. indicative (states a fact, asks a question)

        ii. infinitive (the unbounded, "to" form of the verb)[5]

        iii. imperative (gives a command)

        iv. subjunctive (various uses)

    Exempla Latīna:

        est, sunt

        pulsat [Cap. III]

        cantat [Cap. III]

Participle [Cap. XIV]:

    1. is a verbal adjective: it shares qualities of *verbs* and *adjectives*

    2. like a *verb*, a participle has

        a. tense (present, past, future)

        b. voice (active, passive)

    3. like an *adjective*, a participle has

        a. gender

        b. number

        c. case

    Exempla Latīna:

        dormiēns (*puer*)

        canentem (*gallum*)

        stantem (*servum*)

Adverb [Cap. I]:

    1. qualifies a

        a. verb

        b. adjective

        c. another adverb

---

4.   The present shows continuing action in the present (I am walking), simple present (I walk), emphatic present (I do walk).

5.   The infinitive, like the supine (not included here), is a verbal noun.

> *Exempla Latīna:*
> > *bene*
> > *nōn*
> > *ubi* (interrogative adverb)
> > *num* (interrogative adverb)

Preposition [Cap. I]:
  1. determines the relationship between two nouns
     > *Exempla Latīna:*
     > > *in* (*Italiā*)
     > > *sine* (*rōsīs*) [Cap. V]
     > > *cum* (*Aemiliā*) [Cap. V]

Conjunction [Cap. I]:
  1. joins words, phrases, or clauses
     > *Exempla Latīna:*
     > > *sed*
     > > *et*

Interjection: An exclamation for emphasis [Cap. XXII]:
  > *Exemplum Latīnum:*
  > > *heus!*

Syntactic Terms
[Examples are underlined]
Subject: the focus of the sentence. To find the subject, ask "who" with the verb.

  Julia is singing. Who is singing? Julia (subject)

  > *Exempla Latīna:*

  Rōma in Italiā est.
  Iūlia cantat [Cap. III].

Predicate: the verb and its modifier(s). To find the verb in a sentence, look for the word that denotes an action or state of being.
  - *Rōma in Italiā est*: *est* is the verb/predicate (state of being)
  - *Iūlia cantat*: *cantat* is the action (action)

Predicate nominative: a noun used with a copulative (linking) verb to **restate** the subject.
  - *Corsica īnsula est.*
  - *Tūsculum oppidum Rōmānum est.*

Predicate adjective: an adjective used with a copulative (linking) verb to **qualify** the subject.
  - *Fluvius magnus est.*
  - *Oppidum parvum est.*

Transitive verb: a verb which is completed by a direct object.

Exempla Latīna:

Mārcus nōn <u>videt</u> Quīntum [Cap. III].
Mārcus puellam <u>pulsat</u> [Cap. III].

Intransitive verb: a verb that is not completed by a direct object (which is in the accusative case) or that stands alone (e.g., "I stand," "I sit"). In both examples below, the dative case completes the verb, which is intransitive.

Exempla Latīna:

Pater dormit [Cap. III].
Pater venit [Cap. III].

Direct object: a word in the accusative case that receives the action of the verb.

Exempla Latīna:

Mārcus nōn videt Quīntum [Cap. III].
Mārcus puellam pulsat [Cap. III].

Indirect object: a word in the dative case that tells "to or for whom" the action of the verb is performed.

Exempla Latīna:

Pater <u>filiō</u> <u>suō</u> magnum mālum dat [Cap. VII].
Dominus <u>servīs</u> māla et pira dat [Cap. VII].

Notā Bene:[6] Some verbs which are transitive in English are intransitive in Latin.

---

6.   *Notā Bene* means "note well" or "take note—this is important!"

I. Imperium Rōmānum

Rēs Grammaticae Novae

1. Getting Started: The Roman Empire
2. Using This Book
   a. Pay Attention to Endings
   b. Be Aware of Latin's Flexible Word Order
   c. Concentrate on Meaning and Context
   d. Be Patient: Keep Reading
   e. Answers Often Explain Questions
   f. Look to Context for Word Meaning
3. Morphology
   a. Nouns: Singular/Plural
   b. Antonyms
   c. Adjectives and Substantives
   d. Interrogatives: *num, quid*
   e. Numbers: *mīlle*
4. Points of Style: Latin Concision

Lēctiō Prīma (Section I)

Getting Started: The Roman Empire

In the first chapter, we take you 2,000 years back into the past, to the time when the Roman Empire was at the height of its power, extending from the Atlantic Ocean to the Caspian Sea and from Scotland to the Sahara. We give you a few geographical facts as background for the sketches from life in ancient Rome that follow.

On the map of the Roman Empire facing the first page of the text, you will find all the geographical names occurring in the chapter. After locating the names *Rōma, Italia, Eurōpa, Graecia*, etc., you will understand what is said about the situation of the city of *Rōma* in the first sentence: *Rōma in Italiā est*, and about *Italia* and *Graecia* in the next two: *Italia in Eurōpā est. Graecia in Eurōpā est.* This is said once more in a single sentence: *Italia et Graecia in Eurōpā sunt.* The meaning of *et* should be quite clear, but can you tell why it is now *sunt* instead of *est?* If not, look in the margin and read the next two sentences as well. Have you discovered when to use *est* and when *sunt?* If so, you have learned the first rule of grammar: a singular subject is joined with a singular verb and a plural subject with a plural verb.

If you read LINGUA LATINA, heeding the following suggestions, you'll learn Latin well and easily.

1.   Pay Attention to Endings (e.g., -a, -ā)

Did you also notice the slight difference between *Italia* and *Italiā*, and what little word produces the long *-ā?* This difference is pointed out and explained in the first marginal note:

> *Italia*
> *in Italiā*

2.   Be Aware of Latin's Flexible Word Order (e.g., *est, sunt*)

Another thing worth noticing: here *est* and *sunt* come at the end of the sentence, but you will see that it is not always so; *Rōma est in Italiā* is also correct. The word order is less rigid in Latin than in English.

3.   Concentrate on Meaning and Context (e.g., the negation *nōn*)

Is it really possible, you may ask, to understand everything by just reading the text? It certainly is, provided that you concentrate on the meaning and content of what you are reading. It is sufficient to know where *Aegyptus* is, to understand the statements *Aegyptus in Eurōpā nōn est, Aegyptus in Āfricā est* (l.5). There can be no doubt about the meaning of *nōn* (a so-called negation).

4.   Be Patient: Keep Reading (e.g., *quoque* and *sed*)

Often a sentence is understood only when seen together with other sentences. In the sentence *Hispānia quoque in Eurōpā est* (ll.2–3), you will not understand *quoque* until you read in context: *Italia et Graecia in Eurōpā sunt. Hispānia quoque in Eurōpā est.* (The two preceding sentences might have been *Italia in Eurōpā est* or *Graecia quoque in Eurōpā est.*) If you are still in doubt, just go on reading till the word recurs: *Syria nōn est in Eurōpā, sed in Asiā. Arabia quoque in Asiā est* (l.7). Now you will certainly understand *quoque*—and in the meantime, you have learned the word *sed* almost without noticing it.

5.   Answers Often Explain Questions (e.g., *-ne…?* and *ubi…?*)

In the next paragraph, a number of questions are asked, and each question is followed by an answer. It is often necessary to read the answer before you can be quite sure of the meaning of the question. The first question is *Estne Gallia in Eurōpā?* The particle *-ne* attached to *est* marks the sentence as a question (our question mark [?] was unknown to the ancient Romans). The answer is *Gallia in Eurōpā est.* The next question, *Estne Rōma in Galliā?* is answered in the negative: *Rōma in Galliā nōn est.* (Latin has no single word for "yes" or "no." The sentence—or part of it—must be repeated with or without *nōn*.)

In the question *Ubi est Rōma?* the word *ubi* is intelligible only when you get the answer: *Rōma est in Italiā.*

6.   Look to Context for Word Meaning

After the short survey of the location of the principal Roman provinces, you are told about various localities: *Rhēnus* and *Nīlus*, *Corsica* and *Sardinia*, *Tūsculum* and *Brundisium.* You will find these names on the map, and the text will tell you what they represent. If you are still in doubt about the meaning of the words *fluvius, īnsula,* and *oppidum,* turn back to the picture heading the chapter.

Nouns: Singular/Plural

Note that these words occur in two different forms: *Nīlus* alone is called *fluvius,* but *Nīlus* and *Rhēnus* together are called *fluviī.* In similar circumstances, you will notice the use of the forms *īnsula* and *īnsulae,* as well as *oppidum* and *oppida.* In the section GRAMMATICA LATINA in LINGUA LATINA you will learn that the forms *fluvius, īnsula,* and *oppidum* are called *singulāris,* while *fluviī, īnsulae,* and *oppida* are called *plūrālis*—in English singular and plural.

Lēctiō Altera (Section II)

Antonyms [↔]

As you read on, you will see that *Nīlus* is referred to not only as *fluvius,* but also as *fluvius magnus,* unlike *Tiberis,* which is described as *fluvius parvus.* In the same way, *Sicilia* is referred to as *īnsula magna* as opposed to *Melita* (the modern Malta), which is called *īnsula parva.* In the margin, *magnus* and *parvus* are represented as opposites (sign [↔], "the opposite of"); this will help you to understand the meaning of the words, but note that the endings change: *fluvius magnus,* but *fluviī magnī.* A further example: *Brundisium* is called *oppidum magnum* and *Tūsculum, oppidum parvum,* and when the same words occur in the plural, they are called *fluviī magnī, īnsulae magnae,* and *oppida magna.*

Adjectives and Substantives

A word that shows this variation between the endings *-us, -a, -um* in the singular and *-ī, -ae, -a* in the plural is called an adjective (Latin *adiectīvum*, "added word") because it is added to a noun (substantive), which it qualifies. Other nouns occurring in this chapter are:

prōvincia	*littera*
imperium	*vocābulum*
numerus	

Adjectives occurring in this chapter are:

magnus, -a, -um	*Rōmānus, -a, -um*
parvus, -a, -um	*Latīnus, -a, -um*
Graecus, -a, -um	*prīmus, -a, -um*

Plural adjectives found in this chapter are:

multī, -ae, -a	*paucī, -ae, -a*

Note: The endings of the adjectives depend on the nouns that they qualify; so it is *prōvincia magna* but *imperium magnum*.

More Interrogatives: *num, quid*

The question *Num Crēta oppidum est?* (l.49) must, of course, be answered in the negative: *Crēta oppidum nōn est. Num* is an interrogative (i.e., asking) particle, like *-ne,* but a question beginning with *num* implies a negative answer. The next question is *Quid est Crēta?* Here, again, only the answer, *Crēta īnsula est,* makes the meaning of the question quite plain.

Compare:

Estne Crēta oppidum?	Is Crete a town? (I really don't know, so I'm asking.)
Num Crēta oppidum est?	Crete isn't a town, is it? (I suspect Crete is not a town and expect you to answer "no.")

Remember the other interrogatives in this chapter:

Quid est Crēta?	What is Crete?
Ubi est Crēta?	Where is Crete?

More about Endings

We have seen that, after *in,* the final vowel is *-ā* and not *-a.* Remember that the macron over the *ā* means the vowel is long (see pronunciation guide). We now see that *in* also makes *-um* change to *-ō*:

in imperiō Rōmānō (l.58) *in capitulō prīmō* (l.73)
in vocābulō (l.72)

You will learn more about these forms in *-ā* and *-ō* in Cap. V.

Lēctiō Tertia (Section III)

Mīlle

Mīlle, the word for "a thousand," is an indeclinable adjective; indeclinable means its endings never change. So:

    mīlle numerī   *mīlle vocābula*   *mīlle litterae*

Points of Style: Latin Concision

Latin is a concise language. It can often express in a few words what requires several words in other languages. One of the reasons is that Latin has fewer particles (small, uninflected words) than most modern languages; Latin also has nothing corresponding to the English articles "a" and "the," as in "a river," "the river," etc.

Recēnsiō (Review)

Remember:

1. Pay attention to endings.
2. Be aware of Latin's flexible word order.
3. Concentrate on meaning and context.
4. Be patient: keep reading.
5. Answers often explain questions.
6. Look to context for word meaning.

Important terms:

- Enclitic: word that is appended to another word (*-ne, -que*)
- Particle: small uninflected word
- Indeclinable: word whose endings do not change (*mīlle*)

Studia Rōmāna

The map in the beginning of this chapter shows the Roman Empire (*Imperium Rōmānum*) at its height in the second century AD, the time in which our narrative takes place. This is the time of the *Pax Rōmāna*, the Roman peace (which lasted from the end of the first century BC through the second century AD, from the time of the emperor Augustus through Marcus Aurelius). Rome had begun almost a millennium before our story, in 753 BC, as a hamlet on the hills around the swamp that would eventually become the Roman Forum. It began as a tiny kingdom (753–510 BC), then a republic run by the aristocracy (510–27 BC), and finally an empire which lasted in the west until the fifth century AD and in the east—in Constantinople—until the fifteenth century.

In addition to learning the words for town (*oppidum*) and island (*īnsula*), you learn the word for river (*fluvius*) and the names of a few (*Nīlus, Rhēnus, Dānuvius, Tiberis*). Rivers are very important—for drinking water, for agriculture, for travel, for transport of goods, and as territorial boundaries. So important were rivers that river gods are often shown holding a cornucopia (*cornū cōpiae*, the horn of plenty), emphasizing their gift to agricultural fertility. Latin poets sometimes identify a group living in an area with the river that supplies them water: "the chilly brook Digentia that the folk of Mandela drink" (*Quīntus Horātius Flaccus*, 65–8 BC, *Epist.* 1.18.105); "those who drink the Tiber and the Fabaris" (Vergil, 70–19 BC, *Aen.* 7.715). The Romans helped along natural resources with the building of aqueducts. Appius Claudius Crassus directed that the first one, the Aqua Appia, be built in the fourth century BC (he is also to be credited with the construction of the Via Appia, the major roadway that led from Rome; see Cap. VI). By the time of our narrative, there were ten.[1] Aqueducts fed fountains throughout a town lucky enough to be connected to an aqueduct. The structure of the house (see Cap. V) helped with water collection: rain water could come in through an opening in the roof of the *ātrium*, fall into a pool and be collected in a cistern for later use.

The image of the tablet inscribed with numerals (*numerī*) and letters (*litterae*) that heads Section III in your text represents an important vehicle for writing. It is called a *tabella* (Cap. XXI) and consists of a wooden board with a raised border, with wax (*cēra*) in the middle. The pointed stick you see to the right of the tabella is called a *stilus*. It had a pointed end (for writing on the wax) and a broad, tapered surface on the other with which one could smooth out the wax (hence erasing the writing). There were different varieties of these tablets, including ones small enough to be held in the hand (called *pugillārēs* from *pugnus*, "fist"). In the margins on page 107 (Cap. XIV), you can see a tablet that folded and tied closed (just like *pugillārēs*), as well as a *stilus* and a *rēgula* (ruler). In Cap. II, there is a picture of an ancient book (*liber antīquus*) in the form of a scroll, as well as a *pāgina*, a written page (and the page itself!). You will learn more about writing in Cap. XVIII.

Vocābula Disposita/Ōrdināta

Nōmina (Nouns)[2]

capitulum, -ī	chapter
exemplum, -ī	example, model
fluvius, -ī	river
grammatica, -ae	grammar

---

1.   Frontinus (first century BC) 1.4: *Nunc autem in urbem īnfluunt aqua Appia, Aniō Vetus, Mārcia, Tepula, Iūlia, Virgō, Alsietīna quae eadem vocatur Augusta, Claudia, Aniō Novus.* The Aqua Alexandrina was completed in the early third century AD.

2.   Ignore for now the letters that come after each vocabulary entry; they are there for your later reference and their significance will be clear in the next chapter.

imperium, -ī	command, empire
īnsula, -ae	island
littera, -ae	letter
numerus, -ī	number
ōceanus, -ī	ocean
oppidum, -ī	town
pēnsum, -ī	task
prōvincia, -ae	province
syllaba, -ae	syllable
vocābulum, -ī	word

Verba (Verbs)

est	he/she/it is
sunt	they are

Adiectīva (Adjectives)

Graecus, -a, -um	Greek
Latīnus, -a, -um	Latin
magnus, -a, -um	big, large, great
multī, -ae, -a (*pl.*)	many, a great many
parvus, -a, -um	little, small
paucī, -ae, -a (*pl.*)	few, a few
plūrālis (numerus)	plural (**plūrālis** and **singulāris** are adjectives of the 3rd declension; you will learn about these in Cap. XII)
prīmus, -a, -um	first
Rōmānus, -a, -um	Roman, of Rome
secundus, -a, -um	second, favorable
singulāris (numerus)	singular
tertius, -a, -um	third

Numerī (Numbers)

ūnus	one, only
duo	two
trēs	three
sex	six
mīlle	one thousand

Adverbia (Adverbs)

nōn	not

Praepositiōnēs (Prepositions)

in (*prp. + abl.*)	in, on, at
(*prp. + acc.*)	into, to, against

Coniūnctiōnēs (Conjunctions)

et	and, also
sed	but
quoque	also, too

Vocābula Interrogātīva (Interrogative words)

-ne?   *enclitic added to the emphatic word at*
                             the beginning of a question the answer
                             to which may be either "yes" or "no." It
                             can be used in both direct and indirect
                             questions (Cap. XIX).

num?   if, whether; *expects a "no" answer*

quid? *n.* (see **quis**)   what, anything; *adv.* why

ubi? *interrog. adv.*   where

II. Familia Rōmāna

Rēs Grammaticae Novae

1. Gender: Masculine, Feminine, Neuter
2. Nouns:
    a. Ending in -*us*
    b. Ending in -*a*
    c. Ending in -*um*
    d. Ending in -*er*
    e. Genitive
3. Adjectives:
    a. *cēterī, ae, a*
    b. Possessive
    c. Numbers
4. Pronouns: *quis, quae, quid*
5. Adverbs: Interrogative *quot*
6. Conjunctions
7. *Ecce*
8. Points of Style: Enumerations

The Roman Family

We now introduce you to the people whose daily lives we will follow in the rest of the text. The picture shows them dressed in their best clothes, except for the four who are relegated to the margin—clearly, they are not on the same level as the rest of the family. Be sure to remember their names, for you will soon become so well acquainted with these persons that you will almost feel like a friend visiting a real Roman family 2,000 years ago. And the remarkable thing about it is that you can understand their language! You will find more about the Roman family in the STUDIA RŌMĀNA section at the end of the chapter.

Lēctiō Prīma (Section I)

Gender: Masculine, Feminine, Neuter

Note that the names of these people end in either -*us* (masculine) or -*a* (feminine); none of them end in -*um* (neuter). You will see that the ending -*us* is characteristic of male persons:

Iūlius	*Dāvus*
Mārcus	*Mēdus*
Quīntus	

and -*a* of female persons:

Aemilia	*Syra*
Iūlia	*Dēlia*

This principle also applies to nouns that denote persons. Nouns referring to males generally end in -*us*:

fīlius	*servus*
dominus	

A smaller number of masculine nouns end in -*r* instead of -*us*:

vir	*puer*

Nouns denoting females end mostly in -*a*:

fēmina	*domina*
puella	*ancilla*
fīlia	

No persons are denoted by words ending in -*um*.

Latin groups nouns by gender, not "sex." The word gender comes from the Latin *genus*, which means group or category. The three genders, or categories, are:

neuter (Latin *neutrum*, "neither," i.e., neither masculine nor feminine)

oppidum	*imperium*
vocābulum	

masculine (Latin *masculīnum*, from *mas*, "male")

fluvius	*titulus*
numerus	*liber*

feminine (Latin *fēminīnum*, from *fēmina*)

īnsula	*prōvincia*
littera	*familia*

Genders (in Latin)

masculine (m.): -*us*, -*er*, -*ir*
feminine (f.): -*a*
neuter (n.): -*um*

Nouns: Genitive Case (*cāsus genetīvus*)

The word *familia* refers to the whole household, including all the slaves, *servī* and *ancillae*, who belong to the head of the family as his property. *Iūlius* is the father, *pater*, of *Mārcus, Quīntus,* and *Iūlia*, and the master, *dominus*, of *Mēdus, Dāvus, Syra, Dēlia,* etc. To express these relationships, we need the genitive (Latin *genetīvus*), a form of the noun ending in:

> Singular: *-ī* (m./n.) and *-ae* (f.)
> *Iūlius est pater Mārcī et Quīntī et Iūliae.*
> *Titulus capitulī secundī est "Familia Rōmāna."* (ll.87–88)

> Plural: *-ōrum* (m./n.) and *-ārum* (f.)
> *Iūlius est dominus multōrum servōrum et multārum ancillārum.*
> *In Graeciā et in Italiā magnus numerus oppidōrum est.* (l.56)

To express the idea of the genitive, English uses the word "of" or an apostrophe: *māter Iūliae* = "Julia's mother" or "the mother *of* Julia."

> genitive: "of," "-'s"
>
> | | m./n. | f. |
> |-------|--------|--------|
> | sing. | *-ī* | *-ae* |
> | pl. | *-ōrum* | *-ārum* |

In addition to the category of gender, nouns fall into categories according to their endings. These categories are called declensions (*dēclīnātiōnēs*), according to the ending of the genitive. Nouns whose genitive ends in *-ae* belong to the 1st declension; those whose genitive ends in *-ī* belong to the 2nd declension.

Conjunctions: *Coniūnctiōnēs*

Particles like *et* and *sed* are called conjunctions (Latin *coniūnctiōnēs*, from *con-iungere*, "join together") because they join words and sentences.

Instead of *et*, you often find the conjunction *-que* attached after the second word. *-que* is called an enclitic because it "leans on" (from the Greek ἐγκλίνω) the word in front of it and cannot stand on its own. The mark "-" in front of it signals an enclitic. Both *et* and *-que* mean "and":

> *Dēlia Mēdusque* = *Dēlia et Mēdus.* (l.9)
> *fīliī fīliaeque* = *fīliī et fīliae.* (l.22)

Conjunctions

> *sed*
> *...-que = et...*

Interrogatives: *Quis, Quae, Quid*

Among the new words in Cap. II are the interrogative words *quis* and *quae,* which are used to ask questions about persons (English "who"):

> *Quis est Mārcus?*   masculine *quis* (plural *quī*)
>
> *Quae est Iūlia?*   feminine *quae* (plural *quae*)[1]

In Cap. I, you met the neuter interrogative *quid* (English "what"):

> *Quid est Creta?*   neuter singular.

The genitive of the interrogative for all genders is *cuius* (English "whose"):

> *Cuius servus est Dāvus? Dāvus servus Iūliī est.* (l.35)

	m.	f.	n.
nom.	*quis?*	*quae?*	*quid?*
gen.	*cuius?*		

Quot

Most words in Latin change endings; for example, *fīlius* (one son) and *fīliī* (more than one son). Some words, however, never change form. They are called indeclinable: they always look the same. *Quot* ("how many") is an indeclinable interrogative adverb that asks questions about number:

> *Quot līberī sunt in familiā? In familiā Iūliī sunt trēs līberī.*
>
> *Quot fīliī et quot fīliae? Duo fīliī et ūna fīlia.*
>
> *Quot servī...?...centum servī.* (ll.37–39)
>
> quot? 1, 2, 3...

Numerī

Like *mīlle* (Cap. I) and most numerals, *centum* (100, l.39) is invariable: it does not change its ending (or "decline," the usual term for a change of a noun or adjective's ending). The numbers one (*ūnus*), two (*duo*), and three (*trēs*), however, do decline, they change endings:

- *ūnus* has the familiar endings *-us, -a, -um*
- the feminine of *duo* is *duae* (*duae fīliae*) and the neuter *duo*
- the neuter of *trēs* is *tria* (*tria oppida*); *trēs* refers to both masculine and feminine nouns.

m.	f.	n.
ūnus	*ūna*	*ūnum*
duo	*duae*	*duo*
trēs	*trēs*	*tria*

---

1. Latin, in fact, tended to use *quis* for both masculine and feminine nominative singular.

Lēctiō Altera (Section II)

Genitive (continued)

The number can also be indicated by the noun *numerus* combined with the genitive plural:

> *Numerus līberōrum est trēs.* (ll.43–44)

> *Numerus servōrum est centum.* (l.43)

As *centum* must be said to be a *magnus numerus,* the following sentences are easily understood:

> *Numerus servōrum est magnus.*

> *In familiā magnus numerus servōrum est.*

It appears that *magnus numerus servōrum* is equivalent to *multī servī.* In the same way, *parvus numerus līberōrum* has the same meaning as *paucī līberī.* You will also find the expressions *magnus numerus oppidōrum* and *fluviōrum* meaning *multa oppida* and *multī fluviī.*

> *magnus numerus…ōrum = multī…ī/multa…a*

> *magnus numerus…ārum = multae…ae*

Adjective: *Cēterī, -ae, -a*

The Romans knew only the northern part of the continent of Africa, where there is only one big river, the Nile:

> *In Āfricā ūnus fluvius magnus est: Nīlus.* (l.58)

It goes on:

> *Cēterī fluviī Āfricae parvī sunt.* (l.59)

The adjective *cēterī, -ae, -a,* "the others," recurs several times; thus, the enumeration of the first three of the thirty-five *capitula* is concluded with *cētera:*

> *In Linguā Latīnā sunt multae pāginae et multa capitula: capitulum prīmum, secundum, tertium, cētera.* (l.86)

The sentence might have read *et cētera,* the Latin expression which gives us the abbreviation "etc."

> *cēterī, -ae, -a*

Points of Style: Enumerations

The following rules apply to enumerations in Latin:

1. *et* put between all items: *Mārcus et Quīntus et Iūlia*
2. no conjunction used at all: *Mārcus, Quīntus, Iūlia*

3. *-que* added to the last item: *Mārcus, Quīntus Iūliaque*
That is:

1. *a et b et c*
2. *a, b, c*
3. *a, b, c-que*

Lēctiō Tertia (Section III)

Adjectives: Possessive

The conversation at the end of the chapter (ll.65–79) shows that instead of the genitive, the adjectives *meus, -a, -um* and *tuus, -a, -um* are used to refer to what belongs to the person speaking or the person spoken to (like English "my" and "your").

The adjective always has the same gender (m., f., or n.), number (sing. or pl.), and case (e.g., nominative, genitive) as the noun it modifies. So, Julius says, "*Dēlia est ancilla mea*" (l.71). *Mea* is an adjective agreeing with *ancilla*, so it is feminine nominative singular.

> *meus, -a, -um*
>
> *tuus, -a, -um*

Ecce

On page 16, you come across the word *ecce* (illustrated with an arrow in the margin). It is used when you point to or call attention to something; in this case, it is pointing to the two books.

Nouns Ending in *-er*: *puer, puerī, liber, librī*

Notice the form of an ancient book: a scroll with the text written in columns. The Latin word for such a scroll is *liber*. *Liber*, like *puer* (also in this chapter), ends in *-er* instead of in *-us*. Notice that some nouns (like *puer*) keep an *e* throughout, while others (like *liber*) have *e* only in the nominative (and vocative, the form used when directly addressing someone).[2] The plural of *liber* is *librī*, while the plural of *puer* is *puerī*. These nouns are always masculine.

Notā Bene: Look to the genitive to determine what happens to the *e*:

puer, puerī	(there will be an *e* throughout)
liber, librī	(the *e* is found only in the nominative)

nominative	genitive
liber	*librī*
puer	*puerī*

---

2.   Vocative, Cap. IV.

Recēnsiō: **Grammatical Terms**

Decline: Nouns, adjectives, and pronouns change endings, depending on
their use in the sentence; that is, they are said to decline.

Declensions: Nouns, adjectives, and pronouns are grouped according to
their characteristic vowel into families, called declensions. The vowel
-a characterizes the first declension (e.g., *puella, domina*), while *-o/u*
marks the second declension (e.g., *servus, imperium*).

Enclitic: An enclitic is a word that cannot stand on its own; it attaches itself
to the word it follows.

Gender: Nouns, adjectives, and pronouns fall into three categories called
genders: masculine, feminine, and neuter.

Indeclinable: A word is called indeclinable if it never changes endings.

Studia Rōmāna

One of the first things you will notice about the pictures of the Roman family
is their clothing. Clothing was an important marker of status in the ancient
world. The basic unit of clothing for everyone was the tunic (*tunica*, Cap. XIV).
The tunic was worn in various lengths and was usually belted at the waist. For
men, it reached the knees or mid-calf. Soldiers wore them above the knee.
Julius is shown wearing a *toga* (Cap. XIV) over his tunic. The toga was made
of white wool and was expensive. It was a highly symbolic garment for special
occasions that marked a man as a Roman citizen. A man who was running for
office would send his toga to the cleaner to have it whitened. A shining white
toga is called *toga candida*, and a man running for office was a *candidātus*: our
"candidate." The right arm is left unencumbered, but the left arm is impeded
by the way the toga is worn (which you can see clearly in the image of Cornelius in the margin on p. 15).

Both Marcus and Quintus wear a toga with a purple stripe (the *toga praetexta*, or bordered toga), the normal ceremonial dress of free-born male children (and also of magistrates!) until around the age of fifteen or sixteen, when
they assumed the *toga virīlis* (the toga of manhood, from *vir*) like their father.
Young girls also wore the *toga praetexta* when they were dressed formally, although Julia is shown here with a plain toga over her long tunic.

Over her tunic, Aemilia wears the *palla*, a long, wide, and cloak-like garment. The tunic of both girls and adult women reached to the foot. Over her
tunic but under the *palla*, Aemilia is probably wearing a *stola*, a long, sleeveless
garment that signifies her status as a *mātrōna*, a married woman.

Clothing was made of wool at home by the *māterfamiliās* and her *ancillae*.
In Livy, (59 BC–AD 17) we find Lucretia, a paragon of Roman womanhood,
in the atrium spinning wool with her *ancillae* by lamplight).[3] Suetonius's (c.
AD 75–160) biography of the emperor Augustus tells us that the women in

---

3. *Ab urbe conditā*, 1.57. *Lūcrētiam…nocte sērā dēditam lānae inter lūcūbrantēs ancillās in mediō
aedium sedentem inveniunt.*

his household learned to spin and weave, despite the family's great wealth and power (*Aug.* 64). The republican period epitaph of a woman named Claudia records, among her accomplishments as the *māterfamiliās*, "She looked after the house; she did the wool-working" (*domum servāvit. Lānam fēcit*).

Children also wore protective amulets around their necks. Boys wore the *bulla* (which was round) and girls the *lūnula* ("little moon" and moon shaped). When boys assumed the *toga virīlis*, they dedicated the *bulla* to the household gods known as the *Larēs*. Before their marriage, girls also dedicated the *toga praetexta*, their toys, and the *lūnula* to the *Larēs*. The *Larēs* represented the spirits of deified dead ancestors; you will learn more about them in Cap. IV.

Footwear included *soleae* (sandals) and *calceī* (shoes); *soleae* covered only part of the foot, and were worn indoors and at meals, while the *calceus* (Cap. XIV, p. 106) covered the whole foot and was a sturdier shoe.

We see the slaves, both men and women, wearing short, belted tunics.

Vocābula Disposita/Ōrdināta

Nōmina

  1st declension

ancilla, -ae	female slave, servant
domina, -ae	mistress
familia, -ae	domestic staff, family
fēmina, -ae	woman
fīlia, -ae	daughter
pāgina, -ae	page
puella, -ae	girl

  2nd declension

dominus, -ī	master
fēminīnum, -ī (genus)	feminine
fīlius, -ī	son
genetīvus, -ī (cāsus)	genitive
liber, -brī	book
līberī, -ōrum	children
masculīnum, -ī (genus)	masculine
neutrum (genus)	neuter
puer, -erī	boy
servus, -ī	slave, servant
titulus, -ī	title
vir, -ī	man, husband

  3rd declension (you will learn more about these nouns in Cap. IX)

māter (*f.*)	mother
pater (*m.*)	father

Adiectīva
  1st/2nd declension (-us, -a, -um)
    antīquus, -a, -um   old, ancient, former
    centum (*invariable*)   a hundred
    cēterī, -ae, -a (*pl.*)   the other(s), the rest
    duo, duae, duo   two
    meus, -a, -um   my, mine
    novus, -a, -um   new
    tuus, -a, -um   your, yours
  3rd declension (you will learn more about these adjectives in Cap. XII)
    trēs, tria   three

Prōnōmina
    quis? quae? quid?   who, what
    quī? (*m. pl.*)   what, which
    cuius? (*gen. sing.*)   whose

Adverbia
    quot? (*indecl.*)   how many, (as many) as

Coniūnctiōnēs
    -que   and *enclitic added to the second word of a pair of words in order to link them together*

III. Puer Improbus

Rēs Grammaticae Novae

1. Verbs
   a. The Latin Verb
   b. Transitive/Intransitive
   c. Implied Subject
2. Nouns Subject/Object
3. Pronouns
   a. Personal Pronouns: Accusative Case
   b. Relative and Interrogative Pronouns
4. Adverbs: Interrogatives *cūr, quia*
5. Conjunctions: Negatives
6. Points of Style: Writing Relative Sentences

Sibling Quarrel

Now that you have been introduced to the family, you are going to watch some of their doings. We begin with the children—they are portrayed here as being much the same in ancient times as they are today. So, we are not surprised to learn that Julius and Aemilia's children cannot always get on together. Here, little Julia is the first to suffer, because her singing annoys her big brother. Peace is not restored until Mother and Father step in.

The chapter is divided up into three scenes (*scaena prīma, secunda, tertia*).

Lēctiō Prīma (Section I)

The Latin Verb

Several of the new words in this chapter are verbs. A verb (Latin *verbum*) is a word that expresses an action or a state: that someone does something or that something exists or takes place. The first Latin verb you come across is *cantat* in the opening sentence: *Iūlia cantat*. Other verbs are *pulsat, plōrat, rīdet, videt, vocat, venit*, etc. They all end in *-t*—like *est*, which is also a verb—and mostly come at the end of the sentence.

Verbs

-at	*cantat, pulsat, plōrat*
-et	*rīdet, videt, respondet*
-it	*venit, audit, dormit*

Like nouns, verbs are grouped into categories, called conjugations (*coniugātiōnēs*); verbs in the 1st conjugation have stems ending in -*ā*, in the 2nd in -*ē*, in the 4th in -*ī*. In Cap. IV you will learn some verbs from the 3rd conjugation, which also have a 3rd person singular ending in -*it*; in that conjugation, some verbs have a stem ending in -*ī* and others ending in a consonant.

Nouns: Subject/Object

The first of the two words in the sentence *Iūlia cantat* denotes the person who performs the action. Other sentences of the same kind are:

Iūlia plōrat. (1.9)	*Aemilia venit.* (1.21)
Mārcus rīdet. (1.10)	*Pater dormit.* (1.37)

But it is not always as simple as this. Take, for instance, the sentence that is illustrated by the little drawing in the margin: *Mārcus Iūliam pulsat* (1.8). Here, we are told not only who performs the action, but also at whom the action is aimed. The same pattern is seen in the following sentences, also illustrated by pictures:

Quīntus Mārcum videt. (1.11)	*Mārcus Quīntum pulsat.* (1.14)
Quīntus Mārcum pulsat. (1.13)	*Iūlia Aemiliam vocat.* (1.19)

Subject: The person who performs the action is called the subject of the verb. The subject has the ending -*us*, -*a* (or -*um* for neuter nouns); these forms are called nominative (Latin *nōminātīvus*).

Object: The person toward whom (or the object toward which) the action is directed, the object, takes the ending -*um* or -*am*. The forms -*um* and -*am* are called accusative (Latin *accūsātīvus*).

In other words: *Iūlia* is changed to *Iūliam* when we are told that Marcus hits her, just as *Mārcus* becomes *Mārcum* when he is the victim. In similar circumstances, *puella* changes to *puellam*, and *puer* to *puerum*, and qualifying adjectives get the same ending:

Mārcus parvam puellam pulsat. (1.59)
Iūlius puerum improbum verberat. (1.64)

subject	**object**	**verb**
Mārcus	*Iūliam*	*pulsat*

	m.	f.
nominative:	-*us*	-*a*
accusative:	-*um*	-*am*

Both the nominative (subject) and the accusative (object) are called *cases*: *cāsus nōminātīvus* and *cāsus accūsātīvus*.

Verbs: Transitive/Intransitive

Verbs like *pulsat, videt, vocat*, which can be used with an object in the accusative, are called **transitive**. Verbs without an object—e.g., *plōrat, dormit*—are **intransitive** verbs.

> *Iūlia plōrat* (intransitive: no object) *et Aemiliam vocat* (transitive: accusative object). (l.9)

> *Mārcus nōn videt Quīntum* (transitive). (l.11)

In the following sentence, the first verb (*pulsat*) is transitive and the second (*ridet*) intransitive:

> *Mārcus puellam pulsat—et rīdet!* (l.12)

Notā Bene: You need to pay attention to whether a word is transitive in Latin—which will not always be the same as its English equivalent!

Lēctiō Altera (Section II)

Personal Pronouns: Accusative Case

Instead of accusative nouns in *-am* and *-um*, you sometimes find the words *eam* and *eum*, e.g.:

> *Iūlia plōrat quia Mārcus eam pulsat.* (ll.27–28)

> *Cūr Iūlius Quīntum nōn audit? Iūlius eum nōn audit, quia dormit.* (ll.42–43)

On page 20, you will notice the marginal note "*eam: Iūliam*" means that here, *eam* stands for *Iūliam*.

A word of this kind, which takes the place of a name or noun, is called a pronoun (Latin *prōnōmen*, from *prō* "instead of" and *nōmen* "name" or "noun").

Corresponding to *eum* (him) and *eam* (her), the pronoun *mē* is used when a person is speaking about himself or herself, and *tē* is used about the person spoken to (in English, "me" and "you"):

> *Aemilia: "Quis mē vocat?"*

> *Quīntus: "Iūlia tē vocat."* (ll.24–25)

	m.	f.
acc.	eum	eam
	mē	
	tē	

Implied Subject

In English, we use the pronouns "he" and "she": Where is Julius? Why doesn't *he* come? But in Latin, these pronouns are not needed. When the context shows who the subject is, it need not be repeated (or replaced by a pronoun):

> *"Ubi est Iūlius? Cūr nōn <u>venit</u>?"* (ll.35–36)

Similarly:

> *Iūlius eum nōn audit, quia <u>dormit</u>.* (l.43)

> *"Cūr māter Mārcum verberat?" "Mārcum <u>verberat</u>, quia puer improbus est."* (ll.58–59)

Adverbs: Interrogatives *cūr* and *quia*

The interrogative adverb *cūr* ("why?") is used to ask about the cause (Latin *causa*). A question introduced by *cūr* calls for an answer with the causal conjunction *quia* ("because"):

> <u>*Cūr*</u> *Iūlia plōrat? Iūlia plōrat, <u>quia</u> Mārcus eam pulsat.* (ll.26–28)

> <u>*Cūr*</u> *Mārcus Iūliam pulsat? <u>Quia</u> Iūlia cantat.* (ll.30–31)

> question: *cūr...?*

> answer: *...quia...*

Conjunctions: Negative

The conjunctions *et* and *sed* are not usually combined with a negation; instead of *et nōn* and *sed nōn*, the conjunction *neque* (*ne-que*) is used, i.e., *-que* attached to the original negation *nē* (= *nōn*):

> *Iūlius dormit <u>neque</u> Quīntum audit.*   In English, "and not"

> *Iūlius venit, <u>neque</u> Aemilia eum videt.*   In English, "but not"

> *ne-que = et nōn (sed nōn)*

Lēctiō Tertia (Section III)

Pronouns: Relative and Interrogative

In the sentence *Puer <u>quī</u> parvam puellam pulsat improbus est* (l.63), *quī* refers to *puer* and is called a relative pronoun. The relative pronoun connects ("relates") a subordinate clause to a main clause. The relative pronoun refers to a word in the main clause called an **antecedent**. The pronoun will agree with its antecedent in gender and number, but its case will be determined by the subordinate clause. In the preceding example, *quī* is masculine singular to agree with its antecedent *puer* and nominative because it is the subject of *pulsat* in its own clause.

More examples:

Puer quī rīdet est Mārcus. (l.70)

Puella quae plōrat est Jūlia. (l.71)

As a relative pronoun *quem* is used in the masculine and *quam* in the feminine when it represents the verb's object in its own clause:

Puer <u>quem</u> Aemilia verberat est Mārcus. (ll.75–76)

Puella <u>quam</u> Mārcus pulsat est Iūlia. (ll.72–73)

The examples show that *quī* and *quem* (m.) refer to a masculine noun, and *quae* and *quam* (f.) to a feminine noun.

In Cap. IV (l.75) you will meet *quod*, which refers to a neuter noun:

baculum, <u>quod</u> in mēnsā est

At the end of the chapter (p. 23), you find sentences with both the **interrogative** and the **relative** pronoun, e.g.:[1]

<u>*Quis*</u> *est puer <u>quī</u> rīdet?*   <u>Who</u> (interrogative) is the boy <u>who</u> (relative) is laughing? (l.69)

In the feminine, the two pronouns are identical:

<u>*Quae*</u> *est puella <u>quae</u> plōrat?*   <u>Who</u> (interrogative) is the girl <u>who</u> (relative) is crying? (l.70)

The interrogative pronoun *quis* is *quem* in the accusative:

<u>*Quem*</u> *vocat Quīntus? Quīntus Iūli<u>um</u> vocat.* (l.77)

Points of Style: Writing Relative Sentences

Consider these sentences

- (from Cap. II) *Iūlius est vir Rōmānus. Iūlius est pater Mārcī.* These two independent sentences have equal value. Their common lexical link is *Iūlius*. Substituting the relative for one *Iūlius*, we can make two different complex sentences:
  Iūlius, quī est vir Rōmānus, est pater Mārcī.
  Iūlius, quī est pater Mārcī, est vir Rōmānus.
  In the first sentence, Julius's being a Roman man is made subordinate to his being the father of Marcus, while in the second, his being Marcus's father is the subordinate, or dependent, idea.

- (from Cap. III) *Iūlius eum audit. Iam nōn dormit pater.* (l.48)
  Pater, quī eum audit, iam nōn dormit.   Father, who hears him, is no longer sleeping.

  Iūlius, quī iam nōn dormit, eum audit.   Julius, who is no longer sleeping, hears him.

---

1. See the explanation (p. xv) of when—and why—sentences will be translated.

Since *pater* and *Iūlius* both refer to the same person, we can substitute a relative pronoun for one of the occurrences. The meaning of the sentence changes a bit, depending on how the clauses are combined. The first one suggests (as did the original two independent clauses) that Julius is no longer sleeping because he hears Marcus wailing and that wakes him up. The second implies that he hears Marcus because he is no longer sleeping.

relative pronoun: connects a clause

puer qui̲...

puella quae̲...

	m.	f.	n.
nom.	*quī*	*quae*	*quod*
acc.	*quem*	*quam*	*quod*

interrogative pronoun: asks a question

nom.	*quis*
acc.	*quem*

Recēnsiō: Qu- words

quis? quae? quid?	who, what? (interrogative pronoun)
quī, quae	who (interrogative pronoun, plural)
quia	because (conjunction)
quot	how many? (interrogative adverb)

New Grammatical Terms

Case: The ending of a noun or adjective changes depending on the word's function; each of these alterations is called a "case" (Latin *cāsus*).

Subject: The person (or thing) that performs the action of the verb is called the subject, represented in Latin by the nominative case.

Object: The person (or thing) that completes the meaning of the verb is called the direct object, represented in Latin by the accusative case.

Conjugation: The ending of a verb's stem (*-ā, -ē, -ī, -ĭ,* or consonant) determines the group (conjugation) to which it belongs.

Transitive: A verb is transitive if an accusative direct object completes its meaning.

Intransitive: A verb is intransitive if its meaning is complete without an accusative direct object.

Implied Subject: If the subject is not directly stated, but needs to be supplied from the ending of the verb, it is called an implied subject.

Pronoun: A pronoun takes the place of a noun.

Lexical Entry: The way a word is presented in a lexicon (dictionary), for example *mamma, -ae,* f. The vocabulary entry for verbs and some other words will change in the first part of this book as you learn more morphology (forms of words). For now, verbs are listed as 3rd person singular. Cap. X adds the present infinitive. The actual lexical entry for verbs begins with the 1st person singular, which you will first meet in Cap. XV.

Studia Rōmāna

In the second scene, we see Julius sleeping on a *lectus*, a Roman bed. While it looks pretty uncomfortable, such sleeping couches were common in the ancient world (other images on pp. 74, 78, 187). By our standards, Roman furniture could be sparse. The three most common pieces were the table (*mēnsa*), chair (*sella*), and couch (*lectus*). Storage places in the form of cupboards (*armārium*) and chests (*arca*) were also important. Containers for books (scrolls) went by various names: the *capsa* (also in diminutive form: *capsula*) was a cylinder that can often be seen at the foot of a statue of one who wants to mark himself as learned. The *scrīnium* was a portable chest for holding books and papers. The *cista* (also in diminutive form: *cistula*) was a woven basket used for holding various things, including books; a particular usage for the *cista* was to hold the sacred implements at a religious festival. Oil lamps (*lucernae*) were ubiquitous. They could be carried in the hand and placed on a lamp-stand (*lychnūchus*, λυχνοῦχος).

Furniture—especially tables, of which the Romans were particularly fond—could be a sign of wealth. The beginning of Cap. IV (p. 26) shows Julius sitting at a table that rests on ornately carved legs. Pliny the Elder (first century AD) writes about the Roman mania for tables (*mēnsārum insānia*) made of citrus (cedar) wood (*arbor cītrī, Historia Nātūrālis*, 13.29); elsewhere, he writes of table legs being made of ivory (12.3). You will see at the end of our story that Julius can afford to adorn his dining room with expensive linens for the dining couches (Cap. XXX). Romans sometimes brought their own napkin (*mappa*) or hand towel (*mantēle*) to dinner parties. Catullus (first century BC) complained in the first century BC that someone stole a napkin from him while dining out, which was both expensive and a gift from a friend (Poem 12). The complaint continues to the time period of our narrative. Martial (first century AD) writes about a recent diner, "No one had brought his napkin (*mappa*) since thefts were feared: Hermogenes stole the cloth (*mantēle*) from the table" (Book 12.28: *attulerat mappam nēmō, dum fūrta timentur: / mantēle ā mēnsā surpuit Hermogenes*).

Julius sits on a low stool (p. 22: *scamnum*), but the Romans had a variety of chairs (*sellae*)—including the high-backed chairs that we see in Cap. XIV (p. 110).

In the third scene, as father punishes his son, the sound is represented by *tuxtax* (ll.64, 65), a word meant to imitate the sound of being beaten. Corporal punishment for children was common. Some other colorful Latin expressions:

- *bombax*: an exclamation of surprise
- *babae*: an exclamation of joy and amazement

In the next chapter, you'll meet some other Latin exclamations:

- *fū*: an exclamation of dislike or aversion
- *st*: "shhhhh…"

Vocābula Disposita/Ōrdināta

Nōmina

1st

mamma, -ae	mommy
persōna, -ae	character, person
scaena, -ae	scene, stage

2nd

accūsātīvus, -ī (cāsus)	accusative
nōminātīvus, -ī (cāsus)	nominative
verbum, -ī	word, verb

Verba

-at (1)

cantat	sing
interrogat	ask, question
plōrat	cry
pulsat	strike, hit, knock (at)
verberat	beat, flog
vocat	call, invite

-et (2)

respondet	answer
rīdet	laugh, make fun of
videt	see

-it (4)

audit	hear, listen
dormit	sleep
venit	come

Adiectīva

1st/2nd (-us, -a, -um)

improbus, -a, -um	bad, wicked
īrātus, -a, -um	angry
laetus, -a, -um	glad, happy
probus, -a, -um	good, honest, proper

Prōnōmina
    eam   her
    eum   him
    mē   me
    quae (*f.*)   who, which, she who
    quam (*acc. sing. f.*)   whom, which, she whom
    quem (*acc. sing. m.*) whom, which, he whom
    quī (*m.*)   who, which, he who
    tē   you

Adverbia
    cūr?   why?
    iam   now, already
    hīc   here

Coniūnctiōnēs
    neque   and not, but not, nor, neither
    quia   because

Alia (Cētera)
    ō!   oh!

IV. Dominus et Servī

Rēs Grammaticae Novae

1. Verbs
   a. Conjugations: *coniugātiōnēs*
   b. Mood:
      i.   *modus indicātīvus*
      ii. *modus imperātīvus*
2. Nouns: Vocative Case: *cāsus vocātīvus*
3. Adjectives
   a. Numbers: *numerī*
   b. Possessives: *eius/suus, meus/tuus*
4. Pronouns: Nominative, Genitive Case

We now leave the children for a while and turn to the grown-ups. There is a worried look on Julius's face; it turns out that a sum of money is missing. Who is the thief? The problem is not solved until the end of the chapter, of course—and by then, the culprit has already decamped! Later (in Caps. VI and VIII), you will find out where he is hiding and what he does with the money. But right now, you must set to work to discover who the thief is.

Lēctiō Prīma (Section I)

Verbs: Conjugations

The stem of a Latin verb ends in one of the long vowels *-ā, -ē, -ī*, or in a consonant. The verbs are therefore divided into four classes, called conjugations (*coniugātiōnēs*):

1st conjugation: *ā*-verbs, with stems ending in *-ā*: *vocā-, cantā-, pulsā-*.

2nd conjugation: *ē*-verbs, with stems ending in *-ē*: *tacē-, vidē-, habē-*.

3rd conjugation: consonant-verbs, with stems ending in a consonant: *pōn-, sūm-, discēd-*.

4th conjugation: *ī*-verbs, with stems ending in *-ī*: *venī-, audī-, dormī-*.

To these stems the different verbal endings are added (a vertical stroke [|] is here used to mark the division between stem and ending).

When *-t* is added:

- the last vowel of the stem becomes short: *voca̱|t, vide̱|t, veni̱|t*
- in the consonant-verbs a short *-i-* is inserted before the *-t*: *pōn|i̱t, sūm|i̱t, discēd|i̱t.*

Conjugations

ā-stems	*vocā̱-*
ē-stems	*vidē̱-*
consonant-stems	*pōṉ-*
ī-stems	*venī̱-*

This verbal form is called the **indicative** (Latin *indicātīvus,* "stating," "indicating"). The indicative makes a statement or asks a question.

Verbs: Moods: *Modī*

So far all of our reading has consisted of sentences that make statements or ask questions. In this chapter, you learn how to give commands. These different forms of the verb are called moods (*modus*). As you saw in the previous section, statements and questions fall into the category of the indicative mood (*modus indicātīvus*). Commands in Latin are expressed by the imperative mood (*modus imperātīvus*).

Imperative: *Modus Imperātīvus*

The form of the verb used to give orders is called the **imperative** (Latin *imperātīvus,* from *imperat,* "he, she, it orders"). When giving an order to one person, the Latin imperative consists of the shortest form of the verb called the **stem**, without any ending, e.g., *vocā! tacē! venī!,* or a short *-e* is added when the stem ends in a consonant, as in *pōne̱!* (the stem is *pōn-*). Examples:

Dāvum vocā! (l.24)	*Tacē, serve!* (l.37)
Venī! (l.27)	*Sacculum tuum in mēnsā pōne!* (l.60)

Imperative

vocā! vidē! venī! pōne!

In the following examples, the first verb is an **imperative** (gives an order), the second, **indicative** (makes a statement or asks a question).

vocā: call!	*voca|t*	he, she, it calls
vidē: see!	*vide|t*	he, she, it sees
pōn|e: put!	*pōn|it*	he, she, it puts
audī: listen!	*audi|t*	he, she, it listens

Pronouns: Genitive (*cāsus genetīvus*)

The genitive of *is* (which you will learn in Section II) is *eius* (cf. English "his, her"):

> *In sacculō eius (: Iūliī) est pecūnia.* (l.1)

Possessives: *meus, -a, -um/tuus, -a, -um*

The adjectives *meus, -a, -um* (my), *tuus, -a, -um* (yours) and *suus, -a, -um* (his own, her own, its own) are called **possessive adjectives**. The possessive adjective serves to replace the genitive (for all three genders: masculine, feminine, and neuter).

Possessives: *eius/suus*

English has one set of possessives for the 3rd person: *his, her, its*. Latin has two:

> the genitive pronoun   *eius*
> the possessive adjective   *suus, -a, -um*

Compare the following two sentences:

> *Dāvus sacculum eius sūmit.*   Davus takes *his* (someone else's) bag.
>
> *Dāvus sacculum suum sūmit.*   Davus takes *his own* bag. (l.74)

Both *eius* and *suus, -a, -um* mean *his, her, its*, but they are not interchangeable. To understand the difference, compare the two examples (ll.61–62):

> *Dāvus sacculum suum in mēnsā pōnit.*
>
> *Iam sacculus eius in mēnsā est.*

In the first sentence—*Dāvus sacculum suum in mēnsā pōnit*—the subject is Davus and the money also belongs to Davus; therefore "his" (or "his own") is expressed by the adjective *suum*. When the "his" (or "hers" or "its") refers back to the subject of the sentence, Latin uses the possessive adjective *suus, -a, -um*. In English, the word "own" is sometimes added to make the meaning plain: "his/her own."

In the second sentence—*Iam sacculus eius in mēnsā est*—the subject is *sacculus*, and "his" is expressed by the genitive of the pronoun: *eius*.

Look at another example:

> *Iūlius pecūniam suam sūmit.*   Julius takes his (own) money.

Note that "his own" is feminine, because it modifies *pecūniam*, even though it is translated "his" and refers to Julius. An adjective always has the same gender, number, and case as the noun it modifies.

In other words, when:

- referring to something that belongs to the grammatical subject of the sentence, the **adjective** *suus, -a, -um* is used: *Iūlius servum suum vocat.*
- referring to something that does not belong to the grammatical subject of the clause, the **pronoun** *eius* is used: *Servus eius abest.*

Recēnsiō: Possessive Adjectives and Possessive Pronouns

Compare the following examples:

Ubi est sacculus tuus?	Where is *your* bag? (l.58)
Ecce sacculus meus.	Here is *my* bag. (l.59)
Sūme sacculum tuum.	Take *your* bag. (l.73)
Dāvus sacculum eius sūmit.	Davus takes *his* (someone else's) bag.
Dāvus sacculum suum sūmit.	Davus takes *his own* bag. (l.74)

Nouns: Vocative in -*e*

When one person uses another's name as a form of address, he or she uses the vocative case, the case of "calling" (Latin *vocātīvus*, from *vocat*). We have already seen the characters in our story addressing each other in Cap. III:

Mamma! (l.60)

Mater! Mārcus Quīntum pulsat. (ll.16–17)

Fū, puer! (l.45)

St, puerī! (l.39)

Pater! Pa-ter! (l.41)

In each of these cases, the vocative has the same form as the nominative.

In the vocative of the 2nd declension, however, nouns that end in –*us* have a different form. When a 2nd declension nominative ends in -*us*, the vocative ends in -*e*. Medus calls Davus, crying, "*Dāve!*" (l.25), and when Davus greets his master, he says, "*Salvē, domine!*" and Julius answers, "*Salvē, serve!*" (ll.34–35).

Dāvus (nom.)	→	*Dāve* (voc.)
dominus (nom.)	→	*domine* (voc.)
servus (nom.)	→	*serve* (voc.)

Numbers (*numerī*): 1–10

Of the following cardinal numbers, only one, two, and three decline (see Cap. II); the rest are indeclinable adjectives:

1. *ūnus*: I
2. *duo*: II
3. *trēs*: III
4. *quattuor*: IV
5. *quīnque*: V
6. *sex*: VI
7. *septem*: VII
8. *octō*: VIII
9. *novem*: IX
10. *decem*: X

Lēctiō Altera (Section II)

Pronouns: Nominative

In the second of the two clauses, *Mēdus discēdit, quia is pecūniam dominī habet* (ll.76–77), the nominative *Mēdus* is replaced by the pronoun *is*, which is the nominative corresponding to the accusative *eum* (English "he" and "him"). In English, the pronoun is always used. In Latin, the nominative of this pronoun:

- is used only when it carries a certain emphasis (here, Medus is contrasted with Davus)
- is omitted when the subject is not emphasized ("implied subject," Cap. II)
  Mēdus nōn respondet, quia abest (next section, l.85).

In English, we must mark emphasis by inflection (voice) or underlining (for example) the stressed word:

Medus does not answer because he is not there.	*Mēdus nōn respondet, quia abest.*
Medus leaves because he has the master's money.	*Mēdus discēdit, quia is pecūniam dominī habet.*

Lēctiō Tertia (Section III)

The final reading in this chapter offers further practice of the material introduced in the first two readings. Notice in particular the emphasis of *is*:

Dāvus bonus servus est. Is nōn habet pecūniam meam. (ll.81–82)
Mēdus nōn venit, quia is habet pecūniam tuam. (ll.92–93)
Iūlius īrātus est—is nōn rīdet! (l.94)

Recēnsiō: Grammatical Terms

Stem: the form of the verb without its endings
Conjugation: one of the four groups of verbs: *Coniugātiō*
Mood: the name given to the category of expression of the verb (e.g., makes a statement; gives an order): *Modus*

Indicative: the mood of the verb that asks a question or makes a statement: *Indicātīvus*
Imperative: the mood of the verb that gives an order: *Imperātīvus*
Nominative: the case of the subject: *Nōminātīvus*
Accusative: the case of the direct object: *Accūsātīvus*
Genitive: the case of possession: *Genetīvus*
Vocative: the case of calling, or address: *Vocātīvus*

Studia Rōmāna

The *familia* consists of the master (*dominus*), his wife (*domina*), their children (*līberī*, the "free people"), and the slaves (*servī* and *ancillae*). The *familia* had a shared religious cult: the *lar familiāris* (or plural: *larēs familiārēs*) whose shrine was called a *larārium* (located usually in the *ātrium*, but sometimes also found in the kitchen or peristyle—an inner courtyard lined with rows of columns). *Larēs* are depicted as male dancers, mid-dance (as can be seen from their billowing tunics), carrying a drinking horn or a bowl. They often flank an image of a man with his toga over his head (the garb of someone acting in a priestly function and preparing to perform a sacrifice); this image represents the *genius* (spirit) of the *dominus* of the home. There is also often a snake depicted below the *larēs* and the *dominus*. The *larēs* belonged to and protected the place, and thus united all who lived in that place. In addition to the *larēs* for the homestead (the *larēs familiārēs*), there were also *larēs* for the crossroads in the neighborhood (the gods of the crossroads, honored at the festival of the *Compitālia*) and of the town in general (*larēs pūblicī*)—that is, of nearly every place that was marked as a specific location (as are the home, the crossroads, etc.).

The other important domestic gods were *Vesta* (the goddess of the hearth) and the *Penātēs*. The *Penātēs* were also guardians of the household, with dominion over the household goods, including food. Unlike the *Larēs*, they were associated with the *paterfamiliās* instead of the whole *familia*.

Slavery was an accepted fact of life in the ancient world. As Rome expanded from a series of huts on the Palatine Hill to a massive empire through warfare, prisoners of war became slaves. The children of those slaves (called *vernae*) increased the number. The master had complete control of his slaves' lives. Marriage between slaves was not recognized under Roman law, but they could be given permission to enter into a *contubernium*. Their children belonged to the master and were called *vernae* (home-bred slaves). When a master manumitted ("sent from his hand"; freed) a slave, that slave became a freedman, or *lībertus/līberta*. Although no longer part of the *familia*, the *lībertus* now belongs among his former master's dependents or clients (*clientēs*) and still has obligations to his former master. A slave could earn a small amount of money, a *pecūlium*, for his services; he might eventually save enough to buy his freedom.

The slaves in our story have names that suggest their origin. *Syra* might have come from Asia Minor (Syria and the area around Assyria). Varrō (first-century BC polymath, in *dē Linguā Latīnā*, 8.21) tells us that masters often choose the names of their new slaves either from the name of the person who sold the slave or the region in which the slave was purchased (or he might give the new slave whatever name appealed to him). *Dēlia* is a Greek name (was she bought at Delos, a center of slave trade?), as is *Dāvus*, whose name was popular in Roman comedy. In Cap. XVI, you will learn that Medus is also Greek. There were different types of slaves; the slaves in our story are house-slaves, but Julius owns other slaves who worked in the fields and the mines. There were highly educated slaves who could teach children (and their masters), and act as secretaries and scribes. There were skilled chefs (who were highly prized—and very expensive). One of Aemilia's *ancillae* would have acted as her hairdresser, *ōrnātrīx*. There were *pedisequī* and *pedisequae*, slaves who were in constant attendance on their masters (the name means someone who follows one's footsteps). A Roman involved in public affairs would have walked through the forum with his *nōmenclātor*, a slave whose job it was to tell his master the names of those they encountered in Rome.

Vocābula Disposita/Ōrdināta

Nōmina
  1st

mēnsa, -ae	table
pecūnia, -ae	money

  2nd

baculum, -ī	stick
indicātīvus, -ī (modus)	indicative
imperātīvus, -ī (modus)	imperative
nummus, -ī	coin
sacculus, -ī	purse
vocātīvus, -ī (cāsus)	vocative

Verba
  -ā (1)

accūsat	accuse
imperat (+ *dat.*)	command, order, rule
numerat	count
salūtat	greet

  -ē (2)

habet	have, hold, consider
pāret (+ *dat.*)	obey
tacet	be silent

consonant (3)

discēdit	go away, depart
pōnit	place, put, lay down
sūmit	take

irregular

abest	be absent
adest	be present

Adiectīva

1st/2nd (-us, -a, -um)

bonus, -a, -um	good
decem	ten
novem	nine
nūllus, -a, -um	no, none
octō	eight
quattuor	four
quīnque	five
septem	seven
suus, -a, -um	his, her, their (own)
vacuus, -a, -um	empty

Prōnōmina

eius	his (*gen. sing.* of **is, ea, id**)
is, ea, id	he, she, it, that
quī, quae, quod	who, which, that

Adverbia

rūrsus	again, back
tantum	so much, only

Alia

salvē	hello, good morning (*sing.*)

V. Vīlla et Hortus

Rēs Grammaticae Novae

1. Verbs
   a. Indicative and Imperative Plural
   b. *rīdet/rīdent*
   c. *agit/agunt*
2. Nouns
   a. Accusative Case (plural)
   b. Case Uses: Prepositions with the Ablative
3. Adjectives in *-er*
4. Pronouns: *is, ea, id*
5. Prepositions

The Roman Villa

We have made the acquaintance of what is evidently a prosperous Roman family, to judge from the splendid villa in which they live. The plan on page 33 and the pictures of various parts of the house will give you an impression of the layout of this typical Roman villa. Characteristic features are the atrium, with its opening in the roof and pool for rainwater, and the peristyle, the inner courtyard lined with rows of columns.

Lēctiō Prīma (Section I)

Accusative Case (Plural)

In Cap. III, you learned the accusative singular in *-um* and *-am*; we now learn the **accusative plural** ending in *-ōs* and *-ās*. The plural *fīliī* becomes *fīliōs* when it is the object of the verb: *Iūlius duōs fīliōs habet*; similarly, *fīliae* changes to *fīliās*. E.g.:

> *is multōs servōs habet* (l.6)
>
> *ea multās ancillās habet* (ll.7–8)

The accusative of masculine and feminine nouns always ends:
- in *-m* in the singular and
- in *-s* in the plural

Neuter nouns have the **same ending** in the accusative as in the nominative (sing. *-um*, pl. *-a*):

> *In vīllā sunt duo ōstia.* (nominative, l.25)

> *Vīlla duo ōstia et multās fenestrās habet.* (accusative, l.26)
> **accusative** sing. and pl.

	m.	f.	n.
sing.	-um	-am	-um
pl.	-ōs	-ās	-a

Prepositions with the Ablative Case

Prepositions (Latin *praepositiōnēs*, "placed in front") link a noun (or pronoun) to another word in the sentence. A preposition takes an object (either in the ablative, as here, or in the accusative); the preposition plus its object is called a **prepositional phrase**.

Since the first chapter, you have been using the preposition *in*:

> *Rōma in Italiā est.* (Cap. I, l.1)

> *Germānia in imperiō Rōmānō nōn est.* (Cap. I, ll.58–59)

> *Quot servī sunt in familiā tuā?* (Cap. II, l.74)

> *In sacculō meō* (Cap. IV, l.15)

In this chapter, you learn more prepositions. Like *in*, the prepositions *ab*, *cum*, *ex*, and *sine* cause the following nouns to take the ending *-ō* (m./n.) or *-ā* (f.) and in the plural *-īs*:

in ātriō	*cum līberīs*
ex hortō	*sine rosīs*
ab Aemiliā	

The forms in *-ō*, *-ā*, and *-īs* are called ablative (Latin *cāsus ablātīvus*).

> *ab, cum, ex, in, sine* + *-ō*, *-ā*, *-īs*

ablative	m./n.	f.
sing.	-ō	-ā
pl.	-īs	-īs

Adjectives in -er

You learned in Cap. II that not all masculine nouns end in -*us*; some, like *puer* and *liber*, end in -*er*. Not all adjectives end in -*us*, -*a*, -*um*. Some, like *pulcher, pulchra, pulchrum*, end in -*er*:

> *Syra nōn est fēmina <u>pulchra</u>, neque <u>pulcher</u> est nāsus eius.* (l.17)
>
> *cum rosīs <u>pulchrīs</u>* (l.61)
>
> *Rosae <u>pulchrae</u> sunt.* (l.63)

Notā Bene: pulcher, pulchra, pulchrum, like *liber, librī*, has an *e* only in the nominative singular. Like nouns ending in –*er*, the stem of an adjective ending in –*er* can be determined from the genitive singular; the feminine singular will also tell you if the adjective keeps the *e*: *pulchra*.

Pronoun *is, ea, id*

New forms of the pronoun *is* (masculine) are now introduced: feminine *ea*, neuter *id*; plural *iī* (= *eī*), *eae, ea*.

sing.	**m.**	**f.**	**n.**
nom.	*is*	*ea*	*id*
acc.	*eum*	*eam*	*id*
gen.	*eius*	*eius*	*eius*
abl.	*eō*	*eā*	*eō*
pl.	**m.**	**f.**	**n.**
nom.	*iī, eī*	*eae*	*ea*
acc.	*eōs*	*eās*	*ea*
gen.	*eōrum*	*eārum*	*eōrum*
abl.	*eīs/iīs*	*eīs/iīs*	*eīs/iīs*

Notā Bene:

- In the accusative and ablative, pronoun *is, ea, id* shows the same endings as the noun it represents; remembering the accusatives <u>*eum*</u> and <u>*eam*</u>, you will identify forms like *e<u>ō</u>, e<u>ā</u>* (abl. sing.), *e<u>ōs</u>, e<u>ās</u>* (acc. pl.) and *i<u>īs</u>* (= *e<u>īs</u>*, abl. pl.).
- The genitive plural is *e<u>ōrum</u>, e<u>ārum</u>* (thus, for *dominus serv<u>ōrum</u>*, you find *dominus e<u>ōrum</u>*).
- The genitive singular has a special form *eius,* which is the same for all three genders: you have already had *sacculus <u>eius</u>* (: *Iūliī*), now you find *nāsus <u>eius</u>* (: *Syrae*). (These genitives correspond to the English possessive pronouns "his/her/its/their").

Verbs: Indicative Plural

Lastly, you learn the 3rd person plural form of verbs:

Indicative: when the subject is in the plural (e.g., *puerī*), or is more than one person (e.g., *Mārcus et Quīntus*), the verb ends in *-nt* (cf. *est* and *su<u>nt</u>*):

> *Mārcus et Quīntus Iūliam voca<u>nt</u>.*
>
> *Puerī rīde<u>nt</u>.*
>
> *Multī servī in ūnō cubiculō dorm<u>iu</u>nt.* (l.40)

Notā Bene: In the consonant-verbs (3rd conjugation), a short vowel is inserted before the plural endings of the indicative:

- *-u-* before the indicative ending *-nt*:
  Puerī discēd<u>u</u>nt. (ll.75–76)
- Even in 4th conjugation verbs (*ī*) *-u-* is inserted before *-nt*:
  Puerī veni<u>u</u>nt.

Lēctiō Altera (Section II)

Verbs: Imperative Plural

Imperative: when two or more people are ordered to do something, the plural form of the imperative ending in *-te* is used:

> *Mārce et Quīnte! Iūliam vocā<u>te</u>!* (l.51)
>
> *Audī<u>te</u>!* (l.67)
>
> *Tacē<u>te</u>, puerī!* (l.72)

Notā Bene: As in the indicative, in the imperative plural of the consonant-verbs (3rd conjugation), a short vowel is inserted before the ending:

- *-i-* before the imperative ending *-te*
  Discēd<u>i</u>te, puerī! (cf. l.73)

Imperative and Indicative

		sing	pl.
1. *ā*	imp.	*vocā*	*vocā|te*
	ind.	*voca|t*	*voca|nt*
2. *ē*	imp.	*vidē*	*vidē|te*
	ind.	*vide|t*	*vide|nt*
3. con.	imp.	*pōn|e*	*pōn|ite*
	ind.	*pōn|it*	*pōn|unt*
4. *ī*	imp.	*audī*	*audī|te*
	ind.	*audi|t*	*audi|unt*

Verbs

rīdet/rīdent

Julia's remark, *"puerī mē rīdent"* (l.70), shows that *rīdet*, which is usually an intransitive verb, can take an object in the sense "laugh at": *Puerī Iūliam rīdent.*

rīdet alone	*Puerī rīdent.*	The boys are laughing.
rīdet + acc.	*Puerī me rīdent.*	The boys are laughing at me.

agit/agunt

The consonant-verb *agit, agunt* denotes action in general: *Quid agit Mārcus? Quid agunt puerī?* (English "do"). The imperative of this verb is often put before another imperative to emphasize the command, somewhat like our English "Come on!" or "Get going!" e.g., *Age! venī, serve! Agite! venīte, servī!*

> *age! agite!* + imp.

Recēnsiō: Prepositions with the Ablative

> *in*
> > *Iūlius in magnā vīllā habitat.* (l.1)
> > *Vīlla Iūliī in magnō hortō est.* (l.12)
> > *In hortīs sunt rosae et līlia.* (l.13)
>
> *ex*
> > *Discēdite ex peristȳlō.* (l.73)
> > *Puerī aquam sūmunt ex impluviō.* (l.83)
>
> *ab*
> > *Puerī Iūliam audiunt, neque iī ab Aemiliā discēdunt.* (l.56)
> > *Iūlia plōrat et cum ūnā rosā ab iīs discēdit.* (l.71)
>
> *cum*
> > *Iūlius in vīllā suā habitat cum magnā familiā.* (l.9)
> > *Pater et māter habitant cum Mārcō et Quīntō et Iūliā.* (ll.9–10)
> > *In Italiā sunt multae vīllae cum magnīs hortīs.* (ll.12–13)
>
> *sine*
> > *Aemilia sine virō suō Iūliō in vīllā est.* (ll.44–45)
> > *In oppidō Tūsculō est sine Aemiliā.* (ll.45–46)
> > *Puella sine rosīs pulchra nōn est.* (ll.63–64)

Studia Rōmāna

In this chapter, you learn the features of a Roman country house, called a *vīlla*. You will notice on the diagram on page 33 how many of the rooms are called *cubicula*, or bedchambers. Archaeologists assign the word *"cubiculum"* to small rooms in general. We often are not sure what the rooms were used for; therefore, every room you see marked as a *cubiculum* is not necessarily a bedroom.

The entranceway to a Roman house was called the *vestibulum*. The visitor would pass through this area into the *ātrium*. The *ātrium* usually had an opening in the roof called a *compluvium*, through which rainwater could fall into the *impluvium*—a small pool—below. The *ātrium* is the most public space in the house and it was here that visitors would be welcomed. Tall doors often flanked the room, two on each side, enclosing small rooms and the third set (in the photograph on p. 33, this third set has curtains rather than doors) leading to the *ālae*, or "wings" (the same word is used for birds' wings, as you will learn in Cap. X); these are open alcoves. At the far end of the *ātrium*, opposite the entrance and across the *impluvium*, is the *tablīnum*, or record-room, of the house (the word *tablīnum* is related to *tabula,* the word you met in Cap. I that can mean both "writings" as well as "writing tablet"). In some houses—as it appears from the illustration in your book—the *tablīnum* had a large opening onto the *peristȳlum* and/or *hortus*.

Just as the word *peristȳlum* comes from Greek (meaning "surrounded by columns"), the peristyle was a Greek architectural feature before it was a Roman one. Originally, the Roman house consisted of the *ātrium* and the rooms surrounding it with the garden (*hortus*) in back. The covered walkway created by the colonnade in the peristyle provided shade. At the far end of the peristyle in the diagram, you can see a dining room, called *triclīnium* in Latin. You will read about the *triclīnium* and dinner parties in Caps. XXX–XXXI.

Where was the kitchen (*culīna*, Cap. XXX)? Originally, cooking was done in the *ātrium* with portable braziers. Not every house seems to have had a permanent kitchen. But where we do find kitchens, they are off the peristyle and are simple affairs.

Your text tells you that *Vīlla duo ōstia et multās fenestrās habet* (l.26). Our evidence for windows is slight, but Pliny the Younger (*Gāius Plīnius Caecilius Secundus*), a Roman who lived a little before our narrative (around AD 62–113), includes several mentions of windows in his description of his seaside villa. While Roman houses in towns had either a private façade broken only by the door or an attached shop front (as you will see in Cap. VIII), they did not have windows looking out onto the street. It is most likely that windows were more common in the private parts of houses and when they provided a view. Rooms often had their own internal "view" in the guise of elaborate wall paintings. These ranged from original artworks by skilled craftsmen to less expensive scenes produced by workshops. Mosaics often covered the floor; these, like wall paintings, also ranged from the simple to the exquisite, like the Alexander mosaic in the House of the Faun in Pompeii.

There are other words for "house" besides *vīlla*. A *casa* is a small country cottage; a house is also called a *domus* (Cap. XIX) or, as a building, *aedificium* (Cap. XXV).

Vocābula Disposita/Ōrdināta

Nōmina
  1st

aqua, -ae	water
fenestra, -ae	window
rosa, -ae	rose
vīlla, -ae	country house, villa

  2nd

ablātīvus, -ī (cāsus)	ablative
ātrium, -ī	main room, hall
cubiculum, -ī	bedroom
hortus, -ī	garden
impluvium, -ī	water basin in the atrium for collecting rainwater
līlium, -ī	lily
nāsus, -ī	nose
ōstium, -ī	door, entrance
peristȳlum, -i	peristyle

Verba
  -ā (1)

amat/amant	love
dēlectat/dēlectant	delight, please
habitat/habitant	dwell, live

  consonant (3)

agit/agunt	drive, do, perform
carpit/carpunt	gather, pick, crop

Adiectīva
  1st/2nd (-us/er, -a, -um)

foedus, -a, -um	ugly, hideous
pulcher, -chra, -chrum	beautiful, fine
sōlus, -a, -um	alone, lonely

Prōnōmina

is, ea, id	he, she, it

Adverbia

etiam	also, even, yet

Praepositiōnēs

ab (*prp. + abl.*)	from, by
cum (*prp. + abl.*)	with
ex (*prp. + abl.*)	out of, by
sine (*prp. + abl.*)	without

VI. Via Latīna

Rēs Grammaticae Novae

1. Verbs
    a. *it/eunt*
    b. Passive Voice
2. Nouns
    a. Case Uses
        i. Accusative: Prepositions with the Accusative Case
        ii. Ablative:
            1. Preposition *ab/ā* + Ablative
            2. Ablative of Agent and Means/Instrument
    b. Constructions of Place
3. Correlatives: *tam/quam*

Roman Roads

Road communications were highly developed in the ancient Roman world. The different parts of the Roman Empire were connected by an excellent network of highways. These roads were primarily military, although they were also important to the economy. Not surprisingly, the Romans constructed a good number of roads in Italy during the time of their expansion from the fourth century BC onward. Vitruvius, an engineer and architect who lived at the time of the emperor Augustus, wrote a book called *dē Architectūrā*; he tells us about the careful construction of roads: how the ground is prepared and graded so that water drains properly, the levels beginning with the earth and ending with large paving stones. Wheel-ruts are still visible on many streets in Pompeii.

On the map on page 40 of Lingua Latīna, you see the most important Roman roads in Italy, among them the famous Via Appia, running southward from Rome and continuing all the way to Brundisium. The Via Appia is the oldest paved Roman road; it was built at the end of the fourth century BC from Rome to Capua (see the map). By the middle of the third century BC, it reached all the way to the coastal town of Brundisium.

Running almost parallel to the Via Appia is the Via Latina, built in the third century BC, which passes the town of Tusculum mentioned in the first chapter. Julius's villa stands in the neighborhood of this town, so that anyone going from there to Rome must follow the Via Latina. Therefore, it is not surprising to find Medus walking along this road. You will soon discover what it is that attracts him to the city.

Tusculum lies about 15 miles southeast of Rome, as you can see on the map. Its location—in the countryside but still an easy journey to Rome—made it an attractive place for prominent Romans to have villas. The Greek geographer Strabo (62 BC–AD 24) tells us that Tusculum can be seen from Rome. In the first century BC, Cicero had a home here, about which he speaks often and fondly in his letters, and where he wrote some of his philosophical works, including *Tūsculānae Disputātiōnēs*, or "The Discussions at Tusculum." Julius's estate, as you will learn in Cap. XXVII, lies to the southwest of Tusculum near Lake Albanus, an area that was as fertile as it was lovely (*amoenus*).

Lēctiō Prīma (Section I)

Prepositions with the Accusative Case

In Cap. V, you met some common **prepositions** that take the ablative (see *Recēnsiō* at the end of Cap. V). Most other prepositions take the **accusative**, e.g.:

ad	*ad vīllam*	to the country house (l.19)
ante	*ante lectīcam*	in front of the litter chair (l.33)
apud	*apud eum = cum eō*[1]	with him (l.37)
circum	*Circum Rōmam est mūrus antīquus.*	Around Rome is an ancient wall. (ll.14–15)
inter	*inter Rōmam et Capuam*	between Rome and Capua (ll.3–4)
per	*per portam*	through the gate (l.76)
post	*post lectīcam*	behind the litter chair (l.33)
prope	*prope Rōmam*	near Rome (l.8)

Prepositions *ad* and *ab/ā* (continued)

Ad indicates motion to a place—it is the opposite of *ab* (followed by the ablative), which indicates motion away **from** a place.

The corresponding interrogative adverbs are *quō* and *unde*:

> *Quō it Iūlius? Ad vīllam it.*

> *Unde venit? Ab oppidō.*

---

1. *Apud* most closely resembles French *chez*; it means in the presence of, at, near, as well as with.

quō?	*ad* + acc.
unde?	*ab* + abl.

Instead of *ab*, we often find the shortened form *ā* before a consonant, but never before a vowel or *h-*:

ā vīllā	*ab ancillā*
ā dominō	*ab oppidō*

ab + vowel and *h-*

ā/*ab* + cons. (except *h-*)

Verbs: *it/eunt*

The verb "to go" belongs to the 4th conjugation, but is irregular, as you can see from the difference between *audiunt* (they hear) and *eunt* (they go). An irregular verb is one whose endings don't follow the standard pattern of the four conjugations; the verb "is" (*est/sunt*) is also irregular.

Iūlius ab oppidō ad vīllam suam it.	Julius goes from the town to his country house. (l.20)
Dominus et servī ab oppidō ad vīllam eunt.	The master and slaves are going from the town to the country house. (ll.20–21)

Quō it Iūlius? (l.35)
Ad vīllam it. (l.35)
Iūlius et Cornēlius ad vīllās suās eunt. (l.57)

Correlatives: *Tam/Quam*

Quam is an interrogative adverb:

Quam longa est via Flāminia?	How long is the via Flaminia? (ll.11–12)

Tam answers the question posed in *quam*; together, they are called correlatives. Correlatives are adverbs or adjectives (Cap. VIII) that respond to each other. As you will see in Cap. VII, in Latin, pairs of correlatives often resemble *tam/quam* in that one starts with "t" and the other with "qu," and the rest of the word is the same. *Tam...quam* is best translated into English as "as...as":

Quam longa est via Flāminia?	
Via Latīna nōn tam longa est quam via Appia.	The Via Latina is not as long as the Via Appia. (ll.10–11)

Tiberis fluvius nōn tam longus est quam fluvius Padus. (l.13)
Circum oppidum Tūsculum mūrus nōn tam longus est quam circum Rōmam. (ll.16–17)

Saccī quōs Syrus et Lēander portant magnī sunt, sed saccus quem Syrus portat nōn <u>tam</u> magnus est <u>quam</u> saccus Lēandrī. (ll.27–29)

Lēctiō Altera (Section II)

Nouns: Constructions of Place with Names of Cities and Towns

I. Accusative (place to which) and Ablative (place from which or separation)

Motion **to** or **from** a town mentioned by name is expressed by the name of the town in the accusative or ablative, respectively, **without a preposition**. In Latin, therefore, we speak of traveling *Rōmā—Brundisium* (from Rome to Brundisium), or, if going in the opposite direction, *Brundisiō—Rōmam* (from Brundisium to Rome).

The **accusative** shows the place toward which one moves:

> *Rōmam it.* He is going to Rome. (l.50)
> *Cornēlius nōn Rōmam, sed Tūsculum it.* (ll.54–55)

It is the fundamental function of the **ablative** (with or without a preposition) to denote "place from which." In this function, it is called **ablative of separation** (*<u>abl</u>ātīvus* means "taking away"):

> *Tūsculō venit.* He is coming from Tusculum. (l.49)
>
> *Is nōn Tūsculō, sed Rōmā venit.* (ll.53–54)

Otherwise, prepositions are used:

> *Iūlius ab oppidō ad vīllam suam it.* (l.20)
>
> *Dominus et servī ab oppidō ad vīllam eunt.* (ll.20–21)

II. Locative Case (place in which)

To indicate where something or somebody is, the preposition *in* followed by the ablative is most often used:

> <u>*in*</u> *Italiā*
> <u>*in*</u> *oppidō*
> <u>*in*</u> *hortō*

The following examples show, however, that *in* is no more used with names of towns than *ad* and *ab*:

> *Cornēlius Tūsculī habitat.* (l.59)
> *Mēdus Rōm<u>ae</u> est.* (l.47)

Instead of "*in*," the name takes the ending *-ī* or *-ae* according to whether the nominative ends in *-um/-us* or *-a*. This form is called locative (Latin *locātīvus*, from *locus*, "place"):

| Ubi habitat Cornēlius? Is Tūsculī habitat. | Where does Cornelius live? He lives in Tusculum. (ll.58–59) |
| Rōmam it, quia Lydia Rōmae habitat. | He is going to Rome because Lydia lives in Rome. (ll.77–78) |

Locative *-ī, -ae*

quō? Tūscul<u>um</u> Rōm<u>am</u>

unde? Tūscul<u>ō</u> Rōm<u>ā</u>

ubi? Tūscul<u>ī</u> Rōm<u>ae</u>

Verbs: Passive Voice (*vōx passīva*)

All the verbs you have been using so far are in the active voice (the subject does the acting), e.g.:

Dāvus et Ursus portant Iūlium.

Syrus saccum portat. (l.25)

We can express the same idea differently using the passive voice (the subject receives the action):

Iūlius ab Ursō et Dāvō portātur. (l.62)

Saccus ā Syrō portātur.

Saccī ā Syrō portantur.

Puerī ā puellā videntur.

Active Voice:
- Subject does the acting
- endings *-t, -nt*

Passive Voice:
- Subject acted upon
- endings *-tur, -ntur*
- The person or thing performing the action goes into the ablative (see next section)

In addition to the examples in the text and GRAMMATICA LATINA in LINGUA LATĪNA, consider the following sentences from earlier chapters changed into the passive:
- 1st conjugation
  Puer parvam puellam pulsat (Cap. II, l.29) → Parva puella ā puerō pulsātur.
- 2nd conjugation
  Quīntus Mārcum videt (Cap. II, l.11) → Mārcus ā Quīntō vidētur.

- 3rd conjugation
  Dāvus sacculum in mēnsā pōnit (Cap. IV, l.61) → *Sacculus ā Dāvō in mēnsā pōnitur.*

- 4th conjugation
  Puerī Iūliam audiunt (Cap. V, l.56) → *Iūlia ā puerīs audītur.*

	active	passive
1.	*voca|t*	*vocā|tur*
	voca|nt	*voca|ntur*
2.	*vidē|t*	*vidē|tur*
	vidē|nt	*vidē|ntur*
3.	*pōn|it*	*pōn|itur*
	pōn|unt	*pōn|untur*
4.	*audi|t*	*audī|tur*
	audi|unt	*audi|untur*

Ablative Case (Agent and Means/Instrument)

Consider the following sentence:

Mārcus Iūliam pulsat.   Marcus hits Julia.

If we make that sentence passive, we get:

Iūlia pulsātur ā Mārcō.   Julia is hit by Marcus.

In the second sentence, Marcus is no longer the grammatical subject, but he is still the actor, or **agent**, of the verb. In the passive voice, the name of the person by whom the action is performed, the **agent**, is in the ablative preceded by *ab* or *ā* (*ā Mārcō*). This construction is called the **ablative of personal agent**, that is, when the agent is a person, not a thing or an animal:

Iūlius ab Ursō et Dāvō portātur.	Julius is (being) carried by Ursus and Davus. (l.62)
Saccī quī ā Syrō et Lēandrō portantur magnī sunt.	The bags which are being carried by Syrus and Leander are big. (ll.65–66)

Dominus ā servō malō timētur. (ll.73–74)

Verba Mēdī ā Lydiā laetā audiuntur. (l.95)

When the action is performed by something other than a person—an animal or an inanimate object—the source of the action is expressed by the simple ablative without the preposition *ab/ā*. The simple ablative here indicates means or cause. This construction, called the **ablative of means** (also **ablative of instrument**—Latin *ablātīvus īnstrūmentī*) is very common both in passive and active sentences: e.g.,

Cornēlius equō vehitur.	Cornelius is being transported by a horse. (or, more idiomatically, "he is riding a horse") (ll.68–69)
Iūlius lectīcā vehitur.	Julius is being carried in a litter chair. (l.69)
Lȳdia verbīs Mēdī dēlectātur.	Lydia is delighted by Medus's words. (l.91)
Dominus servum baculō verberat.	
Servī saccōs umerīs portant.	
Mēdus viā Latīnā Rōmam ambulat.	

Sometimes, the agent/means is left unexpressed, e.g.:

Dominī vehuntur.	Masters are carried (or "travel"). (l.70)

In the sentence *Mēdus Lydiam amat et ab eā amātur* (ll.78–79), both active and passive are used.

Vocābula Disposita/Ōrdināta

Nōmina
  1st

amīca, -ae	female friend
lectīca, -ae	litter, sedan
porta, -ae	gate
via, -ae	road, way, street

  2nd

āctīvum, -ī (verbum)	active
amīcus, -ī	friend
equus, -ī	horse
inimīcus, -ī	(personal) enemy
locātīvus (cāsus)	locative
mūrus, -ī	wall
passīvum (verbum)	passive
saccus, -ī	sack
umerus, -ī	shoulder

  3rd (you will learn about this family of nouns later)

praepositiō (*f.*)	preposition

Verba
  -ā (1)

ambulat, ambulant	walk
intrat, intrant	enter
portat, portant	carry

  -ē (2)

timet, timent	fear, be afraid (of)

consonant (3)
  vehit, vehunt   carry, convey, ride, sail, travel
  Irregular
  it/eunt   go

Adiectīva
  1st/2nd (-us/er, -a, -um)
    duodecim   twelve
    fessus, -a, -um   tired, weary
    longus, -a, -um   long
    malus, -a, -um   bad, wicked, evil

Adverbia
    ante   in front of, before
    autem   but, however
    itaque   therefore
    nam   for
    procul   far (*often combines with preposition* **ab**)
    quam   how, as, than
    tam   so, as

Praepositiōnēs
    ā (*prp. + abl.*)   from, of, since, by
    ad (*prp. + acc.*)   to, toward, by, at, till
    ante (*prp. + acc.*)   in front of, before
    apud (*prp. + acc.*)   beside, near, by
    circum (*prp. + acc.*)   around
    inter (*prp. + acc.*)   between, among, during
    per (*prp. + acc.*)   through, by, during
    post (*prp. + acc.*)   behind, after, later
    procul ab (*+ abl.*)   far from
    prope (*prp. + acc.*)   near, nearly

Vocābula Interrogātīva
    quam?   how?
    quō?   where (to)?
    unde?   from where? whence?

VII. Puella et Rosa

Rēs Grammaticae Novae

1. Verbs
   a. Imperative of *esse*
   b. *salvē/salvēte*
   c. Compound Verbs
2. Nouns: Case Uses
   a. Accusative Case: Prepositions
   b. Genitive with *plēnus*
   c. Dative Case
      i. Dative Case *is, ea, id*
      ii. Dative Case: Interrogative and Relative Pronoun
      iii. Dative with Compound Verbs
   d. Ablative: Preposition *ex/ē* + the Ablative Case
3. Pronouns
   a. Reflexive Pronoun
   b. Demonstrative Pronouns: *hic, haec, hoc*
4. Adverbs: Interrogative *num* and *nōnne*
5. Point of Style: *et…et/neque…neque/nōn sōlum…sed etiam*

Julius Returns, with Gifts

Syra comforts a weeping Julia, who is concerned about the appearance of her nose. When Julius comes back from town, he usually brings something with him for the family, so in this chapter, you find out what is in the two sacks that Syrus and Leander have been carrying.

Lēctiō Prīma (Section I)

Reflexive Pronoun

The examples *Puella sē in speculō videt et sē interrogat* (ll.8–9) show that the pronoun *sē* (acc.) is used when referring to the subject in the same sentence; *sē* is called the reflexive pronoun (English "himself/herself/themselves"). Reflexive means it "bends back" toward the subject.

Puella sē in speculō videt et sē interrogat.
   The girl sees herself in the mirror and asks herself. (ll.8–9)
Puella Syram in speculō videt et eam interrogat.
   The girl sees Syra in the mirror and asks her (Syra).
Iūlia Syram post sē in speculō videt, i.e. post Iūliam. (l.15)

When to use what:

When the pronoun refers back to the subject of the sentence:
  • use the **reflexive** *sē* (acc.): himself/herself/themselves

When the pronoun refers to a person or thing **other than** the subject of the sentence:
  • use the personal pronoun *eum/eam/eōs/eās*: him/her/them

Recēnsiō: sē vs. suus, -a, -um

Sē is a pronoun and takes the place of a noun that refers back to the (3rd person) subject of the sentence.

   Iūlia Syram post sē in speculō videt. (l.15) = *Iūlia Syram post Iūliam in speculō videt.*

Suus, -a, -um is a possessive adjective and modifies a noun that belongs to the (3rd person) subject of the sentence.

   Aemilia virum suum amat. (l.4) = *Aemilia virum Aemiliae amat.*

Accusative Case: Prepositions

Compare the sentences:

   Iūlius in vīllā est.
   Iūlius in vīllam intrat.

In the first sentence, *in* takes the ablative (*vīllā*), as we have seen often; in the second, it is followed by the accusative (*vīllam*). The examples show that *in* takes the accusative when there is motion into a place. Therefore we read:

   Syra in cubiculum intrat. (l.14)
   "Venī in hortum, Iūlia!" (l.17)

Place where:

   ubi? in + ablative
   in vīllā, in hortō, in cubiculō

Place to which:

   quō? in + accusative
   in vīllam, in hortum, in cubiculum

Interrogative *num* and *nōnne*

A question introduced with *num* calls for a negative answer; therefore, Julia asks, "*Num nāsus meus foedus est?*" (l.20). The *num* shows she wants a "no!" answer. The opposite effect is obtained by *nōnne*: when Syra asks, "*Nōnne fōrmōsus est nāsus meus?*" (l.26), she certainly expects the answer to be "yes." Nevertheless, Julia says, "*Immō foedus est!*" The word *immō* serves to stress a denial (English "no," "on the contrary").

question:	expected answer:
nōnne…est?	*…est*
num…est?	*…nōn est*

Verbs: Imperative of the Verb *esse*

The imperative of *est* is *es!* (i.e., the stem without an ending; plural *este!*):

> "*Tergē oculōs! Es laeta!*" (l.23)

> *Este bonī* (be good!)

Lēctiō Altera (Section II)

Preposition *Ex/ē* + the Ablative Case

The example *Iūlia ē cubiculō exit* shows the shorter form *ē* of the preposition *ex*. The same rule applies to the use of *ex* and *ē* as to *ab* and *ā*:

- before vowels and *h-*, only *ex* and *ab* are used
- *ē* and *ā* are only used before consonants, never before vowels or *h-*
- *ex* and *ab* can also be used before consonants

Examples with *ex* and *ē*:

- *ē/ex vīllā* (before a consonant, use either *ē* or *ex*)
- *ex ātriō* (before a vowel, use only *ex*)
- *ex hortō* (before an "h," use only *ex*)

Dative Case (*cāsus datīvus*)

I. Nouns

When we are told that Julius gives something to a member of the family, the name of this person ends in *-ō* (*Mārcō, Quīntō, Syrō, Lēandrō*) or in *-ae* (*Aemiliae, Iūliae, Syrae, Dēliae*). This form, ending in *-ō* in the masculine (and neuter) and in *-ae* in the feminine, is called dative (Latin *datīvus*, from *dat*, "gives"):

> *Iūlius Syrō et Lēandrō māla dat.*

In the plural, the dative ends in *-īs* like the ablative:

> *Iūlius servīs māla dat.*

> *Iūlius ancillīs māla dat.*

dative	m./n.	f.
sing.	*-ō*	*-ae*
pl.	*-īs*	*-īs*

Summary of 1st and 2nd Declension Endings

	m. sing.	m. pl.	f. sing.	f. pl.	n. sing.	n. pl.
nom.	*-us*	*-ī*	*-a*	*-ae*	*-um*	*-a*
acc.	*-um*	*-ōs*	*-am*	*-ās*	*-um*	*-a*
gen.	*-ī*	*-ōrum*	*-ae*	*-ārum*	*-ī*	*-ōrum*
dat.	*-ō*	*-īs*	*-ae*	*-īs*	*-ō*	*-īs*
abl.	*-ō*	*-īs*	*-ā*	*-īs*	*-ō*	*-īs*
voc.	*-e*					

II. *is, ea, id*

The dative of the pronoun *is, ea, id* is *eī* in the singular:

> *Iūlius eī* (: *Quīntō/Iūliae*) *mālum dat.*

In the plural, the dative of the pronoun *is, ea, id* is *iīs* (or *eīs*):

> *Iūlius iīs* (: *servīs/ancillīs*) *māla dat.*

The forms are the same for all three genders.

Summary of *is, ea, id* and Reflexive Pronoun *sē*

	sing.			pl.			reflexive
	m.	f.	n.	m.	f.	n.	pronoun
nom.	*i|s*	*e|a*	*i|d*	*i|ī*	*e|ae*	*e|a*	
acc.	*e|um*	*e|am*	*i|d*	*e|ōs*	*e|ās*	*e|a*	*sē*
gen.	*e|ius*	*e|ius*	*e|ius*	*e|ōrum*	*e|ārum*	*e|ōrum*	(Cap. X)
dat.	*e|ī*	*e|ī*	*e|ī*	*i|īs*	*i|īs*	*i|īs*	*sibi*
abl.	*e|ō*	*e|ā*	*e|ō*	*i|īs*	*i|īs*	*i|īs*	*sē*

Salvē/Salvēte

The greeting *Salvē!* expresses a wish for good health. It was understood as an imperative, so it has a plural form in *-te*: "*Salvēte, fīliī!*" (l.31)

sing.	*salvē!*
pl.	*salvē|te!*

Demonstrative Pronouns: *hic, haec, hoc*

Referring to things close to him, Julius says, e.g., <u>hic</u> *saccus* (l.43) and <u>hoc</u> *mālum* (ll.90–91), and Julia says <u>haec</u> *rosa* of the flower that she is holding (l.85). The **demonstrative** (or pointing) pronoun *hic, haec, hoc* (English "this") is treated in Cap. VIII.

Plēnus + the Genitive Case

Note the genitive after *plēnus* ("full <u>of</u>…"):

> *Hic saccus plēnus māl<u>ōrum</u> est.* (ll.43–44)
> *Oculī Iūliae plēnī sunt lacrim<u>ārum</u>.* (l.79)

> *plēnus* + gen.

Verbs: Compound Verbs

Compound verbs often have prepositions as their first element, like <u>ad</u>-est and <u>ab</u>-est. In this chapter, you find <u>in</u>-est, <u>ad</u>-venit, <u>ad</u>-it, <u>ex</u>-it, and in the next, <u>ab</u>-it. Often, the same preposition is put before a noun in the same sentence:

> *Quid <u>in</u>est <u>in</u> saccīs?* (l.39)
> *Iūlius <u>ad</u> vīllam <u>ad</u>venit.* (l.30)
> *Iūlia <u>ē</u> cubiculō <u>ex</u>it.* (ll.82–83)

compounds with prepositions:

> *ad-, ab-, ex-, in-*

Lēctiō Tertia (Section III)

Dative Case (continued): Interrogative and Relative Pronoun

The dative (sing.) of the interrogative and relative pronoun is *cui* (see ll.101–104):

> <u>Cui</u> *Iūlius mālum dat?* (l.101)
> *Puer/puella <u>cui</u> Iūlius mālum dat est fīlius/fīlia eius.* (ll.101–102)

The genitive of the interrogative and relative will be met in Cap. VIII.

Point of Style: *et…et/neque….neque/nōn sōlum…sed etiam*

Note the repetition of the conjunctions *et* and *neque* (ll.50, 57):

> *<u>et</u> Mārcus <u>et</u> Quīntus māla habent.*   English "both…and"
> *Servī <u>neque</u> māla <u>neque</u> pira habent.*   English "neither…nor"

Instead of *et...et*, we often find *nōn sōlum...sed etiam*:

> *nōn sōlum mūla, sed etiam pira.* (l.56)   English "not only...but also"

et...et
neque...neque
nōn sōlum...sed etiam

Recēnsiō: Interrogative Words

Quis? Quid?	Who? What?
Ubi?	Where? In what place?
Quot?	How many?
Cūr?	Why?
Unde?	Whence? From what place?
Quō?	Where? To what place?
-ne?	Asks a question with no expectations.
Nōnne?	Expects a "yes" answer.
Num?	Expects a "no" answer.

Studia Rōmāna

While her brothers attend school (Caps. XIV, XV, XVII, XVIII), Julia remains at home; she is too young for school. Not all girls were educated outside the home, but there is evidence that some girls were—even in the early years of Rome's history (Livy, 3.44).

The amount of education girls received varied greatly. For some girls, education consisted of learning the domestic duties involved in managing a household. Others were clearly well educated and even wrote poetry. Although we have poems remaining only from two women poets (both named Sulpicia), the poets Propertius, Tibullus, and Catullus (all first century BC) refer to women in their poetry as *docta* (learned), a word that suggests they wrote verse. A famous portrait from Pompeii shows a young woman holding a stylus and a tabula, pondering her next words. Clearly her family wanted to publicize her education.

Young girls from prominent families participated in festivals, particularly in the chorus (Catullus 34, "Hymn to Diana"; Horace, *Carmen Saeculāre*). There were priesthoods open to women, most exalted of which were the six Vestal Virgins; a daughter of a patrician father could become one of the two young girls (aged six to ten) who became apprentices to the service of Vesta. Just as Vesta protected the home (see Cap. IV) she was also the guardian of Rome's sacred fire.

Her parents' aspirations for Julia are to be a wife and mother. The age of marriage varied, and while some girls were married very young, not all were. A law that Roman girls could not be married before the age of twelve tells us just how young! A girl required a dowry (*dōs*), money that a family gave to her husband or his family when they were married. If the couple were divorced or if the wife died, the dowry had to be returned.

Girls were expected to be chaste and *mōrigera* (compliant to her father and later to her husband). The Younger Pliny (*Plīnius Secundus,* first century AD) gives us a portrait of ideal young womanhood in a letter he wrote about the death of the young daughter of a friend (*Epist.* 5.16). She was only thirteen and about to be married. Pliny praises her effusively as a bright young woman, an eager reader with a joyful and lovable personality. She combined the virtues of all ages in one: the wisdom of an old woman (*anīlis prūdentia*), the serious-ness of character of a married woman (*gravitās mātrōnālis*), the charm of a young girl and virginal modesty (*suāvitās puellāris cum virginālī verēcundiā*). She bore her illness with restraint (*temperantia*), patient endurance (*patientia*), and self-possession (*cōnstantia*).

Pliny's letter is not an isolated example. When his daughter Tullia died in childbirth, Cicero was distraught and wrote many letters trying to come to terms with his feelings. During the time of our narrative, letters between the emperor Marcus Aurelius (AD 121–180) and his friend *Mārcus Cornēlius Frontō* (c. AD 95–c. 166) contain many references to their love of their children, girls as well as boys. We know from inscriptions (particularly epitaphs), from images on tomb markers as well as from literary representations, that girls were much loved.

Salutations and valedictions in Latin: in this chapter, you learned to say "hello" to one person (*salvē*) and to more than one (*salvēte*). Romans even today say, "Salve!" as an informal greeting. You can also say, *Quid novī est?* or just *Quid novī?*, which means, "What's new?" When leaving, you can say, *Valē* or *Valēte* ("Be well! Fare well!," Cap. XIV).

Vocābula Disposita/Ōrdināta

Nōmina
  1st
    lacrima, -ae   tear
  2nd
    datīvus, -ī (cāsus)   dative
    mālum, -ī   apple
    oculus, -ī   eye
    ōsculum, -ī   kiss
    ōstiārius, -ī   doorkeeper
    pirum, -ī   pear
    speculum, -ī   mirror

Verba
  -ā (1)
    dat, dant   give
    exspectat, exspectant   wait (for), expect
    lacrimat   cry
  -ē (2)
    tenet, tenent   hold, keep (back)
    terget, tergent   wipe
  consonant (3)
    claudit, claudunt   shut, close
    currit, currunt   run
    vertit, vertunt   turn
  -ī (4)
    advenit, adveniunt   arrive
    aperit, aperiunt   open, disclose
  Irregular
    adit, adeunt   go to, approach
    exit, exeunt   go out
    inest, insunt   be in

Adiectīva
  1st/2nd (-us/er, -a, -um)
    fōrmōsus, -a, -um   beautiful
    plēnus, -a, -um (+ *gen./abl.*)   full (of)

Prōnōmina
    hic, haec, hoc   this
    sē, sibi   himself, herself

Adverbia
    immō   no, on the contrary
    illīc   there[1]
    nōn sōlum…sed etiam   not only…but also

Coniūnctiōnēs
    et…et   both…and
    neque…neque   neither…nor

Praepositiōnēs
    ē (*prp. + abl.*)   out of, from, of, since

Vocābula Interrogātīva
    nōnne?   not?

---

1. Accent on the ultima: *illīc*; originally the word was *illīce*, with accent on the long penult; when the *e* dropped, the accent was retained.

VIII. Taberna Rōmāna

Rēs Grammaticae Novae

1. Verbs
    a. 3rd Conjugation "i-stems"
2. Nouns
    a. Case Uses
        i. Ablative of Price (*ablātīvus pretiī*)
        ii. Ablative of Means/Instrument (*ablātīvus īnstrūmentī*) (continued)
        iii. Dative (continued): Indirect Object
3. Adjectives
    a. Interrogative Adjective
    b. Pronoun vs. Interrogative Adjective
    c. Correlatives: *tantus/quantus*
4. Pronouns
    a. Relative Pronoun without an Antecedent
    b. Demonstratives *hic, haec, hoc/ille, illa, illud*
5. Adverbs
    a. *quam*
6. Points of Style: *convenit*

Daily Life: Shopping

In the ancient world, people did their shopping over open counters lining the streets. Passers-by could simply stand on the pavement in front of a shop and buy what they wanted. We can be sure that the shopkeepers gave their customers every encouragement.

Lēctiō Prīma (Section I)

Pronouns

In this chapter, we pay particular attention to some important pronouns:
- the **interrogative** pronoun: *quis, quae, quid* (introduced in Cap. II)
- the **relative** pronoun: *quī, quae, quod* (introduced in Cap. III)

- the **demonstrative** pronouns
  is, ea, id (introduced in Cap. III)
  hic, haec, hoc (introduced in Cap. VII)
  ille, illa, illud

Relative Pronoun without an Antecedent (*Quī = Is quī*)

Instead of saying "he who, etc." or "whoever," Latin sometimes has just "who," e.g.:

> *Quī tabernam habet, tabernārius est = is quī...*
>   Whoever has a shop is a shopkeeper. (ll.3–4)

> *Quī magnam pecūniam habent ōrnāmenta emunt = Iī quī...*
>   Those who have a lot of money buy jewelry. (ll.16–17)

> *Quae nūllam aut parvam pecūniam habent ōrnāmenta aspiciunt
>   tantum, nōn emunt.* (ll.14–15)

> *Pecūniōsus est quī magnam pecūniam habet.* (l.35)

When the relative pronoun is used without an antecedent, a demonstrative pronoun may be understood, that is, *quī* can equal *is quī.*

Demonstrative Pronouns

The demonstrative pronoun *hic, haec, hoc* points to something that is near the speaker (compare the adverb *hīc,* "here") and represents the English "this." In the first reading, we meet only the feminine singular, nominative, accusative/ablative:

> *haec taberna?* (l.2)
> *in hāc viā* (l.11)
> *ad hanc tabernam* (l.16)

Ablative of Means/Instrument (*ablātīvus instrūmentī*) (continued)

You learned the ablative of means or instrument in Cap. VI (in conjunction with the passive voice). Here are more examples of the ablative of instrument (without prepositions):

Fēminae ōrnāmentīs dēlectantur.	Women are delighted by adornments. (ll.12–13)
Gemmīs et margarītīs ānulīsque ōrnantur.	They are adorned by jewels and pearls and rings. (l.24)
Lydia tabernam Albīnī digitō mōnstrat.	Lydia points to the store of Albinus with her finger. (l.43)

Interrogative Adjective

In Cap. II, you learned the interrogative pronoun, which asks the question "who, what?" The interrogative adjective is used before nouns:

quī servus?	what/which slave?
quae ancilla?	what/which slave-woman?
quod oppidum?	what/which town?
Quī vir et quae fēmina? (l.26)	
Quod ōrnāmentum? (ll.30–31)	

Notā Bene: The interrogative pronoun looks the same as the interrogative adjective (and relative pronoun) *except* in the nominative masculine and neuter singular:

quis, quid	nominative m./n. singular interrogative <u>pronoun</u>
quī, quod	nominative m./n. singular interrogative <u>adjective</u>

Recēnsiō: Interrogative Pronoun vs. Interrogative Adjective

Quis clāmat?	Who is shouting? (pronoun)
Quī puer clāmat?	What boy is shouting? (adjective)
Quae ōrnāmentum accipit?	Who receives the jewelry? (pronoun)
Quae fēmina ōrnāmentum accipit?	What woman receives the jewelry? (adjective)
Quid vēndit tabernārius?	What does the shopkeeper sell? (pronoun)
Quod ōrnāmentum vēndit tabernārius?	What piece of jewelry does the shopkeeper sell? (adjective)

Notā Bene:

- You will sometimes find *quis* (i.e., the form of the interrogative pronoun) used instead of *quī* (the form of the interrogative adjective) before a noun (especially a name) in questions of identity: *Quis servus? Mēdus.*
- While we here use *quae* for the nominative feminine singular of the interrogative pronoun, when you read ancient authors, you will usually find *quis* used for both masculine and feminine.

3rd Conjugation "i-stems"

So far you have learned verbs with stems ending in a long vowel (ā, ē, ī,) or a consonant. The final group of verbs has a stem ending in a short ĭ and is grouped with the 3rd conjugation. In this chapter, we see the verbs *accipit* and *aspicit*, which have plural forms in *-iunt*:

> Stem: *accipi-*; *accipit*; *accipiunt*

> Stem: *aspici-*; *aspicit*; *aspiciunt*

The short ĭ appears only before an ending beginning with a vowel, such as *-unt*: *accipiunt, aspiciunt*; otherwise, these verbs behave like consonant-verbs and are regarded as belonging to the 3rd conjugation.

The imperatives of "i-stems" (introduced in Section II of LINGUA LATINA) in *-e, -ite* are just like consonant stems:

> *accipe! accipite!*

> *aspice! aspicite!*

You will learn more about i-stem verbs in Cap. XII. When you have learned all the forms of the verb, it will be easy to distinguish the consonant and i-stems of the 3rd conjugation. Until then, they will be listed separately in the vocabulary.

Lēctiō Altera (Section II)

Demonstrative Pronouns

In this reading, we meet more forms of *hic, haec, hoc*:

> *hae margarītae* (l.49)   *hic ānulus* (l.69)
> *hī ānulī* (l.53)   *hunc ānulum* (l.76)
> *in hīs ānulīs* (l.55)   *huius (ānulī)* (l.75)

We are also introduced to the demonstrative *ille, illa, illud*, which refers to something that is further away from the speaker and is represented by the English "that":

> *illam tabernam* (l.41)   *illum (ānulum)* (l.76)
> *illa ōrnāmenta* (l.42)   *illīus ānulī* (l.75)
> *ille ānulus* (l.70)

Like *hic, haec, hoc* and *ille, -a, -ud*, most pronouns have the endings *-īus* in the genitive and *-ī* in the dative in all three genders (but the *i* is short or consonantal in *eius, cuius, huius, cui, huic*).

The neuter ending *-ud* in *illud* is also found in *alius, -a, -ud* (l.33) and is like the *-od* in *quod*.

See the paradigms for *hic haec hoc, ille illa illud,* and *is ea id* in the *recēnsiō* at the end of the chapter.

Correlatives: *tantus/quantus*

In Cap. VI, you learned the correlatives *tam...quam* (as...as). When talking about size, the adjectives *tantus* and *quantus* are used (instead of *tam magnus* and *quam magnus*). So, *tantus...quantus* stands for *tam magnus quam*. *Tantus...quantus* ("as big as") are correlative adjectives, as *tam...quam* are correlative adverbs (l.75). As adjectives, they agree with the nouns they modify; as correlatives, they respond to one another:

Digitus quārtus nōn tantus est quantus digitus medius.	The fourth finger is not <u>as big as</u> the middle finger. (ll.126–128)
Pretium illīus ānulī tantum est quantum huius.	The price of that ring is <u>as great as</u> that of this one. (l.75)

Tantus and *quantus* can also be used alone:

Tanta gemma sōla octōgintā sēstertiīs cōnstat.	Such a large gem alone costs 80 sesterces. (ll.64–65)
Quantum est pretium illīus ānulī?	How much is the price of that ring? (ll.72–73)

Remember, you have already learned (in Cap. IV) *tantum* as an adverb meaning "only."

Quae nūllam aut parvam pecūniam habent ōrnāmenta aspiciunt tantum, nōn emunt.	Those (women) who have no or little money only look at jewelry, they don't buy. (ll.14–19)

Quam

Quam is also used in exclamations and means "how":

"Ō, quam pulchra sunt illa ōrnāmenta!"	Oh, how beautiful those ornaments are! (ll.41–42)

Recēnsiō: Quam

- relative pronoun: feminine accusative singular
  Puella quam Aemilia videt est Iūlia.
- interrogative pronoun: feminine accusative singular
  Quam videt Aemilia?
- interrogative adjective: feminine accusative singular
  Quam puellam videt Aemilia?
- adverb correlating with *tam* (= as)
  Estne via Latīna tam longa quam Via Aurelia?
- adverb in questions and exclamations (= how)
  Quam pulchra est vīlla Iūliī!

Ablative of Price (*ablātīvus pretiī*)

With the verbs *emit*, *vēndit*, and *cōnstat* (verbs of buying and selling, etc.), the price is in the ablative, called *ablātīvus pretiī* ("ablative of price"). Examples:

> *Hic ānulus centum nummīs cōnstat.*   This ring costs 100 coins. (l.59)

> *Albīnus…Mēdō ānulum vēndit sēstertiīs nōnāgintā.* (ll.116–117)

Dative (continued)

In the last example, *Mēdō* is **dative** with *vēndit*. The dative now occurs also with *ostendit* (ll.46, 52, 58, 83) and *mōnstrat* (l.130). Being transitive, these verbs have an object in the accusative, which is often called the **direct object** to distinguish it from the dative, which is called the **indirect object**. Examples:

Albīnus Lȳdiae margarītās ostendit.
Albinus shows Lydia the pearls. (ll.46–47)

Shows what?	pearls, accusative direct object
Shows to whom?	Lydia, dative indirect object

Albīnus iīs trēs ānulōs ostendit.
Albinus shows them three rings. (l.52)

Shows what?	three rings, accusative direct object
Shows to whom?	them, dative indirect object

Lȳdia, quae Rōmae habitat, Mēdō viam mōnstrat.
Lydia, who lives in Rome, points out the road to Medus. (ll.129–130)

Shows what?	road, accusative direct object
Shows to whom?	Medus, dative indirect object

Points of Style: *Convenit*

Latin is not English. While we all know this, it presents one of the biggest obstacles to understanding the language, especially if you try to put a Latin thought into English! The use of *convenit* in the following examples illustrates important principles to bear in mind. Consider the following two sentences:

> *Tanta gemma ad tam parvum ānulum nōn convenit.*   Such a big gem does not suit such a small ring. (l.81)

> *Hic ānulus ad digitum tuum nōn convenit.*   This ring does not fit your finger. (l.121)

Note that:

1. The syntax of the two languages works differently. In English, both "suit" and "fit" are transitive verbs and take a direct object. In Latin, *convenit* is intransitive and (here) is followed by *ad* + the accusative.

2. The same word often needs to be translated by different English words in different contexts. The concept, if kept in Latin, is perfectly clear: one thing does not "come together well" (*convenit*) with something else (*ad* + accusative). In English, however, we say, "a gem does not suit a ring" rather than "does not come together with." In the second sentence, however, we are more likely to use "fit" for *convenit*.

You will find that you can often understand the Latin more fluently if you *don't* translate, but understand the concept behind the vocabulary and apply that concept to its context. When moving between the two languages, remember to be flexible in your vocabulary and to let go of the expectation that other languages "should" act like English.

Lēctiō Tertia (Section III)

Demonstrative Pronouns

In the final reading, we continue to see more forms of the demonstratives *hic* and *ille*:

huic tabernāriō (l.97)	*haec ōrnāmenta* (l.105)
illī tabernāriī (l.100)	*hōs ānulōs* (l.105)
illae viae (l.102)	*hās gemmās* (l.105)
in illīs tabernīs (ll.103–104)	*hōrum ōrnāmentōrum* (l.107)

Notā Bene: As you can see, with a few exceptions, their declension is already familiar to you. The stem of *hic, haec, hoc* is just *h-*, cf. the plural *hī hae, hōs hās, hōrum hārum, hīs*, but in the singular (and in n. pl. nom./acc.), a *-c* is added. Again, full paradigms are below in the *recensiō* and in the Grammatica Latina in Lingua Latina.

In the Grammatica Latina, you will find that not only *ille, -a, -ud* but also *is, ea, id* are used as adjectives. *Is, ea, id* can be used as a weaker form of *hic* (English "this") or *ille* (English "that"):

is servus   *ea ancilla*   *id ōrnāmentum*

Pronouns Multiplied (examples)

Note the use of both the interrogative and relative pronouns in the same sentence in the following examples:

Quae sunt illae viae in quibus illae tabernae sunt?	Which (interrogative) are those roads in which (relative) there are those shops? (ll.102–104)
Et quae sunt illa ōrnāmenta quae in illīs tabernīs parvō pretiō emuntur?	And which (interrogative) are those jewels which (relative) are sold for such a small price in those shops? (ll.103–104)

Recēnsiō: Pronouns

Personal: takes the place of a noun

is, ea, id

	sing.			pl.		
	m.	f.	n.	m.	f.	n.
nom.	i|s	e|a	i|d	i|ī	e|ae	e|a
acc.	e|um	e|am	i|d	e|ōs	e|ās	e|a
gen.	e|ius	e|ius	e|ius	e|ōrum	e|ārum	e|ōrum
dat.	e|ī	e|ī	e|ī	i|īs	i|īs	i|īs
abl.	e|ō	e|ā	e|ō	i|īs	i|īs	i|īs

Demonstrative: points out as closer (*hic, haec, hoc*) or further away (*ille, illa, illud*)

Hic, haec, hoc

[1]	sing.			pl.		
	m.	f.	n.	m.	f.	n.
nom.	hic	Haec	hoc	hī	hae	haec
acc.	hunc	Hanc	hoc	hōs	hās	haec
gen.	huius	huius	huius	hōrum	hārum	hōrum
dat.	huic	Huic	huic	hīs	hīs	hīs
abl.	hōc	Hāc	hōc	hīs	hīs	hīs

Ille, illa, illud

[2]						
nom.	ill|e	ill|a	ill|ud	ill|ī	ill|ae	ill|a
acc.	ill|um	ill|am	ill|ud	ill|ōs	ill|ās	ill|a
gen.	ill|īus	ill|īus	ill|īus	ill|ōrum	ill|ārum	ill|ōrum
dat.	ill|ī	ill|ī	ill|ī	ill|īs	ill|īs	ill|īs
abl.	ill|ō	ill|ā	ill|ō	ill|īs	ill|īs	ill|īs

Interrogative: Asks a question (*quis/quid*: interrogative pronoun; *qui/quod*: interrogative adjective; all other forms the same)

Quis, quid

	sing.			pl.		
	m.	f.	n.	m.	f.	n.
nom.	*quis/quī*	*quae*	*quid/quod*	*quī*	*quae*	*quae*
acc.	*quem*	*quam*	*quid/quod*	*quōs*	*quās*	*quae*
gen.	*cuius*	*cuius*	*cuius*	*quōrum*	*quārum*	*quōrum*
dat.	*cui*	*cui*	*cui*	*quibus*	*quibus*	*quibus*
abl.	*quō*	*quā*	*quō*	*quibus*	*quibus*	*quibus*

Relative: Connects a dependent clause to a sentence

Qui, quae, quod

	sing.			pl.		
	m.	f.	n.	m.	f.	n.
nom.	*quī*	*quae*	*quod*	*quī*	*quae*	*quae*
acc.	*quem*	*quam*	*quod*	*quōs*	*quās*	*quae*
gen.	*cuius*	*cuius*	*cuius*	*quōrum*	*quārum*	*quōrum*
dat.	*cui*	*cui*	*cui*	*quibus*	*quibus*	*quibus*
abl.	*quō*	*quā*	*quō*	*quibus*	*quibus*	*quibus*

Studia Rōmāna

The pictures of Lydia and Medus shopping reproduce a storefront scene commonly found at Pompeii, Herculaneum, and Ostia, our best sources of town architecture. Pompeii and nearby Herculaneum, at the foot of Mt. Vesuvius (and near to Puteoli on the map on p. 40), were destroyed by the volcanic eruption of 79 AD. Because they were buried for centuries by volcanic ash (Pompeii) and lava (Herculaneum), much remains that gives us a great deal of information about Roman towns in the first century AD. There are also extensive remains from Ostia, the port of Rome (map, p. 40), which was at its peak at the time of our narrative. Many shops such as the one seen in the drawings on pages 54 and 55 are found there. Shops can often be found flanking the entranceways to Roman townhouses and apartment blocks (called *īnsulae*). The shopkeeper and his family lived above the shop in the small quarters on the second floor.

Some shops sold prepared food and drinks over counters accessible both from the street and from the inside (which often had eating areas as well). The counters can be equipped with large built-in jars for storing foodstuffs or jars of wine (*dōlia, ōrum*). Behind the counter, there are often built-in shelves. We find a variety of names for food shops: *thermopōlium* (a Greek word, "cook shop," found in the comic writer Plautus), *taberna, popīna, caupōna* (which was an inn that offered food). There were also a lot of bakeries (*pistrīnae*), often where they not only baked bread, but milled flour as well. Just as at a home, painted *larāria* adorn many walls.

We also see the couple walking on a kind of sidewalk, called *crepīdinēs* after *crepida* (from the Greek word for a sandal, the same as the Latin *solea*). These raised projections helped keep pedestrians away from the traffic (and filth!) of the streets. Another boon to pedestrians were raised stepping-stones that made a kind of ancient crosswalk. In this way, pedestrians were protected from the water that overflowed from the many fountains that provided water to the citizens (only the wealthy had running water in their homes), as well as from the refuse of daily life that found its way into the gutters.

Vocābula Disposita/Ōrdināta

Nōmina
  1st
    gemma, -ae   precious stone, jewel
    līnea, -ae   string, line
    margarīta, -ae   pearl
    taberna, -ae   shop, stall
  2nd
    ānulus, -ī   ring
    collum, -ī   neck
    digitus, -ī   finger
    ōrnāmentum, -ī   ornament, piece of jewelry
    pretium, -ī   price, value
    sēstertius, -ī   sesterce (coin)
    tabernārius, -ī   shopkeeper
  3rd
    prōnōmen, prōnōminis (*n.*)   pronoun

Verba
  -ā (1)
    clāmat, clāmant   shout
    cōnstat, cōnstant   cost, stand firm
    mōnstrat, mōnstrant   point out, show
    ornat, ornant   equip, adorn
  consonant (3)
    cōnsistit, cōnsistunt   stop, halt
    emit, emunt   buy
    ostendit, ostendunt   show
    vēndit, vēndunt   sell
  ĭ-stem (3)
    aspicit, aspiciunt   look at, look
    accipit, accipiunt   receive

    -ī (4)
       convenit, conveniunt   come together, meet, suit
    Irregular
       abit, abeunt   go away

Adiectīva
    1st/2nd (-us/er, -a, -um)
       alius, alia, aliud   another, other
       gemmātus, -a, -um   set with a jewel
       medius, -a, -um   mid, middle
       pecūniōsus, -a, -um   wealthy
       quantus, -a, -um   how large, (as large) as
       quārtus, -a, -um   fourth
       tantus, -a, -um   so big, so great

Numerī (indeclinable unless otherwise noted)
       nōnāgintā   ninety
       octōgintā   eighty
       vīgintī   twenty

Prōnōmina
       ille, illa, illud   that, the one, he

Adverbia
       nimis   too, too much
       satis   enough

Coniūnctiōnēs
       aut   or

IX. Pāstor et Ovēs

Rēs Grammaticae Novae

1. Verbs
    a. *ēst/edunt*
    b. *dūc/dūcite*
    c. Assimilation
2. Nouns: 3rd Declension (Consonant and *i*-Stem)
    a. Declensions
    b. Gender
    c. 3rd Declension
    d. Case Uses
        i. Prepositions *suprā* and *sub*
3. Pronouns: *ipse, ipsa, ipsum*
4. Conjunction: *dum*

The Italian Landscape

We leave the family at the villa for a while and join a shepherd and his dog guarding sheep.

Lēctiō Prīma (Section I)

Third Declension Nouns

By studying the landscape above the chapter, you will learn a great many new Latin nouns. In the words *campus, herba, rīvus, umbra, silva,* and *caelum,* you see the familiar endings *-us, -a,* and *-um.* The remaining words, *collis, pāstor, canis, mōns, sōl,* etc., have quite different endings, not only in the nominative, but also in the other cases.

Words **declined** (i.e., inflected) in this way are said to belong to the **3rd declension** (Latin *dēclīnātiō tertia*), whereas the **1st declension** (*dēclīnātiō prīma*) comprises words in *-a* (like *fēmina*), and the **2nd declension** (*dēclīnātiō secunda*) words in *-us* and *-um* (like *servus* and *oppidum*).

In the Grammatica Latina section of Lingua Latina, you will find examples of these three declensions. Take advantage of this opportunity to review the case-forms of *īnsula* (1st declension) and *servus* and *verbum* (2nd declension), and then study the new 3rd declension (examples: *pāstor* and *ovis*).

The nominative singular of 3rd declension nouns varies. In this chapter, you meet 3rd declension nouns whose **nominative** singular have either:

- no ending
  pāstor
  sōl
  arbor

- or end in -*is*
  ov<u>is</u>   *pān<u>is</u>*
  can<u>is</u>   *coll<u>is</u>*

- or end in -*ēs*
  nūb<u>ēs</u>

- or end in just -*s*
  mōns   *dēn*s

  ▷ This final -*s* causes changes in the stem, which can be seen in the genitive singular, e.g.:

    o When the stem (genitive singular) of *mōns* and *dēns* ends in -*t* (*mont|is, dent|is*)

    o When -*s* is added to a stem ending in -*t*, the -*t* drops and the vowel lengthens (*mont|s* and *dent|s* → *mōns, dēns*)

We can see from the example of *mōns* and *dēns* that the nominative of a 3rd declension word might look quite different from the rest of the cases. The **endings** of the other cases, however, are regular:

- in the singular they have the following endings:
  -*em* in the accusative
  -*is* in the genitive
  -*ī* in the dative
  -*e* in the ablative

- in the plural they have the following endings:
  -*ēs* in the nominative and accusative
  -*um* or -*ium* in the genitive
  -*ibus* in the dative and ablative

Or, schematically:

	sing.	pl.
nom.	-/-(e/i)s	-ēs
acc.	-em	-ēs
gen.	-is	-(i)um
dat.	-ī	-ibus
abl.	-e	-ibus

Notā Bene: There are two possible endings to the genitive plural (*-um* and*-ium*) because there are two different kinds of 3rd declension nouns: **consonant-stems** (ending in *-um* in the genitive plural) and **i-stems** (ending in *-ium* in the genitive plural). The two types differ only in the genitive plural.

> Consonant-Stems
> - nouns with no ending in the nominative, e.g., *pāstor*, have *-um* in the genitive plural (and others to be learned later)
>
> I-Stems
> - m./f. nouns of two syllables ending in *-is, -es*:
>   - ▷ *nūbēs, nūbis* (gen.pl: *nūbium*)
>   - ▷ *ovis, ovis* (gen.pl.: *ovium*)
>   - ▷ *canis, canis* is an exception to this rule; the gen.pl. is *canum*
>
> some m./f. nouns in *-s*
> - nouns in *-ns*:
>   - ▷ *mōns, montis* (gen.pl.: *montium*)
>   - ▷ *dēns, dentis* (gen.pl.: *dentium*)

Examples of all these endings are shown with the nouns *ovis* and *pāstor* (ll.3–7, 11–18).

Gender

The 3rd declension nouns in this chapter are masculine or feminine, but since the endings are the same for the two genders, you cannot determine the gender of such nouns until they are combined with adjectives of the 1st and 2nd declensions (like *magnus, -a, -um*) or until they appear with pronouns (e.g., *hic pāstor*). By looking at the noun/adjective combinations below, you can determine the gender of each noun:

pāstor fessus	*ovis alba*
parvus collis	*magna vallis*
magnus mōns	*multae arborēs*

From the above, you can see that *pāstor, collis,* and *mōns* are masculine and that *ovis, vallis,* and *arbor* are feminine.

Ēst/edunt

The verb in the sentence *Ovēs herbam edunt* (l.8) is a consonant-verb, as shown by the plural ending *-unt*, but the singular is irregular: *Pāstor pānem ēst* (*edit* also appears, but is more rare). The macron (long mark) over the "ē" in *ēst* will distinguish "he/she eats" from *est* "he/she is."

sing.	*ēst*
pl.	*edunt*

Dūc/dūcite

Also note the short imperative *dūc!* of the consonant-verb *dūcit, dūcunt*. The original form, *dūce*, is found in early poets.

    imp.   *dūc! dūc|ite!*

Suprā/sub

New prepositions are *suprā*, which takes the accusative, and *sub*, which takes the ablative (when motion is implied, *sub* takes the accusative).

    suprā + acc.   above
    sub + abl. (acc.)   below

> *Sōl in caelō est suprā campum.* (l.25)
> *Caelum est suprā terram.* (l.26)
> *Sub arbore autem umbra est.* (l.30)
> *Sub arboribus sōl nōn lūcet.* (l.52)

Summary of Declension Endings: 1st, 2nd, 3rd

Sing.	1st	2nd m. ‖ n.	3rd m./f.
Nominative	-a	-us ‖ -um	-s, ----
Accusative	-am	-um	-em
Genitive	-ae	-ī	-is
Dative	-ae	-ō	-ī
Ablative	-ā	-ō	-e
Pl.	1st	2nd m. ‖ n.	3rd m./f.
Nominative	-ae	-ī ‖- a	-ēs
Accusative	-ās	-ōs ‖ -a	-ēs
Genitive	-ārum	-ōrum	-(i)um
Dative	-īs	-īs	-ibus
Ablative	-īs	-īs	-ibus

Lēctiō Altera (Section II)

Dum

So far, the conjunctions you have met join two things—either words, phrases, or independent clauses (a set of words with a subject and a verb that makes complete sense by itself):

et	and	*sed*	but
et...et	both...and	*aut*	or
-que	and (enclitic)	*quod*	because
neque	and not, but not	*quia*	because
neque...neque	neither...nor		

We will now meet a different kind of conjunction. A **temporal** conjunction joins two clauses: a main clause and a subordinate clause that explains the time relationship between the ideas in the two clauses. The temporal conjunction *dum* expresses simultaneousness, that is, that the actions in the two clauses happen at the same time (English "while"):

> <u>Dum</u> *pāstor in herbā dormit, ovis nigra abit.* (l.39)

Dum ("while") shows that the action in the main clause ("the black sheep goes away") is happening at the same time (simultaneously) as the action in the subordinate clause ("the shepherd sleeps in the grass").

Ut

Ut is both an adverb and, as you will learn later, a conjunction. As an adverb, it often represents the English "as":

> *Oculī lupī in umbrā lūcent ut gemmae et dentēs ut margarītae* (l.72–73)

Ipse, ipsa, ipsum

The demonstrative pronoun *ipse* is used for emphasis like English "himself/herself/itself": *Ubi est lupus ipse?* (ll.54–55). It is declined like *ille* apart from the neuter sing. in *-um* (not *-ud*): *ipse, -a, -um.*

nom.	ips|e	ips|a	ips|um	ips|ī	ips|ae	ips|a
acc.	ips|um	ips|am	ips|um	ips|ōs	ips|ās	ips|a
gen.	ips|īus	ips|īus	ips|īus	ips|ōrum	ips|ārum	ips|ōrum
dat.	ips|ī	ips|ī	ips|ī	ips|īs	ips|īs	ips|īs
abl.	ips|ō	ips|ā	ips|ō	ips|īs	ips|īs	ips|īs

Ubi est lupus ipse? — Where is the wolf itself (or "himself")?

Ovis vestīgia lupī in terrā videt, neque lupum ipsum videt. — The sheep sees the tracks of the wolf in the earth, but she does not see the wolf itself.

Ubi est ovis ipsa? — Where is the sheep herself (or "itself")?

Assimilation

The meaning of verbs can be modified or clarified when they are augmented by **prefixes**. The final consonant of the prefix sometimes undergoes a sound change because of the initial consonant of the simple verb with which it is joined. So, for example, when *ad* and *in* enter into compounds with *currit* and *pōnit*, they change to *ac-* and *im-*: *a̲c-currit, i̲m-pōnit.* Such a change, which makes one consonant more similar to another (*m* is a labial consonant like *p*), is called **assimilation** (from Latin *similis*, "similar," "like").

Recēnsiō: Grammatical Terms

Case (*cāsus*): The various forms a noun/adjective/pronoun takes depending on its function in a sentence are called cases. The cases are nominative, accusative, genitive, dative, ablative, and vocative.

Declension (*dēclīnātiō*): a family of nouns/adjectives is called a declension. You have learned the first three of five declensions of nouns.

Decline (*dēclīnāre*): When we recite the paradigm of a noun, adjective, or pronoun by giving each of the cases, we are said to decline the word.

Temporal conjunction (*coniūnctiō temporālis*): a temporal conjunction joins two clauses in a sentence by showing the time relation between them, that is, whether the action in one clause happens before, after, or at the same time as the other.

Independent clause: A group of words with a subject (expressed or implied) and verb expressing a complete thought is called an independent clause ("The shepherd sleeps").

Dependent clause: A group of words with a subject (expressed or implied) and verb that does not express a complete thought is called a dependent clause ("While the shepherd sleeps…").

Assimilation: When a prefix is added to a verb, the initial consonant of the verb may cause the final consonant of the prefix to adapt in sound to its neighbor; that is to say, it undergoes assimilation.

Studia Rōmāna

Shepherds were an important part of the Roman agricultural economy and their lives played a role in ancient literary imagination. The belief that being a shepherd entails vigilance but not a lot of physical labor, and that the life of a shepherd was both simple and lovely, led to an idealized portrait in Greek literature, emulated by Vergil's *Eclogues* in the first century BC, in which shepherds sang songs and played music on rustic reed pipes. Ovid strikes a similar theme (*Remedia Amōris*, 181–182):

> *Pāstor inaequālī modulātur harundine carmen nec dēsunt comitēs,*
> *sēdulus turba, canēs.*

> "The shepherd plays his song on a pipe with reeds of varying lengths, nor does he lack his dogs for companions, that diligent pack."

Both shepherds in the countryside and folks in the city celebrated the *Parīlia* on April 21, a festival dedicated to *Pales*, the god who watched over shepherds. The *Parīlia* is revered for another reason: on that festival day, Romulus, a shepherd himself, dug the *pōmērium*, the ditch that marked the boundaries of Rome and which kept the countryside free from the encroachment of houses. So, Romans considered the *Parilia* Rome's birthday.

Rome's founding myth owes a good deal to shepherds. The legend begins and ends with brothers. The first two are Numitor and Amulius; the elder, Numitor, inherited a kingdom, but was usurped by his younger brother. Amulius also made Numitor's daughter, Rhea Silva, a priestess of the goddess Vesta (a Vestal Virgin), which meant she could not marry (and thus bear legitimate heirs to the throne). The god Mars fathered twin boys with Rhea Silva. Her uncle Amulius ordered them drowned in the Tiber. Since the river was rising and flooding (as it did often in antiquity), the servant left them in a basket by the bank. They were found by a she-wolf (*lupa*) who nursed them and kept them alive. Faustulus, the chief herdsman of the king's flocks, subsequently found and adopted them. The boys, Romulus and Remus, grew to be shepherds like their adoptive father; they also became young men worthy of their kingly grandfather. They reclaimed the kingdom and returned it to Numitor and then went off to found their own city. To determine who would be king, they consulted the flight of birds—called taking the auspices (*auspicium*), a word that comes from the combined roots of "bird" (*avis*) and "watch" (**spec-*), but the practice in Roman culture also covers determining the will of the gods from the weather, from sacred chickens, from four-footed animals, and from unnatural occurrences. (When something happens that suggests the success of a project or event, we still call it auspicious.) Quarreling over the interpretation of the auspices, Romulus killed Remus and became the first king of Rome.

Vocābula Disposita/Ōrdināta

Nōmina
  1st

herba, -ae	grass, herb
silva, -ae	wood, forest
terra, -ae	earth, ground, country
umbra, -ae	shade, shadow

  2nd

caelum, -ī	sky, heaven
campus, -ī	plain
cibus, -ī	food
lupus, -ī	wolf
modus, -ī	manner, way
rīvus, -ī	brook
vestīgium, -ī	footprint, trace

  3rd

arbor, arboris (*f.*)	tree
canis, canis (*m./f.*)	dog
clāmor, clāmōris (*m.*)	shout, shouting

collis, collis (*m.*)	hill
dēclīnātiō, dēclīnātiōnis (*f.*)	declension
dēns, dentis (*m.*)	tooth
mōns, montis (*m.*)	mountain
nūbēs, nūbis (*f.*)	cloud
ovis, ovis (*f.*)	sheep
pānis, pānis (*m.*)	bread, loaf
pāstor, pāstōris (*m.*)	shepherd
sōl, sōlis (*m.*)	sun
timor, timōris (*m.*)	fear
vallis, vallis (*f.*)	valley

Verba

-ā (1)

bālat, -ant	bleat
dēclīnat, -ant	decline, inflect
errat, -ant	wander, stray
lātrat, -ant	bark
ululat, -ant	howl

-ē (2)

| iacet, -ent | lie |
| lūcet, -ent | shine |

Consonant/ĭ (3)

accurrit, -unt	come running
bibit, -unt	drink
dūcit, -unt	guide, lead, draw, trace
impōnit, -unt	place (in/on), put
petit, -unt	make for, aim at, attack, seek, ask for, request
quaerit, -unt	look for, seek, ask (for)
relinquit, -unt	leave

-ī (4)

| reperit, -iunt | find |

Irregular

| ēst, edunt | eat |

Adiectīva

1st/2nd (-us/er, -a, -um)

| niger, -gra, -grum | black |
| albus, -a, -um | white |

Numerī (indeclinable unless otherwise noted)

| ūndēcentum | ninety-nine |

Prōnōmina

| ipse, ipsa, ipsum | myself, yourself, etc; the very, the actual |

Adverbia
    procul   far (from), far away

Praepositiōnēs
    sub (*prp. + abl./acc.*)   under, at the foot of, near
    suprā (*prp. + acc.*)   above

Coniūnctiōnēs
    dum   while, as long as
    ut   like, as

X. Bēstiae et Hominēs

Rēs Grammaticae Novae

1. Verbs
   a. Infinitive Active
   b. Infinitive Active in *-se*
   c. Infinitive Passive
   d. Verbs and Expressions that take an Infinitive
      i. *potest/possunt*
      ii. *necesse est*
      iii. *vult/volunt, audet/audent*
   e. Accusative and Infinitive Construction
2. Nouns
   a. 3rd Declension Masculine and Feminine
   b. 3rd Declension Neuter
   c. *nēmō*
   d. Case Uses
      i. Dative of Interest
      ii. Ablative of Manner (*ablātīvus modī*)
3. Conjunctions
   a. *cum*
   b. *quod*
4. Points of Style
   a. *alius...alius*
   b. active and passive

The Story

After reading about the physical characteristics of animals, humans, and gods, we rejoin Marcus, Quintus, and Julia in the garden.

Lēctiō Prīma (Section I)

3rd Declension Masculine and Feminine

In this chapter, several new 3rd declension nouns are introduced.

- Some of them have peculiar forms in the nominative singular: in *leō*, an *-n* is dropped: gen. *leōn|is*.
- In *homō*, this is combined with a vowel change: gen. *homin|is*.
- The *-s* ending produces the spelling *-x* for *-cs* in *vōx*: gen. *vōc|is*.
- The *-s* ending also produces the loss of *d* in *pēs* (note also the short vowel of the stem): gen. *ped|is*.

From now on, the nominative and genitive of new nouns will be found in the margins of your LINGUA LATINA text, as well as in the vocabulary list at the end of each chapter in this book:

leō leōn|is m. lion   *vōx vōc|is* f. voice
homō homin|is m. person   *pēs ped|is* m. foot

This way of listing a noun (nominative, genitive, gender, meaning) is called the *lexical entry*, since that is the way the word will be listed in a lexicon (dictionary).

Conjunctions

Cum

You have already learned the preposition *cum*, which takes the ablative and means "with." *Cum* is also a **temporal conjunction** (referring to time) meaning when:

Cum avis volat, ālae moventur.   When a bird flies, (its) wings move (are being moved). (l.15)

It is easy to distinguish between *cum* preposition and *cum* conjunction. Look at the following sentences:

Iūlius in vīllā suā habitat cum magnā familiā. (Cap. V, l.9)

Aemilia cum Mārcō, Quīntō Iūliāque in peristȳlō est. (Cap. V, l.47)

Etiam līnea cum margarītīs ōrnāmentum est. (Cap. VIII, ll.8–9)

Cum homō ambulat, pedēs moventur. (Cap. X, l.15)

Cum piscis natat, cauda movētur. (Cap. X, ll.15–16)

Quod

You have learned *quod* as the neuter singular of both the relative pronoun *quī, quae, quod* and the interrogative adjective. *Quod* is also a causal conjunction with the same meaning as *quia* (because):

Hominēs ambulāre possunt, quod pedēs habent. (ll.23–24)

means the same as:

Hominēs ambulāre possunt, quia pedēs habent.

It is easy to distinguish between *quod* pronoun, *quod* interrogative adjective, and *quod* conjunction. Look at the following sentences:

> *Iūlius ambulat ad <u>ōstium</u>, <u>quod</u> ab ōstiāriō aperītur.* (Cap. VII, l.33)
> *Lȳdia ōrnāmentum pulchrum in collō habet. <u>Quod ōrnāmentum?</u>*
>   (Cap. VIII, ll.30–31)
> *<u>Ōrnāmentum quod</u> Lȳdia habet est līnea margarītārum.* (Cap. VIII,
>   ll.31–32)
> *Hominēs volāre nōn possunt, <u>quod</u> ālās nōn habent.* (Cap. X, ll.23–25)
> *Neque avēs neque nīdī avium ab aquilā reperīrī possunt, <u>quod</u> rāmīs
>   et foliīs occultantur.* (Cap. X, ll.89–91)

Potest/possunt

The verb *potest*, which first appears in the sentence *Canis volāre nōn <u>potest</u>* (l.21), denotes ability (English "is able to," "can"). It is a compound with *est*: *pot-est*; the first element *pot-* (meaning "able") is changed before *s* by assimilation to *pos-*: *Hominēs ambulāre po<u>s</u>-sunt* (l.23). More examples:

> *Pāstor duōs pedēs habet, itaque pāstor ambulāre potest.* (ll.22–23)
> *Homō sub aquā spīrāre nōn potest.* (ll.47–48)
> *Nēmō enim sine cibō vīvere potest.* (ll.59–69)
> *Hominēs deōs neque vidēre neque audīre possunt.* (ll.38–39)
> *Piscēs numerārī nōn possunt.* (l.45)
> *Avēs canere possunt, piscēs nōn possunt: piscēs vōcēs nōn habent.*
>   (ll.85–86)

> sing. *pot-est*
> pl. *pos-sunt*

Infinitive Active

Volā<u>re</u> and *ambulā<u>re</u>* are the first examples of the basic verb form that is called the **infinitive** (Latin *īnfīnītīvus*); the infinitive in English is expressed by "to" with the verb. The Latin infinitive active ends in *-re*. In *ā-*, *ē-*, and *ī*-verbs (1st, 2nd, and 4th conjugations), this ending is added directly to the stem:

> *volā|re*: to fly
> *vidē|re*: to see
> *audī|re*: to hear

In consonant-verbs of the 3rd conjugation, a short *e* is inserted before the ending:
> *pōn|<u>e</u>re*: to put
> *sūm|<u>e</u>re*: to take

The infinitive of i-stem verbs of the 3rd conjugation is indistinguishable from that of consonant stems:

accip|ere: to receive
fac|ere: to do, make

From now on, the infinitive will be the form of new verbs shown in the margin of Lingua Latina and in the vocabulary of this book, so that you can always tell to which of the four conjugations the verb belongs: 1. *-āre*; 2. *-ēre*; 3. *-ĕre*; 4. *-īre*. Third conjugation verbs (*-ĕre*) are separated into consonant and *i*-stem in the vocabulary of this book but not in the margins of Lingua Latina.

Lēctiō Altera (Section II)

Infinitive Active in *-se*

The infinitive ending *-ere* developed from an earlier ending (*-se*). That earlier intervocalic *-s-*, i.e., an *-s-* between vowels, was changed to *-r-*, so *-se* became *-re* after a vowel (e.g., *amāre* < *amā|se*). The ending *-se* was kept only in the following infinitives, because it was added directly to the stems *es-* and *ed*:

> *esse* (*est sunt*)
> *ēsse* (*ēst edunt*, with assimilation *ds* > *ss*)
> *posse* (*potest possunt*, Cap. XI)

Examples:

> *Quī spīrat mortuus esse nōn potest.* (ll.108–109)
> *Mārcus et Iūlia Quīntum vīvum esse vident.* (l.122)
> *Esse quoque hominī necesse est.* (l.59)
> *…nēmō enim gemmās ēsse potest.* (l.64)
> *Gemmae edī nōn possunt.* (l.64) (*Notā Bene:* The passive infinitive *edī* of *ēsse* is explained in the next section)

Infinitive *-se*:

> *es|se*
> *ēs|se* (< *ed|se*); passive *edī*
> *pos/se* (<*pot|se*)

Infinitive Passive

The sentence *Hominēs deōs vidēre nōn possunt* becomes in the passive: *Deī ab hominibus vidērī nōn possunt. Vidērī* (to be seen) is the **passive infinitive** corresponding to the active *vidēre* (to see). In the passive, *ā-*, *ē-*, and *ī*-verbs have the ending *-rī* in the infinitive, e.g.:

> *numerā|rī* (l.45)
> *vidē|rī* (l.39)
> *audī|rī* (l.39)

Consonant-verbs have only -*ī*, e.g.:

> *em|ī̆: Sine pecūniā cibus emī̆ nōn potest.* (l.62)

Infinitive

active	passive
āre → ārī: vocā|re	*vocā|rī*
ēre → ērī: vidē|re	*vidē|rī*
ĕre → ī: pōn|ere	*pōn|ī*
īre → īrī: audī|re	*audī|rī*

More examples:

> *Aemilia fīlium suum ā Iūliō <u>portārī</u> videt.* (l.126)
> *Sed Mārcus eum spīrāre nōn videt, neque enim anima <u>vidērī</u> potest.*
>   (ll.109–110)
> *Deī ab hominibus neque <u>vidērī</u> neque <u>audīrī</u> possunt.* (ll.38–39)
> *Gemmae edī nōn possunt.* (l.64)

Necesse est + the Infinitive and Dative of Interest

We have seen that the infinitive occurs as the object of:

> *Potest possunt*

It occurs after other verbs and expressions as well, for example, in this section of the reading, *necesse est*. *Necesse est* is an **impersonal** expression, that is, one without a subject ("it is necessary"):

> *Necesse est cibum habēre.* (l.60)

The person for whom it is necessary to do something is in the dative (**dative of interest**):

> *Spīrāre necesse est hominī̆.* (l.58)

3rd Declension Neuter Nouns

You also meet the first **neuter** nouns of the 3rd declension. The declension of these nouns will be taken up in the next chapter, but for now, here are the nominative and accusative. Remember, the nominative and accusative of neuter nouns (and adjectives) are always the same:

> *flūmen*
> *mare*
> *animal*

Like all neuter nouns, in the nominative and accusative plural, these nouns end in -*a*:

> *flūmina*
> *maria*
> *animālia*

Nēmō

Homō combined with the negation *nē* forms the pronoun *nēmō* (< *nē* + *homō*, "nobody").

Lēctiō Tertia (Section III)

Vult/volunt, audet/audent + infinitive

In addition to *potest/possunt* and *necesse est*, an infinitive also occurs after:

vult volunt	the irregular verb that denotes will
audet audent	a verb that denotes courage

Examples:

> *Iūlia cum puerīs lūdere vult, neque iī cum puellā lūdere volunt.* (ll.74–76)
> *Canis avem…capere vult, neque potest.* (ll.83–84)
> *Quī volāre vult neque potest, ad terram cadit!* (ll.129–130)
> *Fēminae quae pecūniam facere volunt ōrnāmenta sua vēndunt.* (ll.67–68)
> *Avēs canere nōn audent.* (l.88)
> *Mārcus ipse in arborem ascendere nōn audet!* (ll.96–97)

Notā Bene: The form *vult* (he/she wants) lacks a thematic vowel; the verb is irregular.

Accusative and Infinitive Construction

The object of verbs of perception, like *vidēre* and *audīre*, can be combined with an infinitive to express what someone is seen or heard to be doing (active infinitive), or what is being done to someone (passive infinitive). There are several ways of rendering the accusative and infinitive construction in English:

> *Puerī puellam canere vident* (l.80):
>
> > The boys see (that) the girl is singing.
> > The boys see the girl sing/that the girl sings.
> > The boys see (that) the girl does sing.
>
> *Mārcus Quīntum ad terram cadere videt* (l.104):

Marcus sees (that) Quintus is falling to the ground.
Marcus sees Quintus fall to the ground/that Quintus falls to the ground.
Marcus sees (that) Quintus does fall to the ground.

Aemilia fīlium suum ā Iūliō portārī videt (l.126):

Aemilia sees (that) her son is being carried by Julius.
Aemilia sees her son being carried by Julius.

Aemilia Quīntum ā Iūliō in lectō pōnī aspicit (l.131):

Aemilia sees (that) Quintus is being put onto the bed by Julius.
Aemilia sees Quintus being put onto the bed by Julius.

Notā Bene: The word "that" is optional in English translation and is supplied; there is no Latin equivalent to "that" in any of the sentences above.

Ablative of Manner (*Ablātīvus Modī*)

Besides **means** and **cause**, the simple ablative can also denote **manner** (*ablātīvus modī*), e.g.:

magnā vōce clāmat (l.112)
"leō" dēclīnātur hōc modō... (l.169)

Points of Style

1. *Alius...alius*: In line 9, we read, "*Aliae bēstiae sunt avēs, aliae piscēs.*" Repeating a form of *alius, alia, aliud* signals the idiom that represents the English "some...others." So:
   a. *Aliae bēstiae sunt avēs, aliae piscēs*: some creatures are birds, others fish.
   b. *Alius librīs dēlectātur, alius ōrnāmentīs*: one person is delighted by books, another by jewelry.
   c. *Aliī alia dīcunt*: Different people say different things. Or: Some say one thing, others say another.
2. *Cauda movet/movētur*: Another example of how Latin differs from English can be seen in this chapter. In lines 16–17, we find "*Cum piscis natat, cauda movētur*" (when a fish swims, its tail moves). In line 79, we see "*Canis pilam capit et caudam movet*" (the dog catches the ball and wags its tail). In English, the first use is intransitive, the second transitive. Latin, however, expresses the same idea using the passive and active voices, respectively.
3. *enim*: as your marginalia tell you, *enim* is a combination of *is* and *nam*;

it is postpositive, which means it never comes as the first word in its clause:

- *...is enim nūntius deōrum est* (l.30)
- *...nēmō enim sine cībō vīvere potest* (ll.59–60)

Studia Rōmāna

Dogs were valued as guardians of flock (as we saw in the previous chapter) and home, as pets and as hunters. Dogs were important for hunting, a sport Romans loved—there were even hunts (*vēnātiōnēs*) staged in the Circus Maximus and the *Amphitheātrum Flāviānum* (also called the *Colosseum*, as it was built next to a colossal statue of the first-century AD emperor Nero). Romans saw the hunt as a way for men to display their manliness. Horace called it the "customary work for Roman men, useful for reputation, life and limbs" (*Epist.* 1.18.49–50: *Rōmānīs sollemne virīs opus, ūtile fāmae/vītaeque et membrīs*). *Grattius*, a contemporary of Ovid (first century BC–first century AD), wrote the *Cynēgetica* (τὰ κυνηγετικά) a didactic poem (see below) on hunting dogs, only a small portion of which (540 lines of dacytlic hexameter) survives.

Varrō (116–27 BC) in his book about the Latin language (*dē Linguā Latīnā*) says that dogs were called *canēs* because they sing (*canere*) when guarding at night and when hunting. In Cap. XXII, *Cavē Canem* (Beware of the Dog), the opening illustration shows a mosaic flooring in the *vestibulum* depicting a guard dog. In that chapter, we will also meet one of the family's dogs: *canis catēnārius* (the guard dog, who was bound with a chain). Such dogs were also used in wall paintings—in *Petrōnius's Satyricōn* (first century AD), the arriving guests find "not far from the room of the doorkeeper, a huge dog bound with a chain had been painted on the wall and above it was written in capital letters, 'Beware of the dog'."[1] But dogs were also pets: in this chapter, we see Julia playing with her pet dog (l.77). Cicero relates a story of a father going home to find his youngest daughter in tears over the death of her puppy (*dē Dīvīnātiōne*, 1.102). Especially favored by Greeks and Romans alike was a small terrier similar to the Maltese, called *Melitaeus* (from the island Melita, modern Malta).

Wealthy Romans enjoyed fishponds (*piscīnae*) on their estates—both for fresh and salt-water fish, and fish were sometimes tamed and trained to eat from their master's hand (Cicero, *ad Att.* 2.1). There was even a word for someone whose hobby was fish ponds: *piscīnārius*!

Romans were also partial to pet birds and sometimes had private aviaries (*aviāria*). The first-century BC poet Catullus (poems 2, 3) writes about his girlfriend's grief over her dead sparrow (*passer*, quoted in Cap. XXXIV). Ovid (*Amōrēs* 2.6) writes about his girlfriend's dead parrot (*psittacus*). Birds are

---

1. *Satyricōn* 72: "...*nōn longē ab ōstiāriī cellā canis ingēns, catēnā vīnctus, in pariete erat pictus superque quadrāta litterā scrīptum 'cave canem'.*"

sometimes associated with particular divinities: the eagle (*aquila*) was a symbol of *Iūppiter* and the peacock (*pāvō*) of his wife *Iūnō* (you will learn more of *Iūppiter* and *Iūnō* later). The swan (*cȳcnēus*) was the bird of *Apollō*, god of light, learning and literature. Apollo's sister, the huntress *Diāna*, is accompanied by her hunting dogs (although she, too, is associated with birds). And *Venus*, the goddess of love, rides in a chariot drawn by white doves.

In this chapter, you are also introduced to two Roman divinities: *Mercurius*, the messenger of the gods, whose winged cap and sandals might be familiar to you from florist advertisements, which display Mercury in flight carrying flowers (rushing for speedy delivery). Mercury carried a herald's staff, the *cadūceum*. In addition to being the *deus mercātōrum*, Mercury was the god of thieves, of eloquence and of prosperity. He led the souls of the dead to the underworld. Just as Mercury is associated with the Greek god Hermes, Neptune, an ancient Italian god, later became associated with Poseidon, the Greek god of the sea, and thus of journeys on water. There was a festival to Neptune on July 23 called the *Neptūnālia*.

* Didactic Poetry
Didactic poetry is a genre that aims to teach the reader. In the first century BC, Lucretius wrote an epic in six books on Epicurean philosophy (*dē Rērum Nātūrā*); Vergil wrote an epic in four books on farming (*Geōrgica*).

Vocābula Disposita/Ōrdināta

Nōmina
  1st

āla, -ae	wing
anima, -ae	breath, life, soul
aquila, -ae	eagle
bēstia, -ae	beast, animal
cauda, -ae	tail
fera, -ae	wild animal
pila, -ae	ball

  2nd

asinus, -ī	ass, donkey
deus, -ī	god (*pl.* **deī/diī/dī**, *voc.* **deus**)
folium, -ī	leaf
īnfīnītīvus (modus)	infinitive
lectus, -ī	bed, couch
nīdus, -ī	nest
nūntius, -ī	message, messenger
ōvum, -ī	egg
petasus, -ī	hat with a brim

pullus, -ī	young (of an animal)
rāmus, -ī	branch, bough

3rd

āēr, āeris (*m.*)	air
animal, animālis (*n.*)	animal, living being
avis, avis (*f.*)	bird
flūmen, flūminis (*n.*)	river
homō, hominis (*m.*)	human being, person
leō, leōnis (*m.*)	lion
mare, maris (*n.*)	sea
mercātor, mercātōris (*m.*)	merchant
pēs, pedis (*m.*)	foot
piscis, piscis (*m.*)	fish
pulmō, pulmōnis (*m.*)	lung
vōx, vōcis (*f.*)	voice

Verba

-āre (1)

natat, natāre	swim
occultat, occultāre	hide
spīrat, spīrāre	breathe
volat, volāre	fly

-ēre (2)

audet, audēre	dare, venture
movet, movēre	move, stir
sustinet, sustinēre	support, sustain, endure

-ĕre (3)

ascendit, ascendere	climb, go up, mount
cadit, cadere	fall
canit, canere	sing (of), crow, play
lūdit, lūdere	play
vīvit, vīvere	live, be alive

i-stem

capit, capere	take, catch, capture
facit, facere	make, do, cause
parit, parere	give birth to, lay

Irregular

necesse est	it is necessary
potest, possunt, posse	be able
vult, volunt	want, be willing

Adiectīva

1st/2nd (-us/er, -a, -um)

crassus, -a, -um	thick, fat
ferus, -a, -um	wild
mortuus, -a, -um	dead

perterritus, -a, -um	terrified
vīvus, -a, -um	living, alive

3rd (you will learn about these in Cap. XII)

tenuis, -e	thin

Prōnōmina

nēmō	no one

Adverbia

ergō	therefore, so

Coniūnctiōnēs

cum	when
enim	for
quod	because

XI. Corpus Hūmānum

Rēs Grammaticae Novae

1. Verbs
   a. Infinitive in Indirect Statement
   b. *Posse*
2. Nouns
   a. 3rd Declension Neuter
      i. Neuter *i*-stem nouns
   b. Case Uses
      i. Accusative in Indirect Statement
      ii. Ablative of Respect
      iii. Preposition: *dē* + ablative
3. Possessive Adjectives
4. Conjunctions *atque/neque* (*ac/nec*)

Roman Medicine

The art of healing was naturally far more primitive in the ancient world than it is today, although not all the doctors of antiquity were so incompetent as the zealous physician who treats poor Quintus. Blood-letting was used then as a kind of panacea.

Lēctiō Prīma (Section I)

Third Declension Neuter Nouns

Among the names of parts of the body, there are a number of neuter nouns of the 3rd declension. Like all neuters, these nouns have:

- the same form in the nominative and accusative
- the plural nominative/accusative ending in *-a*

In the other cases, they have the well-known endings of the 3rd declension. These nouns are all consonant-stems, like *flūmen, -in|is*:

ōs̲, ō̲r|is	*cor, cord|is*
crū̲s, crūr|is	*iecu̲r, iecor|is*
corpu̲s, corpo̲r|is	*caput, capit|is*
pectu̲s, pecto̲r|is	*viscer|a, -um*

Notā Bene:

- a final *-s* is changed into *r* when endings are added (*-s* between two vowels turns to *-r*)
- *u* can become *o* in the stem, as in *corpus, pectus,* and *iecur*
- *caput, capit\|is* and *cor, cord\|is* are irregular
- *viscer\|a, -um* is only used in the plural

3rd Declension *i*-Stem Nouns

In Cap. X, we met the 3rd declension neuter nouns *mar\|e mar\|is* and *animal -āl\|is*. There are not many of these nouns; they differ from neuter consonant stems in that they have:

- *-ia* in the nom./acc. pl.
- *-ium* in the gen. pl.
- *-ī* in the abl. sing.

The complete declension patterns (or **paradigms**) are shown below and on page 83 of LINGUA LATINA.

	sing.	pl.	sing.	pl.
nom.	*mar|e*	*mar|ia*	*animal*	*animāl|ia*
acc.	*mar|e*	*mar|ia*	*animal*	*animāl|ia*
gen.	*mar|is*	*mar|ium*[1]	*animāl|is*	*animāl|ium*
dat.	*mar|ī*	*mar|ibus*	*animāl|ī*	*animāl|ibus*
abl.	*mar|ī*	*mar|ibus*	*animāl|ī*	*animāl|ibus*

Summary of Declension Endings: 1st, 2nd, 3rd

sing.	1st	2nd m. ‖ n.	3rd consonant m./f. ‖ n.	3rd *i*-stem m./f. ‖ n.
nom.	-a	-us ‖ -um	-s, ----	-s, --- ‖ -e,- al, -ar
acc.	-am	-um	-em ‖ ---[2]	-em ‖ -e, -al, -ar
gen.	-ae	-ī	-is	-is
dat.	-ae	-ō	-ī	-ī
abl.	-ā	-ō	-e	-e ‖ -ī

---

1. The genitive plural occurs only once in extant texts and in the form *marum*, not *marium*.
2. The neuter accusative singular will be the same as the nominative.

pl.				
nom.	-ae	-ī ‖ -a	-ēs ‖ -a	-a ‖ -ia
acc.	-ās	-ōs ‖ -a	-ēs ‖ -a	-a ‖ -ia
gen.	-ārum	-ōrum	-um	-ium
dat.	-īs	-īs	-ibus	-ibus
abl.	-īs	-īs	-ibus	-ibus

Lēctiō Altera (Section II)

Indirect Statement (Accusative and Infinitive Construction)

In sentences like *Iūlius puerum <u>videt</u>* and *Iūlius puerum <u>audit</u>*, we have seen that an infinitive may be added to the accusative *puerum* to describe what the boy is doing or what is happening to him, e.g.:

> *Iūlius puer<u>um</u> vocā<u>re</u> audit.*
> *Iūlius puer<u>um</u> perterritum <u>esse</u> videt.*

Such a construction is called an **accusative and infinitive construction** (*accūsātīvus cum īnfīnītīvō*); in these constructions, the accusative is logically the subject of the infinitive ("subject accusative"). You will find this construction with:

- verbs of perception (e.g., *vidēre, audīre,* and *sentīre*)
  > *Medicus puer<u>um</u> dorm<u>īre</u> videt.* (l.59)
  > *C<u>or</u> eius palpit<u>āre</u> sentit.* (l.112)
- verbs of speaking (e.g., *dīcere*) and thinking (e.g., *putāre*)
  > *Medicus 'puer<u>um</u> dorm<u>īre</u>' dīcit.* (ll.63–64)
  > *Syra e<u>um</u> mortu<u>um</u> esse putat.* (l.108)
- *iubēre*
  > *Dominus 'serv<u>um</u> ven<u>īre</u>' iubet.*
  > *Medicus Quīnt<u>um</u> 'ōs aper<u>īre</u> atque lingu<u>am</u> ostend<u>ere</u>' iubet.* (ll.69–70)
- *gaudēre* (and with other verbs expressing **mood**)
  > *Syra Quīnt<u>um</u> vīv<u>ere</u> gaudet* (= *Syra gaudet quod Quīntus vīvit*) (l.118)
- *necesse est* (and other **impersonal** expressions)
  > *Necesse est puer<u>um</u> dorm<u>īre</u>.* (l.128)

The **accusative and infinitive construction** reports a person's words or thoughts as an **indirect statement**, e.g.:

- Direct statement: *"Puer dormit."*
- Indirect statement: *Medicus 'puer<u>um</u> dorm<u>īre</u>' dīcit.*

In your text, single quotation marks are used to mark indirect speech but not reported thoughts or perceptions, e.g., when Syra sees the unconscious Quintus:

> *Syra eum mortuum esse putat.* (l.108)

In English, indirect statement is generally expressed by a clause beginning with "that": "says/thinks/believes that…"

Conjunctions

Atque/ac

The conjunction *atque* has the same function as *et* and *-que*; the shortened form *ac* is often found (see Cap. XII, l.59):

- before consonants
- but not before vowels or *h-*

In the following sentences, *ac* could be substituted for *atque*:

> *Quīntus oculōs claudit atque dormit.* (l.41)
> *Medicus ad lectum adit atque puerum aspicit.* (ll.56–57)

But in this sentence, *ac* could not be substituted because *horret* begins with *h*:

> *Quīntus sanguinem dē bracchiō fluere sentit atque horret.*
> (ll.100–101)

Neque/nec

Nec, the shortened form of *neque*, is used before consonants as well as vowels:

> *Itaque pedem aegrum habet nec ambulāre potest.* (l.54)

Dē + ablative

Like *ab*, the preposition *dē* expresses motion "from" (mostly "down from") and takes the ablative:

> *dē arbore* (ll.53–54) *dē bracchiō* (l.99)

Ablative of Respect

The ablative in *pede aeger* (l.55) specifies the application of the term *aeger*. It is called **ablative of respect**, as it answers the question "in what respect?"

> *Nec modo pede, sed etiam capite aeger est.* (l.55)

> Quintus is sick "in his foot" and "in his head."

Lēctiō Tertia (Section III)

Posse

We saw in Cap. X that the infinitive of *est, sunt* is *esse*; similarly, the infinitive of *potest*, which is formed from *pot- + est, sunt* is *posse* (*pot + esse*):

> *Aemilia nōn putat medicum puerum aegrum sānāre posse.* (ll.134–135)

.

Possessive Adjectives

In Cap. II, you learned the possessive adjectives *meus, -a, -um* and *tuus, -a, -um*, and in Cap. IV, the reflexive possessive *suus, -a, -um*. Here, we see the plural possessive adjectives *noster, -tra, -trum* (English "our"):

> *Iam fīlius noster nōn modo pede, sed etiam bracchiō aeger est.* (ll.131–132)
> *Ille medicus crassus fīlium nostrum sānāre nōn potest.* (ll.133–134)

In Cap. XII, you will find several examples of the **possessive adjectives** *noster, -tra, -trum* ("our") and *vester, -tra, -trum* ("your").

Studia Rōmāna

The ancient world offered a variety of approaches to medicine—some rooted in tradition, some in religious practice, some in inquiry into the nature of the body and the power of nature to cure the body. During the time of our narrative (second century AD), Rome boasted several medical schools. The hospitals that had originated with the military had spread to the cities. Doctors had a variety of ways of treating patients: rest, diet, herbs, surgery, and, as in our chapter, bloodletting. The purpose of bloodletting was to help the body come into its natural harmony. At this time lived the philosopher and medical scholar *Galēnus* (Galen), who was born in Pergamon (on the west coast of what is now Turkey) and later traveled to and lived in Rome; famous in his lifetime, Galen's work remained highly influential for centuries.

Many of the doctors practicing in Italy were Greeks (both slave and free). They brought with them a developed theoretical approach to medicine. Some of them, such as Antōnius Mūsa, the physician of the emperor Augustus, became famous and wealthy. But, as a culture closely in tune with agriculture, Romans often looked to the plant world for cures.

Cato's treatise on farming (*dē Agrī Cultūrā*, second century BC) and the Elder Pliny's (*Gāius Plīnius Secundus*, first century AD) *Natural History* (*Nātūrālis Historia*), for example, are full of home remedies based on plants and on charms. Cato's *dē Agrī Cultūrā*, for example, promotes cabbage prepared in a variety of ways as a purgative (a treatment of which Romans were particularly fond), as a remedy for aching joints, as a poultice for an open sore, as a preventative of hangover from too much wine. Pliny the Elder's (first century AD) *Natural History* devotes several books to remedies found in nature.

Worship of the god of healing, Aesculapius (Greek spelling: Asclepius), the son of Apollo, continued well into the Roman Empire at his many sanctuaries and shrines. Archaeologists have found many medical instruments and votive tablets offering gratitude for specific cures.

Vocābula Disposita/Ōrdināta

Nōmina
  1st

gena, -ae	cheek
lingua, -ae	tongue, language
vēna, -ae	vein

  2nd

bracchium, -ī	arm
capillus, -ī	hair
cerebrum, -ī	brain
culter, cultrī	knife
labrum, -ī	lip
medicus, -ī	doctor
membrum, -ī	limb
pōculum, -ī	cup

  3rd

auris, auris (*f.*)	ear
caput, capitis (*n.*)	head
color, colōris (*m.*)	color
cor, cordis (*n.*)	heart
corpus, corporis (*n.*)	body
crūs, crūris (*n.*)	leg
frōns, frontis (*f.*)	forehead
iecur, iecoris (*n.*)	liver
ōs, ōris (*n.*)	mouth
pectus, pectoris (*n.*)	chest
sanguis, sanguinis (*m.*)	blood
venter, ventris (*m.*)	stomach
viscera, viscerum (*n. pl.*)	internal organs

  4th (introduced in the next chapter)

manus (*f.*)	hand

Verba
  -āre (1)

aegrōtat, aegrōtāre	be ill
palpitat, palpitāre	beat, throb

putat, putāre	think, suppose
sānat, sānāre	heal, cure
spectat, spectāre	watch, look at
stat, stāre	stand
-ēre (2)	
dēterget, dētergēre	wipe off
dolet, dolēre	hurt, feel pain, grieve
gaudet, gaudēre	be glad, be pleased
horret, horrēre	bristle, shudder (at)
iubet, iubēre	order, tell
sedet, sedēre	sit
-ĕre (3)	
appōnit, appōnere	place (on), serve
arcessit, arcessere	send for, fetch
dīcit, dīcere	say, call, speak
fluit, fluere	flow
tangit, tangere	touch
-īre (4)	
revenit, revenīre	come back
sentit, sentīre	feel, sense, think
Irregular	
potest, posse	be able

Adiectīva

1st/2nd (-us/er, -a, -um)

aeger, -gra, -grum	sick, ill
hūmānus, -a, -um	human
noster, nostra, nostrum	our, ours
ruber, rubra, rubrum	red
sānus, -a, -um	healthy, well
stultus, -a, -um	stupid, foolish

Adverbia

bene	well
male	badly, ill
modo	only, just

Praepositiōnēs

dē (*prp. + abl.*)	(down) from, of, about
īnfrā (*prp. + acc.*)	below
super (*prp. + acc.*)	on (top of), above

Coniūnctiōnēs

atque/ac	and, as, than
nec	and/but not, nor, not

XII. Mīles Rōmānus

Rēs Grammaticae Novae

1. Verbs
   a. *ferre*
   b. Irregular Imperatives
   c. 3rd Conjugation Vowel Stems
2. Nouns
   a. 4th Declension
   b. *plūrāle tantum*
   c. Case Uses
      i. Dative of Possession
      ii. Dative with Intransitive Verbs
      iii. Partitive Genitive
      iv. Accusative of Extent of Space
3. Adjectives
   a. 3rd Declension Adjectives
   b. Comparison of Adjectives
4. *Mīlle/Mīlia*

The Roman Army

The military played an important part in the Roman world. Above this chapter, you find a picture of a *mīles Rōmānus*. The word "military" is derived from *mīles*, whose stem ends in -*t*: gen. *mīlit|is* (so also *pedes -it|is* and *eques -it|is*).

Lēctiō Prīma (Section I)

Dative of Possession

In the sentence *Mārcō ūna soror est* (l.6), *Mārcō* is dative. This **dative of possession** with *esse* is used to express to whom something belongs. These two sentences are different ways of expressing the same thing:

> *Mārcus ūnam sorōrem habet.*   Marcus has one sister.

> *Mārcō ūna soror est.*   Marcus has one sister, or, literally:
>   there is to Marcus one sister.

In the second sentence, *ūna soror* is nominative, and the dative *Mārcō* tells us "to whom" or "for whom" there is a sister. In English, we would still say, "Marcus has one sister." Here are more examples:

> *Quod nōmen est patrī? Eī nōmen est Iūlius.* (ll.9–10)
> *Aemiliae est ūnus frāter, cui "Aemilius" nōmen est.* (l.17)
> *Virō Rōmānō tria nōmina sunt.* (ll.10–11)
> *Fīliīs nōmina sunt "Mārcus Iūlius Balbus" et "Quīntus Iūlius Balbus."*
>   (ll.12–13)

Irregular Verb: *Ferre*

In the verb *fer|re,* the infinitive ending *-re* is added directly to the consonant-stem. The endings *-t* and *-tur* are also added directly to the stem:

Infinitive:

> *fer|re*

Singular:

> *fer|t*
> *fer|tur*

Plural:

> *fer|unt*
> *fer|untur*

The imperative has no *-e:*

> *fer!*
> *fer|te!*

E.g.:

> *Mīles est vir quī scūtum et gladium et pīlum fert.* (ll.33–34)
>
> *Aemilius pīlum tantum fert.* (l.42)
>
> *Gladius eius brevis et levis est—brevior et levior quam is quī ab
>   equite fertur.* (ll.56–57)
>
> *Gladiī…ā Germānīs feruntur.* (ll.57–58)
>
> *Hispānī et Gallī…et alia arma et arcūs sagittāsque ferunt.* (ll.90–91)

Irregular Imperatives

Like *fer!*, a few other verbs lost the original "e" ending of the imperative and are monosyllables:[1]

> *es!* of *esse* (pl. *es|te!*)
> *dūc!* of *dūcere* (pl. *dūc|ite!*)
> *dīc!* of *dīcere* (pl. *dīc|ite!*)
> *fac!* of *facere* (pl. *faci|te!*—*facere* is an *i*-stem: *faci|unt*)

3rd Declension Adjectives

All the adjectives learned so far, e.g., *alb|us -a -um*, follow the 1st and 2nd declensions: the 1st in the feminine (*alb|a*) and the 2nd in the masculine and neuter (*alb|us, alb|um*). A few 1st/2nd declension adjectives, like *niger -gr|a -gr|um*, have *-er*, not *-us*, in the nom. sing. m. (cf. nouns like *liber -br|ī, culter -tr|ī*). Thus:

> aeger, aegra, aegrum   noster, nostra, nostrum
> pulcher, pulchra, pulchrum vester, vestra, vestrum
> ruber, rubra, rubrum

There are also **adjectives of the 3rd declension**, one of which (*tenuis*) you met in Cap. X. Some others are:

> brevis, breve   trīstis, trīste
> gravis, grave   fortis, forte
> levis, leve

In the masculine and feminine, these adjectives are: i-stems, that is, they decline like *ovis*, except:

- *-ī* (not *-e*) in the ablative singular

	sing. m./f.	pl. m./f.
nom.	brev|is	brev|ēs
acc.	brev|em	brev|ēs
gen.	brev|is	brev|ium
dat.	brev|ī	brev|ibus
abl.	brev|ī	brev|ibus

In the neuter, they are declined like *mare*:

- *-e* in the nom./acc. sing.
- *-ī* in the abl. sing.
- *-ia* in the nom./acc. pl.
- *-ium* in the gen. pl.

1. When these imperatives are found in compound verbs e.g., *abdūc* ("lead away!") the accent remains on the ultima, a verbal reminiscence of the form was *abdūce*.

	sing.	pl.
	n.	n.
nom.	*brev|e*	*brev|ia*
acc.	*brev|e*	*brev|ia*
gen.	*brev|is*	*brev|ium*
dat.	*brev|ī*	*brev|ibus*
abl.	*brev|ī*	*brev|ibus*

So in the nominative singular, we have *gladius brevis, hasta brevis,* and *pīlum breve.*

Examples:

> *Itaque trīstis est Aemilia.* (l.20)
> *Cūr tam brevis est gladius? Quod gladius brevis nōn tam gravis est quam gladius longus.* (ll.50–53)
> *Pīlum nostrum breve et leve est.* (l.134)
> *Mīlitēs Rōmānī fortēs sunt.* (ll.118–119)
> *Pīla eōrum brevia et levia sunt, nōn longa et gravia ut Germānōrum.* (ll.136–137)

Lēctiō Altera (Section II)

Nouns: 4th Declension

The noun *exercitus* here represents the **4th declension** (*dēclīnātiō quārta*). All the forms are shown in lines 80–89. This declension does not comprise nearly so many words as the first three.

In the singular:

- the accusative has -*um*
- the genitive -*ūs*
- the dative -*uī*
- the ablative -*ū*

In the plural:

- the nominative and accusative end in -*ūs*
- the genitive in -*uum*
- the dative and ablative in -*ibus*

	sing.		pl.	
nom.	-*us*	*manus*	-*ūs*	*manūs*
acc.	-*um*	*manum*	-*ūs*	*manūs*
gen.	-*ūs*	*manūs*	-*uum*	*manuum*
dat.	-*uī*	*manuī*	-*ibus*	*manibus*
abl.	-*ū*	*manū*	-*ibus*	*manibus*

Fourth declension nouns are regularly masculine, e.g.:

arcus	*metus*
equitātus	*passus*
exercitus	*versus*
impetus	

manus is feminine (*du<u>ae</u> manūs*)

Dative with Intransitive Verbs

Intransitive verbs are those that are not completed by an accusative direct object. The verbs *imperāre* and *pārēre* (first introduced in Cap. IV) are intransitive and take the dative (persons whom you command and whom you obey are in the dative). In the following sentences, *exercituī* and *ducī* are datives:

> *Dux exercit<u>uī</u> imperat.* (l.82)
> *Exercitus ducī su<u>ō</u> pāret.* (l.82)
> *nec Rōmānīs pārent.* (ll.75–76)
> *Hispānī et Gallī iam exercitibus nostrīs pārent.* (ll.88–89)

Notā Bene: Verbs that are transitive in English are not always transitive in Latin. It can be helpful to memorize intransitive verbs with a dative pronoun (*eī*) to help you remember that they do not take an accusative direct object, e.g.:

> *imperāre eī*
> *pārēre eī*

Adjectives: Comparison

A comparison like *Via Latīna nōn tam longa est quam via Appia* can also be expressed *Via Appia long<u>ior</u> est quam via Latīna*. *Longior* is a **comparative adjective** (Latin *comparātīvus*, from *comparāre*, "compare") and *quam* here means "than" (as opposed to "as" in *tam...quam* "as...as," which you learned in Cap. VI).[2]

The comparative:

- ends in *-ior* in the masculine and feminine (*gladius/hasta long<u>ior</u>*)
- ends in *-ius* in the neuter (*pīlum long<u>ius</u>*)
- declines like 3rd declension consonant-stem nouns:
  - ▷ gen. *-iōr|is*; plural - *iōr|um*
  - ▷ nom./acc. pl. *-iōr|ēs* (m./f.) and *-iōr|a* (n.)
  - ▷ abl. sing. *-e -iōr|e*

---

2. The comparative means "too" when there is no comparison expressed or implied.

	sing. m./f.	pl. m./f.	sing. n.	pl. n.
nom.	*brevior|*	*brevior|ēs*	*brevius*	*brevior|a*
acc.	*breviōr|em*	*breviōr|ēs*	*brevius*	*breviōr|a*
gen.	*breviōr|is*	*breviōr|um*	*breviōr|is*	*breviōr|um*
dat.	*breviōr|ī*	*breviōr|ibus*	*breviōr|ī*	*breviōr|ibus*
abl.	*breviōr|e*	*breviōr|ibus*	*breviōr|e*	*breviōr|ibus*

Examples:

> *Gladius equitis longior et gravior est quam peditis.* (ll.53–54)

> The sword of the cavalryman is longer and heavier than that [i.e., the sword] of the foot-soldier.

> *Gladius peditis brevis et levis est—brevior et levior quam is quī ab equite fertur.* (ll.56–57)

> *Etiam gladiī quī ā Germānīs feruntur longiōrēs et graviōrēs sunt quam Rōmānōrum ac pīla eōrum longiōra et graviōra quam nostra sunt.* (ll.57–59)

Comparative (neuter forms, where different from masculine and feminine, are in parentheses)

	sing. m./f. (n.)	pl. m./f. (n.)
nom.	*-ior* (*-ius*)	*-iōrēs* (*-iōra*)
acc.	*-iōrem* (*-ius*)	*-iōrēs* (*-iōra*)
gen.	*-iōris*	*-iōrum*
dat.	*-iōrī*	*-iōribus*
abl.	*-iōre*	*-iōribus*

Genitive Case: Partitive

So far you have encountered the following uses of the genitive case:

- possession (Cap. II)   *Iūlius dominus Mēdī est.*
- with *numerus* (Cap. II)   *Numerus servōrum est centum.*
- with *plēnus* (Cap. VII)   *Hic saccus plēnus mālōrum est.*

In this chapter, we see the genitive expressing the whole of which a part (*pars part\|is* f.) is taken. It is called **partitive genitive**:

> *Prōvincia est pars imperiī Rōmānī, ut membrum pars corporis est.* (ll.64–65)

Lēctiō Tertia (Section III)

Verbs: 3rd Conjugation Vowel Stems

Besides consonant-stems (like *pōn|ere, sūm|ere, dīc|ere*), the 3rd conjugation includes some verbs whose stems end in short *u* or *i*.

U-Stems: The inflection of *u*-stems does not differ from that of consonant-stems, e.g.:

> *flu|ere*: *fluit, fluunt*
> *metu|ere*: *metuit, metuunt*

I-Stems: *I*-stems, too, largely agree with consonant-stems, but they are characterized by having *i* before vowel endings, e.g., *-unt*. In Cap. VIII, you saw the i-stems *accipiunt* and *aspiciunt*. In this chapter, we also see:

> *capi|unt*
> *iaci|unt*
> *fugi|unt*

Notā Bene: Instead of the characteristic *i*, you will find *e*:

- before *r*, e.g., in the infinitive: *cape|re, iace|re, fuge|re*, stem *capi-, iaci-, fugi-*
- and in final position: *cape! iace! fuge!* (imperative)

Plūrāle Tantum

Here, you read about the equipment of a Roman soldier and the layout of a Roman army camp: *castra*. This noun is neuter **plural**, called *plūrāle tantum* ("plural only," cf. "barracks," "entrails," "arms"). Other *plūrāle tantum* nouns:

> *līberī, -ōrum*   *arma, -ōrum*
> *viscera, -um*

Accordingly, though only one camp is meant, you read:

> *castra* <u>*sunt*</u> (l.94)   *in castrīs* (l.97)
> *vāllum castrōrum* (l.101)

Notā Bene: Plūrāle tantum nouns take plural verbs.

Mīlle/mīlia

The common Roman linear measures were:

- *pēs*, "foot" (29.6 cm or 11.65 inches)
- *passus* = 5 *pedēs* (1.48 m or 4.85 feet)

In Cap. I, you learned *mīlle* (one thousand). *Mīlle passūs* (4th decl.), or "1,000 paces," that is, "5,000 feet," equals a "Roman mile" of 1.48 km, a little less than an English mile ("mile" is derived from *mīlia*). In the singular, *mīlle* is an **indeclinable adjective**; the plural is expressed by the **noun** *mīlia -ium* n., e.g., *duo mīlia* (2,000) which is followed by a partitive genitive:

> *mīlle passūs* (adjective agrees with *passūs*)
> *duo mīlia pass<u>uum</u>* (noun + genitive)
> *sex mīlia mīlit<u>um</u>*
> *Ūnus passus est quīnque pedēs, ergō mīlle passūs sunt quīnque <u>mīlia</u> <u>pedum</u>.* (ll.96–97)

Long distances were given in *mīlia passuum* ("Roman miles").

> 1,000 = *mīlle* + noun

For numbers between 1,000 and 2,000, use *mīlle* and an ordinal between 1–999: e.g., *mīlle et ūnum* (1,001), *mīlle ducentī* (1,200). Above 2,000, use *mīlia* + partitive genitive.

Accusative of Extent of Space

The accusative without a preposition is used to indicate extent ("how long?" "how high?"), e.g.:

Gladius <u>duōs pedēs</u> longus est.	The sword is two feet long. (l.49)
Aemilius in castrīs habitat <u>mīlle</u> <u>passūs</u> ā fīne imperiī.	Aemilius lives in a camp one mile from the boundary of the empire. (l.93)
Prope <u>decem pedēs</u> altum est, et <u>duo mīlia passuum</u> longum.	It is almost ten feet high and two miles long. (ll.102–103)

Recēnsiō: 3rd Declension Ablative Singular in *-ī* and *-e*

Ends in *-e*

- consonant-stem nouns of all genders:
  pāstor (m.) abl.: *pāstōre*
  vōx (f.) abl.: *vōce*
  nōmen (n.) abl.: *nōmine*
- masculine and feminine *i*-stem nouns:
  mōns (m.) abl.: *monte*
  nūbēs (f.) abl.: *nūbe*
- comparative adjectives of all genders
  brevior, brevius (from *brevis, breve*): abl.: *breviōre*
  longior, longius (from *longus, longa, longum*), abl.: *longiōre*

Ends in *-ī*

- neuter *i-stem* nouns
  mare (n.), abl.: *marī*

- positive adjectives of all genders
  brevis, breve, abl.: *brevī*
  gravis, grave, abl.: *gravī*

Studia Rōmāna

Avunculus vs. Patruus: We call the brothers of our mother and father "uncle," but the Romans had different names for the mother's brother (*avunculus*) and the father's brother (*pātruus*). Our English word "avuncular" reflects an ancient distinction: to be avuncular is to behave in a kind and generous way toward a young person or someone with less power. The *pātruus* was associated with severity (Cicero's description was *pertrīstis*, "very stern"). There doesn't seem to be the same association with the *amita* (the father's sister) and the *mātertera* (the mother's sister). The name for grandmother (*avia*) and grandfather (*avus*) was the same for the parents of both one's mother and father.

Tria Nōmina: Praenōmen, Nōmen, Cognōmen

Roman men often had three names, called the *tria nōmina*. *Iūlius* is a *nōmen*, or family name: male members of this family are called *Iūlius* and female members *Iūlia*. Besides the family name ending in *–ius*, Roman men have a first or personal name, the *praenōmen*, and a surname, the *cognōmen*, which is common to a branch of the family. The *cognōmen* is often descriptive of the founder of the family, e.g., *Longus, Pulcher, Crassus*; *Paulus* means "small" and *Balbus* "stammering." Sometimes, the *cognōmen* is added to a particular person's name as an honorific or particular marker, for example, *Pūblius Cornēlius Scīpiō*, the victorious general of the Second Punic War, received the honorific *Africānus* and was then known as *Scīpiō Africānus*. Cicero's good friend *Titus Pompōnius Atticus* received his *cognōmen* as a result of his long residence in Athens. Sons adopted into other families would add their father's name, with the suffix *-ānus* to their new family name. For example, *Pūblius Cornēlius Scīpiō*, who did not have a son, adopted one of the sons of *Lūcius Aemilius Paulus*; that son's name became *Pūblius Cornēlius Scīpiō Aemiliānus*. Families with more than one daughter distinguished them with *māior* ("older," Cap. XIX) or *minor* ("younger," Cap. XIX), by numbers (*prīma, secunda, tertia*), or by diminutives (just as *sacculus*, Cap. IV, is the diminutive of *saccus*, Cap. VI) like *Līvilla*, "little *Līvia*."

The number of *praenōmina* is quite small. Including the list in the margin of page 86 in Lingua Latina, the following names were in common use:

A.	Aulus	Mam.	Māmercus
C.	Gāius	N.	Numerius
Cn.	Gnaeus	P.	Pūblius
D.	Decimus	Q.	Quīntus

K.	Kaesō	Ser.	Servius
L.	Lūcius	Sp.	Spurius
M.	Mārcus	T.	Titus
M'.	Mānius	Ti., Tib.	Tiberius

Why are Gāius and Gnaeus abbreviated with a C and why does Kaesō begin with K instead of C? These spellings reflect an early period of the Latin alphabet, when the "g" sound was represented by "c" and "k" had not yet been replaced by "c."

The Roman Soldier

As you can see from the illustration on page 89, the *castra Rōmāna* was a model of organization. It had two main roads connecting four gates; the *via praetōria* led from the main gate to the *principia*, an open space in the camp in front of the general's quarters (*praetōrium*); the *via prīncipālis* ran in front of the *principia* to the other gates. At the end of Cap. XXXIII, you will find more information on the Roman soldier.

Vocābula Disposita/Ōrdināta

Nōmina
  1st

fossa, -ae	ditch, trench
hasta, -ae	lance
patria, -ae	native country/town
sagitta, -ae	arrow

  2nd

adiectīvum (nomen)	adjective
avunculus, -ī	(maternal) uncle
arma, -ōrum (*n. pl.*)	arms
bellum, -ī	war
castra, -ōrum (*n. pl.*)	camp
comparātīvus, -ī (gradus)	comparative
gladius, -ī	sword
pīlum, -ī	spear, javelin
pugnus, -ī	fist
scūtum, -ī	shield
vāllum, -ī	rampart

  3rd

cognōmen, -inis (*n.*)	surname
dux, ducis (*m.*)	leader, chief, general
eques, equitis (*m.*)	horseman
frāter, frātris (*m.*)	brother
fīnis, fīnis (*m.*)	boundary, limit, end
hostis, hostis (*m.*)	enemy

lātus, lāteris (*n.*)	side, flank
mīles, mīlitis (*m.*)	soldier
mīlia, mīlium (*n.*)	thousand
nōmen, nōminis (*n.*)	name
pars, partis (*f.*)	part, direction
pedes, peditis (*m.*)	footsoldier
praenōmen, praenōminis (*n.*)	first name
soror, sorōris (*f.*)	sister

4th

arcus, arcūs	bow
equitātus, equitātūs	cavalry
exercitus, exercitūs	army
impetus, impetūs	attack, charge
metus, metūs	fear
passus, passūs	pace
versus, versūs	line, verse

Verba

-āre (1)

pugnat, pugnāre	fight
mīlitat, mīlitāre	serve as a soldier
expugnat, expugnāre	conquer
oppugnat, oppugnāre	attack

-ere (3)

incolit, incolere	inhabit
dīvidit, dīvidere	divide
metuit, metuere	fear
dēfendit, dēfendere	defend

i-stem

iacit, iacere	throw, hurl
fugit, fugere	run away, flee

Irregular

fert, ferre	carry, bring, bear

Adiectīva

1st/2nd (-us/er, -a, -um)

altus, -a, -um	high, tall, deep
armātus, -a, -um	armed
barbarus, -a, -um	foreign, barbarian
lātus, -a, -um	wide
vester, -tra, -trum	your, yours

3rd

brevis, -e	short
fortis, -e	strong, brave
gravis, -e	heavy, severe, grave

levis, -e	light, slight
trīstis, -e	sad

Praepositiōnēs
contrā (*prp. + acc.*)	against

Coniūnctiōnēs
ac	and, as, than

XIII. Annus et Mēnsēs

Rēs Grammaticae Novae

1. Verbs
   a. Preterite (Imperfect) Tense
   b. *dīcitur* + Nominative Infinitive
   c. Infinitive *velle*
2. Nouns
   a. Case Uses
      i. Ablative of Time When
      ii. Accusative of Duration of Time
   b. 5th Declension
   c. *māne* (noun/adverb)
3. Adjectives
   a. Names of the Months
   b. Comparison of Adjectives
      i. Positive
      ii. Comparative
      iii. Superlative
   c. Numerals
      i. Cardinals
      ii. Ordinals
      iii. Fractions
4. Conjunction: *vel*

Roman Calendar

Today we still use a version of the Roman calendar as it was reformed by *Iūlius Caesar* in 46 BC with twelve months and 365 days (366 in leap years). Before this reform, only four months—March, May, July, and October—had 31 days, while February had 28 and the other months only 29. This made a total of 355 days. It was therefore necessary at intervals to put in an extra month. The Julian calendar was revised under Pope Gregory XIII in 1582 (creating the Gregorian calendar).

As you learn from the reading, in the oldest Roman calendar, March was the first month of the year and December the last. The calendar was agricultural and seems to have skipped the winter months. One of the early kings of Rome, Numa, is credited with adding January and February to make twelve months of the year. This explains the names *September, Octōber, November,* and *December,* which are clearly formed from the numerals *septem, octō, novem, decem.* The fifth month in the old calendar was called *Quīntīlis* (from *quīntus*), but after the death of *Iūlius Caesar*, it was renamed *Iūlius* in memory of him. In the year 8 BC the following month, which until then had been called *Sextīlis* (from *sextus*), was given the name of the Roman emperor *Augustus.*

Lēctiō Prīma (Section I)

Fifth Declension Nouns

The noun *diēs*, gen. *diēī*, here represents the **5th declension** (Latin *dēclīnātiō quīnta*). Only a few nouns belong to the 5th declension. The complete paradigm is shown below and on page 101 in LINGUA LATINA.

- 5th declension nouns have stems in *ē*, which is kept before all endings, except for those noted below. Most 5th declension nouns have *-iēs* in the nominative, like:

  diēs
  merīdiēs
  faciēs
  glaciēs

- A few have a consonant before *-ēs*, e.g., the common word *rēs*, gen. *reī* ("thing," "matter"), which turns up in the next chapter.

- The long *ē* of the 5th declension is shortened only:

  ▷ before the ending of the accusative singular: *-ĕm*

  ▷ in the genitive and dative singular when a consonant precedes (e.g., *rēs, reī*): *-ĕī*

- The nouns of this declension are feminine except for *diēs* (and *merī-diēs*), which is masculine. (In special senses and in late Latin, *diēs* is feminine.)

	sing.	pl.
nom.	di|ēs	di|ēs
acc.	di|em	di|ēs
gen.	di|ēī	di|ērum
dat.	di|ēī	di|ēbus
abl.	di|ē	di|ēbus

Recēnsiō: Declensions

You have now learned all five declensions. The classification is based on the (original) final stem-vowel:

1st declension: *a*-stems, e.g., *āla*, gen. sing. *-ae*

2nd declension: *o*-stems, e.g., *equus, ōvum*

- the "u" in the ending of these nouns was originally an "o"
  equus < equ|os
  ōvum < ōv|om, gen. sing. *-ī (<-oi)*

3rd declension: consonant-stems and *i*-stems, e.g., *sōl, ovi|s*, gen. sing. *-is*

4th declension: *u*-stems, e.g., *lacu|s*, gen. sing. *-ūs*

5th declension: *ē*-stems, e.g., *diē|s, rē|s*, gen. sing. *-ēī, -eī*

Māne

The neuter noun *māne* is indeclinable; it is also used as an adverb (Cap. XIV, l.155)

> *Prīma pars diēī est māne, pars postrēma vesper.* (ll.35–36)
> *Nox est tempus ā vesperō ad māne.* (l.37)

Calendar: Names of the Months

The names of the months are **adjectives**: *mēnsis Iānuārius*, etc., but they are often used alone without *mēnsis* and come to be felt as masculine nouns (with *mēnsis* understood).

- Most of the months belong to the 1st/2nd declension (e.g., *Iānuārius, -a, -um*).
- 3rd declension
  Aprīlis
  ▷ Genitive masculine singular in *-is*
  ▷ Ablative in *-ī*: (*mense*) *Aprīlī*
  September, Octōber, November, December
  ▷ Nominative masculine singular: *-ber*
  ▷ Genitive masculine singular: *-br|is: Septembris, Decembris*, etc.
  ▷ Ablative in *-ī*: (*mēnse*) *Septembrī, Octōbrī*, etc.

Expressions of Time

To express **time when** the ablative (*ablātīvus temporis*) without a preposition is used:

> *mēnse Decembrī*   in the month of December
> *illō tempore*   at that time
> *hōrā prīmā*   at the first hour

Tempore antīquō Mārtius mēnsis prīmus erat. (ll.17–19)
Nocte sōl nōn lūcet. (l.46)
Vēre campī novā herbā operiuntur. (l.92)
"Quandō sōl altissimus est?" "Hōrā sextā vel merīdiē." (ll.107–108)

Time **how long** (duration) is expressed by the accusative:
centum ann<u>ōs</u> vīvere (ll.10–11)

Numerals

Of the Latin **numerals**, you already know the **cardinals** 1–10:

ūn|us, -a, -um	*sex*
du|o, -ae, -o	*septem*
tr|ēs, -ia	*octō*
quattuor	*novem*
quīnque	*decem*

and the **ordinals** 1st–4th. In numbering the months, the first twelve ordinals are needed:

prīm|us, -a, -um	*septim|us, -a, -um*
secund|us, -a, -um	*octāv|us, -a, -um*
terti|us, -a, -um	*nōn|us, -a, -um*
quārt|us, -a, -um	*decim|us, -a, -um*
quīnt|us, -a, -um	*ūndecim|us, -a, -um*
sext|us, -a, -um	*duodecim|us, -a, -um*

The ordinals are also combined with *pars* to form **fractions**:

⅓:	*tertia pars*
¼:	*quārta pars*
⅕:	*quīnta pars* (etc.)

Notā Bene: ½: <u>*dīmidia*</u> *pars.*

Verbs: Preterite (Imperfect) Tense

The preterite comes from a compound of *praeter* ("beyond," Cap. XIV) and the verb *īre* (Cap. XVI)[1] and refers to "what has gone past," or the past tense. The forms *erat, erant* are used instead of *est, sunt* when the past is concerned. Compare the sentences:

<u>*Tunc*</u> (= *illō tempore*)   *Mārtius mēnsis prīmus <u>erat</u>.*
<u>*Nunc*</u> (= *hōc tempore*)   *Mārtius mēnsis tertius <u>est</u>.*

---

1. You learned the verb "*it*," "he/she goes," in Cap. VI, l.20: *Iūlius ab oppidō ad vīllam suam it.*

Erat, erant is called the **imperfect tense**, or *preterite*, while *est, sunt* is the **present tense** ("tense" comes from Latin *tempus* and refers to the relative *time* of the verb). The past tense of other verbs comes later (Cap. XIX).

Comparison of Adjectives

Consider the following examples:

> *Februārius brevis est.*
> *Februārius brevior est quam Iānuārius.*
> *Februārius mēnsis annī brevissimus est.*

Brevis breve (**positive degree**)

- simply describes or limits the noun "February"
- ends in:
    - *-us, -a, -um* (e.g., *longus, -a, -um*)
    - *-is, -e* (e.g., *brevis, -e*)
    - (other endings will be learned later)

Brevior brevius (**comparative degree** of *brevis*)

- compares February with January
- ends in:
    - *-ior, -ius* (e.g., *longior, longius, brevior, brevius*)

Brevissimus -issima, -issimum (**superlative degree**, Latin *superlātīvus*, of *brevis*):

- compares February with all the other months of the year
- ends in:
    - *-issimus, -a, -um* (e.g., *longissimus, -a, -um, brevissimus, -a, -um*)

Quam

Lines 25–30 illustrate the three degrees as well as different uses of *quam*:

> *Quam* (= how) *longus* (positive degree) *est mēnsis November?*
> *November trīgintā diēs longus est. December ūnum et trīgintā diēs habet.*
> *Iānuārius tam longus est quam* (= as…as) *December, sed Februārius brevior* (comparative degree) *est: duodētrīgintā aut ūndētrīgintā diēs tantum habet.*
> *Februārius brevior* (comparative degree) *est quam* (= than) *cēterī ūndecim mēnsēs: is mēnsis annī brevissimus* (superlative degree) *est.*

Vel

The conjunction *vel* was originally the imperative of *velle*; it implies a free choice between two expressions or possibilities. In each of the following, either expression will do:

> *duodecim mēnsēs <u>vel</u> trecentōs sexāgintā quīnque diēs* (l.7)
> *centum annī <u>vel</u> saeculum* (l.9)
> *hōra sexta <u>vel</u> merīdiēs* (l.43)

Vel is distinct from *aut*, which is put between mutually exclusive alternatives. February can have *either* 28 or 29 days:

> *Februārius brevior est: duodētrīgintā <u>aut</u> ūndētrīgintā diēs.* (l.28)

Lēctiō Altera (Section II)

Roman Calendar: Divisons of the Month

Three days in each month had special names; they are all feminine plurals:

kalendae	the 1st
īdūs	the 13th (*īdūs -uum* 4th decl.)
nōnae	the 5th (the 9th day before *īdūs*: inclusive reckoning)

In March, May, July, and October (the four months that originally had 31 days):
>*īdūs* was the 15th
>*nōnae* was consequently the 7th

The following mnemonic may help:
> In March, July, October, May
> The IDES fall on the fifteenth day,
> The NONES the seventh; all besides
> Have two days less for Nones and Ides.

To these names (*kalendae, īdūs,* and *nōnae*) the names of the months are added as adjectives. Thus:

January 1st	*kalend<u>ae</u> Iānuāri<u>ae</u>*
January 5th	*nōn<u>ae</u> Iānuāri<u>ae</u>*
January 13th	*īd<u>ūs</u> Iānuāri<u>ae</u>*

Ablative of Time When

Dates are given in the ***ablātīvus temporis***, e.g.:

kalend<u>īs</u> Iānuāri<u>īs</u>	on January 1st
īd<u>ibus</u> Mārti<u>īs</u>	on March 15th

Giving the Date in Latin

Other dates were indicated by stating the number of days before the following *kalendae, nōnae,* or *īdūs.* The Romans counted inclusively; that is, they counted the beginning and ending day, e.g., since April 21st (Rome's birthday) is the 11th day before *kalendae Māiae* (inclusive reckoning), it should therefore be:

> *diēs ūndecimus ante kalendās Māiās*

but the Romans put the *ante* first with all the following words in the accusative:

> *ante diem ūndecimum kalendās Māiās*
>   usually shortened *a. d. XI kal. Māi.*

Using the table on page 312 of Lingua Latina, you can easily figure out the date.

Dīcitur + Nominative and Infinitive

Note the passive *dīcitur* with an infinitive and the nominative case:

> *Lūna 'nova' esse dīcitur.* (l.52, "is said to be…")

Compare the same thought using the active verb (*dīcunt*) with the accusative and infinitive construction you learned in Cap. XI:

> (*Hominēs*) *lūnam 'novam' esse dīcunt.*

When used with a predicate nominative, *dīcitur* is closer in meaning to "is called."

> *Diēs prīmus mēnsis Iānuāriī dīcitur 'kalendae Iānuāriae.'* (ll.56–57)
> *Item 'īdūs Februāriae' dīcitur diēs tertius decimus mēnsis Februāriī.*
>   (ll.64–65)
> *Diēs octāvus ante kalendās Iānuāriās, quī dīcitur 'ante diem octāvum kalendās Iānuāriās,' est diēs annī brevissimus.* (ll.72–74)

Lēctiō Tertia (Section III)

Velle

The infinitive of *vult, volunt* has the irregular form *velle,* as appears from the acc. + inf. in:

> *Aemilia puerum dormīre velle putat.* (l.140)

Recēnsiō: Expressions of Time and Space: Ablative and Accusative

The ablative represents a point in space or time:

- Space: Where?
  Diēs est dum sōl in caelō est. (l.35)
  In Germāniā hiemēs frīgidiōrēs sunt quam in Italiā. (ll.95–96)
- Time: When? During what time?
  Aestāte diēs longī sunt, sōl lūcet, āēr calidus est. (l.87)
  *Hōc annī tempore diēs nōn tam calidī sunt quam aestāte et noctēs
    frīgidiōrēs sunt.* (ll.120–121)

The accusative represents movement through a block of space or time.

- Space: How long? How high? How deep?
  Gladius duōs pedēs longus est. (Cap. XII, l.49)
  *vāllum castrōrum…prope decem pedēs altum est, et duo mīlia
    passuum longum.* (Cap. XII, ll.101–103)
- Time: How long?
  November trīgintā diēs longus est. (ll.25–26)
  Mārtius ūnum et trīgintā diēs longus est. (ll.30–31)

In both cases, the **accusative** expresses movement through space/time from point A to point B, unlike the **ablative**, which expresses a specific point in space/time.

Studia Rōmāna

The Julian calendar was all our Julius and his family had ever known. Julius Caesar revised the Roman calendar so that it followed the natural year more closely. Revised very slightly in 1582 by Pope Gregory XIII, the Julian calendar (now called the Gregorian calendar) is still the calendar we use today.

The ancients had long known the length of the solar year, but calendars did not strictly follow the natural year until Julius Caesar, in 45 BC, made his reforms law. Before the Julian calendar, the Romans had to periodically insert days into the year in order to "catch up" to the solar calendar. These intercalendary days (or months!) could be a nuisance. Cicero, while governing the province of Cilicia and eager to return to the political scene at Rome, begs his friends to vote against inserting more days into his term of office.

The Romans had two ways of referring to years. Rome was ruled by kings from the founding of the city in 753 BC up to 510 BC, when it became a republic. One way of marking the years was to refer to the number of years *from the founding of the city* (in Latin: *ab urbe conditā*, abbreviated AUC). More commonly, the years were named by the two leaders of the republic, the *cōnsulēs* (after 510 BC); their names appear in the ablative (in a construction you will learn in Caps. XIV and XVI). In the year 70 BC, for example, *Gnaius Pompēius* (Pompey the Great) and *Mārcus Crassus* were consuls, and the year was marked: *Cn. Pompēiō M. Crassō cōnsulibus,* "when Gnaeus Pompey and

Marcus Crassus were the consuls." It was not until 153 BC, however, that January 1st became the start of the consular year (that is, the date when the consuls took office). Our strict notions of time and dates are a relatively recent phenomenon—the marking of precise time was not as important to the Romans.

The illustration at the beginning of the chapter gives you the twelve astrological signs familiar to us today—and familiar to the Greeks and Romans 2,000 years ago. Astrology was adopted by the Greeks from the Babylonians and the Egyptians in the third century BC and from the Greeks was taken up by the Romans. Cicero translated from Greek to Latin a poem about celestial phenomena by Aratus, in which he tells us that the Greeks call the swath of sky divided into the twelve familiar divisions *Zōdiacus* and the Romans the *orbis signifer*.[2] The emperor Augustus is said to have had his horoscope (*hōroscopus*) published as a sign of his destined power. In the first century AD, Manilius wrote *Astronomica*, a long poem in Latin about astrology, and in the second century, the Egyptian polymath Ptolemy and the lesser-known *Vettius Valēns* wrote books on astrology.

In the illustration on p. 96, you can see a sundial (*hōrologium*), an ancient clock. The sundial has twelve divisions, not twenty-four, because it works only during the day. At night, the movement of the heavenly bodies could be consulted and, for use inside, the ancients could use a water clock, in which water poured into a vessel from one on a higher level. Since the days are longer or shorter depending on the time of the year, time in antiquity was flexible. The first hour began with sunrise. You might also have noticed the absence of a word for our "week." The concept of the week, found in the East (where it was important for astrology), seems to have shown up in Rome under the emperor Augustus, but it did not come into common use until the third century AD, after the time of our narrative. The word for it is *septimāna* (Latin) and *hebdomas* (from the Greek). The Romans had other ways of marking the progression of the months. In addition to the Kalends (*Kalendae*), Ides (*Īdūs*) and Nones (*Nōnae*), every ninth day was a market day, called *Nūndinae* (<*novem+dies*). The chart on page 312 of your text lays out the Roman calendar.

In this chapter, you also meet two gods of the Roman state: *Iānus* and *Mārs*. Roman religion existed on several levels: the state, the neighborhood, the family, and the individual. It is also a mixture of native Italian elements and imports from Greece and elsewhere. Janus is a native Italic deity depicted with two heads facing in different directions. The name *Iānus* means passageway (and in Cap. XV you will learn the word *iānua*, which, like *ōstium*, means "door"). Janus is the god of passageways and thus is associated with beginnings (making January an appropriate name for the first month of the year). The doors of the temple of Janus in the Forum were closed in times of peace and open in times of war. Mars, the god of war, is associated with the Greek god

---

2.   *Zōdiacum hunc Graecī vocitant, nostrīque Latīnī orbem signiferum perhibēbunt nōmine vērō.*

of war Ares. As in the illustration in the margin of your text, Mars is shown in battle array. After Iuppiter, Mars is the chief god of the Romans. The Romans credited Mars with fathering Romulus, the founder of Rome, and his brother Remus.

Vocābula Disposita/Ōrdināta

Nōmina

1st

fōrma, -ae	form, shape, figure
hōra, -ae	hour
kalendae, -ārum (*pl.*)	the 1st of the month
lūna, -ae	moon
nōnae, -ārum (*pl.*)	5th/7th of the month
stēlla, -ae	star

2nd

aequinoctium, -ī	equinox
annus, -ī	year
autumnus, -ī	autumn
initium, -ī	beginning
saeculum, -ī	century
superlātīvus, -ī (gradus)	superlative
vesper, vesperī	evening

3rd

aestās, aestātis (*f.*)	summer
hiems, hiemis (*f.*)	winter
imber, imbris (*m.*)	rain, shower
lūx, lūcis (*f.*)	light, daylight
mēnsis, mēnsis (*m.*)	month
nix, nivis (*f.*)	snow
nox, noctis (*f.*)	night
tempus, temporis (*n.*)	time
urbs, urbis (*f.*)	city
vēr, vēris (*n.*)	spring

4th

īdūs, īduum (*f. pl.*)	13th/15th of the month
lacus, -ūs	lake

5th

diēs, -ēī (*m.*)	day, date
faciēs, -ēī	face
glaciēs, -ēī	ice
merīdiēs, -ēī (*m.*)	midday, noon, south
indēclīnābilis	indeclinable
māne	morning

Verba
  -āre (1)
    illūstrat, illūstrāre   illustrate, make clear
    nōminat, nōmināre   name, call
-ere (3)
  i-stem
    incipit, incipere   begin
  -īre (4)
    operit, operīre   cover
  Irregular
    erat, erant   was, were
    vult, velle   want, be willing

Adiectīva
  1st/2nd (-us/er, -a, -um)
    aequus, -a, -um   equal, calm
    calidus, -a, -um   warm, hot, *f.* hot water[3]
    clārus, -a, -um   bright, clear, loud
    decimus, -a, -um   tenth
    dīmidius, -a, -um   half
    duodecimus, -a, -um   twelfth
    exiguus, -a, -um   small, scanty
    frīgidus, -a, -um   cold, chilly, cool
    nōnus, -a, -um   ninth
    obscūrus, -a, -um   dark
    octāvus, -a, -um   eighth
    postrēmus, -a, -um   last
    quīntus, -a, -um   fifth
    septimus, -a, -um   seventh
    sextus, -a, -um   sixth
    tōtus, -a, -um   the whole of, all
    ūndecimus, -a, -um   eleventh
  3rd
    indēclīnābilis, -e   indeclinable

Numerī (indeclinable unless otherwise noted)
    ducentī, -ae, -a   two hundred
    sexāgintā   sixty
    trecentī, -ae, -a   three hundred
    trīgintā   thirty
    ūndecim   eleven

Adverbia
    item   likewise, also
    māne   in the morning

---

3.   When *calida* (f.) is used as a noun, it means *calida aqua* = hot water.

nunc	now
quandō	when, as
tunc	then

Coniūnctiōnēs

igitur	therefore, then, so
vel	or

XIV. Novus Diēs

Rēs Grammaticae Novae

1. Verbs:
   a. *inquit, inquiunt*
   b. Agreement of subject/verb
2. Nouns: Case Uses
   a. Dative of Interest (*datīvus commodī*)
   b. Ablative of Attendant Circumstances
3. Present Participles (*participium praesēns*)
4. Adjectives
   a. *omnis -e*
   b. Numbers *duo, duae, duo* (ablative)
   c. *uter, neuter, alter, uterque*
5. Pronouns: *mihi, mē, tibi, tē* (dative/ablative)
6. Points of Style: *sē habēre*

The New Day

At dawn, Marcus is roused from his morning slumbers by Davus, who also sees to it that he washes properly before putting on his *tunica* and *toga*, the clothes that were the mark of freeborn Roman men and boys.

Lēctiō Prīma (Section I)

Uter, neuter, alter, uterque

Among the new words in this chapter is a group of words that is used only when two persons or things are concerned; they can be used as adjectives or pronouns:

uter?	which (of the two)?
neuter	neither (of the two)
alter	the other (of the two)
uterque	each (of the two)

Uter, utra, utrum is the interrogative used when there are only two alter-natives ("which of the two?"), e.g.:

> *Uter puer, Mārcusne an*   (the conjunction *an*, not *aut*, is put
> *Quīntus?*   between the two in question)

The answer may be:

1. *neuter, -tra, -trum* ("neither"), e.g., *neuter puer, nec Mārcus nec Quīntus.*
2. *alter, -era, -erum* ("one"/"the other"), e.g., *alter puer, aut M. aut Q.*
3. *uter-, utra-, utrum- que* ("each of the two"), e.g., *uterque puer, et M. et Q.*

Uterque

Where English prefers "both" followed by the plural ("both boys"), Latin has the singular *uterque*:

> *Uterque puer cubat in cubiculō parvō, neuter in cubiculō magnō.* (ll.8–9)
> *Uterque puer quiētus est, neuter puer sē movet.* (ll.10–11)

Uterque is singular and followed by a singular verb.

Subject-Verb Agreement

In Cap. I, you learned that a singular subject is joined with a singular verb and in Cap. V, that plural subjects are joined with a plural verb. In this chapter, we see an exception to that rule: the verb is in the singular if there are two subjects separated by *neque...neque, aut...aut,* or *et...et*, as in:

> *et caput et pēs eī dolet.* (ll.3–4)
> *nec caput nec pēs dolet.* (l.66)

The general rule is that two or more subjects:

- take a verb in the plural if they denote **persons**, as in: *Parentēs ā fīliō intrante salūtantur.* (l.91)
- if the subjects are **things**, the verb agrees with the nearest subject, as in:
  > *pēs et caput eī dolet.* (ll.3–4, 64)

Dative of Interest/Reference

In the last example (*pēs et caput eī dolet*), the dative *eī* denotes the person concerned, benefited, or harmed. This use of the dative is called the **dative of interest** or reference (*datīvus commodī*), e.g.:

> *Bracchium quoque dolet Quīntō.* (l.4)
> *Multīs barbarīs magna pars corporis nūda est.* (ll.76–77)

Duo, duae, duo

The ablative of *duo, duae, duo* is:

- masculine and neuter *du<u>ō</u>bus*
  ē du<u>ō</u>bus puerīs (ll.11–12)
  in du<u>ō</u>bus cubiculīs
- feminine *du<u>ā</u>bus*
  ē du<u>ā</u>bus fenestrīs (l.16)

Ablative of Attendant Circumstances

A noun and an adjective in the ablative can show the conditions surrounding the verb, as in:

Mārcus <u>fenestrā apertā</u> dormit.	with the window open (l.15)
Is <u>fenestrā clausā</u> dormit.	with the window shut (l.18)
Quīntus, quī <u>oculīs apertīs</u> iacet.	with his eyes open (ll.21–22)

Notice that the noun comes first; this is the case unless the adjective is being emphasized.

Present Participle (*Participium Praesēns*)

On page 104, a new form of the *verb* is introduced, the **participle** (Latin *participium*) ending in -(*ē*)*ns*:

puer dormiēns = *puer quī dormit* (ll.22–23)
puer vigilāns = *puer quī vigilat* (l.23)

The participle, being part verb and part adjective, was called *participium* (< *pars partis* "part" + *capere* "take" = share, participate). The participle shares in two parts of speech, the adjective and the verb. The participle:

- is a 3rd declension **adjective** with the same ending in the nōminative singular of all genders.
  vigilāns, gen. -*ant|is*
  dormiēns, gen. -*ent|is*
- keeps **verbal** functions, e.g.,
    it may take an object in the accusative:
  Dāvus cubicul<u>um</u> intrā<u>ns</u> interrogat… (l.25)
- has an **ablative singular** in -*e* when it has verbal force, e.g.:
  Parentēs ā fīliō intrant<u>e</u> salūtantur. (l.91)
- has an **ablative singular** in -*ī* only when used only as an adjective, with no verbal force:

> *ibi nocte silentī Ariadnam*   He left Ariadne sleeping there
> *dormientem relīquit.*   during the silent night. (Cap. XXV,
>   ll.99–100)

Silentī is the ablative of the present participle of *silēre*. Here, it is being used only as an adjective describing the night and has no verbal force.

Participle

sing.	m./f.	n.
nom.	*-ns*	*-ns*
acc.	*-ntem*	*-ns*
gen.	*-ntis*	
dat.	*-ntī*	
abl.	*-nte/-ntī*	
pl.		
nom./acc.	*-ntēs*	*-ntia*
gen.	*-ntium*	
dat./abl.	*-ntibus*	

Lēctiō Altera (Section II)

Personal Pronouns: Dative and Ablative

Mihi and *tibi* are the datives corresponding to the accusatives *mē* and *tē*:

> *"Affer <u>mihi</u> aquam!"* (l.43)
> *"<u>Mihi</u> quoque caput dolet!"* (l.65)
> *"<u>Tibi</u> nec caput nec pēs dolet!"* (l.66)

The **ablative** of these pronouns is identical with the accusative: *mē, tē*. When used as the object of the preposition *cum*, the preposition is suffixed:

> *mē-cum*
> *tē-cum*
> *sē-cum*

For example:

> *Dāvus eum <u>sēcum</u> venīre iubet: "Venī <u>mēcum</u>!"* (ll.86–87)
>   *"Mēdus <u>tēcum</u> īre nōn potest."* (l.117)
>   *"Alterum <u>tēcum</u> fer!"* (l.108)
>   *"Cūr ille servus <u>mēcum</u> venīre nōn potest ut solet?"* (l.120)
>   *"…stilum rēgulamque <u>sēcum</u> ferēns ē vīllā abit."* (ll.127–128)

acc.	*mē*	*tē*
dat.	*mihi*	*tibi*
abl.	*mē*	*tē*

Inquit

The verb *inquit*, "(he/she) says," is inserted after one or more words of **direct speech**:

> *"Hōra prīma est,"* <u>*inquit*</u> *Dāvus, "Surge ē lectō!"* (l.40)
>
> *Servus Mārcō aquam affert et "Ecce aqua,"* <u>*inquit.*</u> (l.44)

It is a **defective** verb: only *inquit, inquiunt* and a few other forms of the indicative occur. Neither *inquit* nor *inquiunt* is used to begin accusative + infinitive constructions.

Lēctiō Tertia (Section III)

Omnis, -e

The opposite of *nūllus* is *omnis, -e* ("every," "all"), which more often appears in the plural *omnēs, -ia* (see lines 115 and 119).

Used without a noun, the plural *omnēs* ("everybody") is the opposite of *nēmō* ("nobody"), and the neuter plural *omnia* ("everything") is the opposite of *nihil* ("nothing").

> omnis ↔ nūllus
> omnēs ↔ nēmō
> omnia ↔ nihil

Points of Style: *sē habēre*

Davus asks Quintus, *Quōmodo sē habet pēs tuus hodiē?* (ll.25–26) ("How is your foot today?"). Quintus answers, *"Pēs male sē habet"* (l.27). *Sē habēre* + adverb = to be (in a certain state) and is a regular way of asking how, as we say in English, "someone is doing."

Studia Rōmāna

In Cap. III, you learned *tuxtax* (ll.64, 65), a word meant to represent the sound of being beaten. The sound of the rooster crowing is *"Cucurrū! Cucucurrū!"* (l.19); the verb *cūcūrīre* means "to crow." You read about the ancient approach to time at the end of Cap. XIII. Romans tended to wake and sleep with the rhythms of the sun and noted exceptions. As a marker of his leisurely life, Horace boasts that he likes to sleep in until the fourth hour after sunrise (*Satire* 1.6.122); work done after dark, and hence by lamplight, is called *lūcūbrātiō*, and Cicero coined the verb *ēlūcūbrāre* for working by lamplight. (Of course, Roman lamps are ubiquitous archaeological finds, so clearly, people didn't go to bed as soon as the sun set or always wait for the sun to rise to start their day.)

Davus is in charge of getting the boys off to school and it was Medus's job (before he ran away) to take them to school. It seems these two slaves shared the post of *paedagōgus*, the slave who minded the children at home and watched over them as they went to school. *Paedagōgus* is a Greek word adopted by the Romans; the Latin word *custos* is sometimes found. Quintilian, who wrote a book on the education of the orator (*Īnstitūtiō Ōrātōria*) in the century before our narrative (c. AD 35–100), stresses that a *paedagōgus* should be well educated and should speak both Latin and Greek well. That way, the children will not develop bad habits of speech at home. The *paedagogus* helped with the children's education, supervised homework and monitored their behavior. He was held responsible for their well-being. Quintilian blames bad behavior on lazy *paedagōgī*. Cicero, in a letter to his friend Atticus (*Ad Att.* 12.33), worries about the health of Atticus's daughter, Attica; were not her *paedagogus* beyond reproach, Cicero writes, he would be inclined to blame him for Attica's ill health. Horace's father acted as his son's *paedagogus*, not trusting the job to a slave: *ipse mihi custos incorruptissimus omnīs/circum doctōrēs aderat* (*Sat.* 1.6.81–82: "My father himself, most blameless guardian, was at my side around all my teachers").

When Marcus goes off to school, his father tells him, *"Valē! Bene ambulā!"*(l.130). This expression of farewell goes all the way back at least to the comic playwright Plautus in the second century BC.

Vocābula Disposita/Ōrdināta

Nōmina
1st

rēgula, -ae	ruler
tabula, -ae	writing tablet
toga, -ae	toga
tunica, -ae	tunic

2nd

calceus, -ī	shoe
gallus, -ī	cock, rooster
participium, -ī	participle
stilus, -ī	stylus
vestīmentum, -ī	garment, clothing

3rd

parentēs, -um (*m. pl.*)	parents

5th

rēs, reī (*f.*)	thing, matter, affair

Indeclinable

nihil (*n.*)	nothing

Verba

-āre (1)

cubat, cubāre	lie (in bed)
vigilat, vigilāre	be awake
excitat, excitāre	wake up, arouse
lavat, lavāre	wash, bathe

-ēre (2)

valet, valēre	be strong, be well
solet, solēre	be accustomed
frīget, frīgēre	be cold

-ere (3)

surgit, surgere	rise, get up
mergit, mergere	dip, plunge, sink
poscit, poscere	demand, call for
induit, induere	put on (clothes)
gerit, gerere	carry, wear, carry on, do

-īre (4)

vestit, vestīre	dress

Irregular

affert, afferre	bring (to, forward)
inquit, inquiunt	(he/she) says/said

Adiectīva

1st/2nd (-us/er, -a, -um)

apertus, -a, -um	open
clausus, -a, -um	closed, shut
sordidus, -a, -um	dirty, mean, base
pūrus, -a, -um	clean, pure
nūdus, -a, -um	naked
togātus, -a, -um	wearing the toga
dexter, -tra, -trum	right, *f.* the right (hand)[1]
sinister, -tra, -trum	left, *f.* the left (hand)
neuter, -tra, -trum	neither
alter, -era, -erum	one, the other, second
uter, -tra, -trum?	which (of the two)?
uterque, utraque, utrumque	each of the two

3rd

omnis, -e	all, every

Prōnōmina

mihi	me, myself (dat.)
tibi	you, yourself (dat.)
mēcum	with me

---

1.   When *dextra* (f.) is used as a noun, it means *dextra manus* = right hand; the noun *sinistra* means left hand.

tēcum	with you
sēcum	with himself/herself

Adverbia
prīmum	first
nihil/nīl[2]	nothing, not at all
quōmodo	how
hodiē	today
adhūc	so far, till now, still
deinde/dein	afterward, then

Praepositiōnēs
praeter (*prp. + acc.*)	past, besides, except

Coniūnctiōnēs
an	or (mostly with **ūter: ūter...an**)

Alia
valē, valēte	farewell, goodbye

---

2. *Nihil* acts as an adverb as well as a noun (contracted form is *nīl*). As a noun, it has two forms, the indeclinable *nihil* above and the 2nd declension neuter *nihilum, -ī*.

XV. Magister et Discipulī

Rēs Grammaticae Novae

1. Verbs
   a. Personal Endings: 1st and 2nd Person
   b. *esse*
   c. *posse*
   d. Impersonal Verbs
      i. *convenit*
      ii. *licet*
2. Nouns: Case Uses
   a. Accusative of Exclamation
3. Pronouns
   a. Personal Pronouns
   b. Pronouns vs. Possessive Adjectives
   c. Reflexives in Indirect Statement

Going to School in Ancient Rome

The illustration at the start of the chapter is a drawing of an ancient relief sculpture of a schoolroom. Rome had no public school system. Parents who could afford it sent their young children to an elementary school, *lūdus,* or had them educated at home by a tutor, often a slave. Quintilian (see notes at end of Cap. XIV) writes about the advantages and disadvantages of each, but sees the natural competition and sociability of the schoolroom as a productive atmosphere for learning. The *lūdus* was run as a private enterprise by a *lūdī magister,* who taught the children reading, writing and arithmetic.

We now follow Marcus to school. His teacher tries his best to maintain discipline, but he has some difficulty in keeping these boys in hand. His recourse to corporal punishment seems to have been a familiar feature of the schoolroom: the first-century BC poet Horace called his teacher Orbillius "*plāgōsus*" (full of *plāgae* or blows) and other writers as well testify to the severity of the schoolroom. Quintilian disapproves of corporal punishment and blames the laxity of contemporary *paedagōgī*: it is the job of the *paedagōgus* to monitor the behavior of his charge. He complains that the *paedagōgī* don't do their jobs of making the boys behave and then the boys are punished for not behaving (*Īnstitūtiō Ōrātōria* I.3).

Lēctiō Prīma (Section I)

Personal Endings: 1st and 2nd Person Singular

From the conversation between the teacher and his pupils, you learn that the verbs have different endings as one speaks about oneself (**1st person**), addresses another person (**2nd person**), or speaks about someone else (**3rd person**).

The dialogue in lines 35–40 illustrates the 1st, 2nd, and 3rd singular endings:

> *Titus, quī librum nōn habet, "Ego librum nōn habeō."*
> *Magister: "Quid? Sextus librum suum habet, tū librum tuum nōn habēs?*
>   *Cūr librum nōn habēs?"*
> *Titus: "Librum nōn habeō, quod Mārcus meum librum habet."*

It appears from this that in the singular:

- the 1st person of the verb ends in *-ō* (*habe|ō*)
- the 2nd in *-s* (*habē|s*)
- the 3rd, as you know, in *-t* (*habe|t*)

Personal Pronouns

The verbs in the above examples are preceded by **personal pronouns** in the nominative:

ego	1st pers. sing.	*nōs*	1st pers. pl.
tū	2nd pers. sing.	*vōs*	2nd pers. pl.

But these pronouns are only used when the subject is emphasized, for example (ll.24–26):

> *Sextus: "Num ego discipulus improbus sum?"*
> *Magister: "Immō tū probus es discipulus, Sexte, at Mārcus et Quīntus et*
>   *Titus improbī sunt!"*

Normally, the personal ending is sufficient to show which person is meant, as in these examples (ll.38–39):

> *Magister: "Cūr librum nōn habēs?"*
> *Titus: "Librum nōn habeō."*

Exclamation: Accusative and Vocative

Diodorus expresses his frustration with the students in two different ways:

> *"Ō, discipulōs improbōs…!"* (l.23)
> *"Ō improbī discipulī!"* (ll.101–102)

The first example (*Ō, discipulōs improbōs*) is in the accusative, the second (*Ō improbī discipulī!*) in the vocative. (As you learned in Cap. IV, the vocative plural has the same form as the nominative plural.) What's the difference? The vocative is used to address those present, while the accusative (called the **accusative of exclamation**) exclaims *about* more than *to* the students.

Esse

The verb *esse* is irregular; in the singular, it runs:

> *sum*
> *es*
> *est*

Example:

> *"Cūr tū sōlus es, Sexte?" "Ego sōlus sum."* (ll.20–21)

Lēctiō Altera (Section II)

Personal Endings: 1st and 2nd Person Plural

The dialogue in lines 51–57 illustrates the 1st and 2nd plural endings:

> *Mārcus (ad Sextum et Titum):* "Vōs iānuam nōn pulsātis cum ad lūdum venītis, nec magistrum salūtātis cum eum vidētis. Audītisne id quod dīcō?"
>
> *Tum Sextus et Titus:* "Id quod dīcis," inquiunt, "vērum nōn est: nōs iānuam pulsāmus cum ad lūdum venīmus, et magistrum salūtāmus cum eum vidēmus. Nōnne vērum dīcimus, magister?"

It appears from this that in the plural:

- the 1st person ends in *-mus* (*pulsā|mus, vidē|mus, venī|mus*)
- the 2nd in *-tis* (*pulsā|tis, vidē|tis, dīc|itis venī|tis*)
- the 3rd, as you know, in *-nt* (*pulsa|nt, vide|nt, dīc|unt veni|unt*)

The examples in the section Grammatica Latina in Lingua Latina show how these **personal endings** are added to the various stems in the **present tense**. The way vocabulary is listed at the end of the chapter will also change. From now on, the 1st person singular, not the 3rd, will be given for each verb.

Personal Pronouns (continued)

The plural of the personal pronouns in the nominative:

nōs	1st pers. pl.
vōs	2nd pers. pl.

The accusative of *ego* and *tū* is *mē* and *tē*, but *nōs* and *vōs* are the same in the accusative (ll.119–120):

"Quid <u>nōs</u> verberās, magister?"
"<u>Vōs</u> verberō."

	sing.	pl.	sing.	pl.
nom.	*ego*	*nōs*	*tū*	*vōs*
acc.	*mē*	*nōs*	*tē*	*vōs*

You will learn the forms of the genitive in Cap. XXIX. For now, add the nominative and accusative to the forms you have already learned:

	sing.	pl.	sing.	pl.
nom.	*ego*	*nōs*	*tū*	*vōs*
acc.	*mē*	*nōs*	*tē*	*vōs*
gen.				
dat.	*mihi*	*nōbīs*	*tibi*	*vōbīs*
abl.	*mē*	*nōbīs*	*tē*	*vōbīs*

Overview of Present Active Endings

1st	*-ō, -mus*
2nd	*-s, -tis*
3rd	*-t, -nt*

Notā Bene:

- before *-ō*:
    - ▷ *ā* combines with *-ō*: *puls|ō* (stem *pulsā*)
    - ▷ *ē* and *ī* shorten: *hab<u>e</u>|ō, ven<u>i</u>|ō* (stems *hab<u>e</u>-, ven<u>i</u>-)*
- in 3rd conjugation consonant-stems:
    - ▷ a short *i* is inserted before:
      -s: *dīc|<u>i</u>s* (stem *dīc-*)
      -mus: *dīc|<u>i</u>mus*
      -tis: *dīc|<u>i</u>tis*
      -t: *dīc|<u>i</u>t*
    - ▷ before *nt* we find a short *u*:
      -nt: *dīc|<u>u</u>nt*

- in 3rd conjugation *i*-stems, a short *i* appears before the endings:
  - ▷ *ō*: *faci|ō* (stem *faci-*)
  - ▷ *-unt*: *faci|unt*
  - ▷ Other verbs of this kind that you have met are *accipere, aspicere, capere, fugere, iacere, incipere,* and *parere*.

	1st	2nd	3rd cons.	3rd i-stem	4th
sing. 1	*puls|ō*	*habe|ō*	*dīc|ō*	*faci|ō*	*veni|ō*
2	*pulsā|s*	*habē|s*	*dīc|is*	*faci|s*	*venī|s*
3	*pulsa|t*	*habe|t*	*dīc|it*	*faci|t*	*veni|t*
pl. 1	*pulsā|mus*	*habē|mus*	*dīc|imus*	*faci|mus*	*venī|mus*
2	*pulsā|tis*	*habē|tis*	*dīc|itis*	*faci|tis*	*venī|tis*
3	*pulsa|nt*	*habe|nt*	*dīc|unt*	*faci|unt*	*veni|unt*

The Reflexive in Indirect Speech

Much of the time, changing direct speech to indirect speech is pretty straight-forward. When someone reports his or her own words in the accusative and infinitive construction (indirect speech), the subject accusative is the reflexive *sē*. This is best learned by studying several examples. We have already read an example in Cap. XIV:

> *Dāvus…eum sēcum venīre iubet*: "*Venī mēcum!*": Davus orders him (Marcus) to come with him (Davus): "Come with me!" (Cap. XIV, l.87)

> *Quīntus*: "(*Ego*) *aeger sum*" is reported by Marcus: *Quīntus dīcit "sē aegrum esse.*" Quintus says that he is sick. (l.82)
> *Mārcus*: "*Ego eius librum habeō*" becomes *Mārcus dīcit "sē eius librum habēre.*"

> *Mārcus*: "*Ego,*" *inquit,* "*nōn dormiō*" becomes *Mārcus dīcit "sē nōn dormīre.*"

> *Sextus et Titus*: "*Neque nōs dormīmus,*" *inquiunt.* "*Vigilāmus et omnia verba tua audīmus*" becomes *Sextus et Titus dīcunt "sē nōn dormīre; sē vigilāre et omnia verba eius audīre.*"

Esse (continued)

The verb *esse* is irregular; in the plural, it runs:

> *sumus*
> *estis*
> *sunt*

Example:

> *"Ubi estis, puerī?" "In lūdō sumus."* (ll.113–114)

Esse

	sing.	pl.
1st	*sum*	*sumus*
2nd	*es*	*estis*
3rd	*est*	*sunt*

Convenit

We first met *convenit* in Cap. VIII (see Points of Style in that chapter). *Convenit* comes from *convenīre* and is here used **impersonally**, i.e., in the 3rd person singular.[1] The impersonal *convenit* often has an infinitive subject and a dative of reference:

> *Tergum dolet Mārcō, neque ille lacrimat, nam lacrimāre puerō Rōmānō nōn convenit.* (ll.62–64)

Posse

Compounds of *esse* show the same irregular forms. As you learned in Cap. X, the "*pot*" of the verb:

- remains before the vowel "*e*" in *potes, potest*
- becomes "*pos*" before "*s*" in *possum*

In the singular, *posse* runs:

> *pos-sum*
> *pot-es*
> *pot-est*

Examples (ll.72–73):

> *Mārcus: "Non cōnsīdō, quod sedēre nōn possum."*
> *Diodōrus: "Cūr sedēre nōn potes?"*

Lēctiō Tertia (Section III)

Posse (continued)

In the plural, *posse* runs:

> *pos-sumus*
> *pot-estis*
> *pos-sunt*

---

1. *Convenīre* can also be used personally, i.e., with a subject other than "it."

Examples (ll.124–127):

> *Magister*: *"Quid nōn cōnsīditis?" Discipulī: "Nōn cōnsīdimus, quod sedēre nōn possumus."*
> *Diodōrus*: *"Quid? Sedēre nōn potestis?... Nec enim stantēs dormīre potestis!"*

Licet

The verb *licet* ("it is allowed," "one may") is also (like *convenit*) **impersonal**, i.e., only found in the 3rd person singular. It is often, like *convenit*, combined with a dative: <u>*mihi*</u> *licet* ("It is permitted to/for me," therefore "I may").

- *In lectulō dormīre licet, hīc in lūdō nōn licet dormīre!*
- cf. *necesse est* (Cap. X: "it is necessary"), which, in addition to the accusative and infinitive, also takes the dative and infinitive. In addition to:
  Necesse est tē pūnīre. (l.59–60)
  We might say:
  Necesse est discipulīs aperīre librōs (it is necessary for the students to open [their] books).

Recēnsiō: Pronouns vs. Possessive Adjectives

In this chapter, you learned more forms of the personal pronoun. In Caps. II, IV, V, and XI, you learned the possessive adjective. Review the following forms:

	personal pronouns	possessive adjectives	personal pronouns	possessive adjectives
nom.	*ego*	*meus, mea, meum*	*nōs*	*noster, nostra, nostrum*
acc.	*mē*		*nōs*	
dat.	*mihi*			
abl.	*mē*			
nom.	*tū*	*tuus, tua, tuum*	*vōs*	*vester, vestra, vestrum*
acc.	*tē*		*vōs*	
dat.	*tibi*			
abl.	*tē*			

Studia Rōmāna

After studying with a *lūdī magister* (also called a *litterātus*), boys would go to a *grammaticus* to learn Greek and Latin literature, especially poetry. Students should also learn music and astronomy and philosophy, according to Quintilian (*Īnstitūtiō Ōrātōria*, I.4). The *grammaticus* might also teach rhetoric (the stages of education are not nearly as rigidly defined as ours), the art of public speaking, but this third stage of education was the province of the *rhētor*.

As the sons of a wealthy Roman, Marcus and Quintus would receive a highly literary and rhetorical education, that is, training in the art of speaking. Cato (second century BC) defined the ideal Roman as *vir bonus dīcendī perītus*, a good man skilled in speaking, and this ideal persisted. Cicero wrote several works on oratory (oratory, from *ōrātiō*, is the equivalent Latin word for rhetoric, from the Greek ῥητορικός in the first century BC); Quintilian's first century AD *Īnstitūtiō Ōrātōria* follows in the tradition of Cato (whose *vir bonus dīcendī perītus* he quotes) and Cicero (who receives lavish praise) of preparing a man for an active and honorable life in the state. (His contemporary, the poet *Mārtiālis*, praised Quintilian as the "consummate guide for directionless youth, the glory of the Roman toga."[2])

A rhetorical education encompassed training in literature, philosophy and history, as well as language. It was, in other words, an education in the liberal arts (*artēs* or *doctrīnae līberālēs*). Cicero (*dē Ōrātōre*, 3.127) enumerated these liberal studies as geometry (*geōmētrīa*), music (*mūsica*), knowledge of literature, both prose and poetry (*litterae et poetae*), science (*dē rērum natūrā*), ethics (*dē hominum mōribus*), and statesmanship (*dē rēbus pūblicīs*). Educated people could expect other educated people to have studied the same works of literature. Before the imperial period, young men often went to Greece to study with philosophers. By the time of our narrative, however, the emperors had set up professorships of Greek and Latin at Rome, and there were many Greek philosophers teaching in Rome.

Education was not the province only of the family and paid (or slave) teachers. Mentoring the young was part of Roman culture: young men associated with established ones. Cicero writes about sitting and listening to accomplished orators and jurists when he was young, especially Cotta and Hortensius (e.g., *Brūtus* 189). When he had gained a place for himself among Roman statesmen, he mentored younger Romans. In his defense of the young Caelius Rufus, Cicero tells us that as soon as Caelius assumed the *toga virīlis*, his father brought him to Cicero and Marcus Crassus to continue his education (*prō Caeliō*, 9). At that time, Caelius was surely also training with a teacher. In the second century AD, Pliny the Younger tells us much in his letters about his efforts to ensure the continuing education of young men. And Marcus Aurelius

---

2.   Martial 2.90: *Quīntiliāne, vagae moderātor summe iuventae/Glōria Rōmānae, Quīntiliāne, togae...*

was finished with his formal schooling, was married, with children and was emperor—still, he happily received and wrote letters to Marcus Cornelius Fronto, who had been his teacher of Latin rhetoric. Their correspondence is a testimony to Marcus's continuing education and the importance of the social network.

A good deal of the teaching, both formal and informal, promoted imitation. If you want to be a good orator, read good oratory and listen to good orators and practice. If you want to be a good person, evaluate the examples (*exempla*) of Roman history. Even in the second century BC, Fronto refers to examples from early Roman history (and can assume that Marcus knows just what he is talking about). The *mōs māiōrum*, "the way our ancestors did things," was kept alive though stories of the past and through the tutelage of family, teachers, and other Romans.

Vocābula Disposita/Ōrdināta

Nōmina
  1st

iānua, -ae	door
sella, -ae	stool, chair
virga, -ae	rod

  2nd

discipulus, -ī	pupil, disciple
domī	at home (*locative*)
lūdus, -ī	play, game, school
magister, magistrī	schoolmaster, teacher
tergum, -ī	back
lectulus, -ī	bed

Verba
  -āre (1)

exclāmō, exclāmāre	cry out, exclaim
recitō, recitāre	read aloud

  -ēre (2)

licet, licēre (+ *dat.*)	it is allowed, one may

  -ere (3)[3]

cōnsīdō, cōnsīdere	sit down
dēsinō, dēsinere	finish, stop, end
reddō, reddere	give back, give

  -īre (4)

pūniō, pūnīre	punish

  Irregular

redeō, redīre	go back, return
sum, esse	be

---

3. The first principal part will show you whether a 3rd conjugation verb is a consonant or *i*-stem; they will, therefore, no longer be separated out.

Adiectīva
  1st/2nd (-us/er, -a, -um)
    malus, -a, -um   bad, wicked, evil
    sevērus, -a, -um   stern, severe
    tacitus, -a, -um   silent
    vērus, -a, -um   true, *n.* truth
  Adiectīva Comparātiva (3rd)
    īnferior, -ius   lower, inferior
    posterior, -ius   back, hind, later
    prior, -ius   first, former, front
  Prōnōmina
    ego   I, myself
    tū   you, yourself
    nōs   we, us, ourselves
    vōs   you, yourselves

Adverbia
    nōndum   not yet
    statim   at once
    tum   then

Coniūnctiōnēs
    antequam   before
    at   but
    sī   if
    nisi   if not, except, but
    vērum   but

Vocābula Interrogātīva
    quid?   why?

XVI. Tempestās

Rēs Grammaticae Novae

1. Verbs
    a. Deponent Verbs (*verba dēpōnentia*)
    b. Irregular Verbs
        i. *īre*
        ii. *fierī*
2. Nouns
    a. Pure *i*-Stems
    b. 1st Declension Masculine Nouns
    c. Case Uses
        i. Partitive Genitive
        ii. Ablative of Degree of Difference
        iii. Ablative with *locus*
3. Participles: Ablative Absolute (*ablātīvus absolūtus*)
4. Points of Style: Word Order

Ancient Navigation

When sailing on the high seas, the Roman sailor had to set his course by the sun in the daytime and by the stars at night. So east and west are named in Latin after the rising and the setting sun, *oriēns* and *occidēns,* and the word for "midday," *merīdiēs,* also means "south," while the word for "north" is the name of the constellation *Septentriōnēs* (*septem triōnēs*), "The Seven Plow-Oxen," i.e., "the Great Bear." The location of the port cities in lines 12–19 can been seen on the map on page 40. Medus approaches a captain and arranges to travel on a merchant ship, as there was no equivalent of the modern passenger ship, although larger ships would have room for more passengers. He and Lydia would have had to bring their own food and sleep on deck.

Lēctiō Prīma (Section I)

Pure *i*-Stems

There is a small group of 3rd declension nouns that are called **pure *i*-stems** because they have -*i* throughout, for example, the noun *puppis, -is* (f.), which has:

- -*im* in the accusative (instead of -*em*)
- -*ī* in the ablative singular (instead of -*e*)

Very few *i*-stems are declined in this way, e.g., the river name *Tiberis, -is* (m.):

> *Urbs Rōma nōn ad mare, sed ad Tiber<u>im</u> flūmen sita est.* (ll.7–8)

1st Declension Masculine Nouns

1st declension nouns (in -*a, -ae*) are feminine, except for a few which denote male persons and are therefore masculine, e.g., *nauta: nauta Rōmān<u>us</u>*.

Locus

The ablative of *locus* may be used

- without *in* to denote location ("where"):
  - ▷ *Ōstia sita est eō locō quō Tiberis in mare īnferum īnfluit.* (ll.15–16)
    e<u>ō</u> loc<u>ō</u> = in eō locō (location)
- without a preposition to denote motion "from":
  - ▷ *Mēdus surgere cōnātur, nec vērō sē locō movēre potest.* (ll.140–141)
    loc<u>ō</u> movēre (ablative of separation)

Lēctiō Altera (Section II)

Deponent Verbs (*verba dēpōnentia*)

In Section I, we met *opperīrī* (= *exspectā<u>re</u>*) a passive form with active meaning:

> *necesse est ventum opperīrī* (l.29)

Many of the new words in this chapter are **deponent verbs** (*verba dēpōnentia*). These verbs have no active forms,[1] hence, *verba dēpōnentia*: verbs that "put aside" their passive meanings[2] (Latin *dēpōnere*, "put aside").

---

1. Except for the participle in -*ns*, and one other form you will learn later in Cap. XXIV.

2. As the first-century AD grammarian *Quīntus Remmius Palaemōn* wrote, "*Dēpōnentia sunt, quod dēpōnant passīvitātem et sūmant actīvitātem.*"

The infinitive ends in *-rī, -ī*

-ārī:
cōnārī	attempt, try
cōnsōlārī	comfort
laetārī	be happy

-ērī:
intuērī	look
verērī	fear

-ī:
complectī	embrace
ēgredī	go out
lābī	slip
loquī	speak
proficīscī	set out
sequī	follow

-īrī:
opperīrī	wait for
orīrī	rise

From the following examples, you can see verbs that have **passive** forms but **active** meanings:

> *laetārī = gaudēre*
> *verērī = timēre*
> *ēgredī = exīre*
> *nauta Neptūnum verētur = nauta Neptūnum timet*
> *ventō secundō nāvēs ē portū ēgrediuntur = exeunt*

Participles: Ablative Absolute (*ablātīvus absolūtus*)

In Cap. XIV, we learned about the ablative of attendant circumstances, which was illustrated in that chapter by

> *fenestrā apertā*
> *fenestrā clausā*

In this chapter, we learn more about this construction. In the *marginalia* of Section I, you read that:

> *marī turbidō = dum mare turbidum est* (l.36)
> *ventō secundō = dum ventus secundus est* (l.38)

These are more examples of the ablative used as an adverbial phrase. Such an adverbial phrase, grammatically independent of the rest of the sentence, is called an **ablative absolute** (Latin *ablātīvus <u>absolūtus</u>,* "set free," therefore independent). It represents the <u>circumstances</u> occurring around an action. In each of the following, the ablative gives further information about the verb. We find the ablative absolute with adjectives:

> *Ventō secundō nāvēs ē portū ēgrediuntur.* (ll.38–39)

> The ablative *ventō secundō* tells us <u>under what circumstances</u> the ships put out ("with a fair wind," "when the wind is favorable").

> *Nautae nec marī turbidō nec marī tranquillō nāvigāre volunt.* (ll.36–37)

> The sailors are unwilling to sail "when the sea is rough," "when the sea is calm."

> *plēnīs vēlīs...vehuntur.* (ll.39–40)

> They travel "with full sails."

> *pedibus nūdīs* (Cap. XIV, l.85)

> stands "with bare feet"

The ablative absolute is common with a participle, either present or past:

> Present participle:

> *Sōle oriente nāvis ē portū ēgreditur multīs hominibus spectantibus.* (ll.64–65); "when the sun is rising," "at sunrise" … "while many people are looking on"

> Past participle:

> *fenestrā apertā dormīre* (Cap. XIV, l.15): to sleep "with the window open" (cf. *fenestrā clausā,* Cap. XIV, l.15)

Even two nouns can form an ablative absolute:

> *Sōle duce nāvem gubernō* (l.94); "the sun being my guide," "with the sun as a guide"

The ablative absolute may often be translated with an English temporal clause (when, while), as in the sentences above. It can also show cause (why the verb happens) and even concession (although the verb happens). If you need to translate an ablative absolute into English, it helps to start with "with" and then think about what the relationship of the ablative absolute means to the rest of the sentence.

īre

In the verb *īre* (and its compounds), the 1st person *eō* and 3rd person *eunt* are irregular, e.g.:

> *in patriam nostram īmus* (l.89)
> *"Nōnne gaudēs," inquit, "mea Lydia, quod nōs simul in patriam nostram redīmus?"* (ll.79–81)

īre

	sing.	pl.
1st	*eō*	*īmus*
2nd	*īs*	*ītis*
3rd	*it*	*eunt*

Partitive Genitive

Since Cap. II, you have been seeing the noun *numerus* followed by the genitive; in Cap. XII, you learned about the genitive with *mīlia*:

> *In flūminibus et in maribus magnus <u>numerus</u> pisc<u>ium</u> est.* (Cap. X, ll.41–42)
> *Ergō mīlle passūs sunt quīnque <u>mīlia</u> ped<u>um</u>.* (Cap. XII, ll.96–97)
> *In castrīs Aemiliī sex <u>mīlia</u> mīlit<u>um</u> habitant.* (Cap. XII, ll.97–98)

These genitives give the **whole** of which the noun is a **part**; they are called **partitive genitives** (or genitives of the whole). This chapter begins with the **partitive genitive** of the relative pronoun:

> *Italia inter duo maria interest, <u>quōrum</u> alterum "mare Superum" appellātur*; *quōrum* (= *ē quibus*: "of which one…the other")
>   cf. *nēmō <u>eōrum</u>* (= *ex iīs*, Cap. XVII, l.12).

Quantity terms like *multum* and *paulum* are often followed by a partitive genitive to express "that of which" there is a large or small quantity, e.g.:

> *paulum/multum aqu<u>ae</u>* (ll.9, 117)
> *paulum cib<u>ī</u> nec multum pecūni<u>ae</u>* (ll.61–62)
> *paulum tempor<u>is</u>* (l.108 margin)

Ablative of Degree of Difference

The ablative of *multum* and *paulum* serves to strengthen or weaken a comparative; this is called the **ablative of degree of difference**:

> *Nāvis <u>paulō</u> levior fit, simul vērō flūctūs <u>multō</u> altiōrēs fīunt* (ll.123–124): "a little," "a lot"

The same forms are used with *ante* and *post* (as adverbs) to state the time difference:

> *paulō ante* (l.148)
> *paulō post* (l.91)
> cf. the ablative in *annō post* (Cap. XIX, l.83)
> *decem annīs ante* (Cap. XIX, l.123)

Lēctiō Tertia (Section III)

Fierī

The infinitive *fi|erī* (3rd person *fi|t fi|unt*) is also irregular. This verb functions as the passive of *facere* (see Cap. XVIII); in connection with an adjective, it comes to mean "become":

> *Mare tranquillum fit.* (ll.97–98)
> *Flūctūs multō altiōrēs fiunt.* (l.124)

Points of Style: Word Order

In Cap. XIII, we met the demonstrative *is, ea, id* being used as an adjective with a dependent genitive:

> *Is mēnsis annī brevissimus est.* (l.30)
> *Is diēs annī prīmus est atque initium annī novī.* (ll.58–59)

In both of these examples, we see that the demonstrative generally precedes the noun. In this chapter, we see a similar example:

> *Ea pars caelī unde sōl oritur dīcitur oriēns.* (l.45)

In all these examples, the genitive follows the noun. Another very common word order is for the genitive to come between the qualifier and its noun, as in the following example:

> *Merīdiēs dīcitur ea caelī pars ubi sōl merīdiē vidētur.* (l.48)

Studia Rōmāna

The dangers of sea travel are widely attested in Roman literature. The *gubernātor* (whence we get the name governor and government, those who guide the ship of state) calls upon *Neptūnus*, the god of the sea, about whom you learned in Cap. X. Sailors also called on the twin heroes *Castor* and *Pollūx* (the *Dioscūrī*, or "sons of Zeus") who are associated with the phenomenon we call St. Elmo's Fire, electric currents around the masts of ships during thunderstorms that appear to be balls of heavenly fire.

Both the Greeks and Romans are fond of cursing the first person who put to sea in a boat. The poet Horace wrote a poem begging Castor and Pollux to take care of his good friend, the poet Vergil, who was about to set out to Greece. He says the man who first entrusted a raft to the sea was a hard man whose heart was surrounded three times with bronze (*Ōdēs* 1.3.9–12: *illī rōbur et aes triplex/circā pectus erat, quī fragilem trucī/conmīsit pelagō ratem/prīmus*).

Despite its dangers, sea travel was efficient and lucrative. Ships carrying a wide variety of merchandise could be found at Ostia (*Portus Ōstiēnsis*), the port whence Medus and Lydia depart. Still visible among the remains at Ostia is the Square of the Corporations (called, in Italian, Piazzale delle Corporazioni). This porticus contains many small rooms with mosaic floors that proclaim a variety of trades and guilds (*collēgia*). Among those represented are traders in leather, rope, wood, and several of grain, but many more goods came and left through Ostia. A large number of warehouses (*horrea*) for storing grain attest to the importance of feeding a large population.

At line 119, the *gubernātor* tells his crew, "*Iacite mercēs!*" This *iactūra*, or throwing overboard of the ship's cargo (i.e., jetsam) and thus making the boat less heavy, must have been the ruin of many a small merchant. Shipwreck, *naufragium*, was such a common problem that a law (*iūs naufragiī*) regulated against the appropriation of the discarded cargo (flotsam). Philosophers explored as an ethical problem the decision of what to throw overboard. Which is sacrificed? The expensive racehorse or the cheap slave? Human feeling argues for the latter, preservation of wealth for the former (Cicero, *dē Officiīs*, 3.89).[3]

Horace refers to both *iactūra* and to the saving power of Castor and Pollux in another ode; because he has no attachment to wealth, he has no need to grovel to the gods to save his goods when seas grow stormy. Castor and Pollux will carry him safely in his tiny boat: "It's not my style, if the mast should wail in a hurricane from the south, to run to wretched prayers and bind myself with vows lest my Cyprian and Tyrian goods add wealth to the greedy sea; at such a time, with the help of my two-oared skiff, Pollux and his twin brother will carry me safely on the breeze through the Aegean storm." (*Odes* 3.29.57–64)

Vocābula Disposita/Ōrdināta

Nōmina
  1st
    nauta, -ae (*m.*)   sailor
    ōra, -ae   border, coast
  2nd
    altum, -ī   "the deep": the open sea
    locus, -ī   place

---

3. *Quaerit, sī in marī iactūra facienda sit, equīne pretiōsī potius iactūram faciat an servulī vīlis. Hīc aliō rēs familiāris, aliō dūcit hūmānitās.*

multum, -ī	a lot, a good deal of
paulum, -ī	a little (also, *adv.*)
vēlum, -ī	sail
ventus, -ī	wind

3rd

fulgur, fulguris (*n.*)	flash of lightning
gubernātor, gubernātōris (*m.*)	steersman
merx, mercis (*f.*)	commodity, *pl.* goods
nāvis, nāvis (*f.*)	ship
occidēns, occidentis (*m.*)	west
oriēns, orientis (*m.*)	east
puppis, puppis (*f.*)	stern, poop deck
septentriōnēs, septentriōnum (*m. pl.*)	north
tempestās, tempestātis (*f.*)	storm

4th

flūctus, -ūs (*m.*)	wave
portus, -ūs (*m.*)	harbor
tonitrus, -ūs (*m.*)	thunder

Verba

-āre (1)

appellō, appellāre	call, address
cōnātur, cōnārī	attempt, try
cōnsōlātur, cōnsōlārī	comfort, console
flō, flāre	blow
gubernō, gubernāre	steer, govern
iactō, iactāre	throw, toss about
invocō, invocāre	call upon, invoke
laetātur, laetārī	rejoice, be glad
nāvigō, nāvigāre	sail
servō, servāre	preserve, save
turbō, turbāre	stir up, agitate

-ēre (2)

impleō, implēre	fill, complete
intuētur, intuērī	look at, watch
verētur, verērī	fear

-ere (3)

cernō, cernere	discern, perceive
cōnscendō, cōnscendere	mount, board
īnfluō, īnfluere	flow into
occidō, occidere	fall, sink, set
complectitur, complectī	embrace
ēgreditur, ēgredī	go out
lābitur, lābī	slip, drop, fall
loquitur, loquī	speak, talk
proficīscitur, proficīscī	set out, depart
sequitur, sequī	follow

-īre (4)
    hauriō, haurīre   draw (water), bail
    opperītur, opperīrī   wait (for), await
    oritur, orīrī   rise, appear
Irregular
    interest, interesse   be between
    fit, fierī   be done, become, happen

Adiectīva
  1st/2nd (-us/er, -a, -um)
    āter, -tra, -trum   black, dark
    contrārius, -a, -um   opposite, contrary
    īnferus, -a, -um   lower
    maritimus, -a, -um   seaside, coastal
    serēnus, -a, -um   clear, cloudless
    situs, -a, -um   situated
    superus, -a, -um   upper
    tranquillus, -a, -um   calm, still
    turbidus, -a, -um   agitated, stormy
    dēpōnēns (*gen.* **depōnentis**)   deponent (verb)

Coniūnctiōnēs
    sīve   or, or if

Praepositiōnēs
    propter (*prp. + acc.*)   because of

Adverbia
    iterum   again, a second time
    paulum   a little, little
    praetereā   besides
    semper   always
    simul   at the same time
    vix   hardly
    vērō   really, however, but

XVII. Numerī Difficilēs

Rēs Grammaticae Novae

1. Verbs
   a. Passive Voice
   b. *oportēre* (impersonal)
   c. *dare*
2. Nouns: Case Uses
   a. Double Accusative
3. Adjectives: Numbers
   a. Cardinals
   b. Inflection
   c. Ordinals
4. Pronouns: *quisque*
5. Adverbs

Lēctiō Prīma (Section I)

Roman Coins

To teach his pupils arithmetic, the teacher has recourse to coins. The current Roman coins were:

> *as* (*assis* m.) copper
> *sēstertius* (HS[1]) = 4 *assēs*: brass
> *dēnārius* = 4 *sēstertiī*: silver
> *aureus* = 25 *dēnāriī*: gold (Cap. XXII, l.108)

Quisque, quaeque, quodque

Only the first part (*quis*) of the pronoun *quisque* (each) declines; you will meet the feminine (*quaeque*) and neuter (*quodque*) in Cap. XVIII. Compare:

> *uterque*   each (of two)
> *quisque*   each

---

1. The abbreviation HS represents IIS, or 2 (II) and a half (*sēmis*); originally the *sēstertius* was valued at 2½ *assēs*.

Double Accusative

Note the **two accusatives** with *docēre,* one for the **person(s)** (*puerōs*), the other for the **thing** (*numerōs*) taught:

> *Magister puerōs numerōs docet.* (ll.1–2)

Cardinal Numbers

In Cap. IV, you learned to count to ten:

ūnus, a, um	*sex*
duo, duae, duo	*septem*
trēs, tria	*octō*
quattuor	*novem*
quīnque	*decem*

To be able to count up to a hundred, you must learn the multiples of ten. With the exception of 10 *decem,* 20 *vīgintī,* and 100 *centum,* they all end in *-gintā*:

10 *decem*	60 *sexāgintā*
20 *vīgintī*	70 *septuāgintā*
30 *trīgintā*	80 *octōgintā*
40 *quadrāgintā*	90 *nōnāgintā*
50 *quīnquāgintā*	100 *centum*

The numbers in between are formed by combining multiples of ten and smaller numbers with or without *et,* e.g.:

> 21 *vīgintī ūnus* or *ūnus et vīgintī*
> 22 *vīgintī duo* or *duo et vīgintī*

The cardinals 11–17 end in *-decim,* a weakened form of *decem*:

11 *ūn-decim*	15 *quīn-decim*
12 *duo-decim*	16 *sē-decim*
13 *trē-decim*	17 *septen-decim*
14 *quattuor-decim*	

but 18 and 19 show the pattern numbers will follow:

> 18 *duo-dē-vīgintī* ("two-from-twenty")
> 19 *ūn-dē-vīgintī* ("one-from-twenty")

In the same way, 28 is *duo-dē-trīgintā* and 29 *ūn-dē-trīgintā.* Thus, the last two numbers before each multiple of ten are expressed by subtracting two and one, respectively, from the multiple of ten in question.

Inflection of Numbers

Like *quot,* the interrogative that asks the number ("how many?"), and *tot,* the demonstrative that refers to the number ("so many"), most Latin cardinals are **indeclinable.**

Of the cardinals 1–100, only *ūn|us, -a, -um, du|o, -ae, -o* and *tr|ēs, tr|ia* decline (and those cardinals that end in them: e.g., *ūna et vīgintī nāvēs*: 21 ships). You have already met most forms of these numbers (the genitives, *ūn|īus, du|ōrum, -ārum, -ōrum* and *tr|ium,* will be introduced in Cap. XIX).

	m.	f.	n.	m.	f.	n.	m./f.	n.
nom.	ūn|us	ūn|a	ūn|um	du|o	du|ae	du|o	tr|ēs	tr|ia
acc.	ūn|um	ūn|am	ūn|um	du|ōs	du|ās	du|o	tr|ēs	tr|ia
gen.				du|ōrum	du|ārum	du|ōrum		
dat.	ūn|ī	ūn|ī	ūn|ī	du|ōbus	du|ābus	du|ōbus	tr|ibus	tr|ibus
abl.	ūn|ō	ūn|ā	ūn|ō	du|ōbus	du|ābus	du|ōbus	tr|ibus	tr|ibus

Multiples of 100 (*centum*) end in *-centī* (200, 300, 600) or *-gentī* (400, 500, 700, 800, 900) and are declined like adjectives of the 1st/2nd declension:

200 *du-cent|ī, -ae, -a*   600 *ses-cent|ī, -ae, -a*
300 *tre-cent|ī, -ae, -a*   700 *septin-gent|ī, -ae, -a*
400 *quadrin-gent|ī, -ae, -a*   800 *octin-gent|ī, -ae, -a*
500 *quīn -gent|ī, -ae, -a*   900 *nōn-gent|ī, -ae, -a*

Ordinal Numbers

In Cap. XIII, you learned the ordinal numbers 1st through 12th:

prīm|us, -a, -um   *septim|us, -a, -um*
secund|us, -a, -um   *octāv|us, -a, -um*
terti|us, -a, -um   *nōn|us, -a, -um*
quārt|us, -a, -um   *decim|us, -a, -um*
quīnt|us, -a, -um   *ūndecim|us, -a, -um*
sext|us, -a, -um   *duodecim|us, -a, -um*

The ordinals are adjectives of the 1st/2nd declension; for the multiples of 10, 20–90, and of 100, 100–1,000, they are formed with the suffix *-ēsim|us, -a, -um*:

20th *vīcēsimus, -a, -um*   100th *centēsimus, -a, -um*
30th *trīcēsimus, -a, -um*   200th *ducentēsimus, -a, -um*
40th *quadrāgēsimus, -a, -um*   300th *trecentēsimus*
50th *quīnquāgēsimus,* etc.   1,000th *mīllēsimus*

Notā Bene:

- Cardinals end in:
  11–17 *-decim*
  30–90 *-gintā*
  200, 300, 600 *-cent|ī*
  400, 500, 700, 800, 900 *-gent|ī*
- Ordinals end in:
  20th–90th, 100th–1,000th *-ēsim|us*
  A summary is given on page 308 in Lingua Latina.

Adverbs

The forms *rēctē, prāvē, stultē,* and *aequē* are formed from the adjectives *rēctus, prāvus, stultus,* and *aequus*; this formation will be dealt with in the next chapter.

Lēctiō Altera (Section II)

The Passive Voice

You have been using the passive voice in the 3rd person singular and plural since Cap. VI. Now we see the remaining endings, the 1st and 2nd persons, singular and plural. The following sentences show examples of the passive voice (ll.63–81):

- 1st person:

  singular: *Cūr ego semper ā tē reprehendor, numquam laudor?*

  plural: *Nōs quoque saepe interrogāmur, nec vērō prāvē respondēmus. Itaque nōs ā magistrō laudāmur, nōn reprehendimur.*

- 2nd person:

  singular: *Tū ā mē nōn laudāris, quia numquam rēctē respondēs. Semper prāvē respondēs, ergō reprehenderis!*

  plural: *Et cūr vōs semper laudāminī? Quia id quod vōs interrogāminī facile est—ego quoque ad id rēctē respondēre possum. Vōs numquam reprehendiminī!*

- 3rd person:

  singular: *Mārcus semper ā magistrō reprehenditur, numquam laudātur.*

  plural: *Sextus et Titus ā magistrō semper laudantur, numquam reprehenduntur.*

Forming the Passive Voice

- personal endings

	sing.	pl.
1.	*-r*	*-mur*
2.	*-ris*	*-minī*
3.	*-tur*	*-ntur*

- The 1st, 2nd, and 4th conjugations: add the endings to the stem with the same vowels as in the active.
- The 3rd conjugation (including 3rd *i*-stems): the vowels are the same as in the active, **except** in the 2nd person singular, where the short *i* becomes *e* before *r* (e.g., *reprehenderis*: you are being censured; *caperis*: you are being taken).

- Remember that deponent verbs (Cap. XVI) use these endings as well, as in *largior* and *vereor* in the paradigms that follow.

sing.	-āre	-ēre	-ere	-īre
1st	*laud|or*	*vere|or*	*reprehend|or*	*largi|or*
2nd	*laudā|ris*	*verē|ris*	*reprehend|eris*	*largī|ris*
3rd	*laudā|tur*	*verē|tur*	*reprehend|itur*	*largī|tur*
pl.				
1st:	*laudā|mur*	*verē|mur*	*reprehend|imur*	*largī|mur*
2nd:	*laudā|minī*	*verē|minī*	*reprehend|iminī*	*largī|minī*
3rd:	*lauda|ntur*	*vere|ntur*	*reprehend|untur*	*largi|untur*

Lēctiō Tertia (Section III)

Oportēre (Impersonal)

The verb *oportēre* occurs only in the 3rd person singular, like *licet* and *convenit* (Cap. XV):

> *Prīmum cōgitāre oportet.* (ll.110–111)
> *Nōn oportet respondēre antequam interrogāris.* (ll.115–116)

Dare

The stem of the verb *da\|re* ends in a short *a*: *da\|mus, da\|tis, da\|tur, da\|te!* etc., except in *dā! dā\|s* and *dā\|ns* (before *ns*, all vowels are lengthened).

Studia Rōmāna

When Diodorus puts his students through their mathematical paces, he makes them apply their skills to money. Horace gives us an example of such interrogation: "Roman boys learn through lengthy calculations to divide a copper coin (*as, assis,* m.) into a hundred parts."… "if a 12th part is taken from 5/12, what remains?" … "a third." "Excellent! You'll be able to safeguard your finances!" (*Ars Poētica* 325–29). The *as* could be divided into 12 parts, which were represented by names, not by fractions as we do. The Latin word for 1/12 is *uncia*, whence comes our word ounce. Twelve *unciae*, or ounces, made up the Latin pound (*lībra*). In Cicero's opinion, the goal of mathematics began and ended with its practical value. He had little interest in the theoretical mathematics of the Greeks, among whom geometry held the highest honor and nothing was more respectable than mathematics. The Romans, on the other hand, have set the limit to this art at the expedience of measuring and calculating (*dē Fīnibus* 1.5: *in summō apud illōs honōre geōmētria fuit, itaque nihil mathēmaticīs illustrius; at nōs mētiendī ratiōcinandīque ūtilitāte huius artis termināvimus modum*).

Our monetary system is fiduciary (from *fidēs, fideī*, "belief, trust," Cap. XXXI)—that is, the value of the paper bills or metal coins we use in buying and selling does not equal the face value (it costs as much to produce a $100 bill as a $5 bill), but we all agree that a $100 bill buys 20 times as much as a $5 bill. During the Roman Empire, the state determined the value of coins, but that value reflected the worth of the metal used in producing the coin. The various metals used during the period of our text show this relative value: copper (the *as*) is worth less than brass (*sēstertius*), which in turn is less than silver (*dēnārius*) and gold (*aureus*). Adulteration and devaluation of currency was a problem—by the end of the second century AD (the time of our narrative), the silver *dēnārius* was only about 50 percent silver, and the rest was bronze. As you can see from the image in the margins on page 129, the border of the image embossed on the surface of the coin did not reach to the edge; sometimes, people trimmed off the extra metal before spending the coin.

The study of coins is called numismatics; the images on coins provide a wealth of information. The front of a coin is called the obverse and the back the reverse. Imperial coins often show the head of the emperor (or a member of his family) on the obverse and a significant image on the reverse. For example, *Mārcus Decimus Brūtus*, one of the men who assassinated Julius Caesar on the Ides of March in 44 BC, issued a denarius with his image on the obverse and, on the reverse, a *pilleus* (cap that indicated freedom) flanked by two daggers. In the second century AD, Hadrian (emperor 117–138) issued a gold aureus with his head on the obverse and the inscription *Hadriānus Augustus*; on the reverse is embossed Romulus and Remus nursing at the wolf with the inscription *COS* (= *consul*) and the number four: consul for the fourth time. The reverse of a coin issued by Marcus Aurelius has a reverse with the inscription *PIETAS AUG* (= *pietās Augusta*) showing implements symbolic of sacrifice and priestly office.

Vocabula Disposita/Ordinata

Nōmina
  2nd

dēnārius, -ī	denarius (silver coin)
respōnsum, -ī	answer

  3rd

as, assis (*m.*)	as (copper coin)

Verba
  -āre (1)

cōgitō, cōgitāre	think
computō, computāre	calculate, reckon
dēmōnstrō, dēmōnstrāre	point out, show
interpellō, interpellāre	interrupt
laudō, laudāre	praise

-ēre (2)
  doceō, docēre   teach, instruct
  oportet, oportēre   it is right, one should
-ere (3)
  discō, discere   learn
  prōmō, prōmere   take out
  repōnō, repōnere   put back
  reprehendō, reprehendere   blame, censure
  tollō, tollere   raise, lift, pick up, remove, take away
-īre (4)
  largior, largīrī   give generously
  nesciō, nescīre   not know
  partior, partīrī   share, divide
  sciō, scīre   know

Adiectīva
  1st/2nd (-us/er, -a, -um)
  centēsimus, -a, -um   hundredth
  certus, -a, -um   certain, sure
  doctus, -a, -um   learned, skilled
  incertus, -a, -um   uncertain
  indoctus, -a, -um   ignorant
  industrius, -a, -um   industrious
  largus, -a, -um   generous
  piger, pigra, pigrum   lazy
  prāvus, -a, -um   faulty, wrong
  rēctus, -a, -um   straight, correct
  3rd
  absēns (*gen.* **absentis**)   absent
  difficilis, -e (*sup.* **difficillimus**) difficult, hard
  facilis, -e (*sup.* **facillimus**)   easy
  prūdēns, prūdentis   prudent, clever

Numerī
  trēdecim   thirteen
  quattuordecim   fourteen
  quīndecim   fifteen
  sēdecim   sixteen
  septendecim   seventeen
  duodēvīgintī   eighteen
  ūndēvīgintī   nineteen
  quadrāgintā   forty
  quīnquāgintā   fifty
  septuāgintā   seventy
  quadringentī, -ae, -a   four hundred
  quīngentī, -ae, -a   five hundred
  sescentī, -ae, -a   six hundred

septingentī, -ae, -a	seven hundred
octingentī, -ae, -a	eight hundred
nōngentī, -ae, -a	nine hundred

Prōnōmina

quisque, quaeque, quodque	each

Adverbia

aequē	equally
numquam	never
postrēmō	finally
prāvē	wrongly
quārē	why
rēctē	correctly
saepe	often
tot	so many
ūsque	up (to), all the time

Coniūnctiōnēs

quamquam	although

XVIII. Litterae Latīnae

Rēs Grammaticae Novae

1. Verbs: *facere/fierī*
2. Adjectives
    a. Superlatives (continued)
    b. *frequēns*
    c. *facilis*
3. Pronouns
    a. *īdem, eadem, idem*
    b. *quisque, quaeque, quodque*
4. Adverbs
    a. Positive, Comparative, Superlative Degrees
    b. Numerical Adverbs
5. Conjunction: *cum*
6. Points of Style: idiom *suum cuique*

Pronunciation

In the Classical period, Latin spelling gave a fairly reliable representation of the pronunciation. In some cases, however, letters continued to be written where they were no longer pronounced in colloquial Latin, e.g., *h-*, *-m* in the unstressed endings *-am, -em, -um*, and *n* before *s*. An indication of this is the occurrence of "misspellings" in ancient inscriptions written by people without literary education, e.g., *ora* for *horam*, *septe* for *septem*, and *meses* for *menses*. In his short exercise, Marcus makes several errors of this kind. Quintilian recognized the difficulty Marcus has encountered (*Īnstitūtiō Ōrātōria* I.1.30): "There is no shortcut to learning the syllables; all must be thoroughly learned and the hardest ones must not—as people often do—be put off."[1]

---

1. *Syllabīs nūllum compendium est: perdiscendae omnēs nec, ut fit plērumque, difficillima quaeque eārum differenda ut in nōminibus scrībendīs dēprehendantur.*

Lēctiō Prīma (Section I)

Īdem, eadem, idem

The demonstrative pronoun *īdem, eadem, idem* ("the same," cf. "identical") is a compound, the first element of which is the pronoun *is, ea, id*; the addition of the suffix *-dem* causes the following changes:

- *is-dem* to *īdem*
- *eum-dem, eam-dem* to *eundem, eandem.*[2]

	sing. m.	f.	n.	pl. m.	f.	n.
nom.	*īdem*	*eadem*	*idem*	*iīdem*	*eaedem*	*eadem*
acc.	*eundem*	*eandem*	*idem*	*eōsdem*	*eāsdem*	*eadem*
gen.	*eiusdem*	*eiusdem*	*eiusdem*	*eōrundem*	*eārundem*	*eōrundem*
dat.	*eīdem*	*eīdem*	*eīdem*	*iīsdem*	*iīsdem*	*iīsdem*
abl.	*eōdem*	*eādem*	*eōdem*	*iīsdem*	*iīsdem*	*iīsdem*

Examples:

> *Numerus syllabārum et vōcālium īdem est.* (l.21)
>   *in eādem syllabā* (l.26)
> *Vocābulum prīmum utrīusque sententiae idem est, sed hoc idem vocābulum duās rēs variās significat.* (ll.32–33)
> *Item varia vocābula eandem rem vel eundem hominem significāre possunt.* (ll.33–35)
> *Discipulī eandem sententiam nōn eōdem modō, sed variīs modīs scrībunt.* (ll.56–58)

Quisque, quaeque, quodque

The pronoun *quis-que, quae-que, quod-que* ("each") is declined like the interrogative adjective with the addition of *-que*.

	sing. m.	f.	n.	pl. m.	f.	n.
nom.	*quisque*	*quaeque*	*quodque*	*quīque*	*quaeque*	*quaeque*
acc.	*quemque*	*quamque*	*quodque*	*quōsque*	*quāsque*	*quaeque*
gen.	*cuiusque*	*cuiusque*	*cuiusque*	*quōrumque*	*quārumque*	*quōrumque*
dat.	*cuique*	*cuique*	*cuique*	*quibusque*	*quibusque*	*quibusque*
abl.	*quōque*	*quāque*	*quōque*	*quibusque*	*quibusque*	*quibusque*

2.   The *m* changes to *n* by assimilation—see Cap. X—*n* being a dental consonant like *d*, cf. *septendecim* and *septentriōnēs*.

Examples:

> *Quisque* discipulus in tabulā suā scrībit eās sententiās quās magister eī
> dictat. (ll.49–50)
> *Quisque* puer stilum et rēgulam prōmit et dūcit līneam rēctam in tabulā
> suā. (ll.55–56)
> Discipulus *quamque* litteram *cuiusque* vocābulī sīc legit. (ll.41–42)
> Ita *quodque* vocābulum *cuiusque* sententiae ā discipulō legitur. (ll.43–
> 44)
> *Quaeque* syllaba vōcālem habet. (l.20)

Facere/fierī

The verb *facere* has no passive form. Instead, *fierī* functions as the passive of
facere:

> *Vōcālis syllabam facit; sine vōcālī syllaba fierī nōn potest.* (l.25)
> *Cum syllabae iunguntur, vocābula fiunt.* (l.29)
> *Cum vocābula coniunguntur, sententiae fiunt.* (ll.29–30)

active   *facere: facit, faciunt*
passive   *fierī: fit, fiunt*

Notā Bene: Compounds of *facere* ending in *-ficere,* e.g., *ef-ficere,* can be used
in the passive:

> *stilus ex ferrō efficitur (= fit)*

Conjunction *Cum*

The conjunction *cum* may serve to introduce a sudden occurrence, as in this
example (l.128):

> *Titus sīc incipit, "Magister! Mārcus bis…"—cum Mārcus stilum in
> partem corporis eius mollissimam premit!* (English "when…," "and
> then…")

Frequēns

The adjective *frequēns* follows the pattern of present participles (Cap. XIV);
that is, it has the same nominative in all three genders in the positive degree:

> *κ littera, quae frequēns est in linguā Graecā, littera Latīna rārissima
> est.* (ll.14–15)

id vocābulum est <u>frequentissimum</u>. (l.101)
Y et z igitur litterae rārae sunt in linguā Latīnā, in linguā Graecā <u>frequentēs</u>. (ll.13–14)

Lēctiō Altera (Section II)

Points of Style: Idiom *suum cuique*

Suus, -a, -um cuique is an idiom:

Magister <u>suam cuique</u> <u>discipulō tabulam</u> reddit.	The teacher gives each student back his own tablet. (ll.67–68)
suum cuique	to each his (her) own: proverbial (even in English!)

Superlatives of Adjectives in *-er*

Adjectives in *-er*, e.g., *pulcher* and *piger,* form superlatives by adding *-errim|us, -a, -um* (instead of *-issim|us*) to the nominative masculine singular (instead of the adjective base).[3] In this chapter, you find *pulcherrim|us* and *pigerrim|us,* in the next *miserrim|us* and *pauperrim|us* from *miser* and *pauper.*

adj. *-er,* sup. *-errim|us*

Facilis, -e

The superlative of *facilis* is *facillim|us* (l.102). Only a very few adjectives form their superlatives like *facilis:*

facilis, -e: facillimus, -a, -um	
difficilis, -e: difficillimus, -a, -um	(Cap. XVII)
gracilis, -e: gracillimus, -a, -um	slender (Cap. XIX)
humilis, -e: humillimus, -a, -um	low (Cap. XXV)
similis, -e: simillimus, -a, -um	similar (Cap. XXXV)
dissimilis, -e: dissimillimus, -a, -um	dissimilar, different

Adverbs

Remember:
- Adjectives qualify nouns.
  - ▷ The adjective answers the question: <u>*quālis?*</u>
    - o In the sentence, *Puer stult<u>us</u> est, stultus* is an adjective qualifying the noun *puer (Quālis est puer?).*
- Adverbs (Latin *adverbium,* from *ad verbum*) qualify verbs, adjectives, and other adverbs.

---

3.   That is, the genitive singular minus the ending.

▷ The adverb answers the question: *quōmodo?*

    o In the sentence, *Puer stultē agit*, the word *stultē* belongs to the verb *agit*, which it modifies (*Quōmodo agit puer?*).

In Cap. XVII, we saw the adverbs *rēctē, prāvē, stultē,* and *aequē* from the adjectives *rēctus, prāvus, stultus,* and *aequus.* Similarly, in the sentence, *mīles fortis est quī fortiter pugnat, fortis* is an adjective (qualifying *mīles*) and *fortiter* an adverb (modifying *pugnat*).

Positive Degree

Just as there are three degrees of adjectives, there are three of adverbs: **positive** (e.g., fast), **comparative** (e.g., faster), and **superlative** (e.g., fastest). Positive degree:

Certē pulcherrimae sunt litterae Sextī.	Sextus's letters are certainly very beautiful. (l.73)
Litterae vestrae aequē foedae sunt.	Your letters are equally ugly. (l.78)

Adjectives of the 1st/2nd declension form adverbs ending in *-ē*:

    stult|us -a -um → stultē
    rēct|us -a -um → rēctē
    pulcher -chr|a -chr|um → pulchrē

3rd declension adjectives form adverbs in *-iter*, e.g.:[4]

    fort|is -e → fortiter
    brev|is -e → breviter
    turp|is -e → turpiter

Notā Bene: Bene and *male* are irregular formations from *bonus* and *malus,* whose forms you will learn in Cap. XIX.

Comparative Degree

The **comparative of the adverb** ends in *-ius*. Note that the form of the comparative adverb is the same as the neuter of the comparative of the adjective:

    pulchrius   *fortius*   *rēctius*

---

4.   If the base of an adjectives ends in *nt*, its adverb ends in *nter*, e.g., *frequēns, frequenter.*

Comparative Degree:

> *"Tū, Tite, neque pulchrius neque foedius scrībis quam Mārcus.":* "neither
> more beautifully nor more unattractively" (ll.79–80)
> *"At certē rēctius scrībō quam Mārcus.":* "more correctly" (l.81)

Superlative Degree

The **superlative of the adverb** ending in *-issimē (-errimē)* is formed from the
superlative of the adjective:

> *pulcherrimē   fortissimē   rēctissimē*

Superlative Degree:

> *"Comparā tē cum Sextō, quī rēctissimē et pulcherrimē scrībit.":* "most
> correctly," "most beautifully" (ll.85–86)

When the superlative occurs without the idea of comparison, it can be translated "very":

> *Latīnē pulcherrimē recitās!*   You read Latin aloud very
> beautifully!

Recēnsiō: **Comparison of Adjectives and Adverbs**

Adjectives

Positive Degree	Comparative Degree	Superlative Degree
rārus, rāra, rārum	*rārior, rārius*	*rārissimus, -a, -um*
mollis, molle	*mollior, mollius*	*mollissimus, -a, -um*
pulcher, pulchra, pulchrum	*pulchrior, pulchrius*	*pulcherrimus, -a, -um*
facilis, facile	*facilior, facilius*	*facillimus, -a, -um*
frequēns	*frequentior, frequentius*	*frequentissimus, -a, -um*

Adverbs

Positive Degree	Comparative Degree	Superlative Degree
rārō	*rārius*	*rārissimē*
molliter	*mollius*	*mollissimē*
pulchrē	*pulchrius*	*pulcherrimē*
*facile**	*facilius*	*facillimē*
frequenter	*frequentius*	*frequentissimē*

*more rare: *faciliter*

Lēctiō Tertia (Section III)

Numerical Adverbs

Numerical adverbs are formed with the suffix *-iēs* (or *-iēns*) and denote how many times an action occurs:

> *quīnquiēs* = 5×
> *sexiēs* = 6×
> *septiēs* = 7×, etc.

Only the first four have special forms:

semel: once	*ter*: three times
bis: twice	*quater*: four times

From *quot* and *tot* are formed *quotiēs* and *totiēs*:

> *Mārcus deciēs H scribit: H H H H H H H H H H* (l.119)
> *Quotiēs Mārcus V scribit? Quater tantum V scrībit.* (ll.122–123)
> *Quotiēs? Semel.* (ll.133–134)
> *Mārcus ter rēctē et bis prāvē scrībit.* (ll.125–126)

Studia Rōmāna

You have already learned (Cap. I) about the wax tablets and the *stylus* used for scratching letters into the wax. In the house of Caecilius Iucundus in Pompeii, 154 such wax tablets were found that recorded business transactions. In addition to wax tablets, Romans wrote on *papȳrus*, a plant that came originally from Egypt whose leaves were glued together, and smoothed out and on parchment (*membrāna, ae*), animal skins dried, stretched and polished. Quintilian (*I.O.* 10.3.31) encourages his orators to write on wax tablets since they erase easily. Parchment is easier to read (as the letters are inked, not scratched) but slow, since the pen has to be so frequently re-inked. Into the ink (*ātrāmentum*) was dipped a reed pen, a *calamus* (as you can see in the margins on p. 141 and on the bottom of p. 142). By the sixth century AD, the *penna* (quill-pen, from the word for feather) had come into use—a technology that stayed the same until the nineteenth century.

Marcus wrongfully boasts that he doesn't need to learn how to write because he dictates to Zeno, a slave who knows both Latin and Greek (*et Latīnē et Graecē scit*, l.159). Writing was a valuable skill and could offer a good profession. *Scrībae* (literate professionals) assisted magistrates at various levels. The best post was *scrība quaestōrius*, a post that the poet Horace held, as did at least one of his young friends to whom he wrote a verse letter (*Epistles* 1.8). The young man, Celsus Albinovanus, was abroad with Caesar Augustus's stepson Tiberius as companion (*comes*) and scribe (*scrība*), a post that Horace suggests might have gone to his head ("we'll treat you accordingly as you treat your good fortune!"[5]).

Marcus implies he doesn't really even need to learn to read, since Zeno reads aloud to him (l.160). A slave whose function it is to read aloud (especially at dinner for entertainment) is called an *anagnōstēs* (from Greek: ἀναγνώστης). Zeno seems to be more of a general secretary than just a slave who can read aloud: a *librārius* (there were female *librāriae* as well) or *āmanuēnsis*. As such, he would have been a valued (and valuable) addition to the household. Cicero depended on and became so close to his secretary Tiro that he manumitted him. Tiro remained a part of the household; after Cicero's death, Tiro collected and published his patron's letters, some of his speeches, and a collection of his jokes (which collection does not, unfortunately, survive).

Diodorus complains in his letter that he has not yet been paid for the month. His complaint, "*Mercēs numquam mihi trāditur ad diem*," was common among teachers at all levels. Lucian, a Greek who also lived in the second century AD, also wrote about the financial plight of teachers. His *dē Mercēde Conductīs* ("On Those Hired for Pay"), for example, bemoans the impoverished plight of teachers who attach themselves to wealthy Roman houses as a live-in scholar. Juvenal (*Decimus Iūnius Iūvenālis*), a satiric poet who wrote around the time of our narrative, writes at length about the travails of intellectuals, including teachers of rhetoric and of *lūdī magistrī* (*Satire* 7). Juvenal uses the imagery of the racecourse; although he trains many future jockeys, he will be paid less than the purse for one race:[6]

> *nōn est leve tot puerōrum*
> *observāre manūs oculōsque in fīne trementīs.*
> *'haec' inquit 'cūra; sed cum se verterit annus,*
> *accipe, victōrī pōpulus quod postulat, aurum.'*

Quintilian stresses the importance of a good working relationship between the *paterfamiliās* and the *lūdī magister*. As we shall see, the relationship between Julius and Diodorus is far from amiable and cooperative.

Vocābula Disposita/Ōrdināta

Nōmina
  1st

cēra, -ae	wax
charta, -ae	paper
epistula, -ae	a letter

---

5. ...*ut tū fortūnam, sīc nōs tē, Celse, ferēmus.*

6. It's no easy thing to watch the eyes and hands—trembling at the starting block—of so many boys. "This," says he, "is your business; but at the end of a full year, receive one gold piece—the reward the people demand for the victor in but one race."

māteria, -ae	material
sententia, -ae	opinion, sentence

2nd

adverbium, -ī	adverb
calamus, -ī	reed, reed pen
erus, -ī	master
ferrum, -ī	iron, sword
mendum, -ī	mistake
papȳrus, -ī	papyrus (paper)
zephȳrus, -ī	west wind

3rd

apis, apis (*f.*)	bee
cōnsonāns, cōnsonantis (*f.*)	consonant
mercēs, mercēdis (*f.*)	hire, pay, wages
vōcālis, vōcālis (*f.*)	vowel

Verba

comparō, comparāre	liken, compare; prepare, get ready
dictō, dictāre	dictate
signō, signāre	mark, inscribe, indicate, notice, seal
significō, significāre	indicate, show, mean

-ēre (2)

dēleō, dēlēre	blot out, efface, destroy

-ere (3)

addō, addere	add, join
animadvertō, animadvertere	notice[7]
coniungō, coniungere	connect, unite
corrigō, corrigere	correct
efficiō, efficere	bring about
imprimō, imprimere	seal, emboss
intellegō, intellegere	understand
iungō, iungere	join
legō, legere	pick, read
premō, premere	press
scrībō, scrībere	write

-īre (4)

exaudiō, exaudīre	hear plainly or favorably

Irregular

dēsum, deesse	fall short, be lacking
supersum, superesse	be over and above, remain, survive

Adiectīva

1st/2nd

dūrus, -a, -um	hard
impiger, -gra, -grum	active, energetic

---

7. From *animum adverte*: "turn your mind toward."

rārus, -a, -um	rare
varius, -a, -um	manifold, various

3rd

frequēns (*gen.* **frequentis**)	crowded, numerous, frequent
mollis, molle	soft
quālis? quāle?	(interrogative and relative) of what sort?
tālis, tāle	of such a sort
turpis, turpe	ugly, foul

Prōnōmina

īdem, eadem, idem	the same (*adj./pronoun*)
quisque, quaeque, quodque	each

Adverbia

sīc	so, thus
ita	so, in such a way
quotiēs	as many times
totiēs	so many times
semel	once
bis	twice
ter	three times
quater	four times
quīnquiēs	five times
sexiēs	six times
deciēs	ten times

XIX. Marītus et Uxor

Rēs Grammaticae Novae

1. Verbs
   a. Imperfect of all Conjugations: Active and Passive
   b. Imperfect of *esse*
2. Nouns
   a. *domus*
   b. Case Uses
      i. Genitive of Quality/Description
      ii. Vocatives for Nouns in *-ius*
      iii. Archaic Genitive
3. Adjectives
   a. Irregular Adjectives
   b. Superlative Adjectives
      i. Absolute
      ii. with Partitive Genitive
   c. *nūllus/ūllus/tōtus/sōlus*
   d. Numerals: Genitive of *ūnus, duo, trēs*
   e. 3rd Declension Adjectives of One Termination
   f. *dignus* (Ablative of Respect)
4. Points of Style: Idioms

Julius and Aemilia

Undisturbed by their noisy children, Julius and Aemilia are walking up and down in the beautiful peristyle, which is adorned with statues of gods and goddesses. Romans could take the choice of sculptural decoration very seriously. Letters written by Cicero in the first century BC demonstrate both his zeal to acquire appropriate ornamentation for his several country estates and his annoyance when his agents picked out statues that didn't project the right image: "Really, why a statue of Mars for me, a proponent of peace?" (*Epistulae ad Familiārēs*, VII.23: *Martis vērō signum quō mihi pācis auctōrī?*). Great numbers of statues were imported from Greece; Cicero thanks his friend Atticus for sending a number of statues (which he has not yet even seen, since they were delivered to one of his estates) and details his plans for distributing them among his *villae* (*Epistulae ad Atticum*, I.4).

Among the names of the gods, notice the name of the supreme god *Iūppiter Iov|is*; the stem is *Iov-* (meaning "sky"), and the long nominative form is due to the addition of *pater* weakened to *-piter*. The Roman gods were identified with the Greek, e.g., *Iūppiter*[1] with *Zeus*, his wife *Iūnō* with *Hēra*, *Venus* with *Aphrodītē*, the goddess of love; *Aphrodītē's* son *Erōs* became *Cupīdō* ("desire").

Lēctiō Prīma (Section I)

Irregular Adjectives

Iūppiter has the honorific titles *Optimus Māximus,* which are the superlatives of *bonus* and *magnus.* The comparison of these adjectives and their opposites *malus* and *parvus* is quite irregular. So is the comparison of *multī*: comp. *plūrēs,* sup. *plūrimī.* Look at these examples:

malus (ll.13–16):

> *Nēmō deōrum pēior marītus est quam Iūppiter, neque ūlla dea pēior uxor est quam Venus.*
> *Inter omnēs deōs deāsque Iūppiter pessimus marītus est ac Venus pessima uxor.*

bonus (ll.25–30):

> *Certē Iūlius marītus melior quam Iūppiter est!*
> *Certē Aemilia uxor melior est quam Venus!*
> *Aemila Iūlium "virum optimum" appellat.*
> *Item Iūlius uxōrem suam "optimam omnium fēminārum" vocat.*

magnus and *parvus* (ll.35–37):

> *Quīntus māior est quam Iūlia et minor quam Mārcus.*
> *Māximus līberōrum est Mārcus, minima est Iūlia.*

multī (ll.52, 54):

> *Rōmae plūrēs hominēs habitant quam in ūllā aliā urbe imperiī Rōmānī.*
> *Urbs Rōma plūrimōs hominēs et plūrimās domōs habet.*

bonus, -a, -um	*melior, melius*	*optimus, -a, -um*
malus, -a, -um	*pēior, pēius*	*pessimus, -a, -um*
magnus, -a, -um	*māior, māius*	*māximus, -a, -um*
parvus, -a, -um	*minor, minus*	*minimus, -a, -um*
multī, -ae, -a	*plūres, plūra*	*plūrimī, -ae, -a*

---

1. Also spelled Jupiter.

Superlative + Partitive Genitive; Superlative Absolute

The superlative is often linked with a partitive genitive:

*optimam omn*ium *fēminārum* (l.30)
*pulcherrima omn*ium *deārum* (l.21)

Without such a genitive, the superlative often denotes a **very** high degree (**absolute superlative**):

"*mea optima uxor*" (l.90): "my excellent wife"
vir pessimus (l.110)
"*mī optime vir*" (l.94)
Tunc miserrima eram (l.107)
virgō pauperrima (l.128)

Archaic Genitive

The ending *-ās* in *māter familiās* and *pater familiās* (ll.17, 38) is an old genitive ending of the 1st declension (= *-ae*).

Numerals: *ūnus, duo, trēs*

You have met the other forms of the first three numbers before; in this chapter, you meet the genitive:

Iūlius et Aemilia sunt parentēs trium *līberōrum*: duōrum *fīliōrum et*
ūnīus *fīliae*. (ll.31–32)

The complete paradigms for these three are:

	m.	f.	n.	m.	f.	n.	m./f.	n.
nom.	ūn|us	ūn|a	ūn|um	du|o	du|ae	du|o	tr|ēs	tr|ia
acc.	ūn|um	ūn|am	ūn|um	du|ōs	du|ās	du|o	tr|ēs	tr|ia
gen.	ūn|īus	ūn|īus	ūn|īus	du|ōrum	du|ārum	du|ōrum	tr|ium	tr|ium
dat.	ūn|ī	ūn|ī	ūn|ī	du|ōbus	du|ābus	du|ōbus	tr|ibus	tr|ibus
abl.	ūn|ō	ūn|ā	ūn|ō	du|ōbus	du|ābus	du|ōbus	tr|ibus	tr|ibus

You have met the variation of declension shown in *ūnus* before, in *ille* (gen. *illīus*, dat. *illī*), *hic* (gen. *huius*, dat. *huic*, from *hui-ce*).

Nūllus/ūllus/tōtus/sōlus

Ūnus, -a, -um is one of a small group of pronouns and adjectives whose genitive singulars end in *-īus* and dative singulars in *ī*. You meet some more of these in this chapter:

nūllus, -a, -um   none, not any
ūllus, -a, -um   any (always with a negative)
tōtus, -a, -um   the whole of, all
sōlus, -a, -um   alone, only

All of these adjectives have a genitive *-īus* and dative *-ī* in the singular.

As you know (Cap. III), *et* is not placed before *nōn*; nor is it placed before *nūllus*: instead of *et nūllus*, we find *neque ūllus*:

- *neque ūlla dea pēior uxor est quam Venus.* (l.14)
- *Iūlius…uxōrem suam neque ūllam aliam fēminam amat.* (ll.24–25)
- *Aemilia…marītum suum neque ūllum alium virum amat.* (ll.26–27)

So, we find *ūllus* only with a negative.

Genitive of Quality/Description

A noun + adjective in the genitive can be used to describe a quality (*genetīvus quālitātis* or **genitive of description**). For example:

> *Mārcus octō annōs habet*; *Quīntus est puer septem ann<u>ōrum</u>.* (ll.33–34)
> *Adulēscēns vīgintī du<u>ōrum</u> ann<u>ōrum</u> erat.* (ll.39–40)

Imperfect of All Conjugations: Active and Passive

The last example (*Adulēscēns vīgintī duōrum annōrum erat*) has *erat*, not *est*, because this was ten years ago (he is no longer *adulēscēns*). *Est* describes the present, *erat* the past. Compare the two sentences:

> *Nunc Iūlius Aemiliam ama<u>t</u>.*   (loves, is loving, does love)
> *Tunc Iūlius Aemiliam am<u>ābat</u>.*   (loved, was loving, used to love)

The form *amā|bat* is the **past tense** or **preterite** (Latin *tempus praeteritum*) of the verb *amā|re*, as distinct from *ama|t*, which is the **present tense** (Latin *tempus praesēns*). The preterite or past tense occurring in this chapter is called the **imperfect** (Latin *praeteritum <u>imperfectum</u>*, "incompleted past"). The **imperfect** denotes a past state of things or an action going on (not completed) or repeated in the past. In each of the following examples, the action goes on over a period of time:

> *ūlius et Aemilia Rōmae habit<u>ābant</u>*: used to live; were living
> *Iūlius cotīdiē epistulās ad Aemiliam scrīb<u>ēbat</u>*: used to write (l.76)
> *Iūlius male dormi<u>ēbat</u>*: was sleeping (l.69)
> *Tunc ego tē am<u>ābam</u>, tū mē nōn am<u>ābās</u>.* (l.98)
> *Neque epistulās, quās cotīdiē tibi scrīb<u>ēbam</u>, leg<u>ēbās</u>.* (ll.101–102)

The imperfect is formed by inserting *-bā-* (1st and 2nd conjugations) or *-ēbā-* (3rd and 4th conjugations) between the stem and the person endings: in the active *-m, -mus* (1st pers.), *-s, -tis* (2nd pers.), and *-t, -nt* (3rd pers.).

In Section II of your reading, you will find that the passive is formed the same way, with the passive endings: *-r, -mur* (1st pers.), *-ris, -minī* (2nd pers.), and *-tur, -ntur* (3rd pers.).

Notā Bene: The 1st person ends in *-m* and *-r* (not *-ō* and *-or*) and that *ā* is shortened before *-m*, *-r*, *-t*, *-nt*, and *-ntur* (*amā|ba̱|m, amā|ba̱|r*, etc.).

1st Conjugation (*āre*): stem + *bā* + personal endings:

> *Iūlius ambulat → Iūlius ambulābat*
> *Signa stant → Signa stābant*

2nd Conjugation (*ēre*): stem + *bā* + personal endings:

> *Tēctum columnīs altīs sustinētur → tēctum columnīs altīs sustinēbātur.*
> *Habēsne librum tuum? → Habēbāsne librum tuum?*

3rd and 4th Conjugation (*ere/īre*): stem + *ēbā* + personal endings:

Consonant-stem:

> *Iūlius flōrēs ad Aemiliam mittit → Iūlius flōrēs ad Aemiliam mittēbat.*
> *Cotīdiē epistulās scrībimus → Cotīdiē epistulās scrībēbāmus.*

Vowel-stem:

> *Aemilia flōrēs ā Iūliō accipit → Aemilia flōrēs ā Iūliō accipiēbat.*
> *Nihil faciō → Nihil faciēbam.*

4th Conjugation:

> *Dormītisne? → Dormiēbātisne?*
> *Saepe Rōmānī conveniunt → Saepe Rōmānī conveniēbant.*

Imperfect: stem vowel (1st conj. *-ā* otherwise *-ē*)

	active	passive
sing.	1. *-(ā‖ē)ba|m*	1. *-(ā‖ē)ba|r*
	2. *-(ā |ē)bā|s*	2. *-(ā‖ē)bā|ris*
	3. *-(ā‖ē)ba|t*	3. *-(ā‖ē)bā|tur*
pl.	1. *-(ā‖ē)bā|mus*	1. *-(ā‖ē)bā|mur*
	2. *-(ā‖ē)bā|tis*	2. *-(ā‖ē)bā|minī*
	3. *-(ā‖ē)ba|nt*	3. *-(ā‖ē)ba|ntur*

Imperfect of *esse*

You have already met the 3rd person of the imperfect of the irregular verb *esse*: *era|t, era|nt* (Cap. XIII). Now you learn the 1st and 2nd persons:

1st	*era|m, erā|mus*
2nd	*erā|s, erā|tis*
3rd	*era|t, era|nt*

Compounds of *esse*, e.g., *ab-esse*, including *posse*, show the same forms:

> *ab-era|m, ab-erā|s*, etc.
> *pot-era|m, pot-erā|s*, etc.

Domus

The noun *domus, -ūs* is a 4th declension <u>feminine</u> noun, but it has some 2nd declension endings (underlined in the paradigm below):

nom.	*domus*	*domūs*
acc.	*domum*	*dom<u>ōs</u>*
gen.	*domūs*	*dom<u>ōrum</u>* (or *dom<u>uum</u>*)
dat.	*domuī*	*domibus*
abl.	*dom<u>ō</u>*	*domibus*

The form *domī*, "at home," in Cap. XV (*Is domī est apud mātrem suam*, l.81) is locative; for this form, as well as the accusative *domum* and ablative *domō* used as adverbs without a preposition, see the next chapter.

Lēctiō Altera (Section II)

3rd Declension Adjectives of One Termination

You have already learned (Cap. XII) 3rd declension adjectives that end in *-is, -e* in the nominative, where *-is* is the masculine and feminine ending and *-e* is the neuter ending, e.g.:

> *brevis, breve*
> *fortis, forte*

And in the last chapter, you learned *frequēns*, an adjective with the same ending in the nominative masculine, feminine, and neuter. Other 3rd declension adjectives as well have the same ending in the nominative singular masculine, feminine, and neuter. Such adjectives vary from *brevis, breve* in the nominative *only*. Two such adjectives are:

> *dīves* (*dīvitior, dīvitissimus*: rich)
> *pauper* (*pauperior, pauperrimus*: poor)

Examples:

> *Iūlius dīves erat, nōn pauper.*
> *Aemilia pauper erat, nōn dīves.*

Lēctiō Tertia (Section III)

Vocative for Nouns in *-ius*

In Cap. IV, you learned that 2nd declension words in *-us* have a special form used when addressing a person, the **vocative**, ending in *-e*, e.g., *domine*. When Aemilia addresses her husband by name, she uses the vocative *Iūlī*, "*Ō, Iūlī!*" and she adds, "*mī optime vir!*" (ll.93–94). The vocative of personal names in *-ius* ends in *-ī* (a contraction of *-ie*):

Iūlius → Iūlī
Cornēlius → Cornēlī
Lūcius → Lūcī

The vocative of *meus* is *mī* and of *filius* is *fīlī*:

Ō, mī fīlī! (Cap. XXI, l.30)
mī optime vir (l.94)

Ablative of Respect

In Cap. XI, you encountered the **ablative of respect** (l.55 *pede aeger*). *Dignus, -a, -um* also takes an ablative of respect:

Ille vir pessimus tē dignus nōn erat!: not worthy of you (l.110)
Tu sōlus amōre meō dignus erās: worthy of my love (ll.111–112)

Points of Style: Idioms

Compare:

I. Apposition

   in urbe Rōmā: in the city of Rome (*Rōma* in apposition to *urbs*)
   Rōmae: at/in Rome (locative)

II. *Ante/Post*

   ante decem annōs: *ante* the preposition + the accusative

   decem annīs ante: *ante* as adverb + ablative of degree of difference

     similarly: *paulō ante*, etc.

III. *Ita...ut/ut...ita*

Ut tunc tē amābam, ita etiam nunc tē amō.	As I loved you then, so even now I love you.
Ita est ut dīcis.	It is just as you say.

IV. *Quam*

   relative pronoun: feminine accusative singular (Cap. III)
   interrogative adjective: feminine accusative singular (Cap. III)
   correlative: *tam...quam*: as...as (Cap. VI)
   adverb: how (Cap. VIII)
   in comparisons: than (Cap. XII)

V. *Opus est*

   = *necesse est*; *oportet*
   nōn opus est mē plūs dīcere = *nōn necesse est mē plūs dīcere*

Studia Rōmāna

Both Aemilia and Julius describe themselves as *miser* (*Ergō Iūlius* <u>*miser*</u> *erat et nocte male dormiēbat ... Itaque ea quoque* <u>*misera*</u> *erat,* l.69 and l.73). In Latin love poetry, *miser* is the standard word to describe someone suffering in love. In the image on page 148, we see Julius and Aemilia with their right hands joined—the iconography in art for the bond between husband and wife (the *iūnctiō*[2] *dextrārum,* joining of right hands). There were different ways to be married in Rome. To be married *cum manū* (literally: "with the hand") meant that a woman passed from the jurisdiction of her father's household to that of her husband (or of her husband's father, if he were still alive and the *paterfamilias*). Instead of being her father's daughter, she became as if the daughter of her new family (*in locō fīliae*). If a woman were married *sine manū* ("without the hand"), she remained under her father's jurisdiction even though married. Aemilia's marriage to Julius would most likely have been *sine manū; manus* marriage became a rarity by our time period. The goal of marriage was the birth and rearing of children; *mātrimōnium...hinc līberōrum prōcreātiō hinc ēducātiō.*[3]

The perisyle of the villa, adorned with statuary, demonstrates the wealth and culture of the *dominus. Cupīdō Amor* is the Latin translation of the Greek personification of love *Erōs* (Ἔρως); in Roman culture, he is primarily a literary and artistic motif (hence the statue of Cupid in the peristyle). *Venus,* however, is a different story. She is not only the wife of Vulcan and mother of Cupid, the paramour of Mars and the goddess of love and beauty, but she is a powerful goddess as well. She is *Venus Genetrix,* goddess of fertility and the ancestral goddess of the Romans (because she was the mother of Aeneas). There were several temples and festivals dedicated to Venus at Rome.

Venus's husband, *Vulcānus* (also *Volcānus*) is an ancient Roman god of devastating fire (as opposed to *Vesta,* the goddess of the life-sustaining hearth-fire, whose priestesses—the Vestals—guarded the state-protecting shrine of Vesta in the Roman Forum). Vulcan became associated with the Greek god Hephaistus (and Vesta with the Greek Hestia); he is the god of forge, depicted as burly and lame, and a bit of a trickster.

Jūnō who, like Venus, was an ancient Italic goddess, was Juppiter's wife and, appropriately, the goddess of marriage. Her husband, Juppiter, was (as your text tells you) a terrible husband prone to falling in love with other women. This kind of immorality among the gods was one of the reasons the Greek philosopher Plato wanted to exclude them from the ideal state.

Jūppiter, as a sky god, regulated the weather; once he became associated

---

2. *Iūnctiō* is from *iungere,* Cap. XVIII.

3. Justinian, *Digest* 1.3. The Digest represents the emperor Justinian's (AD 527–565) efforts to bring together all of Roman law in a more accessible way.

with the Greek Zeus, he became the most powerful of all gods, hence *Jūppiter Optimus Māximus*: Juppiter the Best and Greatest. At Rome, Juppiter had a temple called the *Capitōlium* on a hill overlooking the Roman Forum (l.50); hence the hill is called the *Mōns Capitōlīnus*. *Minerva* and *Iūnō* also had shrines in the Capitolium. *Minerva* was an Italic goddess of crafts, who became associated with the Greek Pallas Athena, the daughter of Zeus, also goddess of crafts (and war and wisdom!). Towns often imitated Rome by building their own *Capitōlium*, with the same triad of Juppiter, Juno, and Minerva.

Vocābula Disposita/Ōrdināta

Nōmina

1st

columna, -ae	column
dea, -ae	goddess
mātrōna, -ae	married woman

2nd

dōnum, -ī	gift
forum, -ī	forum
marītus, -ī	husband
praeteritum, -ī (tempus)	past (tense)
signum, -ī	statue, sign
tēctum, -ī	roof
templum, -ī	temple

3rd

adulēscēns, adulēscentis (*m.*)	young person
amor, amōris (*m.*)	love
coniūnx, coniugis (*m./f.*)	spouse
flōs, flōris (*m.*)	flower
praesēns, entis (tempus)	present tense
pulchritūdō, pulchritūdinis (*f.*)	beauty
uxor, uxōris (*f.*)	wife
virgō, virginis (*f.*)	unmarried girl

4th

domus, -ūs (*f.*)	house

Verba

-āre (1)

ōsculor, ōsculārī	kiss

-ēre (2)

augeō, augēre	increase
possideō, possidēre	possess

-ere (3)
    minuō, minuere   diminish
    mittō, mittere   send
    remittō, remittere   send again, send back

-īre (4)
    conveniō, convenīre   come together, fit together; fit

Irregular
    opus esse (+ *inf.* or *abl.*)   to need

Adiectīva
  1st/2nd (-us/er, -a, -um)
    beātus, -a, -um   blessed, fortunate
    dignus, -a, -um (+ *abl.*)   worthy of
    magnificus, -a, -um   magnificent
    miser, misera, miserum   wretched

  3rd
    dīves (*gen.* **dīvitis**)   rich
    gracilis, -e   slender
    pauper (*gen.* **pauperis**)   poor

Irregular
    melior, melius   better
    pēior, pēius   worse
    māior, māius   larger, greater
    minor, minus   smaller
    plūres, plūra   more
    optimus, -a, -um   best
    pessimus, -a, -um   worst
    māximus, -a, -um   largest, greatest
    minimus, -a, -um   smallest
    plūrimī, -ae, -a   most, a great many

Prōnōmina
    ūllus, -a, -um   any (usually only with negation)
    mī   vocative of **meus**

Adverbia
    cotīdiē   daily
    minus   less
    plūs (*adv.* + *n. noun*)   more
    tamen (*adv.* + *conj.*)   nevertheless

Praepositiōnēs
    ergā (*prp.* + *acc.*)   toward

XX. Parentēs

Rēs Grammaticae Novae

1. Verbs
   a. Future Tense: All Conjugations, Active and Passive, and *esse*
   b. *velle/nōlle*
2. Nouns
   a. *domus* (continued)
   b. *carēre* + Ablative of Separation
3. Pronouns: Personal Pronouns: 1st and 2nd Person, Plural: Dative and Ablative
4. Adverbs: *minus/magis*

Julius and Aemilia Look to the Future

A happy event is in store for our Roman family. This gives the parents occasion for thoughts about the future, which in turn gives you a chance to get acquainted with the **future tense** (Latin *tempus futūrum*) of Latin verbs.

Lēctiō Prīma (Section I)

Future Tense

The future is formed by the insertion between the stem and personal ending of:

(1) *-b-* in the 1st and 2nd conjugations, with the following vowel variations:
   a. 1st person singular in *ō*: *amā|b|ō, habē|b|ō*
   b. 3rd plural in *u*: *amā|bu|nt, amā|bu|ntur*
   c. 2nd singular **passive** in *e*: *amā|be|ris*
   d. Otherwise in *i*: *amā|bi|s, amā|bi|t, amā|bi|mus*

Notā Bene: Remember the sequence *-bō, -bi, -bu* (plus the change of *i* to *e* before *r*).

(2)   In the 3rd and 4th conjugations, the sign of the future is:

    a. 1st pers. sing. *-a-* + active ending *m* as in the imperfect, e.g.:

        dīc|a|m, capi|a|m, audi|a|m

        dīc|a|r, capi|a|r, audi|a|r

    b. Otherwise *-ē-*

        dīc|ē|s, capi|ē|s, audi|ē|s

        dīc|ē|ris, capi|ē|ris, audi|ē|ris

    c. But *-ē-* is **shortened** to *-e-* before *-t, -nt, -ntur*:

        dīc|e|t

        dīc|e|nt

        dīc|e|ntur

future

1st and 2nd conjugation					
active	passive	active	passive	active	passive
1. *-b|ō*	*-b|or*	1. *cūrābō*	*cūrābor*	1. *dēbēbō*	*dēbēbor*
2. *-b|is*	*-b|eris*	2. *cūrābis*	*cūrāberis*	2. *dēbēbis*	*dēbēberis*
3. *-b|it*	*-b|itur*	3. *cūrābit*	*cūrābitur*	3. *dēbēbit*	*dēbēbitur*
1. *-b|imus*	*-b|imur*	1. *cūrābimus*	*cūrābimur*	1. *dēbēbimus*	*dēbēbimur*
2. *-b|itis*	*-b|iminī*	2. *cūrābitis*	*cūrābiminī*	2. *dēbēbitis*	*dēbēbiminī*
3. *-b|unt*	*-b|untur*	3. *cūrābunt*	*cūrābuntur*	3. *dēbēbunt*	*dēbēbuntur*
3rd and 4th conjugation					
active	passive	active	passive	active	passive
1. *-a|m*	*-a|r*	1. *alam*	*alar*	1. *exaudiam*	*exaudiar*
2. *-ē|s*	*-ē|ris*	2. *alēs*	*alēris*	2. *exaudiēs*	*exaudiēris*
3. *-e|t*	*-ē|tur*	3. *alet*	*alētur*	3. *exaudiet*	*exaudiētur*
1. *-ē|mus*	*-ē|mur*	1. *alēmus*	*alēmur*	1. *exaudiēmus*	*exaudiēmur*
2. *-ē|tis*	*-ē|minī*	2. *alētis*	*alēminī*	2. *exaudiētis*	*exaudiēminī*
3. *-e|nt*	*-e|ntur*	3. *alent*	*alentur*	3. *exaudient*	*exaudiēntur*

Esse: **future**

	sing.	pl.
1.	*erō*	*erimus*
2.	*eris*	*eritis*
3.	*erit*	*erunt*

Lēctiō Altera (Section II)

Minus/magis

Note irregular adverbs *minus* (less) and *magis* (more), often paired with *quam* (than):

> *Num parvulam fīliam <u>minus</u> amābis <u>quam</u> fīlium?* (ll.57–58)
> *Nēminem <u>magis</u> amābō <u>quam</u> parvulam fīliam.* (l.59)
> *Iam fīliōs tuōs <u>magis</u> amās <u>quam</u> tuam Iūliam fīliolam.* (l.61–62)

Velle/nōlle

You already know the 3rd person present of the irregular verb *velle: vult, volunt.* The 1st and 2nd persons are: *volō, volumus* and *vīs, vultis,* respectively. The negation *nōn* is not placed before the forms *volō, volumus, volunt,* and *velle;* instead, we find the forms *nōlō, nōlumus, nōlunt,* and *nōlle,* which are contracted from *nē* + *volō,* etc.:

> *Ego alteram fīliam habēre <u>volō</u>, plūrēs quam duōs fīliōs <u>nōlō</u>!*: want...do not want (ll.54–55)
> *Cūr tū fīlium habēre vīs, Iūlī?* (l.56)
> *Vōs virī fīliōs modo habēre vultis.* (ll.63–64)
> *Nōs virī etiam fīliās habēre volumus.* (ll.72–73)
> *Iūlia dīcit "sē patre suō carēre nōlle."* (ll.140–141)

present of	*velle*		*nōlle*	
	sing.	pl.	sing.	pl.
1.	*volō*	*volumus*	*nōlō*	*nōlumus*
2.	*vīs*	*vultis*	*nōn vīs*	*nōn vultis*
3.	*vult*	*volunt*	*nōn vult*	*nōlunt*

The **imperative** *nōlī, nōlīte* is used with an infinitive to express a prohibition ("don't...!"), e.g.:

> *Nōlī abīre!* (l.69)
> *Nōlī dīcere "tatam" et "mammam."* (l.157)
> *Nōlīte mē "Iūliolam" vocāre! Id nōmen mē nōn decet.* (ll.160–161)

Lēctiō Tertia (Section III)

Domus (continued)

In Cap. VI, you learned that names of cities and towns express place with the accusative (to which), ablative (from which), and locative (at which). *Domus* follows the same rule: the accusative and ablative of *domus* (*domum* and *domō*) are used without a preposition to express motion to or from one's home, e.g.:

> *domum revertentur* (ll.123–124)
>   *domō abīre* (l.137)

The form *domī* is locative ("at home") e.g.:

> *domī manēre* (l.127)

Notā Bene:

domum	acc.: "to home"
domō	abl.: "from home"
domī	loc.: "at home"

Ablative of Separation

The ablative expressing "place from which" in *domō* and *Tūsculō* is the **ablative of separation**; the verb *carēre* ("be without," "lack") is completed by an ablative of separation (and not an accusative), e.g.:

> *Īnfāns neque <u>somnō</u> neque <u>cibō carēre</u> potest.: somnō…cibō carēre =*
> *sine + abl.: sine somnō et cibō esse* (ll.5–6)
> *Iūlia dīcit "sē <u>patre suō carēre</u> nōlle."* (l.141)

Personal Pronouns *nōs/vōs* (continued)

The personal pronouns *nōs* and *vōs* become *nōbīs* and *vōbīs* in the ablative and dative:

> *Necesse est mihi crās rūrsus ā vōbīs discēdere.* (ll.129–130)
> *Nōlī ā nōbīs discēdere!* (l.136)

You will see the dative (also *nōbīs* and *vōbīs)* in the reading in the next chapter:

> *Prīmum magister nōbīs aliquid recitāvit.* (Cap. XXI, l.91)
> *Tabellam vōbīs ostendam.* (Cap. XXI, l.109)

You will learn the genitive of the personal pronouns in Cap. XXIX.

Recēnsiō: personal pronouns

	1st sing.	1st pl.	2nd sing.	2nd pl.
nom.	*ego*	*nōs*	*tū*	*vōs*
acc.	*mē*	*nōs*	*tē*	*vōs*
dat.	*mihi*	*nōbīs*	*tibi*	*vōbīs*
abl.	*mē*	*nōbīs*	*tē*	*vōbīs*

Recēnsiō

1. Expressions of comparison

...*nōn minus...quam*	no less than
nec plūs nec minus quam opus est	no more or less than is necessary
magis quam	more than

2. *nōn tantum...sed etiam = nōn sōlum...sed etiam*

3. "Emotion" adverbs: *minimē, profectō*

4. Expressions of time:

Eō ipsō tempore	at that very time
Eō tempore	at that time
Tempore praeteritō	in the past; at a past time
Tempore futūrō	in the future; at a future time
Tōtam noctem	for the whole night
Tertiō quōque diē[1]	every third day
Cotīdiē	daily
Herī	yesterday
Hodiē	today
Crās	tomorrow
Decem annīs post	afterward by ten years; ten years later = *post decem annos*: after ten years (the first is an ablative of degree of difference and *post* is an adverb, the second a preposition + the accusative)

Summary of *esse*

Present	Future	Imperfect
sum	*erō*	*eram*
es	*eris*	*erās*
est	*erit*	*erat*
sumus	*erimus*	*erāmus*
estis	*eritis*	*erātis*
sunt	*erunt*	*erant*

Studia Rōmāna

While Aemilia insists she will nurse her own baby, many babies born to wealthier women were nursed by *nūtrīcēs*, who might be slaves or free women. Like our understanding of education, much of our knowledge of early childhood comes from treatises about raising and educating children. The nurse,

---

1. *Quōque* (from *quisque*), not *quŏque* (conjunction: also, too).

according to Quintilian, must speak Latin well and be of the highest character (*ante omnia nē sit vitiōsus sermō nūtrīcibus*: *Īnstitūtiō Ōrātōria*, I.1). Cicero had said the same, claiming a speaker who was not particularly well educated had gained his eloquence from being raised in a home where language mattered (*Brūtus*, 211). After all, the child will learn to speak by listening to the surrounding adults.

But before the baby can be raised, it must be born and acknowledged. After the birth, fires are lit in the house and a couch laden with food for the gods is set in the atrium (such a gift-laden couch for the gods is called a *lectisternium*). The day will be celebrated annually, as we do. The gods who were invoked during the birth will be thanked: *Iūnō* and *Diāna*. Also venerated were the ancient Italic deities of childbirth, *Lūcīna* and the *Carmentēs*. (Lucina is often melded with Juno: *Iūnō Lūcīna*.[2]) After eight days (for a girl) or nine (for a boy) the family celebrates a *lūstrātiō*, or purification, and officially welcomes the child to the family.

Roman writers often emphasize the importance of the mother's role in the raising of children, pointing to famous Roman mothers who greatly influenced their sons. *Titus Līvius* (2.40) gives us one such formidable mother of the fifth century BC. When Marcius Coriolanus was preparing to wage war against Rome, his own city, the women of Rome marched out to the camp to plead with their rebellious sons. Livy recounts Coriolanus's mother Veturia giving a scathing reprimand to her son, thereby stopping the war.

Perhaps the most famous Roman mother of the republican period was *Cornēlia*, the mother of the Gracchi, statesmen renowned for their oratorical skills. Cornelia, who lived in the second century BC, was the daughter of Publius Cornelius Scipio Aemilianus (about whom you will learn more in the second book in this series, *Rōma Aeterna*) and the wife of *Tiberius Semprōnius Gracchus*. Cornēlia bore twelve children, but nine died before adulthood—such infant mortality was not unusual. A story related by *Valerius Maximus*, a writer of the first century AD who compiled historical anecdotes, pays tribute to her character as a mother. To illustrate *maxima ōrnāmenta esse mātrōnīs līberōs*, Valerius tells this story: When a woman from Campania was visiting at the home of Cornelia and showing off her very beautiful jewelry, Cornelia drew out the conversation until her children came home from school and then said, "These are my jewels."[3] Cicero praised the eloquence of her letters (which he had read) by saying, "It appears her sons were raised not as much on the lap of their mother as in conversing with her" (*appāret filiōs nōn tam in gremiō ēducātōs quam in sermōne mātris*, Brutus, 211). Cornelia was so revered as an image of ideal motherhood that a statue of her was set up in the Forum.

---

2. Terence *Andria* 473: *Iūna Lūcīna, fer opem, servā mē!* cries a woman in childbirth.

3. *Cornēlia Gracchōrum māter, cum Campāna mātrōna apud illam hospita ōrnāmenta sua pulcherrima illīus saeculī ostenderet, trāxit eam sermōne, dōnec ē scholā redīrent līberī, et "haec," inquit, "ōrnāmenta sunt mea."*

Vocābula Disposita/Ōrdināta

Nōmina
  1st
    cūnae, -ārum   crib
    fīliola, -ae   diminuitive of **fīlia**
  2nd
    colloquium, -ī   conversation
    domō (*abl.*)   from home
    fīliolus, -ī   diminuitive of **fīlius**
    officium, -ī   duty
    silentium, -ī   silence
    somnus, -ī   sleep
  3rd
    īnfāns, īnfantis (*m./f.*)   baby
    lac, lactis (*n.*)   milk
    mulier, mulieris (*f.*)   woman, wife
    nūtrīx, nūtrīcis (*f.*)   (wet) nurse
    sermō, sermōnis (*m.*)   conversation
  4th
    gradus, -ūs (*m.*)   step

Verba
  -āre (1)
    cūrō, cūrāre   care for
    for, fārī   speak
    postulō, postulāre   demand
  -ēre (2)
    careō, carēre (+*abl.*)   lack
    dēbeō, dēbēre   owe, ought
    decet, decēre (*impersonal*)   be fitting, proper
    maneō, manēre   remain
    sileō, silēre   be silent
  -ere (3)
    advehō, advehere   carry to
    alō, alere   nourish, raise
    colloquor, colloquī   converse
    dīligō, dīligere   love, cherish
    occurrō, occurrere   run up
    pergō, pergere   continue
    revertor, revertī   turn back
  -īre (4)
    vāgiō, vāgīre   wail (of babies)
  Irregular
    nōlō, nōlle   be unwilling, not want
    volō, velle   wish, want

Adiectīva

  1st/2nd (-us/er, -a, -um)

aliēnus, -a, -um	belonging to another
futūrus, -a, -um	future
necessārius, -a, -um	necessary
parvulus, -a, -um	small
praeteritus, -a, -um	past
ūmidus, -a, -um	humid, wet

Adverbia

crās	tomorrow
magis	more
minimē	not at all; very little
mox	soon, next
profectō	surely; for a fact
rārō	rarely

Praepositiōnēs

ad...versus (*prp. + acc.*)	toward
adversus (*prp. + acc.*)	toward
ūnā cum (*prp. + acc.*)	together with

Coniūnctiōnēs

sīve...sīve	whether...or

XXI. Pugna Discipulōrum

Rēs Grammaticae Novae

1. Verbs
   a. Perfect System
      i. Indicative, Active and Passive
      ii. Infinitive
   b. Perfect Passive Participle
   c. Varieties of the Perfect Stem
   d. *crēdere* + Dative Case
2. Nouns:
   a. Locative: *humī*
   b. Neuters of the 4th Declension
3. Pronouns: *aliquis, aliquid*
4. Adjectives:
   a. Substantive Adjectives
   b. Perfect Participles as Adjectives

Marcus Gets into a Fight

The chapter opens with Marcus coming home from school. He seems to be in a bad way: he is wet and dirty, and his nose is bleeding. Whatever can have happened on his way home? This is what you find out reading the chapter. You are reading Marcus's version of the story, and whether it is true or not, you can learn from it the verb forms that are used when you talk about an event that has already taken place.

Lēctiō Prīma (Section I)

Perfect System

We find a new form of the verb *ambulāre—ambulāvit*—in the explanation given for Marcus's wet clothes:

> *Mārcus per imbrem ambulāvit.*   Marcus walked/has walked through the rain. (ll.7–8)

This tense is called the **perfect**, in Latin *tempus praeteritum perfectum*, "past completed," as distinct from the **imperfect** tense or *praeteritum imperfectum*, "past not completed" (Cap. XIX).

The difference is that the imperfect, as we know, describes a state of affairs or an ongoing or repeated (habitual) action in the past, while the perfect tense tells about what once happened and is now finished. Compare the two preterites in the sentences:

> *Iūlia cantābat. Tum*   Julia was singing. Then Marcus hit
> *Mārcus eam pulsāvit!*   her!

The perfect can also denote the present result of a past action ("the present perfect"), e.g.:

> *Iam Iūlia plōrat, quia*   Julia is crying, because Marcus
> *Mārcus eam pulsāvit.*   has hit her.

Context will tell you which sense of the perfect is more appropriate.

The tenses you have thus far learned (present, imperfect, future) have been formed from the **present stem**. The perfect is formed by adding endings (often called "secondary" endings) to the **perfect stem**. In the first section, we find the secondary endings for the 3rd person: *-it* and *-ērunt*.

Examples:

> *Puerī per imbrem ambulāvērunt.* (ll.7–8)
> *Mārcus et Titus Sextum pulsāvērunt.* (ll.13–14)
> *Sordidus est quod humī iacuit.* (ll.19–20)
> *Et Mārcus et Sextus humī iacuērunt.* (ll.21–22)
> *Titus vērō Mārcum vocāre audīvit.* (ll.22–23)
> *nec vērō parentēs eum audīvērunt.* (ll.25–26)

Perfect Passive

The **present stem** has been the basis for the active and passive voice in all tenses you have learned so far (that is, the **present**, **future**, and **imperfect tenses**), e.g.:

> *Sextus Mārcum pulsat/pulsābit/pulsābat.*
> *Mārcus ā Sextō pulsātur/pulsābitur/pulsābātur.*

The active and passive of the **perfect tense**, however, are based on different stems. The passive voice is formed from the **perfect passive participle** in combination with the present of *esse* (*sum, es, est,* etc.). Since the participle is a verbal adjective, the ending of the participle agrees with the subject in gender, number, and case, e.g.:

> *Mārcus ā Sextō pulsātus est.* (l.11)
> *Sextus...pulsātus est.* (ll.14–15)

Iūlia ā Mārcō pulsāta est.
Puerī laudātī sunt.
Litterae ā Sextō scrīptae sunt.

The Perfect Stem: Active Voice

The personal endings of the perfect active are added to the **perfect stem**, which is the familiar **present stem** expanded or changed. Compare the following examples:

	Present Stem	Perfect Stem
1st	*pulsā-*	*pulsāv-*
2nd	*iacē-*	*iacu-*
4th	*audī-*	*audīv-*
3rd	*dīc-*	*dīx-*
3rd	*scrīb-*	*scrīps-*

As you can see, consonant-stems undergo even greater changes in the perfect tense. The varieties of the perfect stem may seem confusing at first, but the stem, in fact, can undergo a limited number of changes. For example:

- 1st and 4th conjugation verbs (present stems ending in *ā* or *ī*) regularly form the perfect stem by the addition of *v*, e.g.:
  pulsā-: pulsāv-
  audī-: audīv-
- 2nd conjugation verbs (stems in -*ē*) frequently drop the *ē* from the stem and add *v* (which becomes *u* when not following a vowel):
  iacē-: iacu-
- 3rd conjugation verbs (with present stems ending in a consonant) show a variety of perfect stem changes, e.g.:
  ▷ by adding *s* to the present stem, which can change the way the stem looks:
  In *scrīb-: scrīps-* voiced *b* changes to voiceless *p*
  In *dīc-: dīx-* only the spelling changes (*x = cs*)

You will learn more about the formation of the perfect passive stem, usually called the supine stem, in the next chapter.

Locative: *humī, rūrī*

You have met the locative form *domī*, "at home," in Cap. XV (l.81) and in the last chapter. In this chapter, we meet the locative *humī*, "on the ground." In Cap. XXVII, you will meet *rūrī*, "in the country(side)." These three nouns are used in the locative (in addition to the names of cities and towns, as you learned in Cap. VI).[1]

> Is <u>domī</u> est apud mātrem suam. (Cap. XV, l.81)
> Sordidus est quod <u>humī</u> iacuit. (ll.19–20)
> <u>In urbe</u> Iūlius semper in negōtiō est, sed <u>rūrī</u> in ōtiō cōgitat dē negōtiīs urbānīs. (Cap. XXVII, ll.65–67)

Lēctiō Altera (Section II)

Perfect Active System (continued)

The perfect active endings for the

- 1st person are *-ī* (sing.) and *-imus* (pl.)
- 2nd person are *-istī* (sing.) and *-istis* (pl.)

Examples:

> Ego illum pulsāvī! (l.40)
> Tūne sōlus Sextum pulsā<u>vistī</u>? (l.41)
> Ego et Titus eum pulsā<u>vimus</u>. (l.42)
> Vōs duo ūnum pulsā<u>vistis</u>? (l.43)

Summary of Endings for the Perfect Active:

	sing.	pl.
1.	*-ī*	*-imus*
2.	*-istī*	*-istis*
3.	*-it*	*-ērunt*

Neuters of the 4th Declension

The two nouns *cornū, -ūs* and *genū, -ūs* are among the rare **4th declension neuters**:

	sing.	pl.	sing.	pl.
nom.	*cornū*	*cornua*	*genū*	*genua*
acc.	*cornū*	*cornua*	*genū*	*genua*
gen.	*cornūs*	*cornuum*	*genūs*	*genuum*
dat.	*cornū*	*cornibus*	*genū*	*genibus*
abl.	*cornū*	*cornibus*	*genū*	*genibus*

---

1. In Cap. XXV, you will learn that this rule applies not only to cities and towns, but to small islands as well.

Aliquis, aliquid

Aliquis, aliquid is an indefinite pronoun, which refers to an undetermined person or thing (English "someone," "something"). It declines just like *quis, quid* with *ali-* added.

> *<u>Aliquis</u> pedibus sordidīs in solō mundō ambulāvit.* (ll.65–66)
> *Prīmum magister nōbīs <u>aliquid</u> recitāvit.* (ll.91–92)

Lēctiō Tertia (Section III)

Esse (continued)

The verb *esse* has a separate perfect stem *fu-*:

> *fu|ī   fu|imus*

Notā Bene: In the perfect, *esse* is completely regular (in fact, all Latin verbs are regular in the perfect system).

Examples:

> *In lūdōne quoque bonus puer <u>fuistī</u>?* (ll.82–83)
> *Profectō bonus puer <u>fuī</u>.* (l.84)
> *Mārcus dīcit, sē bonum puerum <u>fuisse</u>.* (l.85)
> *Malī discipulī <u>fuistis</u>!* (ll.104–105)
> *Certē malī discipulī <u>fuimus</u>.* (l.106)

Perfect Infinitive Active

In Cap. XI, you learned the accusative and infinitive construction using the present infinitive, e.g.:

> *Medicus "puerum dormīre" dīcit = "Puer," medicus inquit, "dormit."*

Dormī|re is called the **present infinitive** (Latin *īnfīnītīvus praesentis*) and corresponds to the present tense *dormi|t*. Compare lines 96–97 in this chapter:

> *Iūlius: "Mārcus dormīvit!"*
> *Iūlius "Mārcum dormī<u>visse</u>" dīcit.*

Dormīv|it is the perfect tense and the corresponding infinitive *dormīv|isse* is called the **perfect infinitive** (Latin *īnfīnītīvus perfectī*); it represents completed action and is formed by the addition of *-isse* to the perfect stem, e.g.:

- *intrāv|isse: Iūlius "Mārcum intrā<u>visse</u>" dīcit.* (l.73)
- *iacu|isse: Nōn dīcit, "eum humī iacu<u>isse</u>."* (ll.73–74)
- *fu|isse: Mārcus dīcit, "sē bonum puerum fu<u>isse</u>."* (l.85)

The **present infinitive** represents an action happening **at the same time** as the main verb, while the **perfect infinitive** represents an action **happening before** the main verb.

present infinitive: *-re*	perfect infinitive: *-isse*
pulsāre	pulsāvisse
iacēre	iacuisse
scrībere	scrīpsisse
audīre	audīvisse
esse	fuisse

Perfect Infinitive Passive

As you have learned (above), the perfect passive indicative is formed from the perfect passive participle and the indicative of esse. Similarly, the **perfect infinitive passive** is formed from the perfect passive participle with the infinitive *esse*:

laudātum esse	to have been praised
scrīptum esse	to have been written
audītum esse	to have been heard

In the accusative + infinitive construction, the participle agrees with the subject accusative, e.g:

> *Mārcus "sē ā magistrō laudā<u>tum</u> <u>esse</u>" dīcit.*
> *Aemilia litter<u>ās</u> ā Mārcō scrīpt<u>ās</u> <u>esse</u> crēdit.* (ll.121–122)
> *Intellegēbam <u>tē</u> nōn cornibus, sed pugnīs pulsā<u>tum</u> esse.* (ll.35–36)

Notā Bene:

- Perfect Infinitive Passive: neuter of the perfect passive participle + *esse*
  laudāt|um esse
- Accusative + Infinitive Construction: participle agrees with the subject
  Iūliam laudātam esse
  Mārcum et Quīntum laudātōs esse

Perfect Passive Participle as an Adjective

The perfect participle is also used as an attributive adjective; it is **passive** in meaning, as opposed to the **present participle** in *-ns,* which is active:

> *puer laudātus = puer quī laudātus est.*
> *puer laudāns = puer quī laudat.*

Adjectives as Substantives

The neuter plural of adjectives and pronouns is often used as a noun (substantively) in a general sense, e.g.:

multa	a great deal, many things (l.90)
omnia	everything, all things (l.95)
haec	these things (l.123)
et cētera	and all the rest

Crēdere

With the intransitive verb *crēdere*, the person whom you trust or whose words you believe is put in the dative:

Mihi crēde! (l.119)

Mārcō nōn crēdit. (l.140)

Cūr nōn crēdis fīliō tuō? (l.146)

Summary of Perfect

Perfect Active

personal endings			1st: *pulsā-*	*pulsāv-*
	sing.	pl.		sing.	pl.
1.	-ī	-imus	1.	*pulsāv -ī*	*pulsāv -imus*
2.	-istī	-istis	2.	*pulsāv -istī*	*pulsāv -istis*
3.	-it	-ērunt	3.	*pulsāv -it*	*pulsāv -ērunt*

2nd: *habē-*	*habu-*		3rd: *scrīb-*	*scrīps*
	sing.	pl.		sing.	pl.
1.	*habu -ī*	*habu -imus*	1.	*scrīps -ī*	*scrīps -imus*
2.	*habu -istī*	*habu -istis*	2.	*scrīps -istī*	*scrīps -istis*
3.	*habu -it*	*habu -ērunt*	3.	*scrīps -it*	*scrīps -ērunt*

4th: *audī-*	*audīv-*		Esse: *fu-*	
	sing.	pl.		sing.	pl.
1.	*audīv -ī*	*audīv -imus*	1.	*fu -ī*	*fu -imus*
2.	*audīv -istī*	*audīv -istis*	2.	*fu -istī*	*fu -istis*
3.	*audīv -it*	*audīv -ērunt*	3.	*fu -it*	*fu -ērunt*

Perfect Passive

<table>
<tr><td colspan="3">personal endings</td></tr>
<tr><td></td><td>sing.</td><td>pl.</td></tr>
<tr><td>1.</td><td>-t|us, -a sum</td><td>-t|i, -ae sumus</td></tr>
<tr><td>2.</td><td>-t|us, -a es</td><td>-t|i, -ae estis</td></tr>
<tr><td>3.</td><td>-t|us, -a, -um est</td><td>-t|i, -ae, -a sunt</td></tr>
</table>

<table>
<tr><td colspan="3">1st:</td><td colspan="3">2nd:</td></tr>
<tr><td>1.</td><td>pulsāt|us, -a</td><td>sum</td><td>1.</td><td>habit|us, -a</td><td>sum</td></tr>
<tr><td>2.</td><td>pulsāt|us, -a</td><td>es</td><td>2.</td><td>habit|us, -a</td><td>es</td></tr>
<tr><td>3.</td><td>pulsāt|us, -a, -um</td><td>est</td><td>3.</td><td>habit|us, -a, -um</td><td>est</td></tr>
<tr><td>1.</td><td>pulsāt |ī, -ae</td><td>sumus</td><td>1.</td><td>habit|ī, -ae</td><td>sumus</td></tr>
<tr><td>2.</td><td>pulsāt |ī, -ae</td><td>estis</td><td>2.</td><td>habit|ī, -ae</td><td>estis</td></tr>
<tr><td>3.</td><td>pulsāt |ī, -ae, -a</td><td>sunt</td><td>3.</td><td>habit|ī, -ae, -a</td><td>sunt</td></tr>
</table>

<table>
<tr><td colspan="3">3rd: scrīb-   scrīpt</td><td colspan="3">4th: audī-   audī-</td></tr>
<tr><td>1.</td><td>scrīpt|us, -a</td><td>sum</td><td>1.</td><td>audīt|us, -a</td><td>sum</td></tr>
<tr><td>2.</td><td>scrīpt|us, -a</td><td>es</td><td>2.</td><td>audīt|us, -a</td><td>es</td></tr>
<tr><td>3.</td><td>scrīpt|us, -a, -um</td><td>est</td><td>3.</td><td>audīt|us, -a, -um</td><td>est</td></tr>
<tr><td>1.</td><td>scrīpt||ī, -ae</td><td>sumus</td><td>1.</td><td>audīt|ī, -ae</td><td>sumus</td></tr>
<tr><td>2.</td><td>scrīpt||ī, -ae</td><td>estis</td><td>2.</td><td>audīt|ī, -ae</td><td>estis</td></tr>
<tr><td>3.</td><td>scrīpt||ī, -ae, -a</td><td>sunt</td><td>3.</td><td>audīt|ī, -ae, -a</td><td>sunt</td></tr>
</table>

Varieties of the Perfect Stem

- suffix *v/u* added to verb stem (*ama-v-*) or to the root (*hab-u-*)
- suffix *s* added to the root; *s* often changes the stem (*dūc-s-* = *dux-*)
- root perfect (see also Cap. XXIII):
  - ▷ the vowel of the root is lengthened; sometimes the vowel changes (*fac → fēc*)
  - ▷ the root is "reduplicated" by repeating the initial consonant of the verb, followed by a vowel (see also Cap. XXIII)
    - ○ usually *e*: *fallere → fefellisse*
    - ○ sometimes the root vowel: e.g., *mordēre, momordisse* (Cap. XXII)
    - ○ Sometimes, perfect and present stem appear identical: *ostendere → ostendisse*
- Some verbs have a perfect stem that cannot be easily understood just by the rules above:
  - ▷ verbs formed from a lost or imaginary stem (*petere → petīvī*, as if from *petīre*)
  - ▷ verbs that have features peculiar to the present stem

- o e.g., *scindere* → *scidisse* has a "nasal infix"[2] only in the present system
  - o inchoative verbs[3] with *-scō* lose the *-scō* in the perfect system (*cognōscere* → *cognōvisse*)
- Note on *emere* and compounds (Cap. XVIII):
  - ▷ *emere* and its compounds have a euphonic *p* before the perfect participle (try saying *emtum* and you'll find that the *p* in *emptum* is a very natural development from that combination)
  - ▷ *sūmere* is a compound of *emere*

Studia Rōmāna

Marcus and Sextus should not have been fighting—they should also not have been walking home on their own, but would have been accompanied by their *paedagōgī* as chaperones, part of whose job was to ensure safe (and street-brawling-free!) travel between home and school. Children enjoyed many games while not in school. From infancy, there were toys: rattles for babies (*crepundia*), pull-toys for toddlers and small children, and dolls (*pūpae*) for girls. In a famous simile, Vergil describes boys intently spinning tops through empty *ātria* (see Cap. V for the *ātrium*): "as sometimes, a top flying under the force of the hurled lash, a top which boys, intent on their game, send round in a circle through the empty atrium."[4] Horace (*Satires* 2.3.247–48) talks about building houses (*aedificāre casās*: "sand-castles"?), hitching mice to small carts (*plostellō adiungere mūrīs*), riding a stick-horse (*equitāre in harundine*), playing a game called *pār impār* ("odds and evens"), in which one player holds a number of small things—coins, nuts, etc.—in his hand and the other player has to guess whether it is an odd or even number. A player could also use small bones (knucklebones, *astragalī* Greek or *tālī* Latin) for *pār impār* as well as for other dice games (a version of our "jacks," for example). Reversible game boards (*tabulae lūsōriae*) have been found with a board for *lūdus lātrunculōrum* (*lātrunculus* means "robber" but also "pawn"—this seems to be a sort of chess game) on one side and on the other, *duodecim scrīpta* (or *lūdus duodecim scrīptōrum*, a kind of backgammon) played with *calculī*, or small stones, as game pieces.

   Although the Latin word is unattested, Roman children surely played hide-and-go-seek (Greek children called it ἀποδιδρασκίνδα). Ball games (*pīlae*) were popular with adults as well as children. The game *trigōn* (τρίγων, triangle, also called *pīla trigōnālis*: a kind of handball played by three people

---

2. The consonants *m* and *n* are sounds formed partially through the nose, and are therefore called nasals. *Tangere* (Cap. XI) shows both the nasal infix and reduplication: *tangere* → *tetigisse*. Note that the "*n*" disappears in the perfect and the reduplication *te* is added to the stem, whose vowel has shortened.

3. An inchoative verb is one that suggests that action of the verb is beginning or undergoing change.

4. *Aeneid* 7.378,-380: *ceu quondam tortō volitāns sub verbere turbō,/quem puerī magnō in gÿrō vacua ātria circum/intentī lūdō exercent.*

standing in a triangle shape) was very popular and often played in the baths. Pliny's villa at Laurentium included a ball court in the baths to accommodate players (called a *sphaeristērium* after the Greek word for ball, *sphaera*, σφαῖρα). Horace (*Satires* 1.6.126) says he played *trigōn* on the Campus Martius, a popular venue for games (as well as for military exercises). Playing at war seems to have been popular as well. In a letter (*Epistles* 1.18.60–64), Horace advises his ambitious young addressee, Lollius, not to turn up his nose at the enthusiasms of his influential friends (like hunting, a popular sport) so that he can write poetry instead. Lollius himself has played at mock battles on his father's estate, reenacting the (naval) Battle of Actium (31 BC), apparently on a lake with small boats, with slaves as soldiers.[5]

It will come as no surprise to learn that Roman society placed a very high value on good faith (*bona fidēs*, (Cap. XXXI). In a useful, if false, etymology, Cicero identifies *fidēs* with *fierī* (Cap. XVI): "*Fidēs*" *enim nōmen ipsum mihi vidētur habēre cum fit quod dīcitur* (*dē Rē Pūblicā* 4.7). Julius and Aemilia should not have to be wary of their son's sincerity. Marcus violates the foundations of propriety when he lies to his parents. In *dē Officiīs*, a book on proper values or duties addressed to his son Marcus (who was studying philosophy in Athens), that continued to be widely read until relatively recently, Cicero examines honorable conduct (*honestum*, Book I), advantageous behavior (*ūtile*, Book II), and the conflict between the two (Book III). Beyond all the quarrels of philosophers, he says, the old, simple proverb holds true: a good person is one with whom you can *in tenebrīs micāre*. *Micāre* is to flash up a number of fingers while another person simultaneously guesses the number; like "rock, paper, scissors," it is both a game and a way of making a decision. A character in the *Satyricon*, Petronius's first-century AD comic novel, includes the same proverb as proof of solid character: someone "upright, dependable, a friend to a friend, a guy with whom you could flash fingers in the dark" (*rēctus...certus, amīcus amīcō, cum quō audacter possēs* [= you could] *in tenebrīs micāre*, 44.8).

Vocābula Disposita/Ōrdināta

Nōmina
1st

causa, -ae	cause, reason
pugna, -ae	fight
tabella, -ae	writing tablet

2nd

humus, -ī (*f.*)	ground
humī (*loc.*)	on the ground
imperfectum, -ī	imperfect (tense)

---

5. *Interdum nūgāris rūre paternō:/partītur lintrēs exercitus, Actia pugna/tē duce per puerōs hostīlī mōre refertur;/adversārius est frāter, lacus Hadria, dōnec/alterutrum vēlōx Victōria fronde corōnet.*

perfectum, -ī (tempus)	perfect (tense)
porcus, -ī	pig
solum, -ī	soil, ground, floor
3rd	
bōs, bovis (*m./f.*)	ox
cruor, cruōris (*m.*)	gore, blood
sordēs, sordis (*f.*)	dirt
often pl. **sordēs, -ium**	
vestis, vestis (*f.*)	clothes, cloth
4th	
cornū, cornūs (*n.*)	horn
genū, genūs (*n.*)	knee

Verba

-āre (1)

(dubitō) dubitāre, dubitāvisse, dubitātum	doubt
(excūsō) excūsāre, excūsāvisse, excūsātum	excuse
(mūtō) mūtāre, mūtāvisse, mūtātum	change, exchange
(nārrō) nārrāre, nārrāvisse, nārrātum	relate, tell

-ere (3)

(cognōscō) cognōscere, -nōvisse, -nitum	get to know, recognize
(cōnspiciō) cōnspicere, cōnspexisse, cōnspectum	catch sight of, see
(crēdō) crēdere, -didisse, -ditum (*intr. + dat.*)	believe, trust, entrust
(fallō) fallere, fefellisse, falsum	deceive
(vincō) vincere, vīcisse, victum	defeat, overcome, win

-īre (4)

(mentior) mentīrī, mentītum	lie

Irregular

(sum) esse, fuisse	be
(āiō) ais, ait, āiunt	say

Adiectīva

1st/2nd (-us/er, -a, -um)

angustus, -a, -um	narrow
candidus, -a, -um	white, bright
falsus, -a, -um	false
indignus, -a, -um (*+ abl. of respect*)	unworthy, shameful
mundus, -a, -um	clean, neat
validus, -a, -um	strong

Prōnōmina
    aliquis, aliquid   someone, something

Adverbia
    interim   meanwhile

Coniūnctiōnēs
    postquam   after, since

Alia
    humī   on the ground (*locative*)
    ain' = ais ne?   you don't say? really?

XXII. Cavē Canem

Rēs Grammaticae Novae

1. Verbs
   a. Supine: Accusative and Ablative
   b. The Three Verbal Stems, or Principal Parts
   c. Relative Time of Infinitives
   d. *ferre*
2. Participles: Ablative Absolute
   a. Relative Time of Participles
3. Pronouns
   a. *quis quid* (from *aliquis, aliquid*)
   b. *iste, ista, istud*
4. Adverbs: *forās, forīs*

Cavē Canem

The picture over the chapter represents an ancient mosaic found inside the front door of a house in Pompēiī. The picture and the warning inscription *Cavē canem!* are evidence of the way the Romans tried to safeguard their houses against intruders. Every house was guarded by a doorkeeper (*ōstiārius* or *iānitor*), who often had a watchdog to help him. So, it is not easy for a stranger to be admitted to Julius's villa. First, he must wake the doorkeeper and then he has to convince him that his intentions are not hostile.

Lēctiō Prīma (Section I)

The Three Verbal Stems, or Principal Parts

From the three verbal stems are derived all forms of the verb:

> the **present stem**
> the **perfect stem**
> the **supine stem**

Knowing the three forms in which these stems are contained will enable you to **conjugate** (i.e., inflect) any Latin verb. These crucial forms are called the **Principal Parts**, given here as the three infinitives:

1. The present infinitive active, e.g., *scrīb|ere*
2. The perfect infinitive active, e.g., *scrīps|isse*
3. The perfect infinitive passive, e.g., *scrīpt|um esse*

The Supine Stem

The stem we use to form the perfect passive system and the supine (below) is usually called the **supine stem**. From this stem we also form the perfect passive participle as well as and the future active participle, as you learn in the next chapter (Cap. XXIII).

The supine stem is regularly (but not always) formed:

- by the addition of *t* to the present stem, e.g.:
  salūtā-: salūtāt-
  audī-: audīt-
  dīc-: dict-
- When phonetics dictate, we find *s* instead of *t*:
  ▷ *dt/tt → s* (usually *ss* after a short vowel and *s* after a long vowel)
  claudere → clausum
  ▷ *gt → ct*
  augēre → auctum
- In *ē*-stems *ē* is changed to *i,* e.g.:
  terrē-: territ-
- There are several other irregularities, especially in 3rd conjugation verbs, where the addition of *t* may cause changes by assimilation, e.g.:
  scrīb-: scrīpt- (*p* is voiceless like *t*)
  claud-: claus- (*dt > tt > ss >s*)

Supine

The supine (Latin *supīnum*) is a verbal noun used only in the accusative (in -*um*) and the ablative (in -*ū*).

Accusative (-*um*)

In this chapter the letter carrier (*tabellārius*) tries to assure the *ōstiārius* with the words:

Ego nōn veniō vīllam oppugnā*tum* sīcut hostis, nec pecūniam
postulā*tum* veniō (ll.33–34).

Oppugnātum and *postulātum* are examples of the **accusative supine**. In the accusative, the supine:

- ends in -*tum*
- is found with verbs of motion, e.g., *īre* and *venīre*
- expresses purpose

Other examples of the **accusative supine** in this chapter are:

salūtātum venīre	to come to greet (in order to greet, with the purpose of greeting) (l.49)
dormītum īre	to go to sleep (in order to sleep, with the purpose of sleeping) (l.50)
ambulātum exīre	to go out to walk (in order to walk, with the purpose of walking) (l.51)
lavātum īre	to go to wash (in order to wash, with the purpose of washing) (l.52)

Ablative (-*ū*)

In addition to the accusative expressing purpose with verbs of motion, the supine is found in the ablative. The **ablative supine** is a rare form used to modify certain adjectives, particularly *facilis* and *difficilis*. The ablative shows the respect in which the adjectives apply (cf. the ablative of respect in Caps. XI and XIX).

The following forms *dictū* and *audītū* are examples of the **ablative supine**:

Nōmen meum nōn est facile dictū. (l.43) = *Nōn est facile meum nōmen dīcere.*
Vōx tua difficilis est audītū. (l.46) = *Difficile est vōcem tuam audīre.*
    Id facilius est dictū quam factū. (l.81) = *Facilius est dīcere quam facere.*

The Supine Versus the Perfect Passive Participle

The **supine**:

- exists in two unchanging forms: the accusative and the ablative
- will always end in -*um* (accusative) or -*ū* (ablative)

The **perfect passive participle**:

- by itself acts as an adjective
- creates the passive voice of the past tense when combined with a finite form of *esse*
- creates the perfect infinitive passive when combined with the infinitive *esse*

    As an **adjective**, the participle exhibits all the forms of a 1st/2nd declension adjective (like *bonus, bona, bonum*). It will agree with the word it modifies in gender, number, and case.

> *Discipulī, ā magistrō*   The students, warned by the teacher,
> *monitī, silent.*   are being quiet.

The perfect passive participle combined with the present tense of *esse* (*sum, es*, etc.) forms the perfect passive tense; the participle will agree with its subject.

> *Discipulī ā magistrō monitī*   The students were warned by the
> *sunt et silent.*   teacher and are being quiet.

The simple perfect infinitive passive (to have been + perfect passive) consists of the neuter singular of the perfect passive participle + the present infinitive of *esse*.

> *monitum esse*   to have been warned

In indirect statement, the perfect infinitive passive must agree with its subject.

> *Puerī sciēbant sē monitōs*   The boys knew they had been
> *esse.*   warned.

The Three Verbal Stems in the Vocabulary

1. The margins of *Familia Romana* and the vocabulary at the back of this book give three verbal stems, or principal parts, as they are commonly called:
   - o present infinitive active
   - o perfect infinitive active
   - o supine (accusative)

2. At the end of each chapter in this book, however, four principal parts will be listed in the vocabulary:
   - o 1st person singular present indicative active
   - o present infinitive active
   - o perfect infinitive active
   - o supine (accusative)

Notā Bene:

- The perfect infinitive passive will be listed without *esse*.
- The perfect infinitive passive will be missing if the verb has no passive, e.g.: *posse potuisse*.
- The deponent verbs show the passive present and perfect infinitives, e.g.: *loquī locūtum esse*.

The forms show various stem mutations, e.g.:

- vowel lengthening, e.g.:
  emere, ēmisse, ēmptum
  venīre, vēnisse
- loss of *n* and *m*, e.g.:
  scindere, scidisse, scissum
  rumpere, rūpisse, ruptum
- reduplication (doubling) of syllables in the perfect, e.g.:
  pellere, pepulisse, pulsum
- occasionally an unchanged perfect stem, e.g.:
  solvere, solvisse, solūtum

To learn such stem varieties, a new exercise is now introduced in PĒNSVM A in Lingua Latina, where the missing perfect and supine stems are to be inserted in the verbs listed. Symbols used: [~] for perfect stem and [≈] for supine stem.

The principal parts (from the margins) to be learned in this chapter follow (the 1st person singular present active indicative is given in parentheses):

(aperiō) aperīre, aperuisse, apertum
(claudō) claudere, clausisse, clausum
(dīcō) dīcere, dīxisse, dictum
(emō) emere, ēmisse, ēmptum
(pellō) pellere, pepulisse, pulsum
(possum) posse, potuisse
(scindō) scindere, scidisse, scissum
(solvō) solvere, solvisse, solūtum
(sūmō) sūmere, sumpsisse, sumptum
(terreō) terrēre, terruisse, territum
(veniō) venīre, vēnisse
(vinciō) vincīre, vīnxisse, vīnctum

Quis, Quid from *Aliquis, Aliquid* (after *sī, num, nisi, nē*)

After *sī, nisi* (Cap. XV), *num,* and *nē,* the indefinite pronoun *aliquis, aliquid* (someone, something) is shortened to *quis quid.* In the following examples, the pronouns *quis, quid* are not interrogative, but **indefinite** (= *aliquis*):

Sī quis vīllam intrāre vult (l.7)	"if anyone"
Num quis hīc est? (ll.27–28)	i.e., not "who," but whether "anyone" is there.
Num quid tēcum fers? (ll.104–105)	i.e., not "what," but "anything" or "something."

If you find mnemonics useful, a good one for this rule is: "after *sī, nisi, num,* and *nē,* all the *alis* go away." Compare these examples:

Aliquis intrāre vult.	Someone wants to enter.

Sī quis intrāre vult.   If someone wants to enter.
Num quis intrāre vult?   Surely no one wants to enter?

Recēnsiō: Declension of *Quis, Quid*

quis	quid	quī	quae	quae
quem	quōs	quās	quae	quae
cuius	cuius	quōrum	quārum	quōrum
cui	cui	quibus	quibus	quibus
quō	quō	quibus	quibus	quibus

Lēctiō Altera (Section II)

Iste, ista, istud

The demonstrative pronoun *iste, -a, -ud* (declined like *ille, -a, -ud*) refers to something connected with the person addressed (2nd person): Tlepolemus says *iste canis* about the doorkeeper's dog (l.86, "that dog of yours") and talking about Tlepolemus's cloak, the doorkeeper says *istud pallium* (l.103).

iste	ista	istud	istī	istae	ista
istum	istam	istud	istōs	istās	ista
istīus	istīus	istīus	istōrum	istārum	istōrum
istī	istī	istī	istīs	istīs	istīs
istō	istā	istō	istīs	istīs	istīs

Recēnsiō

Review the following pronouns/demonstrative adjectives

hic, haec, hoc	this one (over here by me)
iste, ista, istud	that one (over there by you)
ille, illa, illud	that one (over there by him)
is, ea, id	he, she, it/this/that
ipse, ipsa, ipsum	himself, herself, itself

Because of relative nearness of the demonstratives to the speaker (i.e., *hic* → her by me, *ipse* → there by you and *ille* → there by him), they are sometimes called demonstratives of the 1st (*hic, haec, hoc*), 2nd (*ipse, ipsa, ipsum*) and 3rd (*ille, illa, illud*) persons.

Ablative Absolute (continued from Cap. XVII)

Compare the following sentences:

Iānitōre dormiente, canis vigilāns iānuam cūstōdit. (l.23)
Cane vīnctō, tabellārius intrat. (l.119)

Iānitōre dormiente is the ablative absolute with the present participle, which expresses what is happening now, i.e., at the same time (= *dum iānitor dormit…*, "while…").

Cane vīnctō is the ablative absolute with the perfect participle, which expresses what has been done (= *postquam canis vīnctus est…*, "after…").

Relative Time of Participles and Infinitives

The tense of the participle is relative to the main verb:

- **present** participle is happening **at the same time** as the main verb
- **perfect** participle happened **before** the main verb

The English rendering in the sentences below demonstrates the time relationship of the main verb and the participle:

Iānitōre dormiente, canis vigilāns iānuam cūstōdit.	While the doorkeeper sleeps/is sleeping, the watchful dog guards the door.
Iānitōre dormiente, canis vigilāns iānuam cūstōdiebat.	While the doorkeeper slept/was sleeping, the watchful dog was guarding the door.
Cane vīnctō, tabellārius intrat.	When the dog is tied up, the letter carrier enters.
Cane vīnctō, tabellārius intrāvit.	When the dog had been tied up, the letter carrier entered.

The same time relation holds between main verbs and infinitives:

- present infinitive/participle means "same time as main verb"
- perfect infinitive/participle means "time before the main verb"

Adverbs *forās, forīs*

In this section, we meet two new adverbs which both mean "outside":

- *forīs*: place where (cf. *ibi, hīc, illīc*)

    Tandem iānitor forēs aperit et Tlēpolemum forīs in imbre stantem videt (ll.56–57)

    "Manē forīs!" inquit iānitor. (l.68)

- *forās*: place to which (cf. *hūc, illūc*)

    Prius vincī canem et sine mē intrāre! Nōlī iterum mē forās in imbrem pellere! (l.115)

    "Non ego," inquit, "sed hic canis tē forās pepulit." (ll.116–117)

Recēnsiō: Ferre

In this chapter we meet the full conjugation of the irregular verb *ferre* (ll.105ff.). As you can see from the paradigm below, only the present tense of *ferre* is irregular: it lacks a vowel before the personal ending in the 2nd and 3rd persons singular (*fers, fert*), and in the 2nd person plural (*fertis*). In the other tenses, it is completely regular:

Present	Imperfect	Future
ferō	*ferēbam*	*feram*
fers	*ferēbās*	*ferēs*
fert	*ferēbat*	*feret*
ferimus	*ferēbāmus*	*ferēmus*
fertis	*ferēbātis*	*ferētis*
ferunt	*ferēbant*	*ferent*

Studia Rōmāna

The letter carrier (*tabellārius*) is (justifiably!) afraid of the watchdog. In his treatise on agriculture, Columella (first century AD) praises the virtues of the watchdog. What servant is more loving of his master? What companion is more loyal? What guard is more incorruptible? What more wakeful sentinel can be found? What, in short, avenger or defender is more steadfast? (*quis famulus amantior dominī, quis fidēlior comes, quis custos incorruptior, quis excubitor inuenīrī potest uigilantior, quis denique ultor aut uindex constantior? dē Rē Rusticā, 7.12*).

The privacy of the home is guarded not only by the dog, but also by the slaves, including the *iānitor* and the *ōstiārius*. In Book 3 of *dē Ōrātōre*, Cicero tells a funny story about the poet Ennius visiting Scipio Nasica (second century BC): When Nasica arrived at the house of the poet Ennius and asked to see Ennius, a female slave answered that Ennius was not at home. He had the feeling that she had spoken on her master's orders and that Ennius was within. After a few days, Ennius went to see Nasica and asked for him at the door; Nasica cried, "I'm not here!" Ennius then said, "Really? Do I not recognize your voice?" At this, Nasica replied, "You are an impudent man! When I asked after you, I believed your slave woman when she claimed that you were not at home. You do not believe me in person?" For the most part, this is a story you can read! The parts you can't are translated in parentheses. Cicero is talking about jokes where someone seems to not know what he knows—like that one of Nasica (*ut illud Nāsīcae*)

> *Ut illud Nāsīcae, quī cum ad poētam Ennium vēnisset* (when he had come), *eīque ab ostiō quaerentī Ennium ancilla dīxisset* (the female slave had said) *domī nōn esse. Nāsīca sēnsit illam dominī iussū dīxisse et illum intus esse; paucīs post diēbus cum ad Nāsīcam vēnisset* (when

he had come), *Ennius et eum ad iānuam quaereret* (and was asking for), *exclāmat Nāsīca domī nōn esse. Tum Ennius, "Quid? Ego nōn cognoscō vōcem," inquit "tuam?" Hic Nāsīca, "Homō es impudēns: ego cum tē quaererem* (when I asked for you) *ancillae tuae crēdidī tē domī nōn esse, tū mihi nōn crēdis ipsī?"*

Without a post office—never mind a telephone or email—how did the Romans send messages to each other? They often called upon a traveler (particularly if known to them) to take a message. Cicero writes to his friend Marcus Marcellus that he was sending a second letter so soon after a first because there was a carrier at hand and he couldn't pass up the opportunity (*Ad Fam.* 4.9.1). In a letter to his friend Atticus, he alludes to the difficulties of the job of letter-carrier; Atticus's freedman Philogenes had just made a long and rather unsafe journey to bring Cicero a letter (*Ad Att.* 5.20.8: *perlonga et nōn satis tūta via*). Friends, freedmen, slaves: all were pressed into service of carrying letters—generally on foot. Cicero had slaves who seemed reserved expressly for sending letters (*domesticii tabellāriī, Ad Fam.* 2.7.3).

Augustus established what would become the *cursus pūblicus*: a conveyance of official messages from the emperor, magistrates, or the military. Its original purpose was military: to speed communication between Rome and the provinces; "first he set up regular stations of young men (later, carriages) at short distances along the military roads" (Suetonius, *Augustus.* 49.3: *iuvenēs prīmō modicīs intervallīs per mīlitārīs viās, dehinc vehicula disposuit*).

Vocābula Disposita/Ōrdināta

Nōmina
  1st

catēna, -ae	chain

  2nd

aurum, -ī	gold
faber, fabrī	craftsman
lignum, -ī	wood
pallium, -ī	cloak
tabellārius, -ī	letter carrier
supīnum, -ī	supine (grammar)

  3rd

cardō, cardinis (*m.*)	hinge
foris, foris (*f.*)	folding door
iānitor, iānitōris (*m.*)	door keeper = **ōstiārius**
imāgō, imāginis (*f.*)	picture, image
līmen, līminis (*n.*)	threshold

Verba

-āre (1)

| (arbitror) arbitrārī, arbitrātum | think, judge |
| (rogitō) rogitāre, rogitāvisse, rogitātum | keep asking |

-ēre (2)

(caveō) cavēre, cāvisse, cautum	beware
(dērīdeō) dērīdēre, dērīsisse, dērīsum	laugh at
(moneō) monēre, monuisse, monitum	advise, warn
(mordeō) mordēre, momordisse, morsum	bite
(removeō) removēre, remōvisse, remōtum	remove
(retineō) retinēre, retinuisse, retentum	hold on to
(terreō) terrēre, terruisse, territum	frighten

-ere (3)

(accēdō) accēdere, accessisse, accessum	approach
(admittō) admittere, admīsisse, admissum	let in
(cēdō) cēdere, cēssisse, cessum (*intr. + dat.*)	yield
(fremō) fremere, fremuisse, fremitum	growl
(pellō) pellere, pepulisse, pulsum	strike, drive out
(prehendō) prehendere, prendisse, prēnsum	grab hold of
(prōcēdō) prōcēdere, prōcessisse, processum	move forward
(recēdō) recēdere, recessisse, recessum	withdraw
(resistō) resistere, restitisse (*intr. + dat.*)	resist
(rumpō) rumpere, rūpisse, ruptum	break
(scindō) scindere, scidisse, scissum	rip, tear
(sinō) sinere, sīvisse, situm	allow
(solvō) solvere, solvisse, solūtum	loose (also pay)
(tremō) tremere, tremuisse	tremble

-īre (4)

(cūstōdiō) cūstōdīre, cūstōdīvisse, cūstōdītum	guard
(saliō) salīre, saluisse	leap
(vinciō) vincīre, vīnxisse, vīnctum	bind

Irregular
   (ferō) ferre, tulisse, lātum   carry, bear

Adiectīva
  1st/2nd (-us/er, -a, -um)
    aureus, -a , -um   golden
    ferreus, -a, -um   iron
    ligneus, -a, -um   wooden
  3rd
    ferōx (ferōcis)   fierce, ferocious

Prōnōmina
    iste, ista, istud   that one (of yours)
    quis, quid   shortened from **aliquis, aliquid**

Adverbia
    anteā   before
    forās   outside (toward)
    forīs   outside (place where)
    nūper   recently
    posteā   after
    prius   before
    quīn   why not? in fact
    scīlicet   naturally, of course
    sīcut   just as
    tandem   finally

Praepositiōnēs
    extrā (*prp. + acc.*)   outside
    intrā (*prp. + acc.*)   inside, within

XXIII. Epistula Magistrī

Rēs Grammaticae Novae

1. Verbs
   a. Participles
      i.   Future Participle
      ii. *Eō, īre*: Present Participle and Summary
   b. Infinitives
      i.   Future Active Infinitive
      ii. Future Passive Infinitive
   c. *pudēre* (impersonal)
   d. Perfect Stem, Continued (*ferre*, root perfects, reduplicated)
   e. Principal Parts

Julius Responds to Diodorus's Letter

At the end of Cap. XVIII, an angry Diodorus (the schoolmaster) wrote a letter to Marcus's father. In this chapter, you find out what is in that letter. The reproduction heading the chapter shows the kind of handwriting the ancient Romans used. Compare this with the text on page 180 of Lingua Latina, and you will have no difficulty in deciphering the script.

Lēctiō Prīma (Section I)

Recēnsiō: Participles (Sections I and II)

The first two readings in this chapter offer a good review of the participles and infinitives you have learned thus far:

- Present participle in an ablative absolute: *Tacente Mārcō...* (l.55)
- Present participle: *Interim Mārcus pallidus et <u>tremēns</u> patrem <u>legentem</u> spectat.* (ll.34–36)
- Perfect participle: *vidēsne <u>nōmen</u> "Sextī" litterīs plānīs in parte superiōre <u>īnscrīptum</u>?* (ll.63–64)
- Present infinitive active: *Nōlō hās litterās <u>legere</u>.* (l.15)

- Present infinitive passive: *Tūne putās tē hīs litterīs <u>laudārī</u>, Mārce?* (ll.49–50)
- Perfect infinitive active: *Magister plānīs verbīs scrībit, "tē discipulum improbissimum <u>fuisse</u> ac foedē et prāvē <u>scrīpsisse!</u>"* (ll.60–61)
- Perfect infinitive passive: *Tantum sciō epistulam Tūsculō <u>missam</u> et ā tabellāriō ad tē <u>lātam esse</u>.* (ll.8–9)

Ferre

The principal parts of the irregular verb *ferre <u>tulisse</u> <u>lātum</u>* come from different stems and must be memorized. Examples:

> *Ecce epistula quam illinc ad tē <u>tulit</u>.* (ll.3–4)
> *Tantum sciō epistulam Tūsculō missam et ā tabellāriō ad tē <u>lātam esse</u>.* (ll.8–9)

Lēctiō Altera (Section II)

Pudēre (Impersonal)

When Marcus has been caught cheating, his father says, *"Nōnne <u>tē pudet</u> hoc fēcisse?"* (l.79)

The **impersonal** verb *pudet*:

- tells that a feeling of shame affects someone
- the person affected is in the accusative, e.g.:
  mē pudet "I feel ashamed"
- the cause of the feeling of shame can be expressed by an infinitive, as above (l.79), or by a genitive, e.g.:
  Puerum pudet factī suī. (l.82)

Pudēre (it causes shame) is one of a few impersonal verbs[1] that take:

- The accusative of person concerned and either of the following:
  - ▷ genitive of person/thing affected
  - ▷ infinitive that completes the thought

examples:

> *Pudet mē pigritiae meae.*   I'm embarrassed about my laziness.
> *Pudet mē hoc dīcere.*   I'm ashamed to say this.

---

1.   The other verbs are *piget* (it causes revulsion or displeasure), *paenitet* (it causes regret), *miseret* (it causes pity) and *taedet* (it causes boredom).

Lēctiō Tertia (Section III)

The Future Participle

Julius has to answer the letter. So, after putting Marcus in his place, he says, *"Iam epistulam scrīptūrus sum."* (l.125) He could have said, *"Iam epistulam scrībam,"* using the ordinary future tense of *scrībere* (*scrībam*), for *scrīptūrus sum* is merely an extended form (or periphrasis[2]) of the future, which serves to express what someone intends to do or is on the point of doing; it is composed of the present of *esse* and *scrīptūrus,* which is the **future participle** (Latin *participium futūrī*) of *scrībere.*

The **difference** between the simple future and the periphrasis of the future participle with a form of *esse* is one of tone. The simple future means the speaker intends to do something at some point in the future (which point can be made more by use of an adverb or time expression), while the future participle plus *esse* suggests that the subject is on the point of acting.

The future participle:

- is formed by adding ≈*ūr|us, -a, -um* to the participle/supine stem, e.g.:
  pugnāt|ūr|us from *pugnāre*
  pārit|ūr|us from *pārēre*
  dormīt|ūr|us from *dormīre*
- as an adjective means "about to X," "intending to X"
- as an adjective agrees with its noun in gender, number, and case
- combined with *esse* has a verbal force pointing to the immediate future

examples:

pugnātūrus est	he is about to fight, intending to fight, he will fight
pāritūrus est	he about to obey, intending to obey, he will obey
dormītūra est	she is about to sleep, intending to sleep, she will sleep
scrīptūrī sumus	we are about to write, intending to write, we will write

The future participle of *esse* is *futūr|us,* a form you know already from the expression *tempus futūrum.* All of these forms can be seen in context in Marcus's plea to his parents (ll.84–87):

> *Certē malus puer fuī, sed posthāc bonus puer <u>futūrus sum</u>: semper vōbīs <u>pāritūrus sum</u>, numquam <u>pugnātūrus sum</u> in viā nec umquam in lūdō <u>dormītūrus sum</u>.*

---

2.   A grammatical periphrasis uses two words to express a relationship instead of a simple inflected form.

Future Active Infinitive

The **future active infinitive** (*īnfīnītīvus futūrī*) is composed of the future active participle and *esse*. In the following sentence, *scrīptūrum esse* is a future infinitive. Compare Julius's direct remark that he is about to write a letter with the reported statement:

> *"Epistulam scrīptūrus sum."* (l.125)
> *Iūlius dīcit, "sē epistulam scrīptūrum esse."* (ll.125–126)

Other examples are:

> *futūrum esse*   *pugnātūrum esse*
> *pāritūrum esse*   *dormītūrum esse*

These infinitives are all used in the report of Marcus's promises: (ll.89–93)

> *Mārcus "sē malum puerum fuisse" fatētur ac simul prōmittit "sē posthāc bonum puerum futūrum esse, semper sē parentibus pāritūrum esse nec umquam in viā pugnātūrum nec in lūdō dormītūrum esse"—id quod saepe antehāc prōmīsit!*

The future active infinitive (summary):

- is comprised of the future active participle and the infinitive of the verb to be (*esse*)
- when used as a simple infinitive, the participle is neuter and singular:
  dormītūrum esse   to be about to sleep
  ductūrum esse   to be about to lead
- when used in indirect statement, the participle agrees with its subject:
  Puerī dīcunt sē dormītūrōs esse.   The boys say that they are about to go to sleep.

  Puellae dīcunt sē dormītūrās esse.   The girls say that they are about to go to sleep.

Future Passive Infinitive

The **future passive infinitive** is comprised of the supine and the present passive infinitive to the verb to go (*īrī*). This form never changes: it is always the supine + *īrī*. For example:

> *Aemilia Mārcum ā Iūliō*   Aemilia thinks Marcus will be
> *verberātum īrī putat.*   beaten by Julius. (ll.114–115)

> *Ego eum nec mūtātum esse nec posthāc mūtātum īrī crēdō.* (will be changed) (ll.118–119)

The supine, you will remember from the previous chapter (XXII), expresses purpose. When Julius gets up to go, Aemilia suspects mischief and (using the supine with *īre* to express purpose) asks, *"Mārcumne verberātum īs?"* (ll.113–114).

In the accusative and infinitive construction, her misgivings could be expressed by changing the direct *verberātum īs* to the active infinitive and the supine:

> *Aemilia Iūlium Mārcum verberātum īre putat.*

In practice, however, to avoid the ambiguity of two accusatives the passive form is preferred, hence:

> *Aemilia Mārcum ā patre verberā<u>tum īrī</u> putat.* (ll.114–115)

Notā Bene: The supine does not change, regardless of the subject:

> *Dīc eī, "respōnsum meum crās ā Mārcō trādi<u>tum īrī</u>."* (ll.132–133)
> *Dīc eī, "epistulam meam crās ā Mārcō trādi<u>tum īrī</u>."*

Summary: Future Participles and Infinitives

The **future active participle**:
- can be used just as an adjective
  - ▷ exhibits all the forms of a 1st/2nd declension adjective (like *bonus, bona, bonum*)
  - ▷ agrees with the word it modifies in gender, number, and case
- combined with a verb, creates a periphrasis of the future
  - ▷ can be used instead of the future tense
  - ▷ agrees with its subject
- combined with *esse*, creates the **future infinitive active**
  - ▷ neuter singular of the future active participle + the present infinitive of *esse*
  - ▷ in indirect statement, the participle must agree with its subject

The **future passive infinitive**:
- consists of the accusative of the supine and *īrī*
- never changes in form
- is relatively rare in Latin

Recēnsiō: Summary of Infinitives and Participles

Now you have all the infinitives:
- present active and passive
- perfect active and passive
- future active and passive

You also have almost all the participles:

- present active (there is no present passive)
- perfect passive
- perfect active (deponent verbs only: passive forms but active meaning)
- future active
- the gerundive (Cap. XXXIII) is sometimes called the future passive participle

Again, the tense, or time, of infinitives and participles is purely relative: it does not show absolute time. It is relative to the tense of the main verb:

- The present infinitive/participle shows time **simultaneous** with the main verb.
- The perfect infinitive/participle shows time **prior** to the main verb.
- The future infinitive/participle shows time **subsequent** to the main verb.

Summary: Infinitives

	Active	Passive
Present	*-āre*	*-ārī*
	-ēre	*-ērī*
	-ere	*-ī*
	-īre	*-īrī*
Past	Perfect stem + *isse*	Perfect passive participle + *esse*
Future	Supine stem + *ūrum esse*	Supine + *īrī*

Summary: Participles

For contrast, here is a summary of participles.

	Active	Passive
Present	*-āns*	
	-ēns	
	-ēns/iēns	
	-iēns	
Past	See *notā bene*, note 1 below	*-tus, -ta, -tum*
		See *notā bene*, note 2 below
Future	Supine stem + *-ūrus, -ūra, -ūrum*	

Notā Bene:

1. The perfect participle of Latin deponents can be used as the equivalent of the missing perfect active participle, e.g., *locūtus*: "having spoken."

2. The *-tus, -ta, -tum* of the perfect passive participle can undergo changes in verbs that end in certain consonants. For example, the verb *claudere* has *clausus, -a, -um*, which comes from *claudtus, -a, -um*

Eō, īre

The present participle of *īre* looks regular enough: *i|ēns*, but the declension is irregular: acc. *eunt|em*, gen. *eunt|is*, etc. So also compounds, e.g., *red-īre*, part. *red-iēns, -eunt|is*. Examples in ll.106–107.

Present Participle

sing.	m./f.	n.
nom.	*iēns*	*iēns*
acc.	*euntem*	*iēns*
gen.	*euntis*	*euntis*
dat.	*euntī*	*euntī*
abl.	*eunte/ī*	*eunte/ī*

pl.	m./f.	n.
nom.	*euntēs*	*euntia*
acc.	*euntēs*	*euntia*
gen.	*euntium*	*euntium*
dat.	*euntibus*	*euntibus*
abl.	*euntibus*	*euntibus*

Recēnsiō: Forms of the Perfect Stem

In Cap. XXI, you learned that in addition to adding *u/v* to the stem (with or without the stem vowel: *amāvisse/habuisse*), or *s* (e.g., *dīcere, dīxisse < dīcsisse*), perfects are formed from the root of the verb or from the reduplicated root.

Root Perfects: A "root perfect" is a verb that forms the perfect tense by adding the endings directly to the root of the verb without the addition of any intervening tense sign (e.g., *v* or *s*). Root perfects can show:

- vowel lengthening
  legere, lēgisse, lēctum
  fugere, fūgisse
- vowel change
  facere, fēcisse

Reduplicated Perfects: A perfect stem is called reduplicated when it repeats the initial consonant of the verb, as in the verb *dare*. *Dare* is an unusual looking verb because the stem is basically *d*. In the perfect tense, the stem repeats the *d*, separated from the original *d* of the root by another vowel (*d* + *e* + *d*) and adds the endings: *dare <u>de</u>disse*. *Trā-dere* (= *trāns* + *dare*) and *per-dere* (= *per* + *dare*) are compounds of *dare*, which explains the perfect *trā-<u>di</u>disse* and *per-<u>di</u>disse*.

> *perdere, perdidī, perditum*
> *trādere, trādidī, trāditum*

Principal Parts

The principal parts (from the margins) to be learned in this chapter are (the 1st person singular present active indicative is given in parentheses):

> (*afferō* < *ad* + *ferō*) *afferre, attulisse, allātum*
> (*dēbeō*) *dēbēre, dēbuisse, dēbitum*
> (*dūcō*) *dūcere, dūxisse, ductum*
> (*faciō*) *facere, fēcisse, factum*
> (*ferō*) *ferre, tulisse, lātum*
> (*fugiō*) *fugere, fūgisse*
> (*inclūdō* < *in* + *claudō*) *inclūdere, inclūsisse, inclūsum*
> (*legō*) *legere, lēgisse, lēctum*
> (*mereō*) *merēre, meruisse, meritum*
> (*mittō*) *mittere, mīsisse, missum*
> (*ostendō*) *ostendere, ostendisse*
> (*perdō*) *perdere, perdidisse, perditum*
> (*trādō*) *trādere, trādidisse, trāditum*

Recēnsiō: Impersonal Verbs

decet	it is fitting
licet	it is permitted
necesse est	it is necessary
oportet	it is right (morally right)
opus est	it is needed

Studia Rōmāna

We begin letters with Dear X and end with "sincerely," "love" or some similar signal that closes our letters. Roman letter writers followed a pattern similar to that of Diodorus in his letter to Julius: *Diodōrus Iūliō salūtem dīcit*. The name of the writer comes first in the nominative followed by the name of the recipient in the dative and a greeting. Other greetings (sometimes abbreviated):

- *sī valēs, bene est, ego valeō* = s.v.b.e.e.v.
- *sī valēs, bene est* = s.v.b.e.

The younger Seneca (55 BC–AD 39), in a letter (14) to his young friend Lucilius, wrote, "Our ancestors had a custom, preserved up to my time, to add these words to the beginning of a letter: '*sī valēs bene est, ego valeō,*' We say—correctly—'*si philosophāris, bene est.*' For this is precisely what it means to be well"[3] (*philosophārī*: to apply oneself to philosophy).

Diodorus's closing, *Scrībēbam Tusculī kalendīs lūniīs,* demonstrates another common letter convention, giving the place and date of composition. Diodorus uses the imperfect because he is writing from the perspective of the reader. This is called the epistolary imperfect.

When Julius is handed the letter, he immediately recognizes Diodorus's seal (*obsignāre*: seal a letter). Both tablets and papyrus scolls could be sealed; the seal not only identified the sender, but kept the letter private. During the tumultuous late republic, Cicero joked in a letter that he was afraid to write of political matters lest the papyrus itself betray him (*Ad Att.* 2.20): "I will write to you briefly about affairs of state; for at this point, I'm anxious that the very paper I write on might betray us. And so, in the future, if I have more that I must write about, I will conceal it with allegories."[4]

Cicero often wrote his letters to his friends himself, without the services of his secretary. On one occasion, he explained to Atticus that the different handwriting was a clear sign of how busy he was: he had his *librārius* write the letter while he dictated (*Ad Att.* 4.16: *Occupātiōnum meārum vel hoc signum erit quod epistula librārī manū est*). On another occasion, he reveals the mystery of the nearly illegible handwriting in a letter he had written to his brother Quintus (*Ad Quīntum Fratrem,* 2.15): "No, I wasn't busy, upset or angry—just careless. It's my habit to assume that whatever pen I pick up is a good one." He opens the letter with a nice representation of what one did to prepare to write a letter. His reed pen (*calamō*) and ink (*ātrāmentō*) were prepared (*temperātō*—this time, he bothered to check the point of the pen!), and the papyrus had been smoothed with a file made of a tooth (*chartā dentātā*):

> *Calamō et ātrāmentō temperātō, chartā etiam dentātā rēs agētur.*
> *Scrībis enim tē meās litterās superiōrēs vix legere potuisse. In quō nihil*
> *eōrum, mī frāter, fuit quae putās. Neque enim occupātus eram neque*
> *perturbātus nec īrātus alicuī. Sed hoc faciō semper ut, quīcumque*
> *calamus in mānūs meās vēnerit, eō sīc ūtar tamquam bonō.*

Papyrus was expensive and was often reused by whiting over the old writing and beginning anew. Such reused papyri are called *palimpsestī* (παλίμψηστος); the practice continued and several ancient texts have come to light underneath later writings. Cicero chides his friend Trebatius (*Ad Fam.* 7.18), "I commend

---

3.   *Mōs antiquīs fuit, usque ad meam servātus aetātem, prīmīs epistulae verbīs adicere, "Sī valēs bene est, ego valeō." Rectē nōs dīcimus, "Sī philosophāris, bene est." Valēre enim hoc dēmum est.*

4.   *Dē rē pūblicā breviter ad tē scrībam; iam enim charta ipsa nē nōs prōdat pertimēscō. Itaque posthāc, sī erunt mihi plūra ad tē scrībenda, ἀλληγορίαις obscūrābō.*

your frugality in using a palimpsest—but it really makes me wonder what was on that paper (*chartula*) that you preferred to erase rather than not write this letter (literally: these things) to me, unless it was one of your legal briefs. I surely don't think you erase my letters so you can replace them with yours! Perhaps you mean 'nothing is happening, I have no clients; I haven't even any paper!'"

> *Nam quod in palimpsestō, laudō equidem parsimōniam, sed mīror quid in illā chartulā fuerit quod dēlēre mālueris quam haec nōn scrībere, nisi forte tuās formulās; nōn enim putō tē meās epistulās dēlēre ut repōnās tuās. An hoc significās, nihil fierī, frīgēre[5] tē, nē chartam quidem tibi suppeditāre?*

Vocābula Disposita/Ōrdināta

Nōmina
  1st

litterae, -ārum	a letter = **epistula**

  2nd

factum, -ī	deed
prōmissum, -ī	promise
signum, -ī	sign, statue

  3rd

clāvis, clāvis (*f.*)	key
comes, comitis (*m./f.*)	companion
laus, laudis (*f.*)	praise
pudor, pudōris (*m.*)	(good) shame
verbera, um (*n. pl.*)	a lashing

  4th

vultus, vultūs (*m.*)	face, facial expression

Verba
  -āre (1)

(comitor) comitārī, comitātum	accompany
(negō) negāre, negāvisse, negātum	deny, say…not

  -ēre (2)

(contineō) continēre, continuisse, contentum	contain
(dēbeō) dēbēre, dēbuisse, dēbitum	owe, ought
(fateor) fatērī, fassum	acknowledge
(mereō) merēre, meruisse, meritum	earn, deserve
(palleō) pallēre	be pale
(pudet) pudēre, puduit	feel shame (*impersonal*)
(rubeō) rubēre	be red

---

5. *Frīgēre* (to be cold, like re*frige*rator) is the opposite of *calēre* (to be hot, like *calo*rie), not to be confused with *algēre* (to feel cold, for which we say, "I am cold" when we mean, "I feel cold") and *aestuāre* (to feel hot). *Frīgēre* thus means, (as here) "have nothing to do, be disregarded."

-ere (3)

(āvertō) āvertere	turn aside or away
(dīmittō) dīmittere, dīmīsisse, dīmissum	send in different directions
(inclūdō) inclūdere, inclūsisse, inclūsum	shut in
(īnscrībō) īnscrībere, īnscrīpsisse, īnscrīptum	inscribe
(perdō) perdere, perdidisse, perditum	lose
(prōmittō) prōmittere, prōmīsisse, prōmissum	promise
salūtem dīcere	say hi
(solvō) solvere, solvisse, solūtum	loose, pay
(trādō) trādere, trādidisse, trāditum	hand over or down

Adiectīva

1st/2nd (-us/er, -a, -um)

integer, -ra, -rum	whole, undamaged
pallidus, -a, -um	pale
plānus, -a, -um	level, clear
superior, superius	higher

Prōnōmina

quidnam?	what in the world?
quisnam?	who in the world?

Adverbia

antehāc	before this
fortasse	perhaps
herī	yesterday
hinc	from here
illinc	from there
posthāc	after this
umquam	ever (always in neg. context)

Praepositiōnēs

ob (*prp. + acc.*)	on account of

XXIV. Puer Aegrōtus

Rēs Grammaticae Novae

1. Verbs
   a. Pluperfect Tense: Active and Passive
   b. Deponent Verbs: Perfect Tense
   c. *nōscere*
   d. Principal Parts
2. Adjectives
   a. Comparisons
      i. Conjunction *quam*
      ii. Ablative of Comparison
3. Pronouns: Reflexive Pronoun
4. Adverbs: Adverbs in *ō*
5. Points of Style
   a. *quid agis?*
   b. *posse*
   c. Hyperbaton

Quintus Hears about His Brother's Troubles

From his sickbed Quintus calls Syra and asks her to tell him what has been going on while he has been lying alone and feeling left out of things. Syra readily gives him all the details of Marcus's return home and what had gone before.

Lēctiō Prīma (Section I)

Adverbs

In Cap. XVIII you learned about adverbs ending in *-ter* (e.g., *fortiter*) and in *-ē* (e.g., *stultē*). Note the **adverbs** ending in *-ō*:

subitō (l.12)	*rārō*
certō (l.59)	*prīmō* (l.100, "at first")[1]
postrēmō (l.78)	

---

1. Cf. *prīmum*, l.68, adv. "first."

Reflexive Pronoun

Of the **reflexive pronoun**, the form *sē* is accusative and ablative, the **dative** is *sibi* (cf. *tibi, mihi*):

- Syra: *"Doletne <u>tibi</u> pēs adhūc?"*
- *Puer "pedem <u>sibi</u> dolēre" ait: "Valdē <u>mihi</u> dolet pēs."* (ll.23–24)

acc.	*sē*
gen.	See Cap. XXIX
dat.	*sibi*
abl.	*sē*

Comparisons

There are two ways of expressing comparison between two things:

1. The conjunction *quam* ("than") is used after the comparative (adjective or adverb). Comparisons in any case can be made with *quam*, "than;" the second member of the comparison will go into the same case as the first, e.g.:

    Mārcus pigr<u>ior</u> est <u>quam</u> Quīntus.
    Pēs dexter multō <u>māior</u> est <u>quam</u> pēs laevus! (l.6)
    Pulchr<u>ius</u> scrīpserātis et recitāverātis <u>quam</u> Mārcus.
    (ll.113–114)

2. Instead of using *quam*, it is possible to put the second term in the **ablative**. This construction, the **ablative of comparison**, is used <u>only</u> when the first member of the comparison is in the nominative or the accusative case, e.g.:

    Mārcus pigr<u>ior</u> est Quīnt<u>ō</u>.
    Nunc pēs dexter <u>māior</u> est ped<u>e</u> laev<u>ō</u>. (l.30)
    Cēterum in hāc rē is nōn <u>pēior</u> fuerat cēter<u>īs</u>. (l.77)
    Is canis lup<u>ō</u> ferōc<u>ior</u> est! (l.90)
    Melior sum frātr<u>e</u> me<u>ō</u>! (l.108)
    Ego Mārcum bene nōvī, nec putō eum vōb<u>īs</u> stult<u>iōrem</u> esse. (ll.115–116)
    At certē pigr<u>ior</u> est nōb<u>īs</u>! (l.117)

Deponent Verbs (continued from Cap. XVI)

You learned the present tense of deponents in Cap. XVI. Deponent verbs like *cōnārī* and *mentīrī* are always **passive in form**, *except* for the **present** and **future participles**:

cōnāns, mentiēns	trying, lying
cōnātūrus, mentītūrus	about to try, about to lie

Just as the present tense has the form of the present passive, the **perfect tense** has the form of the perfect passive. It is formed by the perfect participle and *esse*. Some examples of perfect participles of deponent verbs:

> *patī: passus: tergī dolōrēs <u>passus est</u>.* (l.47)
> *loquī: locūtus: saepe dē eā <u>locūtus est</u>.* (l.60)
> *verērī: veritus: Tabellārius canem <u>veritus est</u>.* (l.88)
> *fatērī: fassus: Mārcus "sē mentītum esse" <u>fassus est</u>.* (l.101, note the perfect infinitive: *mentī<u>tum esse</u>*)

Compare the present and the perfect tense:

> | | |
> |---|---|
> | *Quīntus surgere cōnā<u>tur</u>.* | Quintus tries to rise. |
> | *Quīntus surgere cōnā<u>tus est</u>.* | Quintus has tried to rise. |
> | *Mārcus mentī<u>tur</u>.* | Marcus is lying. |
> | *Mārcus mentī<u>tus est</u>.* | Marcus has lied. |

The **imperative** of deponent verbs ending in *-re* is treated in the next chapter, but note the following examples of the imperative:

> *Cōnsōlā<u>re</u> mē, Syra!* (l.40)
> *loque<u>re</u> mēcum!* (l.41)
> *immō laetā<u>re</u>* (l.44)

Lēctiō Altera (Section II)

The Pluperfect Tense

Through Syra's report to Quintus, you learn the tense called **pluperfect** (Latin *tempus plūsquamperfectum*). It is used to express that an action comes before some point in the past, i.e., that something <u>had</u> taken place (ll.65–67):

> *Mārcus nōn modo ūmidus erat quod per imbrem ambulā<u>verat</u>, sed etiam sordidus atque cruentus, quod humī iac<u>uerat</u> et ā Sextō pulsā<u>tus erat</u>. Puerī enim in viā pugnā<u>verant</u>.*

The pluperfects explain why Marcus was (*erat*) wet and dirty: he **had** (previously) walked, had lain, had been hit, had fought (*ambulāv|erat iacu|erat, pulsāt|us erat*, and *pugnāv|erant*).

In the active, the pluperfect is formed by the insertion of *-erā-* (shortened *-era-*) between the perfect stem and the personal endings:

1st person	*~era|m, ~erā|mus*
2nd	*~erā|s, ~erā|tis*
3rd	*~era|t, ~era|nt*

ambulā +v+era+m: I had walked (etc.)   *iac +u+era+m*: I had lain (etc.)
ambulā +v+erā+s   *iac +u+erā+s*
ambulā +v+era+t   *iac +u+era+t*
ambulā +v+erā+mus   *iac +u+erā+mus*
ambulā +v+erā+tis   *iac +u+erā+tis*
ambulā +v+era+nt   *iac +u+era+nt*

In the **passive** the pluperfect is composed of the perfect participle and the imperfect of *esse* (*eram, erās, erat*, etc.), e.g.:

> *Mārcus ā Sextō pulsā<u>tus erat</u>. = Sextus Mārcum pulsāverat.*
> *pulsātus, -a, -eram*: I had been hit (etc.)
> *pulsātus, -a, -erās*
> *pulsātus, -a, -erat*
> *pulsātī, -ae, -erāmus*
> *pulsātī, -ae, -erātis*
> *pulsātī, -ae, -erant*

→ In the Grammatica Latina—both of Lingua Latina and at the end of this book—you find examples of all the pluperfect forms of the four conjugations and of *esse* (*fu|era|m, fu|erā|s, fu|era|t*, etc.).

Nōscere

The perfect *nōvisse* of *nōscere* ("get to know") has present force: "be acquainted with," "know," e.g.:

> *Quōmodo Mēdus puellam Rōmānam <u>nōscere</u> potuit?* (ll.57–58)
> *Nesciō quōmodo, sed certō sciō eum aliquam fēminam <u>nōvisse</u>.* (ll.59–60)
> *Canis tē <u>nōvit</u>, ignōrat illum.* (l.94)

Principal Parts

The principal parts (from the margins) to be learned in this chapter are (the 1st person singular present active indicative is given in brackets):

> (*cadō*) *cadere, cecidisse, cāsum*
> (*cognōscō*) *cognōscere, cognōvisse, cognitum*
> (*cōnor*) *cōnārī, cōnātum*
> (*dō*) *dare, dedisse, datum*
> (*eō*) *īre, īvisse* (or *iisse*), *itum*
> (*fateor*) *fatērī, fassum*
> (*frangō*) *frangere, frēgisse, frāctum*
> (*lavō*) *lavāre, lāvisse, lautum* (or *lavātum*)
> (*loquor*) *loquī, locūtum*
> (*lūdō*) *lūdere, lūsisse*

(*mentior*) *mentīrī, mentītum*
(*mordeō*) *mordēre, momordisse, morsum*
(*nōscō*) *nōscere, nōvisse, nōtum*
(*percutiō*) *percutere, percussisse, percussum*
(*reprehendō*) *reprehendere, reprehendisse, reprehēnsum*
(*vereor*) *verērī, veritum*
(*videō*) *vidēre, vīdisse, vīsum*
(*volō*) *velle, voluisse*

Points of Style

Quid agis

Quid agis? = Quōmodo tē habēs?

>   *Syra Quīntō loquitur,*   How are you? Does your foot
>   "*Sed tū quid agis? Doletne*   still hurt? (ll.22–23)
>   *tibi pēs adhūc?*"

Posse

Syra's remonstration to Quintus illustrates the idiomatic use of *posse*:

> *Mīror tē crūs nōn frēgisse. Facile ōs frangere potuistī.* (ll.32–33)

English would have used the perfect of "break" in both clauses: "I'm amazed that you **did not break** your leg. You **could** easily **have broken** a bone." In English, in other words, we would use a subjunctive (could/might have broken). *Posse*, however, works differently. To express what could have happened in the past, but didn't, Latin uses a past indicative tense of the verb *posse* with a present infinitive.

Hyperbaton

When Quintus hears Syra's narration of what Marcus had done, the word order of his question reflects what is uppermost in his mind—his mother's reaction:

> *Māter quid dīxit?* (l.71)

Marcus throws emphasis on the word *māter* by putting it first. Making the word order reflect the emphasis of thought is called **hyperbaton** and is an important feature of Latin style.

Recēnsiō: The Verbal System (thus far)

Verbs have:

person	first, second, third
number	singular, plural

tense	present, future, imperfect, perfect, pluperfect
voice	active (subject acts); passive (subject acted upon)
finite mood	indicative (*Fact*: asks question; makes statements), imperative (*Order*: gives an order; commands)

Outside the finite[2] verbal system, you have thus far learned the following verbal forms:

infinitive

supine

participle

Tense

Tense shows two things:

duration in time (going on or completed)

position in time (past, present, future)

Present tense: what is in progress right now

Future: what will be in progress in the future

Imperfect: what was in progress in the past

Perfect: shows completion in the present (i.e., in relation to present time, the action is completed.

Pluperfect: shows completion in the past (i.e., the action was completed in relation to another completed action)

Examples:

Indicative

I. *Iūlius signum frangit.*	Julius is breaking the seal.
Ā Iūliō signum frangitur.	The seal is being broken by Julius.
Iūlius signum franget.	Julius will break the seal.
Ā Iūliō signum frangētur.	The seal will be broken by Julius.
Iūlius signum frangēbat.	Julius was breaking the seal.
Ā Iūliō signum frangēbātur.	The seal was being broken by Julius.
Iūlius signum frēgit.	Julius broke/has broken the seal.
Ā Iūliō signum frāctum est.	The seal has been broken by Julius.
Iūlius signum frēgerat.	Julius had broken the seal.
Ā Iūliō signum frāctum erat.	The seal had been broken by Julius.
II. *Latīnē loquī cōnor.*	I am trying to speak Latin, I do try, I try
Latīnē loquī cōnābar.	I was trying to speak Latin, I used to try, I tried
Latīnē loquī cōnābor.	I will try to speak Latin.
Latīnē loquī cōnātus/a sum.	I have tried to speak Latin, I tried to speak Latin, I did try

---

2.   Finite: that is, verbs which have a personal ending limiting their meaning.

Latīnē loquī cōnātus/a eram,   I had tried to speak Latin, but
   sed nōn potuī.   I could not.

Participle

I. *frangēns, frangentis*   breaking
   frāctūrus, -a, -um   about to break
   frāctus, -a, -um   having been broken

II. *cōnāns, cōnantis*   trying
   cōnātūrus, -a, -um   about to try
   cōnātus, -a, -um   having tried (notice active meaning!)

Infinitive

I. *frangere*   to break
   frangī   to be broken
   frāctūrum esse   to be about to break
   frāctum īrī   to be about to be broken
   frēgisse   to have broken
   frāctum esse   to have been broken

II. *cōnārī*   to try
   cōnātūrum esse   to be about to try
   cōnātum esse   to have tried

Infinitive in indirect statement

I. Present

  Videō puerōs signum frangere.   I see that the boys are breaking the seal.

  Videō signum ā puerīs frangī.   I see that the seal is being broken by the boys.

  Videō puerōs signum frāctūrōs esse.   I see that the boys will break the seal.

  Videō signum ā puerīs frāctum īrī.   I see that the seal will be broken by the boys.

  Videō puerōs signum frēgisse.   I see that the boys broke/have broken the seal.

  Videō signum ā puerīs frāctum esse.   I see that the seal has been broken by the boys.

II. Past

  Vīdī puerōs signum frangere.   I saw that the boys were breaking the seal.

  Vīdī signum ā puerīs frangī.   I saw that the seal was being broken by the boys.

Vīdī puerōs signum frāctūrōs esse.	I saw that the boys would break the seal.
Vīdī signum ā puerīs frāctum īrī.	I saw that the seal would be broken by the boys.
Vīdī puerōs signum frēgisse.	I saw that the boys had broken the seal.
Vīdī signum ā puerīs frāctum esse.	I saw that the seal had been broken by the boys.

Studia Rōmāna

While Syra and Quīntus are discussing the day's drama around Marcus, other slaves are in the kitchen (*culīna*) preparing for the dinner party you will read about toward the end of the narrative. What people would have eaten varied a lot, depending on where they lived (city? country?), their socioeconomic status, and other factors. Certain festivals and celebrations included special foods. Birthdays, for example, needed a cake (*lībum*) to offer to the gods in thanksgiving. Wealthy people living in a port city would have a wide variety of choices of foods imported from abroad as well as elsewhere in Italy and their homes would include a *culīna*. People living in apartment blocks (*īnsulae*) might have a portable brazier (grill) but not a kitchen.

Breakfast was a very light meal and seems to have been optional. The breaking of the night fast was often the *prandium*, a simple meal taken late morning or noontime. That breakfast (*ientāculum*) was originally called *prandicula*, or little *prandium* (*prandicula antīquī dīcēbant, quae nunc ientācula*[3]), suggests the *prandium* was often the first meal of the day. The poet Horace (65–8 BC), writing about his moderate (and therefore virtuous) habits, claims he rises late and, after a variety of activities, has his first (around midday) meal: "After eating sparingly—as much as keeps me from enduring the day on an empty stomach, I relax at home" (*prānsus nōn avidē, quantum interpellet inānī/ventre diem dūrāre, domesticus ōtior*, Sat. 1.6.127–28). That's fine for Horace, but Martial tells us that early-rising schoolboys grabbed something on their way: "Get up! The baker is already selling breakfast to boys/and the crested birds of daylight are everywhere singing" (*Surgite: iam vendit puerīs ientācula pistor/ Cristātaeque sonant undique lūcis avēs*, 14.223). These meals were simple and probably consisted of bread and vegetables. (The number of bakeries—with and without milling equipment—in Pompeii shows the importance of bread.) A. Cornelius Celsus (first century AD), who wrote an encyclopedia of medicine (*dē Medicīnā*), sensibly remarks that food intake depends on one's age, activity, and the time of year. He suggests one meal a day in winter (if one must

---

3.   Fēstus.

eat *prandium*, skip the meat and wine!) and in summer, one should include the *prandium* (*Aestāte vērō et potiōne et cibō saepius corpus eget; ideō prandēre quoque commodum est*, I.3).

The main meal of the day was called the *cēna*. Generally, the Romans talk about three courses to the *cēna*: *gustātiō* (appetizer), *cēna* (the main course), *secunda mēnsa* (dessert). Again, the poet Horace claims that, at the end of the day, "I go home back home to a bowl of leeks and chickpeas and flatbread" (*inde domum mē ad porrī et ciceris referō laganīque catīnum*, *Sat*. 1.6.114–115). At the other end of the spectrum are the satiric meals, such as a dinner at Trimalchio's house (in Petronius's first-century AD *Satyricon*), which consisted of an absurd number, amount, and variety of foodstuffs. The Romans seem to have eaten a good deal of pork. Fish was a prized delicacy (the fish swimming in the fishponds mentioned in Cap. XI were dinner as well as pets). Two poems of Horace satirizing effete and pretentious "foodies" (*Satires* 2.4 and 2.8) and the survival of a Roman cookery book named after the first-century AD gourmand Apicius (but actually written in the fourth century AD) are some of the many testimonies to the Roman infatuation with *ars culīnāria*. A staple of Roman cookery was *garum*, a sauce produced by fermenting fish with salt out in the sun for several months. *Garum* is also called *liquāmen*, a word which means a liquid mixture, but comes to be synonymous with the famous (and lucrative) sauce. *Aulus Umbricius Scaurus* made so much money producing and selling his *garum* that he put a mosaic depicting a jar of his fish sauce in the atrium of his house. *Garum*, like wine, came in various qualities and was traded all over the Mediterranean. From time to time, the Romans—mostly in vain—enacted sumptuary laws that tried to curtail extravagance in general and at meals in particular.

Vocābula Disposita/Ōrdināta

Nōmina
  2nd
    plūsquam perfectum, -ī (*n.*) — pluperfect (tense)
    sonus, ī (*m.*) — sound
  3rd
    dolor, dolōris (*m.*) — pain, grief
    latus, lateris (*n.*) — side
    os, ossis (*n.*) — bone
  4th
    strepitus, -ūs (*m.*) — noise, din
    tumultus, -ūs (*m.*) — uproar
Verba
  -āre (1)
    (ignōrō) ignōrāre, ignōrāvisse, ignōrātum — not to know, be ignorant of
    (mīror) mīrārī, mīrātum — wonder at

-ēre (2)

(fleō) flēre, flēvisse, flētum   weep

-ere (3)

(convertō) convertere, convertisse,   turn
    conversum

(cupiō) cupere, cupīvisse, cupitum   want, desire

(frangō) frangere, frēgisse, frāctum   break

(nōscō) nōscere, nōvisse, nōtum   get to know; *pf.:* know

(patior) patī, passum   suffer, permit, allow

(percutiō) percutere, percussisse,   strike, hit
    percussum

(recumbō) recumbere, recubuisse   lie down, lie back

Adiectīva

1st/2nd (-us/er, -a, -um)

aegrōtus, -a, -um   sick

cruentus, -a, -um   bloody, gory

laevus, -a, -um   left

subitus, -a, -um   sudden

3rd

impār (*gen.* imparis)   unequal

pār (*gen.* paris)   equal

Coniūnctiōnēs

etsī   even if, although

Adverbia

aliter   otherwise

certō[4]   for certain

cēterum   besides, however

continuō   immediately

dēnuō   anew, again

intus   within

prīmō   at first

subitō   suddenly

valdē   strongly, very (much)

Praepositiōnēs

iūxtā (*prp.* + *acc.*)   next to, beside

---

4.   Cf: *certē*: certainly, at any rate.

XXV. Thēseus et Mīnōtaurus

Rēs Grammaticae Novae

1. Verbs
   a. Imperative of Deponent Verbs
   b. Accusative and Infinitive
      i. *velle*
      ii. *iubēre* (continued)
2. Participle Perfect (deponents)
3. Nouns: Case Use
   a. Locative
      i. small islands
      ii. plural nouns
   b. Ablative of Respect
   c. Ablative of Manner
   d. Objective Genitive
   e. *oblīvīscī* with Genitive/Accusative
4. Adverbs: Adverbs of Place
5. Points of Style
   a. *quī = et is*
   b. *bene/male velle*

Greek Mythology: Theseus and the Minotaur

In this and the next chapter, we will leave the family and read some well-known Greek myths. These thrilling stories have fascinated not only the Romans, but also readers through the ages, and many poets and artists have drawn inspiration from the narrative art of the Greeks.

Lēctiō Prīma (Section I)

Adverbs of Place

In this chapter, we add to your store of adverbs signaling place that respond to the questions:

ubi?
> *hīc* (Cap. III)   *ibi:* <u>*Ibi*</u> *nāvis mea parāta est.* (l.93–94)
> *illīc* (Cap. VII)

Notā Bene: The accent on *illīc* is on the ultima (*illíc*): see Cap. VII.

unde?
> *hinc* (Cap. XXIII)
> *illinc* (Cap. XXIII): *Nēmō quī tāle aedificium semel intrāvit rūrsus*
>   <u>*illinc*</u> *exīre potest.* (ll.30–31)
> *quō?*
> *hūc: Auxiliō huius fīlī* <u>*hūc*</u> *ad mē redībis* (ll.73–74)
> *illūc:* <u>*hūc*</u> <u>*et*</u> <u>*illūc*</u> *currēns* (l.110)

Notā Bene: Illinc and *illūc,* like *illīc,* are pronounced with the accent on the ultima.

Velle + Accusative and Infinitive

Like *iubēre,* the verb *velle* can take the accusative + infinitive construction:
> <u>*Tē*</u> *hīc man<u>ēre</u>* <u>*volō*</u>   want you to… (ll.2–3)
> *Quam fābulam* <u>*mē*</u> *tibi nārr<u>āre</u>* <u>*vīs*</u>?   do you want me to…
>   (ll.2–4)

Ablative of Respect (continued from Cap. XI)

You have learned (Caps. XI, XIX, XXII) that the ablative case is used to show the respect in which something is true:

> *Nec modo* <u>*pede,*</u> *sed etiam* <u>*capite*</u> <u>*aeger*</u> *est.* (Cap. XI, l.55)
> *Tū sōlus* <u>*amōre*</u> <u>*meō*</u> *dignus erās.* (Cap. XIX, l.111)
> *Vōx tua difficilis est* <u>*audītū.*</u> (Cap. XXII, ll.45–46)

Similarly, a new name can be presented with the ablative *nōmin<u>e</u>* ("by name," abl. of respect), e.g.:

> *mōnstrum terribile,* <u>*nōmine*</u> *Mīnōtaurus* (ll.25–26)
> *parva īnsula* <u>*nōmine*</u> *Naxus*

Lēctiō Altera (Section II)

Locative (continued)

Small islands:

You have learned (Caps. VI, XIX) that for the names of cities and towns, and the nouns *domus, rus,* and *humus,* place where, place to which, and place from which are expressed by the plain ablative (*unde*, from where), accusative (*quō*, to where), and locative (*ubi*, where) without prepositions. This rule applies also to the names of small islands, of which Naxos (*Naxus*) is an example:

acc. *Nax<u>um</u> = ad īnsulam Naxum* (l.99)
abl. *Nax<u>ō</u> = ab/ex īnsulā Naxō* (l.100)
loc. *Nāx<u>ī</u> = in īnsulā Naxō* (l.132)

Large islands (like Crete), however, still require prepositions.

Nax<u>ō</u> in Crētam
ē Crētā Athēn<u>ās</u>

Plural nouns

In Cap. VI, you learned about constructions of place with the names of cities and towns. The place-names mentioned in the story can be found on the map of Greece.

Among the names of towns, note the plural forms *Athēn<u>ae</u>* and *Delph<u>ī</u>*:

nom. *Athēn<u>ae</u>, Delph<u>ī</u>*
acc. *Athēn<u>ās</u>, Delph<u>ōs</u>*
abl. *Athēn<u>īs</u>, Delph<u>īs</u>*

The accusative and ablative, as you know, serve to express motion to and from the town: *Athēn<u>ās</u>*, "to Athens," *Athēn<u>īs</u>*, "from Athens."

But the **locative** of plural town names has the same form as the ablative, so that *Athēnīs* can also mean "from Athens" or "in Athens" (e.g., the equivalent of *in urbe Athēnīs*):

Thēseus Athēn<u>īs</u> vīvēbat. (ll.51–52)

Context will tell you when to interpret as locative (place where) or ablative (place from which).

Ablative of Manner (*Ablātīvus Modī*)

The ablative can express the way or manner in which an action is done, as you see in lines 142–143:

Quī multōs annōs Athēnās <u>magnā cum glōriā</u> rēxit. ("with great glory")

We saw this construction much earlier but without a preposition:

Vocābulum "īnsula" dēclinātur <u>hōc modō</u>. ("in this way") (Cap. IX, l.90)

Mārcus perterritus ad vīllam currit et <u>magnā vōce</u> clāmat. ("with a great voice," "loudly") (Cap. X, ll.111–112)

Notā Bene: The preposition *cum* in the *ablātīvus modī* is optional if the noun is modified by an adjective (*magnā cum glōriā, magnā vōce, hōc modō*). If there is no adjective, *cum* must be used (e.g., *cum glōriā*).

Objective/Subjective Genitive

Transitive verbs like *timēre* and *amāre* are generally used with an object in the accusative, e.g.:

> *mort<u>em</u> timēre*
> *patri<u>am</u> amāre*

Nouns and adjectives (including participles used as adjectives) that are derived from verbs, e.g., *timor* (from *timēre*) and *amor* (from *amāre*), can be combined with a **genitive** to denote what is the object of that verb (e.g., fear or love of something/someone).

> *timor mort<u>is</u>*   fear of death (l.77)
> *amor patri<u>ae</u>*   love of country (l.86)

Such a genitive is called an **objective genitive**. Other examples are:

> *timor mōnstr<u>ōrum</u>* (ll.21–22): *timor < timēre*
> *expugnātiō urb<u>is</u>* (ll.45–46): *expugnātiō < expugnāre*
> *cupiditās pecūni<u>ae</u>* (ll.122–123): *cupiditās < cupere*
> *cupidus aur<u>ī</u> atque sanguin<u>is</u>* (ll.44–47) = *quī cupit aurum atque sanguinem*
> *patri<u>ae</u> amāns* (l.51) = *quī patri<u>am</u> amat*

Iubēre + Accusative and Infinitive (continued)

You have seen several examples of the accusative and infinitive with the verb *iubēre*.

An active infinitive expresses what a person is to do:

> *Medicus Quīntum linguam ostend<u>ere</u> iubet.* (Cap. XI, ll.69–70)

A passive infinitive expresses what is to be done to a person, like *dūcī* in:

> [*Rēx*] *eum (ā mīlitibus) in labyrinthum dūcī iussit:* "ordered him <u>to be taken</u> into the labyrinth" (l.59)

Perfect Participle of Deponents

You know (Cap. XIV) that present participles can have an object:

> *Dāvus cubiculum intrāns* (l.25)
> *Mārcus oculōs aperiēns* (ll.37–38)

In the same way, the perfect participle of deponent verbs (being active in meaning) can be used with the subject of the sentence to express what a person has/had done or did:

> haec _locūta_ Ariadna... ("having said/after saying this...") (l.74)
> Thēseus fīlum Ariadnae _secūtus_... ("having followed...") (ll.84–85)
> Aegeus _arbitrātus_... ("who believed...") (ll.137–138)

Compare

An ablative absolute with a perfect passive participle:

> _Hīs dictīs, Ariadna Thēseō fīlum longum dedit_: (_literally_) "these things having been said, Ariadna..."

A nominative feminine singular perfect participle of a deponent verb, which is active in meaning:

> _haec locūta, Ariadna Thēseō fīlum longum dedit_: "Ariadna, having spoken these things..."

Points of Style

Quī = et is

A relative pronoun at the beginning of a sentence functions as a demonstrative pronoun referring to a word in the preceding sentence. That is, the relative can be a transitional, connecting word, e.g.:

> _Thēseus Athēnīs vīvēbat. Quī_ (= "and he") _nūper Athēnās vēnerat._ (ll.51–52)
> _Labyrinthus ā Daedalō, virō Athēniēnsī, aedificātus erat. Quī iam antequam ex urbe Athēnīs in Crētam vēnit, complūrēs rēs mīrābilēs fēcerat._ (l.34)
> _Mīnōs autem fīliam virginem habēbat, cui nōmen erat Ariadna. Quae_ ("and she") _cum prīmum Thēseum cōnspexit, eum amāre coepit cōnstituitque eum servāre._ (ll.60–62)
> _Thēseus rēx Athēniēnsium factus est. Quī multōs annōs Athēnās magnā cum glōriā rēxit._ (ll.141–143)

Bene/male velle

The idiomatic expressions _bene velle_ ("to wish someone well") and _male velle_ ("to wish someone ill") take a dative of person. From the participle (_bene volēns_ and _male volēns_) come the English words "benevolent" and "malevolent." Example:

> _Rēx enim Athēniēnsibus male volēbat._ (ll.48–49)

Lēctiō Tertia (Section III)

Imperative of Deponent Verbs

The **imperative of deponent verbs** ends in:
- *-re* in the singular (cons.-stems *-ere*)
- *-minī* in the plural (cons.-stems *-iminī*)

Notā Bene:
- The plural imperative of deponents *looks identical* to the 2nd plural indicative: *sequiminī*
- The singular imperative of deponents *looks like* a present active infinitive: *sequere*

You have already seen examples of the singular imperative of deponents (ending in *-re*) in Cap. XXIV, e.g.:

> *Intue̱re pedēs meōs, Syra!* (ll.28–29)
> *loque̱re mēcum!* (l.41)
> *immō laetā̱re.* (l.44)

In this chapter, Theseus says to Ariadne (<u>singular</u> <u>imperative</u>):

> *Opperi̱re mē!* (l.75) *Et tū seque̱re mē! Proficīsce̱re mēcum Athēnās!* (ll.95–96)

To his countrymen, Theseus uses the <u>plural</u> <u>imperative</u> (ll.92–93):

> *Laetā̱minī, cīvēs meī!*
> *Intuē̱minī gladium meum cruentum!*
> *Sequi̱minī mē ad portum!*

Oblīvīscī with Genitive/Accusative

The verb *oblīvīscī* can be completed both by an accusative direct object and by the genitive. *Oblīvīscī* can take an accusative when the object is a thing:

> *Quis tam facile <u>prōmissum</u> oblīvīscitur quam vir quī fēminam amāvit?* (ll.119–120)
> *Redeō ad nārrātiōnem fābulae, <u>quam</u> prope oblīta sum.* (ll.129–130)

When *oblīvīscī* means "disregard," "don't be mindful <u>of</u>," it takes a genitive:

> *oblīvīscere illī̱us virī̱!* (l.126)
> *Nōn facile est <u>amōris</u> <u>antīquī</u> oblīvīscī.* (l.128)

Nāvigandum, fugiendum

The forms *nāvigandum* and *fugiendum* (ll.94, 97) will be taken up in Cap. XXVI.

Recēnsiō: Adverbs of Place

ubi?	in what place?	*quō?*	to what place?
ibi	in that place, there	(*eō*: to that place: Cap. XXVIII)
illīc	in that place	*illūc*	to that place[1]
hīc	in this place	*hūc*	to this place

unde?	from what place?
(*inde*: from that place: Cap. XXIX)
illinc	from that place
hinc	from this place

hūc atque illūc	here and there (to this place and to that)
hīc atque illīc	here and there (on this side and that)

More adverbs

brevī (*brevī tempore*)	in a short time
quotannīs	every year
ūnā cum + abl.	together with

Studia Rōmāna

Syra alludes to several famous Greek myths before settling on the story of Theseus and the Minotaur. Greek literature and stories became an integral part of Roman culture (as Horace wrote, "After Greece was captured, she captivated her uncultivated conqueror and brought culture to unsophisticated Latium"[2]). Greek exempla are often put in service of illustrating Roman moral precepts (although Syra uses the narrative of Theseus and Ariadne as a "misery loves company" solace for her own disappointment in love).

The boy who wanted to drive the chariot of the sun god (*an fābulam dē puerō quī cupīvit regere equōs quī currum Sōlis per caelum trahunt?* ll.6–7) was *Phaëthōn*, the son of Helios, the god who drove the chariot of the sun through the sky each day (about whom you will learn more in the next chapter). She next refers to Homer's *Iliad*, the story of the Trojan war and the most famous Greek epic in antiquity. (*An cupis audīre fābulam dē Achille, duce Graecōrum, quī Hectorem, ducem Trōiānum, interfēcit atque corpus eius mortuum post*

---

1. Like *illīc*, *illūc* is accented on the ultima (i.e., originally *illūce*).
2. *Epist.* 2.1.156: *Graecia capta ferum victōrem cēpit et artīs/intulit āgrestī Latiō.*

currum suum trāxit circum moenia urbis Trōiae? ll.8–11). "Achilles, the best of the Greeks, killed Hector, the best of the Trojans, and then dragged his body around the walls of Troy." Finally she asks Quintus if he wants to hear about Romulus, a story you read about in the notes to Cap. IX (*an fābulam dē Rōmulō, quī prīma moenia Rōmāna aedificāvit... ll.11–13*).

The two great heroes of the Greek mainland were Herakles (Latin: Hercules) in the south among the Dorians in the Peloponnese and Theseus among the Athenians in Attica. Inspired by the renown of Herakles's prowess, Theseus looked for his own adventures. Although the twelve labors of Herakles are more famous, Theseus also performed several labors—seven before the defeat of the Minotaur. Afterward, he continued his adventures, many of them with his best friend Pirithous. Their last undertaking together was a journey to the underworld to capture Persephone, where they were trapped. Herakles saved Theseus, but Pirithous remained in Hades. Near the end of the first century BC, the poet Horace used the image of Theseus's inability to free his friend from Hades as a marker of the finality of death (IV.7.27–28):

> *nec Lēthaea valet Thēseus abrumpere cārō*
> *vincula Pīrithoo.*[3]

The prolific Greek writer Plurarch (first–second century AD) wrote parallel biographies of famous Greeks and Romans. His life of Theseus, as founder of Athens, is paired with that of Romulus, as founder of Rome. The Greek playwright Euripides (fifth century BC) wrote a play about Theseus and his son Hippolytus, and Theseus makes frequent appearances in Greek vase painting. Ovid (43 BC–AD 17/18) includes Theseus in several poems (the *Hērōidēs*, the *Ars Amātōria*, the *Metamorphōsēs*).

There are always variations on myths. In one of the variations of the Theseus and Ariadna myth, Ariadna is rescued and marries Dionysius (Roman: Bacchus), the god of wine.

Vocābula Disposita/Ōrdināta

Nōmina
  1st

fābula, -ae	story
glōria, -ae	glory
mora, -ae	delay

  2nd

aedificium, -ī	building
agnus, -ī	lamb
auxilium, -ī	help, aid

---

3.   *Lēthaeus, -a, -um*: belonging to Lēthē, the river from which the dead drink and thereby forget the past; *abrumpere = ab + rumpere* (Cap. XXII); *vinculum = catēnam* (Cap. XXII).

fīlum, -ī	thread
labyrinthus, -ī	labyrinth
mōnstrum, -ī	monster
saxum, -ī	rock
taurus, -ī	bull

3rd

cīvis, cīvis (*m./f.*)	citizen
cupiditās, cupiditātis (*f.*)	desire
expugnātiō, expugnātiōnis (*f.*)	conquest
lītus, lītoris (*n.*)	shore
moenia, moenium (*n. pl.*)	walls
mors, mortis (*f.*)	death
nārrātiō, nārrātiōnis (*f.*)	story
nex, necis (*f.*)	death
rēx, rēgis (*m.*)	king

4th

cōnspectus, -ūs (*m.*)	sight, view
currus, -ūs (*m.*)	chariot
exitus, -ūs (*m.*)	way out, end

Verba

Notā Bene: Not all verbs have all principal parts (e.g., *maerēre* and *patēre* exist only in the present system).

-āre (1)

(aedificō) aedificāre, aedificāvisse, aedificātum	build
(necō) necāre, necāvisse, necātum	kill
(vorō) vorāre, vorāvisse, vorātum	devour

-ēre (2)

(maereō) maerēre	grieve
(pateō) patēre (*intr.*)	lie open
(polliceor) pollicērī, pollicitum	promise

-ere (3)

(cōnstituō) cōnstituere, cōnstituisse, cōnstitūtum	decide, fix
(dēscendō) dēscendere, dēscendisse, dēscēnsum	descend
(dēserō) dēserere, dēseruisse, dēsertum	leave, desert
(incipiō) incipere, coepisse, coeptum	begin
(interficiō) interficere, interfēcisse, interfectum	kill
(oblīviscor) oblīvīscī, oblītum	forget
(occīdō) occīdere, occīdisse, occīsum	kill

(prōspiciō) prōspicere, prōspexisse, prōspectum	look out, look ahead
(regō) regere, rēxisse, rēctum	rule
(trahō) trahere, trāxisse, tractum	drag

Adiectīva

  1st/2nd (-us/er, -a, -um)

cupidus, -a, -um	desirous
parātus, -a, -um	ready
saevus, -a, -um	savage
timidus, -a, -um	timid

  3rd

complūrēs, -e	very many
humilis, -e	low
mīrābilis, -e	wonderful, marvelous
terribilis, -e	terrible

Adverbia

brevī	in a short time
forte	by chance
hūc	to this place
ibi	there, in that place
illūc	to that place
ōlim	once, long ago
quotannīs	every year

XXVI. Daedalus et Īcarus

Rēs Grammaticae Novae

1. Verbs
   a. Future Imperative (*esse*)
   b. *vidērī*
2. Verbal Noun: Gerund (*gerundium*)
3. Adjectives
   a. Adjectives in *-er*
   b. Irregular Superlatives *summus* and *īnfimus*
4. Pronoun
   a. *quisquam*
   b. Summary of Negative Expressions
5. Points of Style: Participles

Daedalus and Icarus

The story of the boy Icarus, who soared up to the scorching sun only to be plunged into the sea as the sun melted the wax that fastened his wings, has always been admired as an image of the penalty for arrogance and rashness. Syra, too, uses the story to warn Quintus to be careful.

Lēctiō Prīma (Section I)

Gerund

The gerund is a verbal noun that corresponds to English verbal nouns in "-ing." It is 2nd declension, singular neuter. You have already met the gerund in Cap. XXV:

> *Ibi nāvis mea parāta est ad nāvigandum.* (ll.93–94)
> *Parāta sum ad fugiendum.* (l.97)

The words *nāvigandum* and *fugiendum* are gerunds. The **gerund**:

- is characterized by *-nd-* added to the present stem
  - ▷ before consonant- and *ī*-stems (3rd and 4th conjugations), a short *e* is inserted before *-nd-*:
    ad vīv|end|um
    ad audi|end|um
- corresponds to English verbal nouns in "-ing"
- exists only in the singular oblique cases (acc., gen., dat., abl.) of the noun:
  - ▷ accusative ends in *-ndum* (*pugna|nd|um*)
  - ▷ the genitive in *-ndī* (*pugna|nd|ī*)
  - ▷ the dative and ablative in *-ndō* (*pugna|nd|ō*)

The infinitive supplies the missing nominative of the verbal noun.

Uses of the Gerund

In this chapter, you find several examples of the gerund in the different cases (except the dative, which is rarely used). The following examples come from the whole chapter, not just *Lēctiō Prīma*:

- The **accusative** is only found after *ad* and expresses **purpose**, e.g.:

Hodiē plūs temporis ad nārrandum nōn habeō.	I do not have more time today for recounting (stories). (ll.10–11)
Haud longum tempus nōbīs reliquum est ad vīvendum.	There is not much time left to us for living. (l.28)
ūna via nōbīs patet ad fugiendum.	one road lies open to us for fleeing. (l.36)

- The **genitive** occurs:
  - ▷ with nouns, e.g.:

fīnem nārrandī facere (= *fīnem nārrātiōnis f.*)	to make an end of telling (l.13)
cōnsilium fugiendī (= *cōnsilium fugae*)	a plan for escaping (ll.55–56)
Haud difficilis est ars volandī.	The art of flying is hardly difficult. (l.72)
Tempus dormiendī est.	It is time for sleeping. (ll.122–123) (= *tempus est dormīre*)

  - ▷ or as an objective genitive with the adjectives *cupidus* and *studiōsus*:

cupidus audiendī studiōsus volandī	desirous of hearing (ll.17–18, cf. l.108) eager for flying (l.43)

▷ *causā* + a preceding genitive of the gerund denotes cause or purpose:

Nōn sōlum dēlectandī	Not only for the sake of delighting,
causā, vērum etiam	but even for the sake of warning,
monendī causā,	is the story being told. (ll.134–135)
nārrātur fābula.	

- The **ablative** of the gerund is found after *in* and *dē*:

in volandō	in flying (l.80)
dē amandō	about loving (l.154)

▷ or alone as the ablative of means or cause:

Puerī scrībere discunt	Boys learn to write by writing.
scrībendō.	
Fessus sum ambulandō.	I am tired out by walking.
	(l.24; cf. ll.129–130)

Adjectives in *-er*

Adjectives that have *-er* in the m. nom. sing. are found among 1st/2nd declension adjectives (as you learned in Cap. V):

niger, gr|a, gr|um
miser, er|a, er|um
līber, er|a, er|um

As well as among 3rd declension adjectives (as you learned in Cap. XIII):

September, (gen.) *Septembris*
Octōber, (gen.) *Octōbris*
November, (gen.) *Novembris*
December, (gen.) *Decembris*

The following are examples of 3rd declension adjectives in *-er* that have three endings in the nominative (*-er, (e)ris, (e)re*):

celer, celer|is, celer|e
ācer, ācr|is, ācr|e

Notā Bene: Look to the feminine and neuter nominative singulars to see whether an adjective in *-er* has the *e* (like *celer, celeris*) or lacks it (like *ācer, ācris*).

Adjectives in *-er* have *-errimus* in the superlative, e.g., *celerrimus, ācerrimus.*

Summary of 3rd Declension Adjective forms

Third declension adjectives exhibit three different nominative groups:

    a. One nominative form: adjectives ending in *-ns* and *-x*, like *prūdēns* and *audāx* (gen. *prūdent|is, audāc|is*) have the same form in the nominative masculine, feminine, and neuter:

vir/fēmina/cōnsilium prūdēns
vir/fēmina/cōnsilium audāx

b. Two nominative forms: adjectives ending in *-is, -e*, like *brevis, breve* or *gravis, grave*, have one form for the masculine and feminine, and one for the neuter:

vir/fēmina gravis; cōnsilium grave
hōra/mēnsis brevis; tempus breve

c. Three nominative forms: adjectives ending in *-er* (see above) have a different nominative ending for masculine, feminine, and neuter:

Vir ācer; fēmina ācris; cōnsilium ācre

Negative Expressions

In Cap. III, you learned that Latin uses the conjunction *neque* to express "and not, but not" (instead of *et nōn* and *sed nōn*). Similarly, in Cap. XIX, we found *neque ūllus* for "and no one," **not** "*et nūllus*." This chapter adds two more such negations:

- The pronoun *quis-quam, quid-quam* ("anyone," "anything") is likewise used in a negative context. Latin does not express "and no one" and "and nothing" by *et nēmō, et nihil*, but by *neque quisquam* (l.26, "and no one"), *nec quidquam* (Cap. XXVII, l.106, "and nothing");

  ▷ *Quidquam* is changed by assimilation to *quicquam*

- Similarly, *et* is avoided before *numquam* by using *neque umquam* (Cap. XXIII, l.26, "and never").

Summary

and not/but not	*neque/nec*
and no one	*neque/nec ūllus*
and no one	*neque/nec quisquam*
and nothing	*neque/nec quicquam*
and never	*neque umquam*

āēr

The 3rd declension masculine noun *āēr* is borrowed from the Greek and keeps its Greek ending *-a* in the acc. sing. *āer|a* (l.22 = *āer|em*).

nom.	*āēr*
acc.	*āer|a*
gen.	*āer|is*

Lēctiō Altera (Section II)

Irregular Superlatives *summus* and *īnfimus*

- *summus* (l.79) comes from *super(us), -era, -erum* (comparative *superior*)
- *īnfimus* (l.77) comes from *īnfer(us), -era, -erum* (comparative *īnferior*)

Future Imperative

Instead of the short imperative *es! es|te!* of *esse*, the longer form in *-tō, -tōte* is often preferred: *es|tō! es|tōte!*

> *Cautus estō, mī fīlī!* (l.81; cf. l.138)

In other verbs, this so-called **future imperative** is not very common (it will be treated in Cap. XXXIII).

Lēctiō Tertia (Section III)

Vidērī

Vidērī, the passive of *vidēre*, is used (with nom. + inf.) in the sense of "seem (to be)," e.g.:

> *īnsulae haud parvae sunt, quamquam parvae esse <u>videntur</u>.*
> (ll.92–94)

In this function, a dative is often added, e.g.:

> *Mēlos īnsula nōn tam parva est quam <u>tibi</u> <u>vidētur</u>.* (ll.94–95,
>   = *quam tū putās*; cf. ll.96–97, 125);
> *puer <u>sibi</u> vidētur volāre* (ll.143–145, = *sē volāre putat*).

Points of Style: Participles

This chapter offers many examples of how participles contribute to the strongly verbal nature of Latin:

> <u>Daedalus</u> *in labyrinthō <u>inclūsus</u> errābat.* (l.19)
> *Nēmō <u>nōs</u> <u>volantēs</u> persequī poterit.* (l.42)
> *Tum puerum <u>ōsculātus</u>, "Parātī sumus ad volandum," inquit.*
>   (ll.75–76)
> *Haec verba <u>locūtus</u> Daedalus cum fīliō sūrsum ē labyrinthō ēvolāvit.*
>   (ll.83–84)
> *Aliquī pāstor, quī forte <u>suspiciēns</u> eōs tamquam magnās <u>avēs</u> <u>volantēs</u>*
>   *vīdit.* (ll.85–86)
> *novā lībertāte <u>dēlectātī</u>* (l.89)

Īcarus <u>dēspiciēns</u> multitūdinem īnsulārum mīrātus est. (ll.90–91)
    dēspiciēbat <u>mīrāns</u> (l.106)
<u>*Sōlem*</u> *in caelō serēnō <u>lūcentem</u> suspexit.* (ll.107–108)
Puer <u>territus</u>, lacertōs nūdōs <u>quatiēns</u>, in mare cecidit. (ll.115–116)
lībertātem <u>quaerēns</u> mortem invēnit. (l.122)
    quī currum patris regere <u>cōnātus</u> item dē summō caelō cecidit
    (ll.127–128)
Hīs verbīs <u>puerō</u> <u>monitō</u> (l.141)
Neque Quīntus <u>eam</u> <u>abeuntem</u> revocat. (l.142)

Studia Rōmāna

The fall of Icarus was a very popular motif in ancient literature, and enjoyed a
long afterlife in art and literature. The most famous representation is perhaps
Pieter Brueghel the Elder's (sixteenth century) painting, *The Fall of Icarus*.
Ovid tells the story of Daedalus and Icarus at length in the *Metamorphōsēs*
(Book 8), but the stories about Daedalus go all the way back to Homer's *Iliad*.

At the close of the narrative, Syra follows Roman practice by drawing a
moral lesson for Quintus: *ecce omnem fābulam habēs dē puerō temerāriō quī
lībertātem quaerēns mortem invēnit* (ll.121–122). Daedalus, along with Hercules, also figures as an example of human arrogance in one of Horace's *Odes*
(1.3.34–40)

> *expertus vacuum Daedalus āera*
> *pinnīs nōn hominī datīs;*
> *perrūpit Acheronta Herculeus labor.*
> *nīl mortālibus arduī est:*
> *caelum ipsum petimus stultitiā neque*
> *per nostrum patimur scelus*
> *īrācunda Iovem ponere fulmina.*

Vocabulary

āēr, Cap. X; *vacuus*, Cap. IV; *pinna = penna*; *perrumpere < per + rumpere*
(Cap. XXII); *Acheron, Acherontis*, m.: a river in the underworld; *Acheronta*
is accusative; *Herculeus, -a, -um*: of Hercules; *labor, -ōris*, m.: labor, work
(Cap. XXVII); *mortālis, -e*: mortal (Cap. XXVIII); *arduus, -a, -um*: difficult
(Cap. XXXIII); *stultitia, -ae < stultus, -a, -um* (Cap. XI); *patī, passum*: Cap.
XXIV; *scelus, sceleris*, n.: crime, wickedness (Cap. XXXI); *īrācundus, -a, -um*
= prone to anger (cf. *irātus*, Cap. III); *fulmen, fulminis*, n.: lightning bolt (cf.
Cap. XVI *fulgur*: flash of lightning); *ponere = dēponere*: put down, set aside.

Notes
Expertus: understand *est*

Nil arduī: cf Cap. XVI: Partitive genitive with *paulum, multum; nīl = nihil*

Iūppiter, king of the gods, is declined as follows

> *Iūppiter*
> *Iovem*
> *Iovis*
> *Iovī*
> *Iove*

Quintus says the story of Icarus delights him more than the one about the son of the sun god (ll.125–129 and 25.6–7). He refers to *Phaëthōn*, the son of Helios (the sun god) and a mortal woman, *Clymenē*. Helios promised to give Phaethon whatever he wanted. Phaethon wanted, as it were, the keys to the chariot of the sun, even though driving the four horses across the sky was far beyond his strength and experience. When the boy began driving erratically, bringing the sun now too close to, now too far from the earth, Juppiter had no choice but to strike the boy from the sky. Cicero (*dē Officiīs* 3.94) uses the story of Phaethon as an example of promises that should not be kept because they are harmful to the recipient. He ends with *quantō melius fuerat in hōc promissum patris nōn esse servātum*: "how much better it would have been in this case had the promise of the father not been kept!"

Vocābula Disposita/Ōrdināta

Nōmina
  1st

fuga, -ae	flight, a running away
nātūra, -ae	nature
paenīnsula, -ae	peninsula
penna, -ae	feather, wing

  2nd

cōnsilium, -ī	plan
gerundium, -ī	gerund
lacertus, -ī	arm

  3rd

ars, artis (*f.*)	art, skill
carcer, carceris (*m.*)	prison
ignis, ignis (*m.*)	fire
lībertās, lībertātis (*f.*)	freedom
multitūdō, multitūdinis (*f.*)	large number, multitude
opus, operis (*n.*)	work
orbis, orbis (*f.*)	circle, orbit

  4th

cāsus, -ūs (*m.*)	fall, event, (grammatical) case

Verba

-āre (1)

(aberrō) aberrāre, aberrāvisse, aberrātum   wander away, stray

(ēvolō) ēvolāre, ēvolāvisse, ēvolātum   fly away

(excōgitō) excōgitāre, excōgitāvisse, excōgitātum   think out, devise

(imitor) imitārī, imitātum   imitate

(iuvō) iuvāre, iūvisse   help, delight

(levō) levāre, levāvisse, levātum   lift, raise

(revocō) revocāre, revocāvisse, revocātum   call back

-ēre (2)

(videor) vidērī, vīsum   be seen, seem

-ere (3)

(accidō) accidere, accīdisse   happen, occur

(cōnsūmō) cōnsūmere, cōnsūmpsisse, cōnsūmptum   consume, spend

(cōnsequor) cōnsequī, cōnsecūtum   follow, overtake

(cōnficiō) cōnficere, cōnfēcisse, confectum   make, accomplish

(dēspiciō) dēspicere, dēspexisse, dēspectum   look down (at)

(effugiō) effugere, effūgisse   escape

(fīgō) fīgere, fīxisse, fīxum   fix, fasten

(perficiō) perficere, perfēcisse, perfectum   complete, accomplish

(persequor) persequī, persecūtum   follow, pursue

(quatiō) quatere   shake

(suspiciō) suspicere, suspexisse, suspectum   look up (at)

(ūrō) ūrere, ussisse, ustum   burn

-ire (4)

(inveniō) invenīre, invēnisse, inventum   come upon, find

(molliō) mollīre, mollīvisse, mollītum   make soft, soften

Adiectīva

1st/2nd (-us/er, -a, -um)

cautus, -a, -um   cautious

īnfimus, -a, -um   lowest

līber, lībera, līberum   free

propinquus, -a, -um   near, close

reliquus, -a, -um   remaining, left

studiōsus, -a, -um (+ *gen.*)   interested in

summus, -a, -um	highest
temerārius, -a, -um	reckless
3rd	
audāx (*gen.* **audācis**)	bold
celer, celeris, celere	swift
ingēns (*gen.* **ingentis**)	huge, vast

Prōnōmina
quisquam, quidquam	anyone, anything

Adverbia
deorsum	down
haud	not, scarcely
paene	nearly, almost
quidem	indeed
quoniam	since
sūrsum	up
tamquam	as, like, as though
vērum	but

Coniūnctiōnēs
sīn	but if

Praepositiōnēs
trāns (*prp. + acc.*)	across

XXVII. Rēs Rūsticae

Rēs Grammaticae Novae

1. Verbs
   a. Moods in Latin
   b. Subjunctive Mood
      i. Present Subjunctive: Active/Passive
      ii. Verbs of Demanding and Effecting: *verba postulandī et cūrandī*
      iii. Present Subjunctive of Irregular *esse*
   c. Translating the Subjunctive
2. Nouns: Case Uses
   a. Ablative
      i. Ablative of Instrument
      ii. Ablative of Separation
      iii. Prepositions with Ablative
         1. *prae*
         2. *prō*
         3. *abs*
   b. Accusative: *Preposition circā*
   c. Locative: Summary
3. Adverb: *parum*
4. Conjunctions
   a. *ut*
   b. *quam* + the Superlative
5. *Alia*
   a. *nē...quidem*: not...even
   b. *locus, locī/loca*

Julius's Estate

Julius is the owner of a large estate in the Alban Hills, *Mōns Albānus,* near Tusculum and the Alban Lake, *Lacus Albānus.* The running of the farm is left to tenant farmers, *colōnī.* Julius follows their work with great interest when he is in residence in his Alban villa. A typical wealthy Roman, he divides his time between Rome and his country estate. Here we meet him walking in his fields and vineyards, questioning his men about the quality of the crops.

Lēctiō Prīma (Section I)

Ablative of Instrument (*Ablātīvus Īnstrūmentī*) (continued)

The **ablative of instrument** (Caps. VI and VIII) appears in the discussion of the use of the farmers' tools (*īnstrūmentum*) (ll.18–20):

> *Frūmentum falce metitur.*
> *Quō īnstrūmentō serit agricola?*

The verb *ūtī* ("use") takes the ablative of instrument, not the accusative (ll.20–22):

> *Quī serit nūllō īnstrūmentō ūtitur praeter manum.*
> *Quī arat arātrō ūtitur.*
> *Quī metit falce ūtitur.*
> *Quī serit manū suā ūtitur.*

In addition to "use," *ūtī* also means "enjoy," "treat," etc.:

> *Amīcīs meīs bene ūtor.*   I treat my friends well.
> *Vīnō numquam ūtor.*   I never use (drink, enjoy) wine.

Locus, plural: *locī/loca*

Instead of the regular plural *locī* of *locus*, you often find the neuter form *loca, -ōrum* (l.30), which is usual in the concrete sense (places, localities); *locī* is used for passages in books, topics, and points of argument.

> *Italia est terra fertilis, sed multa <u>loca</u> Italiae nōn arantur.* (ll.30–31)
> *Theophrastus cum tractat <u>locōs</u> ab Aristotele ante tractātōs...;* "when
>   Theophrastus treats subjects previously treated by Aristotle..."[1]

Lēctiō Altera (Section II)

Summary: Locative

	sing.	pl.	Examples
1st	-ae	-īs	*Rōmae, Athēnīs*
2nd	-ī	-īs	*Tūsculī, humī*
3rd	-ī/-ĕ		*rūrī, Karthāgine*
			domī

---

1. Cicero, *de Finibus* 1.2.6.

Subjunctive Mood

In addition to many new words, you learn important new verb forms in this chapter. Compare the sentences:

Servus tacet et audit.
Dominus imperat ut servus tace<u>at</u> et audi<u>at</u>.

The first sentence uses the **indicative mood** (Latin *modus indicātīvus*)—*tace|t* and *audi|t*—to tell us what the slave actually does. The second sentence uses the **subjunctive mood** (Latin *modus coniūnctīvus*)—*tace|at* and *audi|at*—to express what the master wants his slave to do. *Taceat* and *audiat* are the **present subjunctive** (Latin *coniūnctīvus praesentis*) of *tacēre* and *audīre*.

Moods (*Modī*) in Latin

Remember, language is an attempt to express thought. So, the mood used in a sentence reflects the way the speaker conceives that thought.

- The **indicative** (*modus indicātīvus*) makes a statement or asks a question.[2] The attitude of the speaker is a simple "fact" or "question."
- The **imperative** (*modus imperātīvus*) gives a direct command.
- The **subjunctive** (*modus coniūnctīvus*) has various functions, such as expressing the will (volitive) or wish (optative) of the speaker. The subjunctive is used in dependent (subordinate) and independent clauses.
  - ▷ Common subjunctive uses in **dependent** clauses:
    indirect commands (Cap. XXVII)
    noun clauses (substantive clauses) (Cap. XXVII)
    final (purpose) clauses (Cap. XXVIII)
    consecutive (result) clauses (Cap. XXVIII)
    cum temporal, *cum* causal, *cum* concessive (Cap. XXIX)
  - ▷ Common subjunctive uses in **independent** clauses:
    deliberative questions (Cap. XXIX)
    wishes (Cap. XXXII)

Present Subjunctive

Forms of present subjunctive:

- 2nd, 3rd, and 4th conjugations insert *-ā/a* between the present stem and the personal endings:

active	passive
-a|m	*-a|r*
-ā|s	*-ā|ris*

---

2.   In Cap. XXIX you will learn about questions in the subjunctive (deliberative questions).

```
-a|t              -ā|tur
-ā|mus            -ā|mur
-ā|tis            -ā|minī
-a|nt             -a|ntur
```

- 1st conjugation verbs, whose stems, as you know, end in *-ā-*, have *-ē/e-* before the personal endings in the present subjunctive:

```
-e|m              -e|r
-ē|s              -ē|ris
-e|t              -ē|tur
-ē|mus            -ē|mur
-ē|tis            -ē|minī
-e|nt             -e|ntur
```

→ In the section Grammatica Latina of Lingua Latina and at the back of this book, you will find examples of verbs with all these endings.

Breviter: The present subjunctive is formed with an *e* in 1st conjugation verbs, and an *a* in the other conjugations.

Translating the Subjunctive: The best way to read Latin is not to translate, but to understand in Latin. That requires knowing how your own language works as well as Latin! Then you can say to yourself, *How does this work in my language?* That may mean there are several ways to translate any given construction. The English translations below aim at showing the variety of interpretations possible. Some may seem rather literal and strained, others too free.

Verba postulandī

While the indicative is used to express that something does actually happen, the subjunctive expresses a desire or effort that something shall happen. Such an **indirect command** can be introduced by verbs that express an order (*verba postulandī*):

```
imperāre              ōrāre
postulāre             monēre
```

These *verba postulandī*—verbs that order, ask, warn, etc.—are often followed by object clauses introduced by *ut*, or, if they are negative (see Section III), by *nē* (or *ut nē*); the verb will be in the subjunctive. Examples can be found in the account of Julius's dealings with his men, e.g.:

Iūlius colōnō <u>imperat</u> <u>ut</u> mercēdem solv<u>at</u>.	Julius orders the farmer to pay his fee/gives an order to the farmer that he pay/commands the farmer in order that he pay. (ll.81–82)

Vōs <u>moneō</u> <u>ut</u> industriē in vīneīs labōr<u>ētis</u>. (l.126)

Complements in *Verba Postulandī*

Notice that the person commanded in each of the three sentences is expressed in a different case:

> *Iūlius <u>colōnō</u> imperat ut mercēdem solvat.* (ll.81–82)
> *Colōnus <u>eum</u> ōrat ut patientiam habeat.* (ll.92–93)
> *Num uxor <u>abs tē</u> postulat ut tū prō mātre īnfantēs cūrēs?* (ll.100–101)

The case of the person ordered depends on the verb used.
  Dative (intransitive verbs):

> imperāre eī ut
> persuādēre eī ut

Ab + ablative (the following verbs suggest "seek from"):

> *quaerere ab eō ut*
> *petere ab eō ut*
> *postulāre ab eō ut*

Accusative (transitive verbs):

> *rogāre eum ut*
> *ōrāre eum ut*
> *monēre eum ut*

Notā Bene: Iubēre (order) does not regularly take an indirect command, but the accusative and infinitive construction. Compare:

> *Vōs <u>moneō</u> <u>ut</u> industriē in vīneīs labōr<u>ētis</u>.* (ll.125–126)
> *<u>Iubeō</u> vōs industriē in vīneīs labōr<u>āre</u>.*
> *Medicus Quīntum ōs aper<u>īre</u> atque linguam ostend<u>ere iubet</u>.*
>   (Cap. XI, ll.69–70)
> *Medicus Quīntō <u>imperat</u> ut ōs aper<u>iat</u> atque linguam ostend<u>at</u>.*

Ut

Most Latin *ut*-clauses with the subjunctive correspond to English "that"-clauses.
  Remember: *ut* is also a comparative conjunction, meaning "like" or "as," and is followed:

- by the indicative:
  <u>ut</u> tempestās mare tranquillum turbā<u>vit</u>, <u>ita</u> (as…thus)… (ll.8–9)
  ut spēr<u>ō</u> (l.149)
  Cūr ille servus mēcum venīre nōn potest <u>ut</u> solet? (Cap. XIV, l.120)
- by a noun adjective:
  Oculī lupī in umbrā lūcent <u>ut</u> gemmae et dentēs <u>ut</u> margarītae.
    (Cap. IX, ll.72–73)

Puer quiētus super lectum iacet <u>ut</u> mortuus. (Cap. XI, ll.103–104)
Gallia autem prōvincia Rōmāna est, <u>ut</u> Hispānia, Syria, Aegyptus.
   (Cap. XII, ll.63–64)
<u>ut</u> saxa…vorāginēs…praedōnēs (Cap. XXVIII, ll.131–132)

Nē…quidem

The negation *nē* is also used in *nē…quidem* ("not even"):

> *Nē in Campāniā quidem plūrēs vīllae sunt.* (l.55)
> *Nē assem quidem habeō.* (l.86)
> *Nē verbum quidem dīc!*

Prae, prō, abs

The prepositions *prae* and *prō* take the ablative; the basic meaning of both is "before," from which other meanings are derived (*prae* ll.63, 83; *prō* ll.71, 72):

> *Arātor duōs validōs bovēs quī arātrum trahunt <u>prae sē</u> agit.* (ll.13–14)
> *Quamquam nūllō modō labōrem agricolārum sordidum indignumve esse exīstimat, tamen sē <u>prae agricolīs</u> beātum esse cēnset.* (ll.61–63)
> *Colōnus pallidus <u>prae metū</u> loquī nōn potest.* (l.83)
> *Colōnus est agricola quī nōn suōs, sed aliēnōs agrōs <u>prō dominō absentī</u> colit.* (ll.71–72)
> *Mercēdem dominō solvit <u>prō frūgibus</u> agrōrum.* (l.72)

Abs for *ab* is found only before *tē*: *abs tē*:

> *Cūr nōndum solvistī mercēdem quam ter quaterve iam <u>abs tē</u> poposcī.*
>   (ll.79–80 = *ā tē*).

Ablative of Separation

Note the ablative of separation (without *ab*) with:

> <u>*pellere*</u>: *ut tē agrīs meīs pellant.* (l.89)
> <u>*prohibēre*</u>: *Nōlī mē officiō meō prohibēre!* (ll.173–174)

Parum

The adverb *parum* often means not "a little" but "too little," as in the following examples:

> *<u>Parum</u> temporis habeō ad opus rūsticum.* (ll.98–99)
> *Imber brevis quem hodiē habuimus frūmentō prōfuit quidem, sed <u>parum</u> fuit.* (ll.130–131)

Lēctiō Tertia (Section III)

Verba cūrandī

Verba cūrandī (verbs that show an effort to get something done) can be used to give commands as well:

cūrāre:	*cūrā ut*	*facere:*	*fac ut*
labōrāre:	*labōrā ut*	*cavēre:*	*cavē nē*
efficere:	*effice ut*		

    Verba cūrandī are not always in the imperative, however, but are often followed by object clauses,[3] e.g.:

Calor sōlis nōn ipse per sē efficit ut vīnum bonum sit.	The heat of the sun does not itself through its own agency bring it about that/effect that/accomplish that the wine is good/does not make the wine good. (ll.124–125)
Faciam ut tergum eī doleat.	I will make his back hurt (*literally*: I will bring it about that the back to him hurts). (l.153)

Like *verba postulandī*, *verba cūrandī* are often followed by object clauses introduced by *ut,* or, if they are negative, by *nē* (or *ut nē*) and the subjunctive.

Prīmum cūrā ut uxor et līberī valeant, tum vērō labōrā ut pecūniam solvās.	First of all take care that/make sure that (your) wife and children be well/are well, then surely work to pay the money/work so that you can pay the money. (ll.111–113)

    Fac ut ovēs ex agrīs agantur! (ll.175–176)
    Officium tuum est cūrāre nē ovēs aberrent nēve ā lupō rapiantur.
      (ll.161–162)

    As appears from the last example, the second of two negative clauses is introduced by *nē-ve,* i.e., *nē* with the attached conjunction *-ve,* which has the same value as *vel.*
    Summary:

ut + subjunctive	command, ask that something happen
nē/ut nē + subjunctive	command, ask that something not happen

---

3.   An "object clause" is a dependent clause that functions as the object of the verb.

Subjunctive of *esse*

In lines 151–152, we find an example of the irregular present subjunctive of *esse*:

> *Ego vērō cūrābō nē ille pāstor neglegēns <u>sit</u> nēve dormiat!*

Here are the other forms:

sim	*sīmus*
sīs	*sītis*
sit	*sint*

Quam + the superlative

Quam + superlative (with or without *posse*) denotes the highest possible degree:

> *Pāstor <u>quam celerrimē potest</u> ad ovēs suās currit.* as quickly as possible
> (ll.177–178)

Studia Rōmāna

We read about Julius's villa in Cap. V and now learn that around the *hortus* lie the fields that support the farm. Iūlius has no doubt inherited the many villas and the house in Rome that had belonged to his father (*Pater lūliī…magnam pecūniam habēbat multāsque vīllās magnificās possidēbat praeter domum Rōmānam*, Caps. XIX, XXX). It was not unusual for wealthy Romans to own more than one estate (Cicero had several), as agriculture was *the* noble profession and capital rooted in land was the mark of a gentleman. This attitude persists through Roman history. In the second century BC, Cato had written in his treatise *dē Rē Rūsticā*, "Our ancestors, when they praised a man as being good, were praising him on these merits: a good farmer and good husbandman" (*Māiōrēs nostrī… virum bonum quom* (= *cum*) *laudābant, ita laudābant, bonum agricolam bonumque colōnum*). In the first century BC, Cicero, in his book *On Duties* (*dē Officiīs*), writes, "Of all the pursuits, from which something is acquired, nothing is better than farming, nothing richer, nothing sweeter, nothing worthier of a free man" (*Omnium autem rērum, ex quibus aliquid adquīritur, nihil est agrī cultūrā melius, nihil ūberius, nihil dulcius, nihil homine līberō dignius*). Columella (first century AD) still sees agriculture as the only way of making a living worthy of a freeborn man.[4]

Vergil wrote a four-book didactic epic (see Cap. X) on farming, called the *Geōrgica* (Γεωργικά, *Concerning Farming*) after his bucolic poems (see Cap. IX) and before his more famous *Aenēis* (*Aeneid*). In the beginning of Book II, he praises the life of farmers, beginning with (II.458–460):

---

4.   1.10: *superest…genus līberāle et ingenuun reī familiāris augendae, quod ex agricolātiōne contingit.*

Ō fortūnātōs nimium, sua sī bona nōrint,
   agricolās! quibus ipsa procul discordibus armīs
   fundit humō facilem uictum iustissima tellūs.

Vocabulary

nimium = nimis
nōrint = noverint (condition about which you will learn in *Rōma Aeterna*): "if they would come to know their good fortune"
discors (genitive: *discordis*): discordant, harsh
fundere: pour, pour out
victus, ūs: sustenance, nourishment (do not confuse with *victum* from *vincere*)

Of course, the situation was not so idyllic for the *colōnī*, as we see in this chapter. A *colōnus* is a tenant farmer who signs a lease with the landowner (Julius). Sometimes, the tenant farmers paid the owner for the right to farm; sometimes, they remunerated the owner by giving him part of the produce. *Colōnī*, as the one in our chapter, can wind up in debt to the farmer and be driven from the farm.

This chapter highlights three important aspects of Roman culture: *officium* (duty, responsibility: from *opus* + *facere*: a labor or duty which one performs), *ōtium* (leisure time, freedom from responsibility), and *negōtium* (literally: the lack of *ōtium*; business, employment). We have already seen the idea of *officium* in Cap. XX, when Aemilia declares of her coming baby, (l.83–84): "*Māter ipsa eum cūrāre et alere dēbet—hoc est mātris officium!*" Julius's inspection of his estate is part of what he sees as his *officium* (Cap. XX, l.96–97: *Meum officium est pecūniam facere ac magnam familiam alere*).

A Roman active in city life (as Julius is with his frequent trips to Rome, Cap. XX) would see his *praedium* not only as the backbone of his finances, but also as an opportunity for *ōtium*, away from the pressures of city life. At his estate, a *paterfamilās* has the *ōtium* after lunch to nap, take a stroll, and bathe (*prīmum quiēscit, tum ambulat, dēnique lavātur*, ll.1–2). But he also must check his farm. In this he also follows Cato's advice: When the master has come to the villa, when he has greeted the household god, let him take a tour of the farm on the same day, if he can; if not the same day, then the day after.[5] His farm would have been managed by a combination of slaves and tenant farmers, freemen who pay Julius rent (ll.70–73). Julius behaves himself exactly as Columella teaches: he is stern but not unreasonable with his farmhands (although we might consider beating the shepherd less than reasonable).

---

5.   2.1: *Paterfamilās ubi ad vīllam vēnit, ubi lārem familiārem salūtāvit, fundum eōdem diē, sī potest, circumeat; sī nōn eōdem diē, at postrīdiē.*

Cato's advice to greet the household god (*larem familiārem salūtāre*) refers to the protective spirit who guarded the place. You read about the *lar familiāris* in the notes to Cap. IV.

Vocābula Disposita/Ōrdināta

Nōmina

1st

agricola, -ae (*m.*)	farmer
cōpia, -ae	abundance
cūra, -ae	care, concern
lāna, -ae	wool
patientia, -ae	patience
ūva, -ae	grape
vīnea, -ae	vineyard

2nd

ager, agrī	field
arātrum, -ī	plow
colōnus, -ī	(tenant) farmer
coniūnctīvus	subjunctive
frūmentum, -ī	grain
īnstrūmentum, -ī	tool, instrument
negōtium, -ī	business
ōtium, -ī	leisure
pābulum, -ī	fodder
praedium, -ī	estate
vīnum, -ī	wine

3rd

calor, calōris (*m.*)	heat
falx, falcis (*f.*)	sickle
frīgus, frīgoris (*n.*)	chill, cold
frūgēs, frūgum (*f. pl.*)	crops
grex, gregis (*m.*)	herd
labor, labōris (*m.*)	labor, toil
pecus, pecoris (*n.*)	livestock, cattle
precēs, precum (*f. pl.*)	prayers
regiō, regiōnis (*f.*)	region
rūs, rūris (*n.*)	countryside
sēmen, sēminis (*n.*)	seed
vītis, vītis (*f.*)	vine

Verba

-āre (1)

(arō) arāre, arāvisse, arātum	plow
(rigō) rigāre, rigāvisse, rigātum	water
(labōrō) labōrāre, labōrāvisse, labōrātum	work, toil

(exīstimō) exīstimāre, exīstimāvisse, exīstimātum	think
(ōrō) ōrāre, ōrāvisse, ōrātum	beg, pray

-ēre (2)

(cēnseō) cēnsēre, cēnsuisse, cēnsum	think
(noceō) nocēre, nocuisse (*intr. + dat.*)	harm
(prohibeō) prohibēre, prohibuisse, prohibitum	keep off, prevent

-ere (3)

(cingō) cingere, cīnxīsse, cīnctum	bind round, surround
(colō) colere, coluisse, cultum	cultivate
(crēscō) crēscere, crēvisse	grow
(invehō) invehere, invēxisse, invectum	import
(metō) metere, messuisse, messum	reap, harvest
(neglegō) neglegere, neglēxisse, neglēctum	neglect
(pāscō) pāscere, pāvisse, pāstum	to pasture
(prōiciō) prōicere, prōiēcisse, prōiectum	throw forward
(quiescō) quiescere, quiēvisse	rest
(rapiō) rapere, rapuisse, raptum	tear away, carry off
(serō) serere, sēvisse, satum	sow
(spargō) spargere, sparsisse, sparsum	sprinkle
(ūtor) ūtī, ūsum (+*abl.*)	use

Irregular

(prōsum) prōdesse, prōfuisse (+*dat.*)	to be profitable, of advantage

Adiectīva

1st/2nd (-us/er, -a, -um)

amoenus, -a, -um	pleasant (of places)
gravidus, -a , -um	heavy, weighty, pregnant
immātūrus, -a, -um	not ripe
inhūmānus, -a, -um	inhumane
mātūrus, -a, -um	ripe, early
rūsticus, -a, -um	of the country, rustic
siccus, -a, -um	dry
suburbānus, -a, -um	near the city
trīcēsimus, -a, -um	30th
urbānus, -a, -um	of the city, sophisticated

3rd

fertilis, -e	fertile
neglegēns (*gen.* neglegentis)	careless
patiēns (*gen.* patientis)	enduring, patient
rudis, -e	rough

Irregular
nēquam/nēquior, nēquius/   worthless
   nēquissimus, -a, -um

Prōnōmina
quīdam, quaedam, quoddam   a certain

Adverbia
  circā   around
  dēnique   finally
  parum   little, too little, *also indecl. noun*
  prae   before
  tantum   only, so much, *also indecl. noun*

Coniūnctiōnēs
  nē   *negative conjunction*
  -ve   or (=*vel*)

Praepositiōnēs
  abs = **ā, ab** (*before* **te**)
  circā (*prp. + acc.*)   around
  prae (*prp. + abl.*)   before, in front of, in comparison with
  prō (*prp. + abl.*)   before, in front of, on behalf of

XXVIII. Perīcula Maris

Rēs Grammaticae Novae

1. Verbs
   a. Imperfect Subjunctive: Active and Passive
   b. Tense in the Subjunctive
   c. Uses of the Subjunctive
      i. Purpose (Final) Clauses
      ii. Result (Consecutive) Clauses
   d. Indirect Statement vs. *verba postulandī*
   e. *velle, nōlle, mālle*
   f. *īre* (Present Subjunctive)
2. Pronoun: Reflexive (continued)

Medus and Lydia at Sea

In this chapter and the next, you hear more about Medus and Lydia. When the violent storm dies down, their ship sails on over the open sea. Lydia shows Medus the little book that she has brought with her and reads aloud from it, and in this way, you become acquainted with the oldest Latin translation of the New Testament, used by St. Jerome in the fourth century in his Latin version of the Bible (the so-called Vulgate, *Vulgāta,* the "popular" version).

Lēctiō Prīma (Section I)

Imperfect Subjunctive

When Lydia explains the power of Jesus Christ to Medus, she uses *verba cūrandī*:

> *Quī medicus verbīs sōlīs potest <u>facere ut</u> hominēs caecī <u>videant</u>, surdī <u>audiant</u>, mūtī <u>loquantur</u>, claudī <u>ambulent</u>?* (ll.30–32)

Compare what happens to the verb in the subjunctive clause when the main verb is in the past:

In Iūdaeā Iēsūs nōn sōlum <u>faciēbat ut</u> caecī <u>vidērent</u>, surdī <u>audīrent</u>, mūtī <u>loquerentur</u>, vērum etiam verbīs <u>efficiēbat</u> ut mortuī <u>surgerent</u> et <u>ambulārent</u>. (ll.34–37)

When the main verb refers to the past, the tense of the subjunctive changes as well. Just as the present subjunctive tells us the verb is incomplete in present time, the imperfect subjunctive tells us the verb is incomplete in past time (see below, Sequence of Tense).

Forming the Imperfect Subjunctive

The imperfect subjunctive is formed by inserting -*rē*- (in consonant-stems -*erē*) between the present stem and the personal endings. The imperfect subjunctive thus looks exactly like the present infinitive plus personal endings.

1st, 2nd, and 4th conjugations insert -*rē*-/-*re* between the present stem and the personal endings, e.g.:[1]

ambulā|re|m	*vidē|re|m*	*audī|re|m*
ambulā|rē|s	*vidē|rē|s*	*audī|rē|s*
ambulā|re|t	*vidē|re|t*	*audī|re|t*
ambulā|rē|mus	*vidē|rē|mus*	*audī|rē|mus*
ambulā|rē|tis	*vidē|rē|tis*	*audī|rē|tis*
ambulā|re|nt	*vidē|re|nt*	*audī|re|nt*

3rd conjugation inserts -*erē*-/-*ere* between the present stem and the personal endings:

surg|ere|m	*fac|ere|m*
surg|erē|s	*fac|erē|s*
surg|ere|t	*fac|ere|t*
surg|erē|mus	*fac|erē|mus*
surg|erē|tis	*fac|erē|tis*
surg|ere|nt	*fac|ere|nt*

Summary of Imperfect Subjunctive Endings

active			
sing.	1st	-(*ā, ē, e, ī*) *re|m*	
	2nd	-(*ā, ē, e, ī*) *rē|s*	
	3rd	-(*ā, ē, e, ī*) *re|t*	
pl.	1st	-(*ā, ē, e, ī*) *rē|mus*	
	2nd	-(*ā, ē, e, ī*) *rē|tis*	
	3rd	-(*ā, ē, e, ī*) *re|nt*	

---

1. Remember: short *e* before -*m*, -*t*, -*nt*, -*r*, -*ntur*.

passive

sing.	1st	-(ā, ē, e, ī) re|r
	2nd	-(ā, ē, e, ī) rē|ris
	3rd	-(ā, ē, e, ī) rē|tur
pl. 1st		-(ā, ē, e, ī) rē|mur
	2nd	-(ā, ē, e, ī) rē|minī
	3rd	-(ā, ē, e, ī) re|ntur

esse: present and imperfect subjunctive

sing.	present	imperfect
1st	*sim*	*esse|m*
2nd	*sīs*	*essē|s*
3rd	*sit*	*esse|t*
pl.		
1st	*sīmus*	*essē|mus*
2nd	*sītis*	*essē|tis*
3rd	*sint*	*esse|nt*

→ Examples of all the forms of the four conjugations, active and passive, and of *esse* are found in the section Grammatica Latina of Lingua Latina and at the back of this book.

Tense in the Subjunctive

Just as with infinitives and participles, time (tense) in the subjunctive is not about absolute time as much as relation. The present and imperfect subjunctives in dependent clauses represent **incomplete action** relative to the main verb.

If the main verb:

- is present or future, use the present subjunctive to indicate incomplete action
- refers to the past (perfect, imperfect, or pluperfect), the imperfect subjunctive indicates incomplete action[2]

Compare the sentences:

Magister mē monet (/monēbit) ut taceam et audiam.
Magister mē monēbat (/monuit/monuerat) ut tacērem et audīrem.

---

2. A perfect tense main verb can be followed by the present subjunctive if the perfect tense represents a present state (e.g., I have arrived=I am here), e.g., Cap. XXXIV, l.31–32: *nisi tam fortiter pugnāvit ut spectātōrēs eum vīvere velint.*

Sequence of Tense

Main Verb	Subordinate Verb	
	Incomplete Action	Completed Action
present future	present subjunctive	(Cap. XXXII)
past tense	imperfect subjunctive	(Cap. XXXIII)

Lēctiō Altera (Section II)

Uses of the Subjunctive: Result

The subjunctive, introduced by *ut*, is used in clauses that tell the consequence of the main clause. These are called **result clauses**. The main clause that introduces the result clause usually contains a word (note below *tam, ita*) that signals the result. Result clauses are also called consecutive clauses (*cōnsecūtīvus, -a, -um < cōnsequī*) as they show what naturally follows from the idea in the main clause.

Result clauses (show tendency or effect):

Num quis <u>tam</u> stultus est <u>ut</u> ista vēra esse crēd<u>at</u>?	*ut…crēdat* tells the consequence of anyone being so stupid: For who is <u>so</u> stupid <u>that</u> he would believe these things are true? (ll.90–91)
Nam trēs diī, Neptūnus, Iūppiter, Plūtō, mundum ūniversum <u>ita</u> inter sē dīvīsērunt <u>ut</u> Iūppiter rēx caelī <u>esset</u>.	For three gods, Neptune, Jupiter, Pluto, divided the whole world among themselves <u>in such a way that</u> Jupiter was king of the sky. (ll.85–87)

There are more examples in Cap. XXIX.

Reflexive *sē* (continued)

In *ut/nē*-clauses expressing an indirect command, the reflexive pronouns *sē, sibi, suus* refer to the subject of the main verb, i.e., the person ordering, requesting, etc. Compare:

Dāvus eum <u>sēcum</u> venīre iubet.: i.e., *eī imperat ut <u>sēcum</u> (cum Dāvō) veniat* (Cap. XIV, l.86–87)

Pāstor dominum ōrat nē <u>sē</u> verberet.: i.e., *nē pāstōrem verberet* (Cap. XXVII, ll.158–159)

Mēdus eam rogat ut aliquid <u>sibi</u> legat.: i.e., *ut Mēdō legat* (ll.56–57)

[Iaīrus] Iēsum rogāvit ut fīliam <u>suam</u> mortuam suscitāret. (l.65–66)

Lēctiō Tertia (Section III)

Uses of the Subjunctive: Purpose (Final)

The subjunctive, introduced by *ut*, is used in clauses that tell the end or goal of the main clause. These are called purpose, or final (*fīnālis*), clauses.

Purpose clauses (show intention):

Praedōnēs nāvēs persequuntur,	Pirates follow the ships <u>in</u>
<u>ut</u> *mercēs et pecūniam rapi<u>ant</u>*	<u>order to</u> (or just "<u>to</u>") seize
nautāsque occīd<u>ant</u>.	and kill. (ll.132–134)

Petrus ambulābat super aquam, <u>ut</u> venī<u>ret</u> ad Iēsum. (ll.102–103)
ē vīllā fūgī, <u>ut</u> verbera vītā<u>rem</u> atque <u>ut</u> amīcam meam vidē<u>rem</u> ac semper cum eā <u>essem</u>. (ll.162–163)

Indirect Statement versus *Verba Postulandī* (Indirect Commands)

Note the difference between:

- *verba dīcendī et sentiendī,* which are combined with the acc. + inf.
- *verba postulandī,* which take an *ut*-clause in the subjunctive.

Some verbs can have both functions, e.g., *persuādēre* in these two examples:

Mihi nēmō persuādēbit homin<u>em</u> super mare ambulāre <u>posse</u>.:
    no one will persuade/convince me <u>that</u>… (ll.110–111)
Mēdus mihi persuāsit <u>ut</u> sēcum venī<u>rem</u>.: Medus persuaded me <u>to</u>…
    (ll.174–175)

In both senses, *persuādēre* takes the dative (intransitive, like *oboedīre, impendēre, servīre, prōdesse,* and *nocēre*).

Īre: Present Subjunctive

In ll.145–146 we meet the present subjunctive of *īre*:

cūrābō ut salvī in Graeciam <u>eāmus</u>,

Īre:

Indicative	Subjunctive
eō	*eam*
īs	*eās*
it	*eat*
īmus	*eāmus*
ītis	*eātis*
eunt	*eant*

Velle, nōlle, mālle

In addition to *velle* (Caps. X, XIII), *nōlle* (= *nōn velle*, Cap. XX), this chapter presents *mālle* (*magis velle*), to "want more," or "prefer." *Mālle* is often followed by *quam*:

> *Ego Rōmae vīvere mālō quam in Graeciā.* (ll.150–151)
> *Nōs cīvēs Rōmānī morī mālumus quam servīre!* (ll.154–155)

Volō, velle, voluisse to be willing, want		*Nōlō, nōlle, nōluisse* to be unwilling, not want		*Mālō, mālle, māluisse* to prefer	
volō	volumus	nōlō	nōlumus	mālō	mālumus
vīs	vultis	nōn vīs	nōn vultis	māvīs	māvultis
vult	volunt	nōn vult	nōlunt	māvult	mālunt

Recēnsiō: Subordinate Subjunctive Clauses

Verba postulandī et cūrandī + *ut/nē* subjunctive:

> *Quī medicus verbīs sōlīs <u>potest facere ut</u> hominēs caecī videant, surdī audiant, mūtī loquantur, claudī ambulent?* (ll.30–32)

> *In Iūdaeā Iēsūs nōn sōlum <u>faciēbat ut</u> caecī vidērent, surdī audīrent, mūtī loquerentur, vērum etiam verbīs efficiēbat ut mortuī surgerent et ambulārent.* (ll.34–37)

> *Ille <u>cūrāvit ut</u> nōs ē tempestāte servārēmur nēve mergerēmur—vel potius nōs ipsī quī mercēs ēiēcimus.* (ll.127–129)

> *<u>Cūrābō ut</u> omnia perīcula vītēmus ac salvī in Graeciam eāmus.* (ll.145–146)

> *"Legam tibi," inquit, "dē virō claudō <u>cui</u> Iēsūs <u>imperāvit ut</u> surgeret et tolleret lectum suum et domum ambulāret."* (ll.58–60)

> *Modo dīxistī, "Chrīstum etiam <u>mortuīs imperāvisse ut</u> surgerent et ambulārent."* (ll.61–62)

> *In Italiā dominō sevērō serviēbam quī <u>ā mē postulābat ut</u> opus sordidum facerem nec mihi pecūlium dabat.* (ll.158–160)

> *Sī quid prāvē fēceram, dominus <u>imperābat ut</u> ego ab aliīs servīs tenērer et verberārer.* (ll.160–161)

> *Multīs prōmissīs <u>eī persuāsī ut</u> mēcum ex Italiā proficīscerētur, Lydia enim Rōmae vīvere māvult quam in Graeciā.* (ll.163–165)

> *Certē nōn laetō animō Rōmā profecta sum, et difficile fuit <u>mihi persuādēre ut</u> amīcās meās Rōmānās dēsererem.* (ll.172–174)

> *Num dominus ille sevērus, quī <u>tibi imperābat ut</u> opus sordidum facerēs, tantum pecūlium tibi dabat prō opere sordidō?* (ll.181–183)

Reflexive *sē, sibi, suus* in indirect command:

> *Mēdus, quī legere nōn didicit, Lydiae librum reddit <u>eam</u>que <u>rogat</u> <u>ut</u> aliquid <u>sibi</u> legat.* (ll.56–57)

> *Audī igitur quod scrīptum est dē Iaīrō, prīncipe quōdam Iūdaeōrum, quī <u>Iēsum</u> <u>rogāvit</u> <u>ut</u> fīliam <u>suam</u> mortuam suscitāret.* (ll.64–66)

> *Nec prōmissīs sōlīs Mēdus <u>mihi</u> <u>persuāsit</u> <u>ut</u> <u>sēcum</u> venīrem, sed etiam dōnō pulcherrimō.* (ll.174–175)

Purpose/final clause: *ut/nē* + subjunctive (*fīnālis -e* < *fīnis*, "end," "purpose"):

> *Praedōnēs maritimī quī nāvēs persequuntur, <u>ut</u> mercēs et pecūniam rapiant nautāsque occīdant.* (ll.132–134)

> *Ōstiā igitur hanc nāvem cōnscendimus, <u>ut</u> in Graeciam nāvigārēmus.* (ll.165–167)

> *Sed herī ē vīllā fūgī, <u>ut</u> verbera vītārem, atque <u>ut</u> amīcam meam vidērem ac semper cum eā essem.* (ll.161–163)

Result/consecutive clause: *ut* + subjunctive:

> *Tanta ūnīus deī potestās nōn est. Nam trēs diī, Neptūnus, Iūppiter, Plūtō, mundum ūniversum <u>ita</u> inter sē dīvīsērunt, <u>ut</u> Iūppiter rēx caelī esset, rēx maris esset Neptūnus, Plūtō autem rēgnāret apud Īnferōs, ubi animae mortuōrum velut umbrae versārī dīcuntur.* (ll.85–89)

> *Num quis <u>tam</u> stultus est <u>ut</u> ista vēra esse crēdat?* (ll.90–91)
> *Num tū <u>tam</u> stultus es <u>ut</u> haec crēdās?* (ll.109–110)

Compare

Indirect statement: *verba dīcendī et sentiendī* → accusative + infinitive:

> *Mihi nēmō persuādēbit hominem super mare ambulāre posse!* (ll.110–111)

> *Nōnne id tibi persuāsit eum habēre potestātem maris et ventōrum?* (ll.115–116)

Studia Rōmāna

The strait (between Sicily and mainland Italy) through which Medus and Lydia are traveling was notoriously dangerous and considered the location of the infamous Scylla and Charybdis: *dextrum Scylla latus, laeuum implācāta Charybdis/obsidet* (Vergil, *Aeneid* 3.420–21). Charybdis was a fierce whirlpool, personified as female that sucked down ships in its vortex. Scylla occupied the rocks opposite Charybdis; she is variously described, but she often appears as a woman from the waist up, a pack of dogs that grab and devour sailors from the waist down. Ovid gives a sympathetic version of the myth in the *Metamorphoses* (Books 13–14): Scylla was a beautiful young girl turned into a monster by the witch Circe, jealous of her beauty and angry because the handsome Glaucus loved Scylla instead of her.

Medus, living as a house slave in Tusculum, would have been less likely to meet Christians than Lydia, who lived in Rome, where there were growing numbers of Christians. We can learn more about early Christians from inscriptions and archaeology than from Latin authors. By the time of our narrative, there were several texts available to Christians like Lydia, in Koine Greek (which, due to its simplicity, both she and Medus could read) as well as Latin translations (the earliest of which to survive is from the fourth century AD). Matthew was written around AD 70, and by the middle of the second century, all four Gospels had been written, along with the Acts of the Apostles and the letters of Paul. From these texts, from inscriptions, and from the (somewhat later) catacombs and their wall painting, we can get some idea about a growing Christian church.

Around this time, *Quīntus Septimius Flōrens Tertulliānus* was born in Carthage in Roman Africa. The first Christian author in Latin, Tertullian came from the educated classes and brought considerable rhetorical skill to his writings. At the turn of the century we have also the narrative of Perpetua and Felicity, two young Christian martyrs at Carthage, put to death in the persecutions of the early third century.

Our story presents us with a credible scenario: the presumably uneducated *gubernātor* holds firm to traditional stories of the realms of Juppiter, Neptune, and Pluto. Medus, although he has never heard of Jesus Christ, is very interested to hear about a new god who might offer him something, and Lydia is a young Christian eager to share her faith. By the time of our story, the Christians had suffered sporadic persecution, most horribly under Nero, who used Christians as a scapegoat, blaming them for the great fire in Rome in AD 64, but also under Domitian (AD 81–96). From the reign of the emperor Trajan (AD 98–117), we have a *commercium epistulārum* between Trajan and Pliny. Pliny did not understand Christian insistence on an allegiance to a god that would not allow them to demonstrate loyalty to the state gods, and especially to the emperor (a loyalty demonstrated by offering a sacrifice of wine and incense, in violation of Christian principles). It is clear from these letters that Christians were suspect as disloyal to the empire and they were at risk of being informed upon by others.

Vocābula Disposita/Ōrdināta

Nōmina
  1st

fāma, -ae	report, reputation
nāvicula, -ae	small boat
turba, -ae	crowd
vigilia, -ae	night watch

  2nd

animus, -ī	mind, emotion, courage
dictum, -ī	saying
fretum, -ī	strait, channel
libellus, -ī	small book
mundus, -ī	world
pecūlium, -ī	money (given to slaves), "slave stipend"
perīculum, -ī	risk, danger

  3rd

phantasma, phantasmatis (*n.*)	ghost, apparition
potestās, potestātis (*f.*)	power, ability
praedō, praedōnis (*m.*)	robber, pirate
prīnceps, prīncipis (*m.*)	chief, leader, head man
tībīcen, tībicinis (*m.*)	flute player
tranquillitās, tranquillitātis (*f.*)	tranquility
vorāgō, vorāginis (*f.*)	abyss, whirlpool

Verba
  -āre (1)

(adōrō) adōrāre, adōrāvisse, adōrātum	adore, worship
(admīror) admīrārī, admīrātum	wonder at
(cessō) cessāre, cessāvisse, cessātum	cease, stop
(memorō) memorāre, memorāvisse, memorātum	relate, recall
(rēgnō) rēgnāre, rēgnāvisse, rēgnātum	rule
(rogō) rogāre, rogāvisse, rogātum	ask
(salvō) salvāre, salvāvisse, salvātum	make safe
(spērō) spērāre, spērāvisse, spērātum	hope for
(suscitō) suscitāre, suscitāvisse, suscitātum	wake up, rouse
(tumultuor) tumultuārī, tumultuātum	make an uproar
(versor) versārī, versātum	move about, be present
(vītō) vītāre, vītāvisse, vītātum	avoid

  -ēre (2)

(habeor) habērī, habitum	be held, be considered

(impendeō) impendēre, impendisse (*intr. + dat.*)	threaten
(persuādeō) persuādēre, persuāsisse (*intr. + dat.*)	persuade, convince

-ere (3)

(apprehendō) apprehendere, apprehendisse, apprehēnsum	seize
(disiungō) disiungere, disiūnxisse, disiūnctum	unyoke, separate
(ēiciō) ēicere, ēiēcisse, ēiectum	throw out, eject
(ēvolvō) ēvolvere, ēvolvisse, ēvolūtum	unroll
(extendō) extendere, extendisse, extentum	extend
(morior) morī, mortuum	die
(nāscor) nāscī, nātum	be born

-īre (4)

(oboediō) oboedīre, -īvisse/ iisse (+ *dat.*)	obey
(pereō) perīre, periisse	perish
(perveniō) pervenīre, pervēnisse	arrive
(serviō) servīre, -īvisse/iisse, -ītum (+ *dat.*)	be a slave to, serve

Irregular

(mālō) mālle, māluisse	prefer

Adiectīva

1st/2nd (-us/er, -a, -um)

attentus, -a, -um	attentive
caecus, -a, -um	blind
claudus, -a, -um	lame
mūtus, -a, -um	mute
perīculōsus, -a, -um	dangerous
quadrāgēsimus, -a, -um	40th
salvus, -a, -um	safe
surdus, -a, -um	deaf
tūtus, -a, -um	safe
ūniversus, -a, -um	the whole of, entire

3rd

cōnstāns (*gen.* cōnstantis)	steady, firm
immortālis, -e	immortal
mortālis, -e	mortal

Adverbia

potius	rather
utrum	whether

Coniūnctiōnēs

velut	as, as if

XXIX. Nāvigāre Necesse Est

Rēs Grammaticae Novae

1. Verbs
   a. Uses of the Subjunctive
      i. Deliberative Questions
      ii. Indirect Questions
   b. *Cum* Clauses
      i. *Cum* Temporal (Indicative)
      ii. *Cum* Temporal and Causal (Subjunctive)
   c. Compound Verbs
2. Nouns: Case Uses
   a. Genitive of Value
   b. Genitive of the Charge
   c. Partitive Genitive: *Nostrum* and *Vestrum*
3. Pronouns: Personal (continued)

"What Shall I Do?"

The Roman merchant, who is ruined because his goods had to be thrown overboard during the storm to keep the ship afloat, cannot fully share the joy of the others at being saved.

Lēctiō Prīma (Section I)

Deliberative Questions

In his distress, the merchant exclaims, *"Heu, mē miserum!"* (acc. in exclamation, Cap. XV) and asks in despair (ll.22–23):

> *Quid faciam?* What am I to do? What can I do?
> *Quid spērem?* What am I to hope for? What can I hope for?

In this kind of deliberative question, when you ask irresolutely what to do, the verb is usually in the subjunctive. Deliberative questions expect to get a directive as an answer, either in the form of the imperative or the subjunctive, or no answer at all (that is, they are questions asked in desperation with no hope of an answer).

Further Examples:

Quōmodo uxōrem et līberōs al<u>am</u>? (l.23)

Gubernātor perterritus exclāmat, "Ō dī bonī! Quid <u>faciāmus</u>?" (ll.198–199)

Sed quōmodo <u>vīvāmus</u> sine pecūniā? Quōmodo cibum et vestem <u>emam</u> īnfantibus meīs? (ll.51–52)

Quid ergō <u>faciam</u>? Ipse dē nāve <u>saliam</u>, an in eādem nāve <u>maneam</u> vōbīscum? (ll.56–57)

Genitive of Value

In order to indicate how much you value something, genitives like *magnī, parvī, plūris, minōris* are used with verbs that evaluate (e.g., *aestimāre* or *facere* in the same sense). Examples:

Mercātōrēs mercēs suās <u>magnī</u> aestimant, vītam nautārum <u>parvī</u> aestimant! (ll.6–7)

Nōnne līberōs <u>plūris</u> aestimās quam mercēs istās? (ll.26–27)

Lēctiō Altera (Section II)

Clauses with the Subordinate Conjunction *cum*

You first learned the conjunction *cum* in Cap. X. Depending on the force of the conjunction, *cum* is used with a verb either in the indicative (as you have met many times) or the subjunctive.

After *cum*, the verb is in the **indicative:**[1]

- in temporal clauses, meaning "when." We met this use of *cum* in Cap. X:

    Cum avis volat, ālae moventur. (Cap. X, l.15)

    Cum syllabae iunguntur, vocābula fīunt. (Cap. XVIII, l.29)

    Cum vocābula coniunguntur, sententiae fīunt. (Cap. XVIII, ll.29–30)

- in clauses describing something that happens usually or repeatedly,[2] e.g.:

    Semper gaudeō <u>cum</u> dē līberīs meīs cōgit<u>ō</u>. (l.47)

    Tū numquam mē salūtābās, <u>cum</u> mē vidē<u>bās</u>. (Cap. XIX, ll.99–100)

---

1. When the *cum*-clause follows the main clause and provides the main focus of the sentence, the indicative is used. This construction is called *cum inversum*. Compare the force of the two English sentences: When I was reading, the phone rang; I was reading when the phone rang. In both sentences, the focus of the sentence is on the phone ringing.

2. *Cum* in this function is called "*<u>cum</u>*" *<u>iterātīvum</u>* (from *iterāre*, "repeat").

After *cum*, the verb is in the **subjunctive**:

- when *cum* means "since," "because," or "as," the subjunctive can be present tense (with a present main verb) or imperfect (with a past tense main verb):

  Gubernātor, cum omnēs attentōs <u>videat</u>, hanc fābulam nārrat. (ll.76–77)

  <u>Cum</u> iam vītam dēspērā<u>ret</u>, id ūnum ōrāvit. (ll.88–89)

  Ānulum abiēcit, <u>cum</u> sēsē nimis fēlīcem esse cēns<u>ēret</u>. (ll.156–157)

  Polycratēs, <u>cum</u> ānulum suum recognōsc<u>eret</u>, māximā laetitiā affectus est. (ll.171–172)

- when the *cum* refers to the past and means "when," its verb is mostly in the imperfect subjunctive, e.g.:

  <u>Cum</u> Ariōn ex Italiā in Graeciam nāvigā<u>ret</u> magnāsque dīvitiās sēcum hab<u>ēret</u>... (ll.78–80)

  <u>Cum</u> haec falsa nārrā<u>rent</u>, Ariōn repente appāruit. (ll.110–111)

Indirect Questions

When questions are reported, that is, they are indirect, the verb goes into the subjunctive. Compare Lydia's (direct) question with her reminder (indirect) of that question in this chapter:

"Nōnne tua <u>erat</u> ista pecūnia?"	"Wasn't that your money?" (Cap. XXVIII, l.187)
"Modo tē interrogāvī tuane <u>esset</u> pecūnia."	"I just asked you if that was your money." (ll.127–128)

As the object of the verb *interrogāre*, the verb in an **indirect question** goes into the subjunctive. Similarly, *Num haec fābula vēra est?* after *dubitāre* becomes:

  dubitō num haec fābula vēra <u>sit</u>. (ll.116–117)

Notā Bene: You will find *dubitāre* with *an* more frequently than with *num*, as you can see in this sentence from the Younger Pliny (*Gāius Plīnius Secundus*):

  Quibus ex causīs, ut suprā scrīpsī, <u>dubitō</u> <u>an</u> īdem nunc tibi quod tunc mihi suādeam.

Consider the implied levels of questions in (ll.105–106):

  "Ubi <u>est</u> Ariōn et quid <u>facit</u>?" (direct question)

  Scītisne ubi <u>sit</u> Ariōn et quid <u>faciat</u>? (indirect question)

  Rēx eōs <u>interrogat</u> "num sci<u>ant</u> ubi <u>sit</u> Ariōn et quid <u>faciat</u>?" (indirect, present main verb)

  Rēx eōs <u>interrogāvit</u> "num sc<u>īrent</u> ubi <u>esset</u> Ariōn et quid fac<u>eret</u>?" (indirect, past main verb)

Notā Bene: Sometimes the reported question is deliberative (see above); context will make this clear:

> *Vir ita perturbātus est ut sē interroget, utrum in mare saliat an in nāve remaneat.* (ll.57–59) = a result clause introducing an indirect deliberative question; what he originally asked himself was: "Should I leap into the sea or remain on the boat," and this becomes: "The man is so distressed that he asks himself whether he should leap into the sea or remain on the boat."
>
> *Mēdus rubēns nescit quid respondeat.* (Cap. XXVIII, l.184): "Medus, blushing, does not know what he should respond." Medus originally asks himself, "what should I respond?"

More Result Clauses

We met consecutive clauses (clauses of result) in the last chapter. Here are further examples from this chapter:

> *Vir ita perturbātus est ut sē interroget...* (ll.57–58)
> *Arīōn tam pulchrē fidibus canēbat ut alter Orpheus appellārētur.* (ll.66–67)
> *An tam ignārus es ut etiam Orpheus tibi ignōtus sit?* (ll.67–68)
> *Is fidicen nōbilissimus fuit quī tam pulchrē canēbat ut bēstiae ferae, nātūram suam oblītae, accēderent.* (ll.70–72)
> *Nautae precibus eius ita permōtī sunt ut manūs quidem ab eō abstinērent.* (ll.86–87)
> *Tanta erat potestās eius, tanta glōria tantaeque dīvitiae, ut nōn sōlum aliī tyrannī, sed etiam dī immortālēs eī invidērent.* (ll.158–160)
> *Piscem cēpit quī tam fōrmōsus erat ut piscātor eum nōn vēnderet.* (ll.167–168)

Words that signal result clauses

tantus, -a, -um so great		adjective of magnitude, quantity
talis, tale	of such a sort	adjective of quality
eius modī	of such a sort	descriptive genitive
tot so many	adjective of quantity	
sīc in this way	adverb	
ita so, in such a way		adverb
adeō	for far, to such an extent	adverb
tam	so	adverb: only with adjs. and other advs.

Under Grammatica Latina, examples are shown of typical *ut-* and *nē*-clauses.

Summary: Purpose and Result

- **Purpose** clauses show the goal of the main verb (in order to); result clauses describe the consequence of the modified (*tam, tantus, ita*) word.

- **Purpose** clauses are negated by *nē*; result clauses are negated by *ut* plus a negative.

	Negative Purpose	Negative Result
that...not	*nē*	*ut...nōn*
that...no one	*nē quis*	*ut...nēmō*
that...nothing	*nē quid*	*ut...nihil*
that...never	*nē umquam*	*ut...numquam*

Lēctiō Tertia (Section III)

Genitive of the Charge

With *accūsāre*, the charge is in the genitive:

> *Lydia pergit eum fūrtī accūsāre.*: accuses him <u>of theft</u> (l.137)

Partitive Genitive (continued)

A partitive genitive may qualify a pronoun, e.g.:

> *aliquid pecūliī* (l.135)
> *nihil malī* (l.157)
> *quid novī?* (Cap. XXXI, ll.2–3)

The partitive genitive of *nōs, vōs* is *nostrum, vestrum*:

> *nēmō <u>nostrum</u>/<u>vestrum</u>* (ll.39, 42–43)

Personal Pronouns (continued from Cap. XX)

There are two forms for the genitive plural of the personal pronouns. The forms *meī, tuī, nostrī, vestrī,* and *suī* (used for singular and plural) are generally used as **objective genitives**, e.g.:

amor meī	love of me (as opposed to *amor meus*: my love)
timor vestrī	fear of you (as opposed to *timor vester*: your fear)

The forms *nostrum* and *vestrum*, as you learned in the previous section, are partitive. It is helpful to distinguish the two by memorizing a phrase. A good one is the partitive phrase Cicero often uses when addressing his audience: *quis vestrum?* (who of you?)

Recēnsiō: Personal Pronouns

	1st sing.	1st pl.	2nd sing.	2nd pl.	Reflexive
nom.	*ego*	*nōs*	*tū*	*vōs*	
acc.	*mē*	*nōs*	*tē*	*vōs*	*sē*
gen.	*meī*	*nostrī/nostrum*	*tuī*	*vestrī/vestrum*	*suī*
dat.	*mihi*	*nōbīs*	*tibi*	*vōbīs*	*sibi*
abl.	*mē*	*nōbīs*	*tē*	*vōbīs*	*sē*

Compound Verbs

Many verbs are formed with **prefixes**, mostly prepositions. Examples in this chapter:

dē-terrēre	*per-movēre*
ā-mittere	*sub-īre*
in-vidēre	*ex-pōnere*
per-mittere	*re-dūcere* (*re-* means "back" or "again")

Prefixes cause a short *a* or *e* in the verbal stem to be changed to *i*. Thus from:

facere is formed	*af-, cōn-, ef-, per-ficere*
capere	*ac-, in-, re-cipere*
rapere	*ē-, sur-ripere*
salīre	*dē-silīre*
fatērī	*cōn-fitērī*
tenēre	*abs-, con-, re-tinēre*
premere	*im-primere*

Similarly, in compounds, *iacere* becomes *-iicere,* but the spelling *ii* is avoided by writing *-icere,* e.g.:

ab-, ad-, ē-, prō-icere

Recēnsiō: Indicative/Subjunctive

Indicative

Ut Orpheus cantū suō ferās ad sē alliciēbat, ita[3] tunc Ariōn canendō piscēs allēxit ad nāvem. (ll.93–95)
Subitō mercātor ē dīvitissimō pauperrimus factus est. (ll.17–18)
Ita spērābat sē magnum lucrum factūrum esse. (l.15)
Laetitia vestra mē nōn afficit. (l.45)
Nec quisquam nostrum trīstitiā tuā afficitur. (ll.46–47)
Quisnam est Ariōn? Nē nōmen quidem mihi nōtum est. (ll.63–64)

---

3.   For *ut...ita,* see Cap. XIX.

*Mercātōrēs mercēs suās magnī aestimant, vītam nautārum parvī
    aestimant!* (ll.6–7)
Nōnne līberōs plūris aestimās quam mercēs istās? (ll.26–27)
Sī fūrtum fēcī, tuā causā id fēcī. (l.139)
*Nāvis autem vēlīs sōlīs nōn tam vēlōciter vehitur quam ante
    tempestātem, nam vēla ventō rapidō scissa sunt.* (ll.191–193)
*"Per deōs immortālēs!" inquit gubernātor, cum prīmum nāvem
    appropinquantem prōspexit. "Illa nāvis vēlōx nōs persequitur."*
    (ll.187–189)

Subjunctive

Purpose (final clauses)

*Is laetus Ōstiā profectus est cum mercibus pretiōsīs quās omnī pecūniā
    suā in Italiā ēmerat eō cōnsiliō ut eās māiōre pretiō in Graeciā
    vēnderet.* (ll.12–15)
Eō enim cōnsiliō nummōs surripuī ut dōnum pretiōsum tibi emerem.
    (ll.139–141)
Rēctē dīcis: meae mercēs ēiectae sunt, ut nāvis tua salva esset!
    (ll.34–35)
Mercēs iēcimus ut nōs omnēs salvī essēmus. (ll.36–37)
*Orpheus etiam ad Īnferōs dēscendit ut uxōrem suam mortuam
    inde redūceret.... Sed perge nārrāre dē Arīone.* (ll.73–75)

Verba Postulandī

Nōlī tū mē cōnsōlārī quī ipse imperāvistī ut mercēs meae iacerentur!
    (ll.30–32)
*Quid iuvat deōs precārī ut rēs āmissae tibi reddantur? Frūstrā hoc
    precāris.* (ll.54–55)
Sed tamen imperāvērunt ut statim in mare dēsilīret! (ll.87–88)
At nōlīte mē monēre ut laetus sim, postquam omnia mihi ēripuistis!
    (ll.43–45)
*Hāc fābulā monēmur ut semper bonō animō sīmus nēve umquam
    dē salūte dēspērēmus. Dum anima est, spēs est.* (ll.122–124)
*Ille vērō, cōnsiliō eōrum cognitō, pecūniam cēteraque sua nautīs dedit,
    hoc sōlum ōrāns ut sibi ipsī parcerent.* (ll.81–83)
Itaque gubernātor imperat ut nāvis rēmīs agātur. (l.193)

Studia Rōmāna

Travel was extensive in the period of our narrative and travel narratives were
a growing genre. The Greek historian Arrian of Nicomedia (on the west coast
of Turkey near Istanbul) wrote *Periplūs Pontī Euxīnī*, a Latin translation of

Περίπλους τοῦ Εὐξείνου Πόντου, a travel narrative about sailing around the Black Sea. Arrian, while governor of the province of Cappadocia, addressed his narrative to the emperor Hadrian (emperor AD 117–138). A contemporary of Arrian, the Greek Pausanias, wrote a guide in ten volumes detailing what he saw and heard on his travels through Greece. Pausanias remains a valuable reference for Roman Greece in the second century AD.

In both this and the previous chapter, the helmsman expresses his fear of pirates. Piracy had been one of the many dangers of sea travel during the republican period (and thus Pompey the Great was given extraordinary military powers to rid the seas of pirates in 67 BC, about which you will read in Cap. XXXII). During the empire, attacks by pirates would be countered by the Roman navy, and sea travel was a good deal safer (although not completely safe). Although large-scale piracy had ceased to exist, it lived on in the popular imagination. More dangerous was the sea itself and shipwreck was not unknown. The *iactūra* of goods was a common practice when shipwreck threatened: the chance of staying afloat was increased by lightening the load. This real danger posed grounds for the following ethical discussion reported in Cicero's *dē Officiīs* (Cicero is reporting a discussion led by Hecaton, a prominent Stoic philosopher from Rhodes of the first century BC): Question: "If one is forced to make a *iactūra* at sea, which should one throw overboard? An expensive horse or a cheap slave?" Response: financial considerations lead in one direction, humane sensibility in the opposite. "What if a foolish man has grabbed a board floating from the shipwreck—will the philosopher grab it away if he can?" No, because it would be wrong. "What about the owner of the ship? Will he grab the plank—it belongs to him." Not at all, not any more than he would toss a passenger overboard because the boat was his. Until they arrive at the ship's destination, the boat belongs not to the owner, but to the passengers (3.23.89–90).

In this chapter, you also read two well-known Greek stories: about the poet Arion and the tyrant Polycrates. The fifth century Greek historian Herodotus writes about both. The famous seventh–century BC Greek lyre-player Arion (Herodotus 1.23–24) was sailing from southern Italy back to Corinth in Greece when he was thrown overboard and rescued by a dolphin. Herodotus (3.40–43) also records the story of Polycrates (the tyrant of Samos in the sixth century BC) who, on the advice of his friend Amasis, the king of Egypt, threw away his signet ring, a valuable emerald set in gold. This last story reflects a common theme that the gods are displeased by too much good fortune; by throwing away the ring, Polycrates hopes to restore the balance of human fortune. That he is unsuccessful signals the magnitude of his ultimate downfall (Polycrates was eventually killed in a way Herodotus finds too horrible to reveal, and when dead, his corpse was crucified for all to see). Pliny the Elder in his *Natural History* (37.2) claims that the gem in Polycrates' ring was on display, set in a golden horn, in the temple of Concord, given to the temple as a gift from Augustus' wife Livia.

The *gubernātor*'s words (124–124) "*Dum anima est, spēs est*" echo Cicero (*Ad Atticum* 9.10) *ut aegrōtō, dum anima est, spēs esse dīcitur.*

Vocābula Disposita/Ōrdināta

Nōmina

1st

dīvitiae, -ārum	riches
fortūna, -ae	fortune
iactūra, -ae	throwing away, loss
invidia, -ae	envy, ill will
laetitia, -ae	happiness
trīstitia, -ae	sadness
vīta, -ae	life

2nd

beneficium, -ī	good deed
delphīnus, -ī	dolphin
dorsum, -ī	back
fundus, -ī	bottom
fūrtum, -ī	theft
lucrum, -ī	profit
maleficium, -ī	evil deed
rēmus, -ī	oar
tyrannus, -ī	tyrant

3rd

carmen, carminis (*n.*)	song, poem
fēlīcitās, fēlīcitātis (*f.*)	happiness
fidēs, fidium (*f. pl.*)	lyre
fidicen, fidicinis (*f.*)	lyre-player
fūr, fūris (*m.*)	thief
nāvigātiō, nāvigātiōnis (*f.*)	sailing
piscātor, piscātōris (*m.*)	fisherman
salūs, salūtis (*f.*)	safety

4th

cantus, -ūs (*m.*)	song

5th

spēs, -eī (*f.*)[4]	hope

Verba

-āre (1)

(aestimō) aestimāre, -āvisse, -ātum	value, estimate
(appropinquō) appropinquāre, -āvisse (*intr. + dat.*)	approach
(dēspērō) dēspērāre, -āvisse, -ātum	lose hope

---

4.   Like *rēs* (Cap. XIV), *spēs* has a short ĕ in the genitive and dative singular (see Cap. XIII for the rules): *spĕs, spĕī.*

(dōnō) dōnāre, -āvisse, -ātum   give, present with
(perturbō) perturbāre, -āvisse, -ātum   disturb
(precor) precārī, precātum   pray, beg
(secō) secāre, secuisse, sectum   cut

-ēre (2)

(abstineō) abstinēre, abstinuisse,   keep off
   abstentum
(appāreō) appārēre, appāruisse   appear
   (*intr. + dat.*)
(cōnfiteor) cōnfitērī, cōnfessum   confess
(dēterreō) dēterrēre, dēterruisse,   deter
   dēterritum
(invideō) invidēre, invīdisse   envy, grudge
   (*intr. + dat.*)
(permoveō) permovēre, permōvisse,   move deeply
   permōtum
(remaneō) remanēre, remānsisse,   remain
   remānsum
(stupeō) stupēre, stupuisse   be aghast
(suādeō) suādēre, suāsisse   advise
   (*intr. + dat.*)

-ere (3)

(abiciō) abicere, abiēcisse, abiectum   throw away
(adiciō) adicere, adiēcisse, adiectum   add
(afficiō) afficere, affēcisse, affectum   affect, stir
(alliciō) allicere, allēxisse, allectum   attract
(āmittō) āmittere, āmīsisse, āmissum   lose
(dētrahō) dētrahere, dētrāxisse,   pull off
   dētractum
(ēripiō) ēripere, ēripuisse, ēreptum   snatch away, deprive
(expōnō) expōnere, exposuisse,   put out, expose
   expositum
(parcō) parcere, pepercisse   spare
   (*intr. + dat.*)
(permittō) permittere, permīsisse   allow, permit
   (*intr. + dat.*)
(queror) querī, questum   complain
(recognōscō) recognōscere,   recognize
   recognōvisse, recognitum
(redūcō) redūcere, redūxisse,   lead back
   reductum
(surripiō) surripere, surripuisse,   steal
   surreptum

-īre (4)

(dēsiliō) dēsilīre, dēsiluisse   jump down
(fīniō) fīnīre, fīnīvisse, fīnītum   finish

Irregular
   (subeō) subīre, subiisse   undergo

Adiectīva
  1st/2nd (-us/er, -a, -um)

celsus, -a, -um	tall, high
ignārus, -a, -um	ignorant, unaware
ignōtus, -a, -um	unknown
maestus, -a, -um	sad
mīrus, -a, -um	surprising, strange
nōtus, -a, -um	known
pretiōsus, -a, -um	precious
rapidus, -a, -um	rapid

  3rd

fallāx (*gen.* fallācis)	false, deceitful
fēlīx (*gen.* fēlīcis)	lucky, fortunate
nōbilis, -e	well-known, famous
vēlōx (*gen.* vēlōcis)	swift

Prōnōmina

nōnnūllī, -ae, -a	several
sēsē	intensive form of **sē**

Adverbia

frūstrā	in vain
inde	from there
nōnnumquam	often
prōtinus	immediately, at once
quasi	as if
repente	suddenly

XXX. Convīvium

Rēs Grammaticae Novae

1. Verbs
   a. Uses of the Subjunctive
      i. Hortatory Subjunctive
   b. Future Perfect Indicative Tense
   c. *miscēre/aspergere*
   d. *fruī*
2. Nouns
   a. *sitis* (Pure *i*-Stem)
   b. *vās*
3. Adjectives
   a. Distributive Numbers
4. Adverbs from 3rd Declension Adjectives (continued)

Convīvium (Dinner Party)

In this and the following chapter, you read about a dinner party at the home of Julius and Aemilia. The guests are good friends of the family. The dinner begins at the early (to us) hour of four o'clock in the afternoon (*hōra decima*), a normal time for the principal meal of the Romans. We hear about the arrangement of a typical Roman dining-room, the *triclīnium,* where the guests reclined on couches. Such a dining-room was not designed for large parties, as not more than three guests could lie on each of the three couches grouped around the little table.

Lēctiō Prīma (Section I)

Fruor, fruī

Like *ūtī, ūsum esse* (Cap. XXIII) the deponent verb *fruī* ("delight in," "enjoy") takes the ablative:

> *Ego numquam īnstrūmentō rūsticō ūsus sum.* (1.38)
>   *ōtiō fruor* (1.23)

279

> *Orontēs…vītā rūsticā nōn fruitur* (l.35)
> *cotīdiē bonō vīnō fruor* (l.59)

Adverbs from 3rd Declension Adjectives (continued)

3rd declension adjectives in *-ns* form adverbs in *-nter*, e.g.:

> *cōnstāns -ant|is* → *cōnsta<u>nter</u>* (contraction of *cōnstantiter*)
> *prūdēns -ent|is* → *prūde<u>nter</u>*
> *dīligēns -ent|is* → *dīlige<u>nter</u>*
> *patiēns -entis* → *patie<u>nter</u>*

Examples:

> *dīlige<u>nter</u> cūrō ut colōnī agrōs meōs bene colant.* (ll.33–34)
> *Prūde<u>nter</u> facis.* (l.35)
> *Patie<u>nter</u> exspectā, dum servī lectōs sternunt.* (l.82; cf. Cap. XXXIII, l.120)

Lēctiō Altera (Section II)

Distributive Numbers

When using repetitive numbers to say, for example, how many guests are reclining on each couch, we might say in English, "three to a couch," or "three each/apiece," or "in threes." Latin does not use the usual numerals *ūnus, duo, trēs,* but the numbers *singulī, bīnī, ternī*:

In <u>singulīs</u> lectīs aut <u>singulī</u> aut <u>bīnī</u> aut <u>ternī</u> convīvae accubāre solent.	Dinner guests usually recline on individual couches in ones or twos or threes. (ll.74–75)

These distributive numerals:

- are adjectives of the 1st/2nd declension
- all end in *-<u>n</u>|ī -ae -a*, except *singul|ī -ae -a*
- are used when the same number is used repetitively, that is, applies to more than one person or thing, e.g.:
  > *bis <u>bīna</u>* (2×2) *sunt quattuor*
  > *bis <u>terna</u>* (2×3) *sunt sex*
  > *In vocābulīs "mea" et "tua" sunt <u>ternae</u> litterae et <u>bīnae</u> syllabae.*

Future Perfect Indicative

To indicate that an action will not be completed until some point in the future, the **future perfect** is used (Latin *futūrum perfectum*), e.g.:

Cēnābimus cum prīmum cocus cēnam parāverit et servī triclīnium ōrnāverint. (ll.83–84)

Although all three acts will happen in the future, the future perfect shows that the cooking and dining room preparation will be finished *before* the guests will eat.

Cum prīmum meum vīnum pōtāveritis, Falernun pōtābitis! (ll.145–146)

The guests will drink the Falernum wine as soon as they will have drunk the wine from Julius's vineyard. Both will happen in the future, but the action in the future perfect tense will be completed before the action in the future tense takes place.

To form the future perfect:

- Active: to the perfect stem add the following endings:

1st	~er|ō	~eri|mus
2nd	~eri|s	~eri|tis
3rd	~eri|t	~eri|nt

- Passive: the perfect participle and the future of *esse* (*erō, eris, erit,* etc.), e.g.:

  Brevī cēna parāta et triclīnium ōrnātum erit. (ll.84–85; cf. l.14)

This tense is especially common in conditional clauses (beginning with *sī*) in cases where some future action must be completed before something else can take place, e.g.:

Discipulus laudābitur, sī magistrō pāruerit.

Further examples of this use will be found in the section GRAMMATICA LATINA.

Lēctiō Tertia (Section III)

Independent Subjunctive: Hortatory

When at last the servant announces that dinner is ready, Julius says:

Triclīnium intrēmus! Let us enter the dining room! (ll.86–87)

At table he raises his glass with the words:

Ergō bibāmus! Therefore, let us drink! (l.120)

The forms *intrēmus* and *bibāmus* are the present subjunctive (1st pers. pl.) of *intrāre* and *bibere*; accordingly, they denote an action that is intended or encouraged, in this case an exhortation ("let's…"). In the next chapter, you will find further examples of this **hortatory** subjunctive (Latin *hortārī*, "exhort").

Sitis/vās

Sitis, -is f. is a pure *i*-stem (see Cap. XVI):

acc.	*-im* (*sitim patī*, l.55)
abl.	*-ī* (*sitī perīre*, l.57)

Vās, vās\|is n. follows the 3rd declension in the singular but the 2nd declension in the plural: *vās\|a, -ōrum* (l.93: *ex vāsīs aureīs*).

Miscēre/aspergere

Wine was not often drunk undiluted (*merum*); it was customary to mix (*miscēre*) one's wine with water. The verb *miscēre* (to mix) can be completed by an accusative and ablative or dative and accusative. The Latin expression is either:

accusative and ablative
vīnum aquā (*cum aquā*) *miscēre*   mix wine with water (l.115)

dative and accusative
mel vīnō miscēre   mix honey (in)to wine (l.132)

Aspergere (to sprinkle) follows the same pattern:
cibum sāle aspergere   sprinkle food with salt (l.111)
sālem carnī aspergere   sprinkle salt (on)to meat (l.109–110)

Recēnsiō: Cum

Cum referring to the future: Indicative

Cēnābimus cum prīmum cocus cēnam parāverit et servī triclīnium ōrnāverint. (ll.82–84)
Tum dēmum hoc vīnum cum illō comparāre poterimus, cum utrumque gustāverimus. (ll.143–144)

Cum iterative: Indicative

Nec vērō omnēs mercātōrēs domī remanent, cum mercēs eōrum nāvibus vehuntur. (Cap. XXIX, ll.8–9)
Cum igitur paucissimī sunt convīvae, nōn pauciōrēs sunt quam trēs, cum plūrimī, nōn plūrēs quam novem—nam ter ternī sunt novem. (ll.75–78)

Cum strict temporal: Indicative

"Per deōs immortālēs!" inquit gubernātor, cum prīmum nāvem appropinquantem prōspexit. (Cap. XXIX, ll.187–188)
Octō diēs iam sunt cum Rōmae nōn fuī. (Cap. XXXI, l.3)

Sex hōrae iam sunt cum cibum nōn sūmpsī. Venter mihi contrahitur
  propter famem. (ll.40–42)
"Haec carō valdē mihi placet," inquit Fabia cum prīmum carnem
  gustāvit. (ll.106–107)
Cum prīmum meum vīnum pōtāveritis, Falernum pōtābitis! (ll.145–
  146)

Cum circumstantial: Subjunctive

Cum Arīōn, nōbilissimus suī temporis fidicen, ex Italiā in Graeciam
  nāvigāret magnāsque dīvitiās sēcum habēret, nautae pauperēs, quī
  hominī dīvitī invidēbant, eum necāre cōnstituērunt. (Cap. XXIX,
  ll.78–81)
Respondērunt "hominem, cum inde abīrent, in terrā Italiā fuisse
  eumque illīc bene vīvere, aurēs animōsque hominum cantū suō
  dēlectāre atque magnum lucrum facere." (Cap. XXIX, ll.106–109)

Cum causal: Subjunctive

Gubernātor, cum omnēs attentōs videat, hanc fābulam nārrat.
  (Cap. XXIX, ll.76–77)
Ibi homō territus, cum iam vītam dēspērāret, id ūnum ōrāvit ut sibi
  licēret vestem ōrnātam induere et fidēs capere et ante mortem carmen
  canere. (Cap. XXIX, ll.187–188)
Ānulum abiēcit, cum sēsē nimis fēlīcem esse cēnsēret. (Cap. XXIX,
  ll.156–157)
Polycratēs, cum ānulum suum recognōsceret, māximā laetitiā affectus
  est. (Cap. XXIX, ll.171–172)
Midās enim, quamquam terram, lignum, ferrum manū tangendō
  in aurum mūtāre poterat, fame et sitī moriēbātur, cum cibus quoque
  et pōtiō, simul atque ā rēge tācta erat, aurum fieret. (Cap. XXXI,
  ll.38–42)
Opus nōn est vetus exemplum Graecum afferre, cum complūrēs fābulae
  nārrentur puerīs quī ita servātī sunt. (Cap. XXXI, ll.154–156)

Studia Rōmāna

Julius joins his guests after bathing: *Tum Iūlius lautus et novā veste indūtus
intrat* (l.15). *Lautus, -a, -um* is a perfect passive participle from *lavāre*, to wash,
bathe (the verb has three variations of the participle; in Cap. XXII, you met
lavātum, the participle you would expect from *lavāre*[1]). *Lautus* is rarely used to

---

1.   The third variation on the participle's form is *lōtum*.

mean simply "having been washed, i.e., clean." Rather, it suggests the impression one gives who has the leisure and resources to bathe: "elegant, refined."

Introduced from Greece via Greek Southern Italy, baths were an important feature of Roman life. Private baths in the home are called *balneum*,[2] (in the republican period, they were also called *lavātrīna*, shortened to *lātrīna*). There were also public baths (mostly privately owned) called *balneae* and, in the imperial period, enormous public baths called *thermae*. The Augustan period architect Vitruvius tells us the various rooms for a bath, although archaeological remains show a great deal of variation: the hot room (*caldārium*, also spelled *calidārium*), the warm room (*tepidārium*), the sweating room (*sūdātōrium*, *lacōnicum*), a room with a cold bath (*frīgidārium*), as well as a changing room (*apodȳtērium*). The natural starting place is the *apodȳtērium*; from there, one visited rooms of increasing warmth and finished in the *frīgidārium*. While baths were ideally placed in a part of the house that would receive the most warmth, they were also kept warm by the use of hypocausts (*hypocaustum*): flooring raised on short brick pillars through which the heat of an external furnace could flow.

Julius entertains his friend Cornelius (familiar to you from Cap. VI) and his wife Fabia, along with Orontes and his wife Paula. Orontes, a freedman (*lībertīnus*), is reminiscent of the freedmen at Trimalchio's dinner party in the first century AD novel written by Petronius, *Satyricon,* and of various Greek freedmen in the satires of Juvenal (first–second century AD). Orontes exhibits the stereotypes of literature and illustrates Roman ambivalence toward the Greeks.

The *triclinium* consists of three couches that can hold three diners each. The diners would recline facing a central communal table. Wealthy houses might have more than one *triclinium*. Generally, the way the mosaic floors and (often elaborate) wall paintings are arranged identifies a room as a *triclinium* and shows where the couches and table were set up. Of the three couches shown in the photo at the beginning of the chapter, the slave is kneeling on what is called the *lectus īmus*, or lowest couch (the order of the couches is shown in the illustration in the margin). This is usually the couch where the host sits, although in our chapter, Julius and Aemilia are sitting on the middle couch, the *lectus medius*, usually reserved for the guest of honor. The host would sit in the highest position (always on the right side of the couch as you face it) on the *lectus īmus* (called *summus in īmō*), and the guest of honor would sit on the lowest position (to the far left of the couch) on the *lectus medius* (called *īmus in mediō*)—that is, next to the host.

The *cēna* (lines 100–103) consists of the three courses described in Cap. XXIV, beginning with eggs for the appetizer (*gustātiō*), moving on to fish

---

2.   In the singular, baths are neuter (*baleum*); in the plural, usually feminine (*balneae*), although the neuter plural is also found.

and pork for the *cēna* proper, and ending with nuts and fruit for the *secundae mēnsae*. The poet Horace describes a full dinner as *ab ōvō ad māla* (*Sat.* 1.3.6)—so Julius's dinner is typical (as you will see in the next chapter, ll.185–186: *Nōnne tē pudet ita ab ōvō ūsque ad māla fābulārī?*). Wine was an important component of the *cēna* and indeed of Roman culture. There were inexpensive everyday wines and aged, expensive wines that Pliny in his *Historia Nātūrālis* calls *vīnum nōbile*. Pliny would agree with Julius that *Falernum... vīnum Italiae optimum habētur* (l.123). Pliny writes, *Nec ūllī nunc vīnō māior auctōritās; sōlō vīnōrum flamma accenditur* (14.8.62) "no wine today has a greater reputation; a flame can be kindled from it alone." That is, Falernian wine was the only one with a high enough alcohol content to be flammable. The next best wines, according to Pliny, come from the area around Julius's farm, the Alban region close to Rome. Cornelius (ll.126–127) is clearly being polite in preferring Julius's Alban wine to Falernum.

Vocābula Disposita/Ōrdināta

Nōmina

1st

cēna, -ae	dinner
convīva, -ae (*m./f.*)	dinner guest
culīna, -ae	kitchen

2nd

argentum, -ī	silver
balneum, -ī	bath
bonum, -ī	blessing, a good
cocus, -ī	cook
convīvium, -ī	dinner party
merum, -ī	unmixed wine
minister, -rī	attendant (cf. **magister**)
triclīnium, -ī	dining room

3rd

carō, carnis (*f.*)	meat
famēs, famis (*f.*)	hunger
genus, generis (*n.*)	kind, sort
holus, holeris (*n.*)	vegetable
hospes, hospitis (*m./f.*)	guest, stranger
iter, itineris (*n.*)	journey, trip
mel, mellis (*n.*)	honey
nux, nucis (*f.*)	nut
sāl, salis (*n.*)	salt
sitis, sitis (*f.*; *acc.* sitim)	thirst
vās, vāsis (*n.*) (*pl.* vāsa, -ōrum)	container

Verba

-āre (1)

(accubō) accubāre	recline at the table
(apportō) apportāre, -āvisse, -ātum	carry to
(cēnō) cēnāre, -āvisse, -ātum	dine
(exōrnō) exōrnāre, -āvisse, -ātum	decorate
(gustō) gustāre, -āvisse, -ātum	taste
(līberō) līberāre, -āvisse, -ātum	set free
(nūntiō) nūntiāre, -āvisse, -ātum	announce
(parō) parāre, -āvisse, -ātum	get, prepare
(pōtō) pōtāre, -āvisse, -ātum (or **pōtum**)	drink

-ēre (2)

(compleō) complēre, -plēvisse, -plētum	fill up
(misceō) miscēre, miscuisse, mixtum	mix
(placeō) placēre, placuisse, placitum (*intr. + dat.*)	please
(salvēre iubeō)	greet

-ere (3)

(accumbō) accumbere, accubuisse	recline at the table
(aspergō) aspergere, aspersisse, aspersum	sprinkle/strew on
(contrahō) contrahere, -trāxisse, -tractum	contract
(coquō) coquere, coxisse, coctum	cook
(ēligō) ēligere, ēlēgisse, ēlectum	pick out, choose
(fruor) fruī, fructum (+ *abl.*)	enjoy
(fundō) fundere, fūdisse, fūsum	pour
(recipiō) recipere, recēpisse, receptum	receive
(requiēscō) requiēscere	rest
(sternō) sternere, strāvisse, strātum	spread, strew
(vīsō) vīsere	go to see, visit

-īre (4)

(exhauriō) exhaurīre, exhausisse, exhaustum	drain, drink up

Irregular

(praesum) praeesse, praefuisse (*intr. + dat.*)	be in charge over
(perferō) perferre, pertulisse, perlātum	carry through
(prōferō) prōferre, prōtulisse, prōlātum	bring forward

Adiectīva

  1st/2nd (-us/er, -a, -um)

    acerbus, -a, -um   bitter

    acūtus, -a, -um   sharp

    argenteus, -a, -um   made of silver

    bīnī, -ae, -a   two at a time

    calidus, -a, -um   hot

    glōriōsus, -a, -um   full of glory

    īmus, -a, -um   bottom of

    inexspectātus, -a, -um   unexpected

    iūcundus, -a, -um   pleasant, agreeable

    lībertīnus, -a, -um   freed

    medius, -a, -um   middle of

    merus, -a, -um   unmixed, pure

    molestus, -a, -um   annoying

    singulī, -ae, -a   one at a time

    tardus, -a, -um   late, tardy

    ternī, -ae, -a   three at a time

  3rd

    dīligēns (*gen.* **dīligentis**)   careful, accurate

    dulcis, -e   sweet

Adverbia

    dēmum   finally

    diū   for a long time

    equidem   indeed

    paulisper   for a short time

    prīdem   some time ago, previously

    sānē   certainly, truly

Praepositiōnēs

    circiter (*prp. + acc.*)   around, near (*adv.* approximately)

XXXI. Inter Pōcula

Rēs Grammaticae Novae

1. Verbs
   a. Uses of the Subjunctive
      i.   Optative Subjunctive
      ii. Hortatory Subjunctive (continued)
      iii. Jussive Subjunctive
   b. *ōdisse*
   c. Semi-deponents
2. Nouns: Case uses
   a. Dative of Agent
   b. Ablative with the Preposition *cōram*
   c. Ablative with the Preposition *super*
3. Adjectives
   a. Verbal Adjective: Gerundive (*gerundīvum*)
   b. Passive Periphrastic
4. Pronouns: Indefinite Relative Pronouns

An Enthusiastic Dinner Conversation

As the wine flows, the conversation among the guests proceeds more freely. The room echoes with discussions, stories, and the latest gossip.

Lēctiō Prīma (Section I)

Indefinite Relative Pronouns

We have seen relative pronouns without an antecedent express the idea of "whoever" and "whatever" (where one might have expected *is quī…, id quod*), e.g.:

Quī spīrat vīvus est.	Whoever breathes is alive. (Cap. X, ll.48–49)
Quod Mārcus dīcit vērum nōn est.	What (or whatever) Marcus says is not true. (Cap. XV, l.58–59)

The same idea is expressed by the **indefinite relative pronouns** *quis-quis* and *quid-quid* ("whoever" and "whatever"), e.g.:

> *Quisquis amat valeat!* (l.196)
> *Dabō tibi quidquid optāveris.* (l.29)

Quidquid is often changed to *quicquid* by assimilation.

Future Perfect Tense (continued)

This chapter offers many more examples of the future perfect tense, used to express an action that must be completed *before* another future action:

> *Nēmō tibi quidquam scrībet dē rēbus urbānīs, nisi prius ipse epistulam*
> *scrīpseris.* (ll.7–8)
> *"Dabō tibi," inquit, "quidquid optāveris." Statim Midās. "Ergō dā mihi,"*
> *inquit, "potestātem quidquid tetigerō in aurum mūtandī."[1]* (ll.29–31)
> *Profectō eum verberābō atque omnibus modīs cruciābō, sī eum invēnerō*
> *priusquam Italiam relīquerit. Nisi pecūniam mihi reddiderit, in cruce*
> *fīgētur!* (ll.63–66)

Lēctiō Altera (Section II)

Ōdisse

The defective verb *ōdisse* ("to hate") has no present stem, but the perfect has present force: *ōdī* ("I hate") is the opposite of *amō*; *ōdisse* and its opposite, *amāre*, are contrasted in *Servī dominum clēmentem amant, sevērum ōdērunt* (ll.93–94).

Cf. *nōvisse* (Cap. XXIV), perfect of *nōscere* ("get to know"), meaning "know": *nōvī*, "I know."

Cōram/Super

The preposition *cōram* ("in the presence of," "before") takes the ablative:

> *cōram exercitū* (l.122)

Super usually takes the accusative ("above"); but when used instead of *dē* in the sense "about," "concerning," *super* takes the ablative:

> *super Chrīstiānīs* (l.147)
> *super fēminā falsā et īnfidā* (l.200)

---

1.   The future perfect is here used with a present tense main verb as *potestātem mūtandī = poterō mūtāre.*

Lēctiō Tertia (Section III)

Gerundive

In Cap. XXVI, you learned about the **gerund** (Latin *gerundium*), a **verbal noun** with forms in the accusative, genitive, dative, and ablative of the neuter singular; it is active in meaning. The **gerundive** (Latin *gerundīvum*) is a **verbal adjective**. Orontes's "*Vīvant omnēs fēminae amandae!*" (ll.172–173) offers an example of the gerundive, which:

- is formed like the gerund by adding -*nd*- or -*end*- to the present stem
- is an adjective of the 1st/2nd declension (*ama|nd|us, -a, -um* < *amāre*)
- is passive in meaning
- expresses what a person or thing is fit for (*fēminae amandae*, above) or what is to be done to a person or thing

The gerundive can be used as an adjective or with the verb *esse* to express obligation.

- As an **adjective**:

fēmina amanda	worthy of being loved; a lovely, charming, or lovable woman
discipulus laudandus	(< *laudāre*) worthy of praise, a praiseworthy or hardworking pupil
liber legendus	(< *legere*) worthy of being read, a good book, a must-read

- Most frequently, the gerundive is used with some form of the verb *esse* to express what must or should happen. This construction is called the **passive periphrastic**:

  Pater quī īnfantem exposuit ipse necandus est! (ll.132–133): "should/ must be killed"

  Ille servus nōn pūniendus, sed potius laudandus fuit. (ll.161–162): "should not have been punished, but rather praised"

  Nunc merum bibendum est! (l.177): "must be drunk"

The gerundive is a passive form; **agent** (the person by whom the action is to be performed) is expressed by the **dative** (not *ab* + ablative):

  Quidquid dominus imperāvit servō faciendum est. (ll.159–160): "must be done"

The passive periphrastic can be used without a subject:

Bibendum nōbīs est!	We must drink!
Tacendum est!	It is necessary to be quiet! (l.178)
Dormiendum omnibus est!	Everyone must sleep!

Remember:

- Gerund: active noun used only in the accusative, genitive, dative, and ablative of the neuter singular.
- Gerund<u>ive</u>: pass<u>ive</u> adject<u>ive</u> with all forms of 1st/2nd declension; expressing what is suitable/necessary and takes a dative of agent.

Optative, Hortatory, Jussive Subjunctives Compared

Orontes, who has had quite a bit to drink, illustrates three related uses of the subjunctive: optative, hortatory, and jussive. All three are expressions of the will of the speaker.

- **Optative**: an expression of wish (may he/she/they) (more in Cap. XXXII)
  Vīvat fortissimus quisque! Vīv<u>ant</u> omnēs fēminae amandae! (ll.172–173)
  "*Quisquis amat val<u>eat</u>! Per<u>eat</u> quī nescit amāre! Bis tantō per<u>eat</u> quisquis amāre vetat!*" (ll.196–197, *per-eat* is the present subjunctive of *per-īre*)
- **Hortatory** (see Cap. XXX): an expression of encouragement or exhortation in the 1st person plural ("let us")

Gaude<u>āmus</u> atque am<u>ēmus</u>!	Let us rejoice and let us love! (l.173)
Vīv<u>āmus</u> omnēs et bib<u>āmus</u>. (ll.183–184)	
Pōcula funditus exhauri<u>āmus</u>. (l.184)	
Rede<u>āmus</u> ad meum Mēdum servum.	Let's get back to my slave Medus.
- **Jussive**: a command expressed in the 3rd person ("let him/her, let them")

Quisquis fēminās amat, pōculum toll<u>at</u> et bib<u>at</u> mēcum!	Whoever loves women, let him lift up his cup and drink with me! (ll.176–177)

The optative subjunctive expresses a wish, hortatory an exhortation, jussive a command. For all three, the negative is *nē*:

Nē pereat!	May he not perish!
Nē pōcula funditus exhauriāmus!	Let us not drain our glasses dry!
Nē bibat!	Let him not drink!

Quisque + Superlative

When *quisque* and the superlative are used together, the phrase means "all the X." Cicero spoke of *optimus quisque*, "all the best men." Orontes cries:

| *Vīvat fortissimus quisque!* | May all the bravest men live! (l.172: i.e., "everyone according as he is the bravest," "all the bravest men") |

Semi-Deponents

There are a very few verbs in Latin that are called semi-deponent. The semi-deponent verb *audēre*, for example, has an active form in the present (*audeō, audēre*), but its form is passive in the perfect: *ausum esse* (to have dared):

> *Ille iuvenis fēminam illam pulcherrimam abdūcere <u>ausus est</u>.*
> (ll.168–169)
> *Perterritus Quīntus cultrum medicī sentit in bracchiō, nec oculōs aperīre <u>audet</u>.* (Cap. XI, ll.97–98)

Conversely, usually *revertī* is deponent in the present tense (*revertor revertī*), but has active forms in the perfect: *revertisse*; thus *revertitur* (she returns) but *revertit* (she returned).[2]

Graffiti

The inscription on page 259 is a **graffito** (Italian for "a scratching") that a love-sick youth has scratched on a wall in Pompeii. It will help you to decipher the characters when you know that the inscription contains the two verses quoted by Orontes (ll.196–197; only the first syllable is missing).

Studia Rōmāna

Roman attitude toward their slaves varied considerably. Were Seneca the Younger (first century AD) at Julius's dinner, he would have argued with his host's view of slaves. Seneca would remind Julius of what he had written to his young friend Lucilius (letter 47): that anyone can become enslaved (through war, kidnapping, etc.) and that he should treat his slaves in a mild and friendly manner. Slaves treated badly will fear and hate their masters. Aemilia reminds Julius of the proverb "*Dominō sevērō tot esse hostēs quot servōs.*" This proverb comes from Seneca's letter: *Eiusdem arrogantiae prōverbium iactātur, totidem hostēs esse quot servōs: nōn habēmus illōs hostēs sed facimus* (47.5).[3]

The mention of crucifixion gives Aemilia the chance to voice her outrage at parents who expose (*ēpōnere*) their infants. It was the right of the *paterfamilias* to decide whether to raise a child or expose it. Although child exposure is a popular theme in literature (particularly the Greek novel), it's not at all

---

2. *Revertere* exists in both active and deponent forms (*reverto, revertere, revertī* and *revertor, revertī, reversus sum*); in the present the deponent forms are more common, in the perfect, the active forms.

3. Of this same haughty attitude, the proverb, "There are as many enemies as slaves," is tossed about: we don't possess them as enemies, but we make them so.

clear how often it happened in real life. There is literary evidence that seriously deformed babies were at greater risk of exposure. But it is clear that, outside of myths like Romulus and Remus, children were not left out in the expectation that they would be eaten by wild beasts, but rather were left in places where they were likely to be picked up and raised by others.

Orontes continues his boorish ignorance, but his tone-deaf responses to the conversation give us the opportunity to explore more myths. There were many sources for and variations of Greek myth, but as it happens, both of the myths that Orontes brings up can be found in Hyginus's *Fābulae*, a simplistic compendium of Greek mythology probably from the second century AD.[4] Also thought to be from the second century AD is the *Bibliothēkē* (or *Library*) of Apollodorus, another compendium of Greek myth. The existence of many handbooks of, in addition to innumerable literary allusions to, Greek myth attests to the vitality of myth in the ancient world.

Cornelius refers to a historical figure of near-mythical status: Solon, Athenian lawgiver and one of the seven sages (wise men) of Greece, lived in the seventh–sixth century BC. When asked why there was no law against parricides, he responded that he was of the opinion that no one would ever commit the crime (Cicero, *dē Rosciō Amerīnō*, 70.5: [*Solōn*] *cum interrogārētur cūr nūllum supplicium cōnstituisset in eum quī parentem necāsset, respondit sē id nēminem factūrum putāsse*). The Romans, however, did have a law against parricide and (at least during the republic) a gruesome punishment for it: the culprit was tied up in a sack with a dog, a cock, a viper, and an ape (Justinian, *Digest* 48.9).[5] By the time of our narrative, the emperor Hadrian had decreed if the sea were not available, the murderer would be thrown to beasts.

Vocābula Disposita/Ōrdināta

Nōmina

  1st

iniūria, -ae	injury, injustice
memoria, -ae	memory
nūgae, -ārum	trifles
parricīda, -ae (*m./f.*)	murderer of a near relative or head of state
poena, -ae	punishment

  2nd

praemium, -ī	reward
supplicium, -ī	punishment

---

4. The story of Midas is Hyginus 191 and of Paris, 91.

5. Justinian's *Digest* 48.9: *Poena parricīdiī mōre maiōrum haec īnstitūta est, ut parricīda uirgīs sanguineīs uerberātus deinde culleō īnsuātur cum cane, gallō gallīnāceō et uīperā et sīmiā: deinde in mare profundum culleus iactātur.*

3rd

crux, crucis (*f.*)	cross
iūs, iūris (*n.*)	law, right; *also* gravy, soup
iuvenis, iuvenis (*m./f.*)	young person (*not an i-stem*)
lēx, lēgis (*f.*)	law, motion, bill
mōs, mōris (*m.*)	custom, habit; *pl.* behavior, morals
mūnus, mūneris (*n.*)	service, duty, gift
pōtiō, pōtiōnis (*f.*)	drink
rūmor, rūmōris (*m.*)	rumor
scelus, sceleris (*n.*)	crime, wickedness
senex, senis (*m.*)	old man (*not an i-stem*)

5th

fidēs, -eī[6]	loyalty, good faith

Verba

-āre (1)

(**cruciō**) **cruciāre, cruciāvisse, cruciātum**	torture
(**ēducō**) **ēducāre, ēducāvisse, ēducātum**	train, educate, rear
(**fābulor**) **fābulārī, fābulātum**	chat, tell a story
(**interpellō**) **interpellāre, interpellāvisse, interpellātum**	interrupt, break in
(**optō**) **optāre, optāvisse, optātum**	choose, wish for
(**vetō**) **vetāre, vetuisse, vetitum**	forbid

-ēre (2)

(**lateō**) **latēre, latuisse**	lie hidden, lurk

-ere (3)

(**abdūcō**) **abdūcere, abdūxisse, abductum**	lead away, carry off
(**aufugiō**) **aufugere, aufūgisse**	run away, escape
(**cōnfīdō**) **cōnfīdere, cōnfīsum** (+ *dat.*)	trust
(**fīdō**) **fīdere, fīsum** (+ *dat.*)	trust, rely on
(**ignōscō**) **ignōscere, ignōvisse, ignōtum** (+ *dat.*)	forgive
(**ōdī**) **ōdisse, ōsum**	hate
(**retrahō**) **retrahere, retrāxisse, retractum**	draw back, withdraw
(**statuō**) **statuere, statuisse, statūtum**	fix, determine

Irregular

(**auferō**) **auferre, abstulisse, ablātum**	carry off

---

6. Like *rēs* (Cap. XIV) and *spēs* (Cap. XXIX), *fidēs* has a short ĕ in the genitive and dative singular (see Cap. XIII for the rules): *fidēs, fideī*.

Adiectīva
  1st/2nd (-us/er, -a, -um)
    asinīnus, -a, -um   asinine
    avārus, -a, -um   greedy
    ēbrius, -a, -um   drunk
    fīdus, -a, -um   loyal, faithful
    fugitīvus, -a, -um   fugitive
    īnfīdus, -a, -um   treacherous
    iniūstus, -a, -um   unjust
    invalidus, -a, -um   weak
    iūstus, -a, -um   just
    nimius, -a, -um   too big
    nōnāgēsimus, -a, -um   ninetieth
    scelestus, -a, -um   wicked
  3rd
    clēmēns (*gen.* **clēmentis**)   merciful
    crūdēlis, -e   cruel
    dēbilis, -e   weak
    impatiēns (*gen.* **impatientis**) impatient
    īnfēlīx (*gen.* **īnfēlīcis**)   unlucky
    praesēns (*gen.* **praesentis**)   present
    sapiēns (*gen.* **sapientis**)   wise
    vetus (*gen.* **veteris**)   old

Prōnōmina
    quisquis, quidquid   whoever, whatever, each, all

Adverbia
    aliquantum (*adv.*)   to some extent
    funditus   utterly (from the root)
    ideō   for that reason
    namque   for in fact (strong **nam**)
    nimium/nimis (*adv.*)   too much
    priusquam   before, sooner, rather
    quantum (*as adv.*)   so much as, as much as
    quamobrem   why? therefore

Praepositiōnēs
    cōram (*prp. + abl.*)   in the presence of, face to face (with)
                          (also *adv.*)
    super (*prp. + abl.*)   over (also *adv.*)

XXXII. Classis Rōmāna

Rēs Grammaticae Novae

1. Verbs
   a. Perfect Subjunctive: Active and Passive
      i.   Perfect Subjunctive in Indirect Questions
      ii. Prohibitions: Perfect Subjunctive in Negative Commands
   b. Uses of the Subjunctive
      i.   Optative Subjunctive (Continued)
      ii. Fear Clauses
      iii. Noun Clauses: *fit/accidit ut* + Subjunctive
   c. Verbs of Remembering and Forgetting
   d. *velle*: Present Subjunctive
2. Nouns: Cases Uses
   a. Ablative of Description
   b. Ablative of Separation
   c. *vīs/vīrēs*
   d. Partitive Genitive: *sēstertius*
3. Pronouns: *aliquis/aliquid*

Medus and Lydia at Sea

The fear of pirates gives rise to a long discussion on board the ship. Medus tells the story of the circumstances in which he was sent to prison and sold as a slave. This story mollifies Lydia, so when finally the danger is over, the two are once more on the best of terms.

Lēctiō Prīma (Section I)

Subjunctive with Noun Clauses

You have already seen clauses acting as the objects of verbs (Cap. XXVIII). A clause can also act as the subject of a verb. The impersonal expressions *fit* and *accidit* may be followed by an *ut*-clause with the subjunctive telling what happens; the *ut*-clause is the subject of *fit*:

Rārō fit ut nāvis praedōnum in marī internō appāreat. (ll.42–43)

Ablative

of Description

A noun + adjective in the ablative can be used to describe a quality (*ablātīvus quālitātis* or **ablative of description**):

> *tantā audāciā sunt* (l.49)
> *bonō animō esse* (Cap. XXIX, ll.122–123)

(cf. genitive of description, Cap. XIX)

of Separation

We saw the ablative of separation with *carēre* in Cap. XX, and with *pellere* and *prohibēre* in Cap. XXVII. With *līberāre* and with *opus esse* as well we find the ablative of separation without a preposition:

> *servitūte līberābantur* (l.6)
> *Quid opus est armīs?* (l.78)
> *...seu pecūniā seu aliā rē mihi opus erit.* (l.118)
> *Quid verbīs opus est?* (l.195)

Vīs

The noun *vīs* ("strength," "force," "violence") has only three forms in the singular:

> nom.   *vīs*
> acc.   *vim* (l.13)
> abl.   *vī* (l.77)

The plural *vīrēs, vīrium* means physical strength:

> *Nautae omnibus vīribus rēmigant.* (l.53, ll.65–66)

Lēctiō Altera (Section II)

Verbs of Remembering and Forgetting

In Cap. XXV, you learned *oblīvīscī* can take a genitive as object:

> *Nōn facile est amōris antīquī oblīvīscī.* (Cap. XXV, l.128)
> *Numquam beneficiī oblītus sum.* (l.26)

Its opposites, *reminīscī* and *meminisse*, meaning "to remember," also can take a genitive as an object:

> *Nec vērō quidquam difficilius esse vidētur quam beneficiōrum*
>   *meminisse.* (ll.125–126)
> *Eius temporis reminīscor.* (ll.155–156)

Like *oblīvīscī*, both *reminīscī* and *meminisse* can also take accusative objects:

> *Duōs versūs reminīscor ē carmine.* (ll.101–102)
> *Tūne nōmen eius meministī?* (ll.106–107)

Reminīscī and *meminisse* will take an accusative when they mean "remember" in the literal sense of "retain in memory" but the genitive when they mean "be mindful of," just as *oblīvīscī* takes the accusative when "forget" means "remove from memory" (mostly used of things) and the genitive when it means "disregard."

Note: meminisse is a defective verb which, like *ōdisse* (Cap. XXXI), has no present stem: the perfect form *meminī* ("I remember") is the opposite of *oblītus sum* ("I have forgotten").

Velle

The present subjunctive of *velle*:

Indicative		Subjunctive	
volō	*volumus*	*velim*	*velīmus*
vīs	*vultis*	*velīs*	*velītis*
vult	*volunt*	*velit*	*velint*

Perfect Subjunctive

During the discussion, the merchant quotes two verses without giving the poet's name. The helmsman does not ask a direct question: *"Quī poēta ista scrīpsit?"* with the verb in the indicative, but uses an indirect question with the subjunctive:[1] *"Nesciō quī poēta ista scrīpserit"* (l.106). *Scrīps|erit* is the **perfect subjunctive** (Latin *coniūnctīvus perfectī*) of *scrībere*.

This tense is formed in the **active** by inserting *-eri-* between the perfect stem and the personal endings:

1st sing.	*~eri|m*
2nd	*~eri|s*
3rd	*~eri|t*
1st pl.	*~eri|mus*
2nd	*~eri|tis*
3rd	*~eri|nt*

Notā Bene: The perfect subjunctive looks like the future perfect indicative **except** for the 1st person singular *~erim* (where the future perfect has *~erō*).

---

1. First seen in Cap. XXIX: *Modo tē interrogāvī tuane esset pecūnia* (ll.127–128) and *dubitō num haec fābula vēra sit* (ll.116–117).

In the **passive**, the perfect subjunctive is composed of the perfect participle and the present subjunctive of *esse* (*sim, sīs, sit*, etc.):

> *Iūlius dubitat num Mārcus ā magistrō laudātus sit* (= *num magister Mārcum laudāverit*).

Perfect Subjunctive

active	perfect stem + *eri* + endings
passive	participle stem + present subjunctive of *esse*

Recēnsiō: *Ferre*

For review, compare the present, imperfect, and perfect subjunctives of *ferō, ferre, tulisse, lātum:*

Tense	Active	Passive
Present	*feram*	*ferar*
	ferās	*ferāris*
	ferat	*ferātur*
	ferāmus	*ferāmur*
	ferātis	*ferāmini*
	ferant	*ferantur*
Imperfect	*ferrem*	*ferrer*
	ferrēs	*ferrēris*
	ferret	*ferrētur*
	ferrēmus	*ferrēmur*
	ferrētis	*ferrēmini*
	ferrent	*ferrentur*
Perfect	*tulerim*	*lātus, -a sim*
	tuleris	*lātus, -a sīs*
	tulerit	*lātus, -a, -um sit*
	tulerimus	*lātī, -ae sīmus*
	tuleritis	*lātī, -ae sītis*
	tulerint	*lātī, -ae, -um sint*

Perfect Subjunctive in Subordinate Clauses

You have learned (Cap. XXVIII) that the present and imperfect subjunctives represent incomplete action in subjunctive subordinate clauses. The present subjunctive is used with a present or future tense main verb and the imperfect with a past tense main verb.

The perfect subjunctive represents completed action in a subjunctive subordinate clause when the main verb is present or future.

Sequence of Tense

Main Verb	Subordinate Verb	
	Incomplete Action	Completed Action
present future	present subjunctive	perfect subjunctive
past tense	imperfect subjunctive	(Cap. XXXIII)

Perfect Subjunctive in Indirect Questions

The perfect subjunctive is used in indirect questions concerning completed actions, when the main verb is in the present, present perfect, or future tense, as in the above examples (*scrīpserit, laudātus sit, laudāverit*) and the following:

> *Haud sciō an ego ita dīxerim.*   I might say that.[2] (l.84)
> *Nesciō quī poēta ista scrīpserit.* (l.106)
> *Mīror unde pecūniam sūmpseris ut aliōs redimerēs.* (ll.132–133)
> *Ego mīror cūr id mihi nōn nārrāveris.* (l.134)
> *Sed nesciō cūr hoc vōbīs nārrāverim.* (ll.154–155)
> *Scīsne quantum pīrātae ā Iūliō Caesare captō postulāverint?*
>   (ll.168–169)
> *Mīlitēs ignōrant quī homō sīs et quid anteā fēceris.* (ll.215–216)
> *Iamne oblītus es quid modo dīxeris?* (l.82): Here *oblītus es* is followed
>   by a perfect subjunctive because it represents the present perfect,
>   where the mental focus is the present result of a past action
>   (Cap. XXI).
> *Nārrābō vōbīs breviter quōmodo amīcum ē servitūte redēmerim atque*
>   *ipse ob eam grātiam servus factus sim.* (l.137)

Sēstertius

After *mīlia*, the partitive genitive plural of *sēstertius* has the shorter ending *-um* in instead of *-ōrum*:

> *decem mīlia sēstertium* (ll.91, cf. l.170)

Lēctiō Tertia (Section III)

Perfect Subjunctive in Prohibitions (Negative Command)

With *nē*, the 2nd person of this tense expresses a prohibition:

> *Nē timueris! Nē timueritis!* (ll.215, 199 = *nōlī/nōlīte timēre!*)
> *Nē dēspērāveris!* (l.162)
> *Nē eum abiēceris!* (l.182)
> *Nē oblīta sīs mē servum fugitīvum esse.* (ll.211–212)

---

2. *Haud sciō an* is an idiom meaning "I think x is probably the case" (the same is true of *nesciō an* and *dubitō an*).

Remember: As you learned in Cap. XX, prohibitions can also be expressed with *nōlī/nōlīte* and the infinitive.

Optative Subjunctive (continued)

In Cap. XXXI, we saw that the subjunctive can express a wish (optative subjunctive). Wishes are often introduced by the adverb *utinam*, e.g.:

Utinam aliquandō līber patriam videam!	May I sometime see my country as a free man! (l.157)
Utinam ille ānulus vītam tuam servet!	May that ring save your life! (ll.182–182)
Utinam salvī in Graeciam perveniant! (l.223)	

Utinam can be left untranslated in English ("may I see my country") or be translated by "I wish that" or similar.

The optative subjunctive to express a wish that something *not* happen uses *nē* to negate the clause, e.g.:

Utinam nē pīrātae mē occīdant! (ll.179–180)

Clauses Expressing Fear

An expression of fear that something may happen implies a wish that it may <u>not</u> happen; this is why the construction with verbs expressing fear, *timēre*, *metuere*, and *verērī* might seem counterintuitive:

- A fear that something <u>will</u> happen is expressed by *nē* + subjunctive, e.g.:
  Timeō nē pīrātae mē occīdant.   I fear the pirates may kill me.
- A fear that something <u>will not</u> happen is expressed with *ut* + subjunctive, e.g.:
  Timeō ut ille veniat.   I fear he may not come.

If you separate the two clauses, you can see how the sentences work:

Timeō (I am afraid) *nē pīrātae mē occīdant* (may the pirates not kill me!) becomes: I fear that the pirates may kill me.

Timeō (I am afraid) *ut ille veniat* (may he come!) becomes: I fear he may not come.

The Prefix *ali-*

The prefix *ali-* serves to make interrogative words indefinite:

quot?	how many?	*ali-quot*: some, several
quandō?	when?	*ali-quandō*: at some time or other, once

| *quantum?* | how much? | *ali-quantum*: a certain amount |
| *quis? quid?* | who? what? | *ali-quis, ali-quid*: someone, something |

Recall, however, that *quis, quid* is used (without *ali-*) as an indefinite pronoun after *sī, nisī, num,* and *nē* (Cap. XXII):

> *Nihil cuiquam nārrāvī dē eā rē, <u>nē quis</u> mē glōriōsum exīstimāret.* (ll.135–136)
>
> *Vērum hōc ānulō <u>sī quis</u> servārī potest, nōn ego, sed amīca mea servanda est.* (ll.180–181)

Recēnsiō: "Qu" words

aliquī, aliqua, aliquod	some (*indefinite adj.*)
aliquis, aliquid	someone, something (*indefinite pronoun*)
quī, quae, quod	who, which, he who (*relative pronoun*)
quī, quae, quod (…?)	what, which (*interrogative adj.*)
quia	because (*conjunction*)
quid	what, anything (*n.* of **quis**, below)
quid (…?)	why (*adv.*)
quīdam, quadam, quoddam	a certain, some (*indefinite pronoun*)
quidem	indeed, certainly (*adv.*)
nē…quidem	not even (*adv.*)
quidnī (…?)	why not (*interrogative adv.*)
quisquis, quidquid/quicquid	whatever, anything that (*indefinite pronoun*)
quis, quae, quid (…?)	who, what (*interrogative pronoun*)
quis, quid (si/num/ne…)	anyone, anything (= **aliquis**)
quisnam, quidnam (…?)	whoever?/whatever? (*strengthened interrogative*)
quisquam, quidquam	anyone, anything (*indefinite pronoun*)
quisque, quaeque, quodque	each (*distributive pronoun*)
quisquis, quidquid	whoever/whatever, anyone who/anything who (*generalizing relative pronoun*)
quō	where (to) (*adv.*)
quod	because, that (= **quia**) (*conjunction*)
quod	what, which, that which (*n.* of relative **quī** above)
quōmodo	how (*adv.*)
quoniam	as, since (*conjunction*)
quoque	also, too (*adv.*)
quot (…?)	how many (*interrogative and relative adj.*)

Studia Rōmāna

The story of Caesar and the pirates (ll.6–9), related more fully by the *gubernātor* (ll.166–177) is told by Plutarch (first–second century), in his biography of Caesar. Piracy (robbery on the sea) was an inveterate problem. According to Thucydides (fifth-century BC Athenian historian), King Minos of Crete (Cap. XXV, l.44) was the first person to establish a navy; he then established colonies around the island, gained control of the waters, and stopped piracy. Rome did not become powerful at sea until the Punic Wars (third century BC). As mentioned briefly in the notes to Cap. XXIX, the Roman navy had made great strides toward policing the seas and keeping them safe from pirates: Pompey in 67 BC (ll.16–41) was granted special military power (*māius imperium*) to combat the pirates. Augustus set up permanent naval stations at *Mīsēnum* and *Ravenna* (*Mīsēnum* is on the point west of *Puteolī* on the map on p. 40 of your text; *Ravenna* is just north of *Arīminum* on the same map). Under the empire, control of the coastline around the Mediterranean facilitated safe seas.

Medus, as a runaway slave, a *fugitīvus,* has a lot to worry about. Should he be caught, it would be up to Julius to decide what to do with him—he could indeed, as he had threatened, have him crucified or, as Medus worries, thrown to beasts. We know both from what the Romans wrote and from artifacts that slaves ran away with some frequency. Archaeologists have found shackles, chains, and slave collars that mark the wearer as a slave, with inscriptions with variations of "hold on to me" (*tenē mē…tenē mē quia fugiō et revocā mē in…*)—the same kind of collars that Romans put on their dogs. Instructions are often included for returning the slave. A runaway slave was a thief (he did not belong to himself but to his master). Someone who finds a runaway slave and does not return him is also a thief and a criminal. During the empire, the Romans employed slave catchers (*fugitīvāriī*) to help them retrieve their property. During the republic, slave-owners had to rely on their network of friends.

We have a *commercium epistulārum* (a correspondence of letters) between Cicero and his friends about a runaway slave named Dionysius (an *anagnostēs*: a slave who read aloud to the master and his guests, so educated with a good voice and therefore expensive, cf. Cap. XVIII). Cicero writes to his friend Publius Sulpicius Rufus, proconsul in Illyria, for help in recovering his Dionysius, who was in charge of Cicero's (very valuable) library; he stole many valuable books and, knowing he would not get away with it, ran away. Spotted in Illyria by several of Cicero's friends, Dionysius claimed he had been set free by Cicero. (For a *fugitīvus* to claim to be *līber*, according to Justinian's Digest of Roman Law, was an even more serious offense, *Dig*est 11.4.2.). Cicero pleads with Sulpicius to do all he can to have Dionysius returned—a small matter, he says, but his grief at losing the books is great (*Ad Fam.* 13.77). At this point, you can read most of it as well! What you can't yet read is translated in parentheses:

*Praetereā ā tē petō in māiōrem modum prō nostrā amīcitiā et prō
tuō perpetuō* (everlasting*) in mē studiō ut in hāc rē etiam ēlabōrēs
(= labōrēs): Dionȳsius, servus meus, quī meam bibliothēcen*[3]
*multōrum nummōrum tractāvit (= cūrāvit), cum multōs librōs
surripuisset* (had stolen) *nec sē impūnē* (without punishment)
*lātūrum putāret, aufūgit. Is est in prōvinciā tuā. Eum et M. Bolānus,
familiāris* (friend) *meus, et multī aliī Narōnae* (at Narona) *vīdērunt,
sed cum sē ā mē manū missum esse dīceret, crēdidērunt. Hunc tū sī
mihi rēstituendum* (will be restored) *cūrāris* (you will take care that)*,
nōn possum dīcere quam mihi grātum futūrum sit. Rēs ipsa parva
sed animī meī dolor magnus est. Ubi sit et quid fierī possit Bolānus
te docēbit. Ego, sī hominem per tē reciperārō* (will have regained)*,
summō mē ā tē beneficiō affectum arbitrābor.*

From these letters, it is clear that not all slaves wore identifying marks and
that some were so integral a part of their master's homes that visitors to those
homes would recognize them elsewhere, so a runaway ran great risks.

Vocābula Disposita/Ōrdināta

Nōmina
  1st

amīcitia, -ae	friendship
audācia, -ae	boldness
grātia, -ae	favor, gratitude, thanks (*pl.*)
incola, -ae (*m./f.*)	inhabitant
inopia, -ae	lack
pīrāta, -ae (*m.*)	pirate
poēta, -ae (*m.*)	poet
victōria, -ae	victory

  2nd

amphitheātrum, -ī	amphitheater
populus, -ī	the people (*not* a person)
talentum, -ī	a talent (sum of money)

  3rd

classis, classis (*f.*)	fleet
condiciō, condicōnis (*f.*)	agreement, contract, condition
gēns, gentis (*f.*)	tribe, nation
servitūs, servitūtis (*f.*)	slavery
victor, victōris (*m.*)	victor
vīrēs, vīrium (*f. pl.*)	strength
vīs (*f.*)	force, power
voluntās, voluntātis (*f.*)	will, desire, good will

3. *Bibliothēcen*: Greek βιβλιοθήκη, Latin *bibliothēcam.*

4th
 cursus, -ūs (*m.*)   running, forward movement; course

Verba
 -āre (1)
 (adiuvō) adiuvāre, adiūvisse,   help
  adiūtum
 (armō) armāre, armāvisse, armātum   arm
 (minor) minārī, minātum   threaten
 (rēmigō) rēmigāre, rēmigāvisse,   row back
  rēmigātum
 (repugnō) repugnāre, repugnāvisse   fight back (mostly *intr.*)
 -ēre (2)
 (dissuādeō) dissuādēre, dissuāsisse   dissuade
 (tueor) tuērī, tuitum and **tūtum**   see, watch, protect
 -ere (3)
 (contemnō) contemnere,   think little of, scorn
  contēmpsisse, contēmptum
 (dēsistō) dēsistere, dēstitisse   leave off, cease
 (ēdūcō) ēdūcere, ēdūxisse, ēductum   lead out
 (flectō) flectere, flexisse, flectum   bend
 (meminī) meminisse (+ *gen.* or *acc.*)   keep in mind, remember
 (praepōnō) praepōnere,   put (*acc.*) before (*dat.*), in charge of
  praeposuisse, praepositum
 (percurrō) percurrisse, percursum   run through
 (redimō) redimere, redēmisse,   buy back
  redēmptum
 (reminīscor) reminīscī   call to mind, recollect
  (+ *gen.* or *acc.*)
 (submergō) submergere, -mersisse,   sink, submerge
  -mersum
 Irregular
 (offerō) offerre, obtulisse, oblātum   offer, present
 (praeferō) praeferre, praetulisse,   prefer
  praelātum
 (referō) referre, rettulisse, relātum   bring back, return

Adiectīva
 1st/2nd (-us/er, -a, -um)
 adversus, -a, -um   opposed, adverse
 cārus, -a, -um   dear
 cūnctus, -a, -um   all
 ēgregius, -a, -um   outstanding
 grātus, -a, -um   grateful, pleasing
 īnfēstus, -a, -um   dangerous
 internus, -a, -um   internal, domestic
 mercātōrius, -a, -um   mercantile

mūtuus, -a, -um	on loan
nūbilus, -a, -um	cloudy
proximus, -a, -um	closest
superbus, -a, -um	lofty, arrogant

3rd

commūnis, -e	shared, common
inermis, -e	(in + arm) unarmed
vīlis, -e	cheap

Adverbia

aliquandō	some time or other, finally
aliquot	some, several
dōnec	until
etiamnunc	even now
intereā	meanwhile
ubīque	anywhere, everywhere
utinam	if that, only that, would that

Coniūnctiōnēs

neu	or not, and not (**nēve…nēve**)
seu	or if, or (**sive…sive**)

XXXIII. Exercitus Rōmānus

Rēs Grammaticae Novae

1. Verbs
   a. Pluperfect Subjunctive
   b. Uses of the Subjunctive
      i. Pluperfect Subjunctive in Subordinate Clauses
      ii. Optative Subjunctive: Unfulfilled Wishes
      iii. Contrafactual Conditions
   c. Passive of Intransitive Verbs
   d. Future Imperative
   e. *velle*: Imperfect Subjunctive
2. Nouns: Case Uses
   a. Ablative of Respect (continued)
3. Adjectives
   a. Gerundive Attraction
   b. Distributive Numerals (continued)

Aemilia Writes to Her Brother

The chapter consists mainly of a letter to Aemilia from her brother, who is in Germania on military service. From this letter, you learn more military terms.

Lēctiō Prīma (Section I)

Distributive Numerals (continued)

In Cap. XXX, you learned that distributive numbers are those used repetitively (e.g., in multiplication or groups of certain numbers). Here are more distributive numerals:

10	*dēnī, -ae, -a* (l.2)	
4	*quaternī, -ae, -a* (l.3)	
5	*quīnī, -ae, -a* (l.3)	
6	*sēnī, -ae, -a* (l.3)	

Nouns that occur only in the plural, i.e., *pluralia tantum*, use distributive numbers, e.g.:

bīna castra	two camps
bīnae litterae	(= *duae epistulae*)

When distributive numbers are used with nouns that are *plūrālia tantum*, *ūnī, -ae, -a* and *trīnī, -ae, -a* are used instead of *singulī, -ae, -a* and *ternī, -ae, -a*, e.g.:

ūnae litterae	(= *ūna epistula*)
trīnae litterae	(= *trēs epistulae*)

Quaeris ā mē cūr tibi ūnās tantum litterās scrīpserim, cum interim trīnās quaternāsve litterās ā tē accēperim. (ll.90–92)

Velle, nōlle, mālle (continued)

The imperfect subjunctive of *mālle* and *nōlle* follows the (perfectly regular) pattern of *velle* (margin, p. 274). Review the forms of the present indicative and present and imperfect subjunctive:

Indicative		Subjunctive Present		Subjunctive Imperfect	
volō	*volumus*	*velim*	*velīmus*	*vellem*	*vellēmus*
vīs	*vultis*	*velīs*	*velītis*	*vellēs*	*vellētis*
vult	*volunt*	*velit*	*velint*	*vellet*	*vellent*
nōlō	*nōlumus*	*nōlim*	*nōlīmus*	*nōllem*	*nōllēmus*
nōn vīs	*nōn vultis*	*nōlīs*	*nōlītis*	*nōllēs*	*nōllētis*
nōn vult	*nōlunt*	*nōlit*	*nōlint*	*nōllet*	*nōllent*
mālō	*mālumus*	*mālim*	*mālīmus*	*māllem*	*māllēmus*
māvīs	*māvultis*	*mālīs*	*mālītis*	*māllēs*	*māllētis*
māvult	*mālunt*	*mālit*	*mālint*	*māllet*	*māllent*

Lēctiō Altera (Section II)

Optative Subjunctive: Wishes Unfulfilled in the Present

In Cap. XXXI, you learned that the present subjunctive (with or without *utinam*) expresses a wish for the future. When we express a wish for the present, it has to be one that isn't true for the present (e.g., "I wish I weren't in class right now!"). There are various names for such wishes (which are optative subjunctive): unfulfilled, unrealistic, and contrafactual (contrary to fact). The verb is in the imperfect subjunctive, e.g., Aemilius's unreal (contrafactual) wishes:

Utinam ego Rōmae <u>essem</u>! (l.67)
Utinam hic amnis Tiberis <u>esset</u> et haec castra <u>essent</u> Rōma! (ll.70–71)

Aemilius is not, in fact, in Rome; the river is not the Tiber and the camp is not Rome. The verb is not in the present, but in the imperfect subjunctive.

Conditions in the Subjunctive: Present Unreal (Contrafactual)

Just as wishes can be unfulfilled (contrafactual), so too can conditions. The following sentences express a condition that can never be realized; here, too, the imperfect subjunctive is used to express unreality:

Sī Mercurius <u>essem</u> ālāsque habērem, in Italiam volārem!	If I were Mercury and had wings, I would fly into Italy (but I'm not Mercury and I don't have wings). (ll.73–75)

Nisi nōs hīc <u>essēmus</u> fīnēsque imperiī <u>dēfenderēmus</u>, hostēs celeriter Dānuvium et Alpēs <u>trānsīrent</u> atque ūsque in Italiam <u>pervenīrent</u>, nec vōs in Latiō tūtī <u>essētis</u>. (ll.82–85)

Sī mihi tantum <u>esset</u> ōtiī quantum est tibi, in epistulīs scrībendīs nōn minus dīligēns <u>essem</u> quam tū. (ll.93–95)

Gerundive Attraction

A gerund is a verbal noun with an active sense and thus can take an accusative direct object. But in practice, the gerund is usually not found with a direct object. Instead, most writers preferred to substitute a phrase consisting of a noun and the gerundive; the meaning is the same in each case. Some examples:

cupidus sōlem propius aspiciendī (Cap. XXVI, l.108)	*cupidus sōlis propius aspiciendī*
cupidus patri<u>am</u> videndī	*cupidus patri<u>ae</u> videnda<u>e</u>* (l.80)
fessus longās fābulās audiendō (Cap. XXVI, l.123)	*fessus long<u>īs</u> fābul<u>īs</u> audiend<u>īs</u>*

Compare: when adding an object to a gerund prepositional phrase, Latin writers consistently use a gerundive/noun combination (not the gerund plus object), e.g.:

Gerund prepositional phrase	Gerundive/noun phrase
ad scrībendum: "for writing"	*ad epistulam scrībendam*: "for writing a letter" (ll.97–98)
in scrībend<u>ō</u>: "in writing"	*in epistul<u>īs</u> scrībend<u>īs</u>*: "in writing letters" (ll.94–95)
ad dēfendend<u>um</u>	*ad castr<u>a</u> dēfendend<u>a</u>* (l.116)
ad persequend<u>um</u>	*ad e<u>ōs</u> persequend<u>ōs</u>* (= *ut eōs persequerentur*) (l.132)

Lēctiō Tertia (Section III)

Passive of Intransitive Verbs

Intransitive verbs, you have learned, do not take an accusative direct object. Intransitive verbs can still be used in the passive, but only if they are used impersonally (that is, in the 3rd person with no subject: "it"). The intransitive verb *pugnāre* is used impersonally in the following examples:

> *ā Rōmānīs fortissimē pugnātum est = Rōmānī fortissimē pugnāvērunt.*
> *Mediā nocte in castra nūntiātum est...* (l.105)

Cum complūrēs hōrās ita fortissimē ā nostrīs, ab hostibus cōnstanter ac nōn timidē pugnātum esset.	literally: "when there had been fighting by our men...by the enemy," but more idiomatically, "when our men and the enemy had fought..." (ll.119–121)

Pluperfect Subjunctive

The last remaining tense of the Latin subjunctive is the **pluperfect** (Latin *coniūnctīvus plūsquamperfectī*). It is formed in the **active** by inserting *-issē-* (shortened *-isse-*) between the perfect stem and the personal endings. In other words, just as the imperfect subjunctive can be formed by adding the personal endings to the present infinitive, the **pluperfect subjunctive** can be formed by adding the personal endings to the perfect infinitive:

1st sing.	*~isse|m*
2nd	*~issē|s*
3rd	*~isse|t*
1st pl.	*~issē|mus*
2nd	*~issē|tis*
3rd	*~isse|nt*

The **pluperfect subjunctive passive** is composed of the perfect participle and the imperfect subjunctive of *esse* (*essem, essēs, esset,* etc.).

Pluperfect Subjunctive in Subordinate Clauses

Just as the perfect subjunctive signifies completed action in a subordinate clause after a present or future tense verb, the pluperfect subjunctive signifies completed action after a past tense main verb.

Sequence of Tense

Main Verb   Subordinate Verb

Incomplete Action Completed Action
present future   present subjunctive   perfect subjunctive
past tense   imperfect subjunctive   pluperfect subjunctive

The pluperfect subjunctive occurs in subordinate clauses such as:

- *cum*-clauses (where *cum* + pluperf. subj. = *postquam* + perf. ind.)
  Quī cum arma cēpissent et vāllum ascendissent (= *postquam…
  cēpērunt/ascendērunt), prīmō mīrābantur quamobrem mediā nocte
  ē somnō excitātī essent…* (ll.109–111)
  Cum complūrēs hōrās ita fortissimē ā nostrīs…pugnātum esset.
  (ll.119–121)

- indirect questions concerning completed action in the past, i.e., with
  the main verb in the preterite (imperfect, perfect, or pluperfect).
  Ego quoque dubitāre coeperam num nūntius vērum dīxisset. (ll.112–
  113)

Optative Subjunctive: Wishes Unfulfilled in the Past

Just as the imperfect subjunctive expresses a wish that is not coming true in
the present, the pluperfect subjunctive expresses a wish that didn't come true
in the past, as in Aemilius's final remarks:

Utinam patrem audīvissem!   If only I had listened to my
                                     father (but I didn't)! (l.166)

Conditions in the Subjunctive: Past Unreal (Contrafactual)

The imperfect subjunctive expresses a condition unfulfilled in the present,
while the pluperfect subjunctive expresses a condition unfulfilled in the past, e.g.:

Sī iam tum hoc intellēxissem,   If I had understood…I would
certē patrem audīvissem nec   have listened and I would not
bellum profectus essem.   have set out. (ll.181–182)

Malus amīcus fuissem, nisi   I would have been a bad friend,
lacrimās effūdissem super   had I not shed tears, since he
corpus amīcī mortuī, cum   would have shed…. (ll.163–165)
ille sanguinem suum prō mē
effūdisset.

More examples can be found in Grammatica Latina.

Thus, the **imperfect subjunctive** expresses a wish/condition that is not
true in the present. The **pluperfect subjunctive** expresses a wish/condition
that was not true in the past:

utinam veniat	"may he come" (in the future) or "may he be coming (presently)"
utinam venīret	"would that he were coming" (but he is not)
utinam vēnisset	"would that he had come" (but he did not)

Ablative of Respect (continued)

The **ablative of respect** (which answers the question "in what respect?") was introduced in Cap. XI (*pede aeger*, l.55), Cap. XIX (*amōre dignus*, ll.111–112), and again in Cap. XXV (*nōmine Mīnōtaurus*, l.26). In the expression *hostēs numerō superiōrēs* (l.144), *numerō* shows in what way the enemy are superior: "in number," "numerically."

Future Imperative

Aemilius ends his letter with some requests (ll.187–189). Here he uses what is often called the **future imperative**. While all imperatives refer to the future, forms in *-tō* (sing.), *-tōte* (pl.) do not imply "immediately." They are often, therefore, used in legal language.

To form the future imperative, the following endings are added to the present stem:

- Vowel Stems
  - ▷ *-tō* (sing.), *-tōte* (pl.)
  - ▷ *nārrā|tō -tōte*
- Consonant Stems
  - ▷ *itō -itōte*
  - ▷ *scrīb|itō -itōte*
- Irregular
  - ▷ *es|tō, es|tōte* from *esse*
  - ▷ *fer|tō, fer|tōte* from *ferre*

Recēnsiō

I. Summary of Conditions

With the indicative

- Present Indicative:

Sī iam hoc intellegis, certē patrem audīs.	If you already understand this, you are certainly listening to your father. (cf. ll.181–182)

  Sī aeger est, in lūdum īre nōn potest. (cf. Cap. XV, l.83)

- Future or Future Perfect Indicative:

  Sī hoc intellēxeris, certē   If you will have understood this,
  patrem audiēs.   you will certainly listen to your
                                        father.

Nōnne laetus eris, sī fīliolam habēbis? (cf. Cap. XX, ll.153–154)

Profectō eum verberābō atque omnibus modīs cruciābō, sī eum invēnerō priusquam Italiam relīquerit. (Cap. XXXI, ll.63–65)

- Past Indicative:

  Sī iam tum hoc intellēxistī,   If you already at that time
  certē patrem audīvistī.   understood this, you certainly
                                        listened to your father.

Sī quid prāvē feceram, dominus imperābat ut ego ab aliīs servīs tenērer et verberārer. (cf. Cap. XXVIII, ll.160–161)

With the subjunctive

- Present Subjunctive (ideal: "should…would"):[1]

  Sī hoc intellegās, certē   If you should understand this,
  patrem audiās.   you would certainly listen to
                                       your father.

  Sī quid prāvē faciam,   If I should do something wrong,
  dominus imperet ut ego   my master would order…
  ab aliīs servīs tenear et
  erberer.

- Imperfect Subjunctive (present unreal: "were…would"):

  Sī iam hoc intellegerēs, certē   If you already understood this
  patrem audīrēs.   (but you clearly don't), you
                                       certainly would be listening to
                                       your father (but you aren't).

- Pluperfect Subjunctive (past unreal):

  Sī iam tum hoc intellēxissēs,   If you had already then
  certē patrem audīvissēs.   understood this (but you clearly
                                       didn't), you certainly would have
                                       listened to your father (but you
                                       didn't).

II. Some Subjunctive Signals

Ut

- Purpose
  - ▷ incomplete action: present or imperfect subjunctive

---

1. *Notā Bene*: There are no examples of this type of condition in your text.

- Result
  - ▷ incomplete action: present or imperfect subjunctive
- Optative
  - ▷ present subjunctive for a future wish or a present wish (when the outcome is uncertain)
  - ▷ imperfect subjunctive for a wish unfulfilled in the present
  - ▷ pluperfect subjunctive for a wish unfulfilled in the past
- Indirect command
  - ▷ incomplete action: present or imperfect subjunctive
- Indirect question
  - ▷ main verb refers to present or future:
    - ○ present subjunctive if subordinate verb expresses incomplete action
    - ○ perfect subjunctive if subordinate verb expresses completed action
  - ▷ main verb refers to past:
    - ○ imperfect subjunctive if subordinate verb expresses incomplete action
    - ○ pluperfect subjunctive if subordinate verb expresses completed action
- Negative fear (i.e., fear that something will not happen/has not happened)
  - ▷ main verb refers to present or future:
    - ○ present subjunctive if subordinate verb expresses incomplete action
    - ○ perfect subjunctive if subordinate verb expresses completed action
  - ▷ main verb refers to past:
    - ○ imperfect subjunctive if subordinate verb expresses incomplete action
    - ○ pluperfect subjunctive if subordinate verb expresses completed action

Utinam
- Wish (see optative subjunctive)

Nē
- Negative Purpose
  - ▷ incomplete action: present or imperfect subjunctive
- Optative (Negative)
  - ▷ present subjunctive for a future wish
  - ▷ imperfect subjunctive for a wish unfulfilled in the present
  - ▷ pluperfect subjunctive for a wish unfulfilled in the past

- Hortatory (Negative)
  - ▷ present subjunctive
- Indirect command (Negative)
  - ▷ incomplete action: present or imperfect subjunctive
- Prohibition
  - ▷ perfect subjunctive
- Affirmative fear (*nē* or *nē nōn*) (i.e., fear that something will happen/has happened
  - ▷ main verb refers to present or future:
    - o present subjunctive if subordinate verb expresses incomplete action
    - o perfect subjunctive if subordinate verb expresses completed action
  - ▷ main verb refers to past:
    - o imperfect subjunctive if subordinate verb expresses incomplete action
    - o pluperfect subjunctive if subordinate verb expresses completed action

Nē...nōn
- Fear (see above, Affirmative fear)

Ut...nōn
- Negative Result
  - ▷ incomplete action: present or imperfect subjunctive

Cum
- Circumstances: subjunctive
- Causal: subjunctive
- (+ ablative: preposition)
- (Pinpointing the time: indicative)
- (Repeated action: "whenever": indicative [usually])

Studia Rōmāna

It's not clear exactly what aspect of *litterae* Aemilius's father pursued and had in mind for his son. We learned in Cap. XXIX that Aemilius's family was poor. Generally, a career in literature was beyond the reach of people of lower socio-economic status. Even writers like Juvenal and Martial who complain constantly of their poverty were poor only in relation to the wealthy elite. He might have been a *scrība* and as such, one of the *appāritōrēs* (free-born attendants to Roman magistrates). Such *scrībae* were public officials; they earned a salary and were part of a *collēgium*, or society, of men who performed the same role. They mixed with more powerful people who could assist their upward mobility.

They were also part of the larger world of letters: the poet Horace (first century BC) was a *scrība quaestōrius*. There is a good amount of evidence, literary and inscriptional, to show the potential for this kind of *studium litterārum*.

One Roman senator who combined the life of a statesman, *studium litterārum* and the military was *Sextus Iūlius Frontīnus*, who lived in the first century AD. His most famous work is his treatise on aqueducts (*dē Aquaeductū Urbis Rōmae*) but he also wrote two works that would have been read by Aemilius's commanders, if not Aemilius himself. *Dē Rē Mīlitārī*, a treatise on military theory, has not survived, but we do have the *Stratēgmata*, a collection of useful examples of stratagems as a continuation of his work on military theory. One section offers examples of clever ways generals (both Greek and Roman) have roused dispirited soldiers. The republican general Aulus Postumius, for example, while fighting against the Latins, told his exhausted troops that two men on horseback were the Dioscuri (Cap. XVI); at the sight of the "gods," his soldiers revived:

> *Aulus Postumius proeliō quō cum Latīnīs conflīxit, oblātā speciē duōrum in equīs iuvenum animōs suōrum ērexit, Pollūcem et Castōrem adesse dīcens, ac sīc proelium rēstituit.*

By Aemilius's time as a soldier, the Roman army had undergone great changes. In the first century BC, the general Marius began the practice of having soldiers carry all of their weapons and equipment, instead of having baggage mules (thereby greatly speeding up the military march). These soldiers got the nickname "Marius's mules." The very efficient practice persisted. The army comprised volunteer soldiers who served for twenty-five years. During this time, they were not allowed to marry (although some had unofficial wives and children). The soldiers' physical training was extensive and difficult. They had to be able to march fast carrying heavy loads, to move in formation, and to wield weapons skillfully. They built the roads they would march on into new territory; at the end of a long day of marching, they built overnight camps, pitched their tents, cooked their meals, and had to be ready to start all over again the next day. Aemilia's brother was part of a legion (*lēgio, legiōnis*, f.), which consisted of ten cohorts (*cohors, cohortis*, f.), which in turn consisted of six companies, called centuries (*centuria, -ae*, f.) of about eighty men. Centuries were led by centurions (*centuriōnēs*). Aemilius was a *pedes* (foot soldier), but he could in time have been promoted to an *eques* (cavalryman), which would have meant a new round of training. The constant trouble with the Germans meant a large number of soldiers were needed in Germany.

The emperor Augustus turned the Roman army into a standing, professional force that policed the boundaries of the Roman world. Inscriptional evidence tells us that Augustus's system stayed remarkably stable for hundreds of years. Soldiers were Roman citizens; auxiliary troops were not. The *stīpendium* (whence our word "stipend") referred both to a term of military service and the recompense earned from that service (*stīpendia merēre* means both "to serve in the military" and "to earn a wage for serving in the military").

Most of what we know about soldiers on the Roman frontiers comes from inscriptions and archaeology. A recent discovery of a number of letters, written on very thin, folded wooden tablets, has been found at Vindolanda, a fort along Hadrian's Wall in Northern England. The discovery of these tablets has revised our view of letter writing, adding thin, wooden tablets inscribed with ink to papyrus and wooden tablets covered with wax and inscribed with a stylus. http://vindolanda.csad.ox.ac.uk/

Vocābula Disposita/Ōrdināta

Nōmina
  1st
    rīpa, -ae   riverbank
  2nd
    gaudium, -ī   joy
    lēgātus, -ī   envoy, delegate
    legiōnārius, -ī   legionary
    proelium, -ī   battle
    stipendium, -ī   salary
    studium, -ī   interest, study
  3rd
    aetās, aetātis (*f.*)   age
    agmen, agminis (*n.*)   army on the march, file
    amnis, amnis (*m.*)   river
    caedēs, caedis (*f.*)   slaughter
    cohors, cohortis (*f.*)   cohort
    ēnsis, ēnsis (*m.*)   sword
    imperātor, imperātōris (*m.*) general, emperor
    legiō, -ōnis (*f.*)   legion
    ōrdō, ōrdinis (*f.*)   order
    pāx, pācis (*f.*)   peace
    ratis, ratis (*f.*)   raft
    valētūdō, valētūdinis (*f.*)   health
    virtūs, virtūtis (*f.*)   virtue
    vulnus, vulneris (*n.*)   wound
  5th
    aciēs, -ēī   line of battle

Verba
  -āre (1)
    (circumdō) circumdare,   surround
      circumdedisse, circumdatum
    (commemorō) commemorāre, mention
      -āvisse, -ātum

(convocō) convocāre, -āvisse, -ātum	call together
(cōpulō) cōpulāre, -āvisse, -ātum	join, connect
(dēsīderō) dēsīderāre, -āvisse, -ātum	long for, miss
(fatīgō) fatīgāre, -āvisse, -ātum	tire out, weary
(hortor) hortārī, hortātum	encourage, urge
(praestō) praestāre, praestitisse	furnish, fulfill
(properō) properāre, -āvisse, -ātum	hasten, hurry
(vulnerō) vulnerāre, -āvisse, -ātum	wound

-ēre (2)

| (studeō) studēre, studuisse (+ *dat.*) | devote oneself to |

-ere (3)

(adiungō) adiungere, adiūnxisse, adiūnctum	add to, join
(caedō) caedere, cecīdisse, caesum	beat, fell, kill
(cōgō) cōgere, coēgisse, coāctum	compel, force
(effundō) effundere, effūdisse, effūsum	pour out
(ērumpō) ērumpere, ērūpisse, ēruptum	break out
(excurrō) excurrere, excucurrisse or excurrisse, excursum	run out, rush out
(īnstruō) īnstruere, īnstrūxisse, īnstrūctum	draw up, arrange
(prōcurrō) prōcurrere, prōcucurrisse or procurrisse, prōcursum	run forward, charge
(prōgredior) prōgredī, prōgressum	go forward, advance

-īre (4)

| (mūniō) mūnīre, mūnīvisse, mūnītum | fortify |

Irregular

fore	= **futurum esse**
(trānsferō) trānsferre, trānstulisse, trānslātum	transfer, transport
(trānseō) trānsīre, trānsīvisse	cross, pass

Adiectīva

1st/2nd (-us/er, -a, -um)

arduus, -a, -um	steep
dēnī, -ae, -a	ten at a time
dīrus, -a, -um	dreadful
horrendus, -a, -um	dreadful
idōneus, -a, -um	suitable
ōtiōsus, -a, -um	leisured, idle
posterus, -a, -um	next, following
prīvātus, -a, -um	private
pūblicus, -a, -um	public

quaternī, -ae, -a	four at a time
quīnī, -ae, -a	five at a time
rīdiculus, -a, -um	laughable, funny
sēnī, -ae, -a	six at a time
trīnī, -ae, -a	three at a time
ūnī, -ae, -a	one at a time

3rd

citerior, citerius	nearer
incolumis, -e	unharmed, safe
mīlitāris, -e	military
ulterior, ulterius	farther, more distant

Prōnōmina

plērīque, plēraeque, plēraque	most

Adverbia

diūtius	longer (*comp.* of **diū**)
etenim	and indeed, for
ferē	about, almost
praecipuē	especially
prīdiē	the day before
quamdiū	how long, as long as
tamdiū	so long, as long

Praepositiōnēs

citrā[2] (*prp. + acc.*)	on this side
secundum[3] (*prp. + acc.*)	along
ultrā (*prp. + acc.*)	on that (the far) side

---

2.   Although not used so in this book, *citrā* can also be used as an adverb.

3.   Although not used so in this book, *secundum* can also be used as an adverb.

XXXIV. Dē Arte Poētica

Rēs Grammaticae Novae

1. Verbs
   a. Intransitive Verbs
   b. Contraction
2. Nouns
   a. "Poetic Plural"
   b. Case use: *in* + Accusative
3. Meter
   a. Syllables
      i. Quantity
      ii. Division
   b. Metric Feet
      i.   Hexameter
      ii. Pentameter
      iii. Elegiac Couplet
      iv. Hendecasyllables
4. Points of Style: Idiom for "to marry"

Latin Poetry

By now you have advanced so far that you can begin to read Latin poetry. In this chapter, you find poems by Catullus (*Gāius Valerius Catullus*, c. 86–54 BC), Ovid (*Pūblius Ovidius Nāsō*, 43 BC–AD 17), and Martial (*Mārcus Valerius Mārtiālis,* c. AD 40–104). At the party, Cornelius starts by quoting a line from Ovid's *Ars Amātōria,* which encourages Julius and Cornelius to quote passages from a collection of love poems, *Amōrēs,* by the same poet. Julius goes on to read aloud some short poems by Catullus and a selection of Martial's witty and satirical epigrams (*epigrammata*). These epigrams are short poems in elegaic couplets (see below).[1]

---

1. Divisions between epigrams are marked in the text by a dash (—).

Reading Poetry

When you first start reading poetry in Latin, you may, temporarily, have to disregard the verse form and concentrate on the content. Poetry's freer word order, in which word groups are often separated can present an obstacle to understanding until you grow accustomed to it. The inflectional endings will show you what words belong together; in some cases, you will find marginal notes to help you, e.g., *ut ipsae spectentur* (l.57), *nōbilium equōrum* (l.62), *amor quem facis* (l.65), *meae puellae dīxī* (l.71). Some supplementary (implied) words are given in italics. However, the important thing is to visualize the situation and enter into the poet's ideas. The comments the guests have made on the poems will be useful for this purpose.

Meter

As you grow accustomed to reading verse, you will be better able to understand the meaning and content of the poems as you read. It is also important for you to study the structure of the verses, that is, the **meter**, which is intrinsic to the poetry. Meter is explained in the GRAMMATICA LATINA section. The following is a summary of the rules:

   Syllabic Quantity: The decisive factor in Latin verse structure is the length or **quantity** of the syllables. Syllables ending in a short vowel (*a, e, i, o, u, y*) are short and are to be pronounced twice as quickly as long syllables, i.e., syllables ending in a long vowel (*ā, ē, ī, ō, ū, ȳ*), a diphthong (*ae, oe, au, eu, ui*), or a consonant. In other words: a syllable is short if it ends in a short vowel; all other syllables are long. A long syllable is marked [—] and a short syllable [∪].

   Syllabic Division: For the division into syllables, each **verse** (*versus*, "line") is treated like one long word:

- **A consonant at the end of a word is linked with a vowel (or h-) at the beginning of the next.** In a word like *satis*, therefore, the last syllable is short if the next word begins with a vowel or *h-*, e.g., in the combination *satis est*, where *-s* is linked with the following *e* in *est*: *sa-ti-s⌢est*—whereas the syllable *tis* is long in *satis nōn est*: *sa-tis-nō-n⌢est.*

- **A vowel (and -am, -em, -im, -um) at the end of a word is dropped before a vowel (or h-) beginning the next word,** e.g., *atque oculōs*: *atqu'oculōs*; *modo hūc*: *mod'hūc*; *passerem abstulistis*: *passer'abstulistis* (in *est* and *es*, the *e* drops, e.g., *sōla est*: *sōla'st*; *vērum est*: *vērum'st*; *bella es*: *bella's*). This is called elision: the vowel is said to be **elided** (Latin *ē-līdere*, "strike out," "squeeze out").

Metric Feet: Each verse can be divided into a certain number of feet (Latin *pedēs*) composed of two or three syllables. The commonest feet are:

- the **trochee** (Latin *trochaeus*), consisting of one long and one short syllable [— ∪]
- the **iamb** (Latin *iambus*), one short and one long [∪ —]
- the **dactyl** (Latin *dactylus*), one long and two short syllables [— ∪∪]
- The two short syllables of the dactyl are often replaced by one long syllable, making a foot consisting of two long syllables [— —], which is called a **spondee** (Latin *spondēus*).

Hexameter: The favorite verse with Latin poets is the **hexameter**, which consists of six feet, the first four of which are dactyls or spondees—the 5th, however, is almost always a dactyl, and the 6th a spondee (or trochee). The last syllable "counts" as long, regardless of its actual length, which is indicated below by an asterisk (*) in the final position:

$$— \underset{\smile}{\smile}\smile| — \underset{\smile}{\smile}\smile| — \underset{\smile}{\smile}\smile| — \underset{\smile}{\smile}\smile| — \smile\smile| — \,^{*}$$

Pentameter: The hexameter often alternates with the slightly shorter **pentameter**, which can be divided into two halves of 2½ feet, each conforming to the beginning of the hexameter (but there are no spondees in the second half):

$$— \underset{\smile}{\smile}\smile| — \underset{\smile}{\smile}\smile| — \| — \smile\smile| — \smile\smile| —$$

Elegiac Couplet: The pentameter never stands alone, but always comes after a hexameter (in the text the pentameters are indented). Such a couplet, consisting of a hexameter and a pentameter, is called an **elegiac couplet** because it was used in **elegies**, i.e., poems expressing personal sentiments, mainly love poems.

Hendecasyllables: Catullus frequently uses the **hendecasyllable** (Latin *versus hendecasyllabus*, "eleven-syllable verse"), which consists of these eleven syllables:

$$— — — \smile\smile — \smile — \smile — \,^{*}$$

It can be divided into a spondee, a dactyl, two trochees, and a spondee (or trochee). (Occasionally the first syllable is short.)

Reading Verse Aloud

Latin verse rhythm is marked by the regular alternation of long and short syllables. Just as a long vowel takes twice the time to pronounce as a short vowel (cf. English "ăha!" versus "fāther"), a long syllable is equivalent to two short syllables. As you read Latin verse aloud, the quantity of the syllables is important. But! If you read the Latin naturally (as you have been doing throughout the book, aided by the text's marking of long vowels with macrons), the rhythm of the verse will emerge. Latin poetry was meant to be heard—so practice reading it aloud. After enumerating the various demands of reading poetry, Quintilian (*I.O.* 1.8) gives this advice for successfully reading verse: *ūnum est igitur quod in hāc parte praecipiam, ut omnia ista facere possit: intellegat* ("There is, therefore, one thing that I would advise on this topic, so that he can do all those things: let him understand [what he reads]").

Plural for Singular

The Roman poets sometimes use the plural ("poetic plural") instead of the singular, especially forms in *-a* from neuters in *-um*, when they are in need of short syllables, e.g., *mea colla* (l.75 for *meum collum*) and *post fāta* (l.180 for *post fātum*). Like other authors, a Roman poet may also use the 1st person plural (*nōs, nōbīs, noster*) about himself. You see this when Catullus calls his friend *venuste noster* (l.152) and when Martial, in his epigram on the response of the public to his books, calls them *libellōs nostrōs* and concludes with the words *nunc nōbīs carmina nostra placent* (ll.163, 166).

In + accusative → against

Martial, who himself writes poems *in inimīcōs*, says about the poet Cinna: *versiculōs in mē nārrātur scrībere Cinna* (l.172). Here *in* + accusative has "hostile" meaning (= *contrā*, cf. the phrase *impetum facere in hostēs*).

Nominative and Infinitive with Passive Verbs

The passive *nārrātur*, like *dīcitur* (Cap. XIII, l.52), is combined with the nom. + inf.: *Cinna scrībere nārrātur/dīcitur* = *Cinnam scrībere nārrant/dīcunt*.

Intransitive Verbs

Besides *imperāre* and *pārēre*, you have met many other verbs that take the **dative**:

crēdere	*appropinquāre*
nocēre	*placēre*
oboedīre	*(cōn)fīdere*
impendēre	*ignōscere*
servīre	*resistere*
(per)suādēre	*minārī*
invidēre	*studēre*
parcere	

Several compounds with *-esse* also take a dative:

prōd-esse	*de-esse* ("fail")
prae-esse	*ad-esse* ("stand by," "help")

In this chapter, you find further examples:

> *favēre* (l.40)
> *nūbere* (l.126)
> *plaudere* (l.217)

The impersonal verb *libet*—like *licet*—is usually combined with a dative:

> *mihi libet* (l.35, "it pleases me," "I feel like," "I want")
> cf. *mihi licet,* "I may," "I am allowed"

Contractions

- A double *i* (*ii, iī*) is apt to be contracted into one long *ī*, as you have seen in the form *dī* for *diī*.
- When *h* disappears in *mihi* and *nihil*, we get the contracted forms *mī* and *nīl* (e.g., ll.118, 174).
- You also find *sapīstī* for *sapiistī* (l.190)—the latter form being a contraction of *sapīvistī*; the final *v* of the perfect stem tends to disappear, so that:
  -īvisse becomes *-iisse/-īsse*
  -āvisse becomes *-āsse*
  -āvistī becomes *-āstī* (Cap. XXVIII, l.106)
  nōvisse becomes *nōsse*
  nōverat becomes *nōrat*

This last form, the pluperfect of *nōscere*, comes to mean "knew," e.g.:

> *Ovidius ingenium mulierum tam bene <u>nōverat</u> quam ipsae mulierēs.* (ll.54–55)
> *suamque <u>nōrat</u> ipsam (: dominam) tam bene quam puella mātrem* (ll.93–94)

Points of Style

The idiom for "marry" is gendered in Latin, as is clear from the chapter:

> *Catullus Lesbiam <u>uxōrem dūcere</u> cupiēbat, nec vērō illa Catullō <u>nūpsit</u>, etsī affirmābat 'sē nūllī aliī virō <u>nūbere</u> mālle* (l.125–127)

A man "leads a woman (home)" into marriage (*in mātrimōnium dūcere*), whereas a woman "covers herself" (i.e., veils herself) for her husband (*nūbere*). In post-classical prose, *nūbere* can also be used for a man. But in classical Latin, the distinction allows Martial to make the following disparaging joke (in addition to those you read at ll.190–191 and 192–193):

> Uxōrem quārē locūplētem dūcere nōlim,
>   Quaeritis? Uxōrī nūbere nōlo meae.
> Inferior mātrōna suō sit, Prisce, marītō:
>   Nōn aliter fīunt fēmina virque pārēs.

VIII.12

(locūples, -ētis = dīves, -itis)

Studia Rōmāna

Scrībimus indoctī doctīque poēmata passim: Everyone is writing poetry, both hacks and laureates; so says Horace in his verse letter to Augustus (*Epist.* 2.1.117), written at the close of the first century. The Romans came late to poetry. Livius Andronicus, a Greek slave, gets the credit for first translating Homer into Latin in the middle of the third century (c. 240 BC). He needed texts with which to teach his Roman students, but the Romans had no poetry. Livius adapted Greek plays to Latin, both tragedies (*tragoediae*) and comedies in Greek dress (*fābulae palliātae*). The Romans harbored some ambivalence toward Greeks and Greek culture (an ambivalence that persisted, as the comment about Orontes "*sed is Graecus est atque lībertīnus*" (30.117) shows). But just as Greek myths captivated the Roman imagination (Cap. XXV), so too did Greek literature, art, and philosophy work its way into Roman culture. Many Romans were bilingual in Greek and Latin. For some, bilingual meant knowing as much Greek as they needed to do business (or to live as a soldier abroad in Greek-speaking lands). The well educated might be truly bilingual.

The Romans translated, they adapted, they imitated. Ennius, in the late third or early second century BC, translated the fourth-century BC Greek writer Euhemerus into Latin. Plautus, in the second century BC, adapted Greek comedies for a Roman audience; he jokes that his play, *The Twin Menaechmi*, imitates Greek—not the highbrow Greek comedy of Athens, but the farcical Greek comedies of Sicily (*Menaechmi*, 11–12):

> *Atque adeō hoc argūmentum graecissat, tamen*
> *nōn atticissat, verum sicilicissitat.*

Graecissat and *atticissat* were colloquial speech. *Sicilicissitat* appears only here; it is a punch line. In Plautus's plays, we find the exuberance of one culture joyfully playing with the literature of another. Romans quickly became more refined and subtle in their interpretation of Greek literature. Plautus's younger contemporary Terence (*Pūblius Terentius Āfer*), a freed slave from North Africa, wrote a smooth and polished Latin, and defended his way of adapting Greek plays in argumentative prologues. By the time of the late republic, Roman writers had learned to look to Greek models as inspiration for a literature that was new, learned, and Roman. The influence of Greek eloquence inspired the Romans to look at Latin with an eye to taking their language to a new level. In the first century BC, Julius Caesar wrote a book on linguistic analogy; Cicero wrote extensively on orators and oratory; *Mārcus Terentius Varrō* wrote a book on the Latin language. It seemed everyone wrote poetry—just not everyone wrote it well (see the Horace quotation above).

The poets in our chapter cover a long time-span. Aemilia likes Plautus, who would, by the second century AD, be one of the ancients, having lived over three centuries prior to our narrative. Catullus wrote in the middle of the first century BC. A contemporary of Cicero (who also wrote poetry), Catullus greatly admired the poets of Hellenistic Greece (that is, Greece during and after Alexander the Great), as well as the—by his time—ancient Greek poets. Catullus and the other "New Poets" favored closely worked, allusive poetry. The citation of poets at the dinner begins with Ovid, one of the greatest poetic geniuses of the Roman world. Ovid was a much younger and greatly admiring contemporary of Vergil and Horace; he heard Horace read his poetry aloud, but only saw Vergil (*Tristia* 4.10.49–51: *et tenuit nostrās numerōsus Horātius aurēs/dum ferit Ausonia carmina cultā lyrā./Vergilium vīdī tantum*). Martial, the final and most quoted poet in the chapter, lived in the first century AD and is the closest to the time of our narrative.

The poets of the late republic and early empire remained unsurpassed in the power and virtuosity of their poetry. By the time of our narrative Vergil and Horace were studied in school as classic texts. The poetry of the first century AD boasted, in addition to Martial and Juvenal, the great epic poet Lucan, who wrote an epic in ten books about the great civil war between Julius Caesar and Pompey the Great. Martial died c. AD 104 and Juvenal c. AD 130; after them, almost no Latin verse from our time period (second century AD) has been preserved. *Studium litterārum*, however, was by no means finished. Educated Roman amateurs were still writing verse and holding recitations, either at private parties or at larger readings in *auditōria*. Pliny the Younger (AD 61–113) tells us much about these reading in his letters.

Our friends at the dinner party read the poetry of others, but we know people composed extemporaneous verse at dinner parties. Catullus tells us of playing a game of one-up-manship with his friend *Licinius Calvus* (another renowned poet of the time whose work—with the exception of a few lines—is unfortunately lost). They took turns writing lines of verse (Catullus 50). The Younger Pliny sends his friend a collection of verse in the hendecasyllabic meter (a favorite of Catullus) that he wrote "while riding in a carriage, while in the bath, while eating dinner, delightfully passing my leisure time" (*Epist.* 4.14: *Accipiēs cum hāc epistulā hendecasyllabōs nostrōs, quibus nōs in vehiculō in balineō inter cānam oblectāmus ōtium temporis*).

Cornelius claims he carries a copy of the poet Martial around with him at all times. By the time of our narrative, books in *cōdex* form (that is, resembling more closely our own books) had become common. In a volume of poetry containing epigrams attached to party favors, known as *apophorēta* (ἀποφόρητα), or "take away presents," Martial himself describes several of such small codices. Here's one (14.186) that claims to contain all of Vergil (*Pūblius Vergilius Marō*, hence, *Marōnem*) on its parchment (*membrana*):

> *Quam brevis inmensum cēpit membrāna Marōnem!*
> *Ipsīus vultūs prīma tabella gerit.*

Vocābula Disposita/Ōrdināta

Nōmina
  1st

arānea, -ae	spider, cobweb
aurīga, -ae (*m.*)	charioteer, driver
cōmoedia, -ae	comedy
dēliciae, -ārum (*f. pl.*)	delight, pet
lucerna, -ae	lamp
nota, -ae	mark, sign
opera, -ae	effort, pains
palma, -ae	palm
tenebrae, -ārum (*f. pl.*)	darkness

  2nd

bāsium, -ī	kiss
cachinnus, -ī	laugh, guffaw
circus, -ī	circle, orbit, Circus Maximus
fātum, -ī	fate
gremium, -ī	lap
ingenium, -ī	nature, character
lūdus, -ī	play, game, school
ocellus, -ī	(little) eye
odium, -ī	hatred
prīncipium, -ī	beginning
scalpellum, -ī	scalpel, surgical knife
theātrum, -ī	theatre

  3rd

certāmen, certāminis (*n.*)	contest, fight
gladiātor, -tōris (*m.*)	gladiator
mēns, mentis (*f.*)	mind
opēs, opum (*f. pl.*)	wealth
passer, passeris (*m.*)	sparrow
ratiō, ratiōnis (*f.*)	reason
rēte, rētis (*n.*)	net

spectātor, spectātōris (*m.*)	spectator
testis, -is (*m.*)	witness

4th

anus, -ūs (*f.*)	old woman
rīsus, -ūs (*m.*)	laughter, laugh
sinus -ūs (*m.*)	fold (of toga)

Indeclinable

nīl	nothing (= **nihil**)

Grammatica

dactylus, -ī	dactyl
dipthongus, -ī	dipthong
epigramma, epigrammatis (*n.*)	epigram
hendecasyllabus, -ī	"eleven-syllable verse"
hexameter, hexametrī	having six metrical feet
iambus, -ī	iamb
pentameter, pentametrī	having five metrical feet
spondēus, -ī	spondee
trochaeus, -ī	trochee
versiculus, -ī	a little line of verse (*diminuitive* of **versus, -ūs**)

Verba

-āre (1)

(**affirmō**) **affirmāre, affirmāvisse, affirmātum**	assert, affirm
(**certō**) **certāre, certāvisse, certātum**	contend, fight
(**conturbō**) **conturbāre, conturbāvisse, conturbātum**	mix up, confound
(**dēvorō**) **dēvorāre, dēvorāvisse, dēvorātum**	swallow up, devour
(**excruciō**) **excruciāre, excruciāvisse, excruciātum**	torture, torment
(**implicō**) **implicāre, implicuisse, implicitum**	enfold
(**ōscitō**) **ōscitāre, ōscitāvisse, ōscitātum**	gape, yawn
(**pīpiō**) **pīpiāre, pīpiāvisse, pīpiātum**	chirp

-ēre (2)

(**faveō**) **favēre, fāvisse**	favor, support (+ *dat.*)
(**libet**) **libēre**	it pleases (+ *dat.*)
(**lūgeō**) **lūgēre, lūxisse**	mourn

-ere (3)

(**accendō**) **accendere, accendisse, accēnsum**	light, enflame
(**ēlīdō**) **ēlīdere, ēlīsisse, ēlīsum**	break thoroughly, omit, elide
(**ērubēscō**) **ērubēscere, ērubuisse**	blush

(laedō) laedere, laesisse, laesum	injure, hurt
(nūbō) nūbere, nūpsisse (+ *dat.*)	marry
(plaudō) plaudere, plausisse, plausum (+ *dat.*)	clap, applaud
(requīrō) requīrere, requīsīvisse, requīsitum	seek, ask
(sapiō) sapere, sapīvisse	be wise, have sense

-īre (4)

(circumsiliō) circumsilīre, circumsiluisse	hop about
(prōsiliō) prōsilīre, prōsiluisse	spring forth

Adiectīva

1st/2nd (-us/er, -a, -um)

bellus, -a, -um	lovely, pretty
dubius, -a, -um	undecided, doubtful
geminus, -a, -um	twin
gladiātōrius, -a, -um	gladiatorial
iocōsus, -a, -um	humorous, funny
mellītus, -a, -um	sweet
misellus, -a, -um	poor, wretched
niveus, -a, -um	snow white
perpetuus, -a, -um	continuous, permanent
poēticus, -a, -um	poetical
scaenicus, -a, -um	theatrical
sērius, -a, -um	serious
tenebricōsus, -a, -um	dark
turgid(ul)us, -a, -um	swollen
ultimus, -a, -um	most distant, last
venustus, -a, -um	charming

3rd

ācer, -cris, -cre	keen, active, fierce
circēnsis, -e	of the circus

Adverbia

dein	afterward, then
interdum	now and then
libenter	with pleasure, gladly
plērumque	mostly

Coniūnctiōnēs

dummodo	provided that, if only

XXXV. Ars Grammatica

Now that you have worked your way through all the declensions and conjugations of the Latin language, it is time to pause and take a comprehensive look at the grammatical system. To give you an opportunity to do this, we present, in a slightly abbreviated form, a Latin grammar, the *Ars Grammatica Minor,* written by the Roman grammarian Dōnātus, c. AD 350. This grammar is based on the works of earlier grammarians, rearranged in the form of question and answer, so it gives us an idea of the teaching methods used in antiquity—and much later, for the "*Donat*" was a favorite schoolbook in Europe throughout the Middle Ages. Now it is up to you to show that you have learned enough to answer the questions on grammar put to schoolchildren in the Roman Empire. Apart from omissions, marked […], the text of Donatus is unaltered (in the examples on p. 303 of LINGUA LATINA, some infrequent words have been replaced by others).

The Latin grammatical terms are still in use. However, the **part of speech** (*pars ōrātiōnis*) that the Roman grammarians called *nōmina* is now divided into **nouns** (or **substantives**) and **adjectives**. The term *nōmen adiectīvum* dates from antiquity, but it was not till medieval times that the term *nōmen substantīvum* was coined (in English "noun substantive" as opposed to "noun adjective"). As a matter of fact, several of the Latin grammatical terms are adjectives that are generally used "substantively" with a noun understood, e.g.:

- (*cāsus*) *nōminātīvus*
- (*numerus*) *plūrālis*
- (*modus*) *imperātīvus*
- (*gradus*) *comparātīvus*
- (*genus*) *fēminīnum* (*masculīnum, neutrum, commūne*)

Genus is "gender" in English; Donatus counts four genders because he uses the term *genus commune* about words that may be both masculine and feminine, e.g., *sacerdōs -ōtis,* "priest/priestess" (other examples are *cīvis, incola, īnfāns, testis, bōs, canis*).

The hexameter quoted by Donatus (l.212) to illustrate the use of *super* with the ablative is taken from the end of the first book of the *Aeneid*, the famous poem in which Vergil recounts the adventures of the Trojan hero Aeneas (*Aenēās*) during his flight from Troy (*Trōia*). Driven by a storm to Africa, he is received in Carthage (*Carthāgō*) by Queen *Dīdō,* who questions him about the fate of the other Trojans, King Priam (*Priamus*) and his son Hector.

Vocābula Disposita/Ōrdināta

Nōmina
  1st
    īra, -ae   anger
    mūsa, -ae   a muse (one of the nine daughters
                                                    of Memory)

  2nd
    scamnum, -ī   stool
  3rd
    admīrātiō, admīrātiōnis (*f.*)   wonder, admiration
    ōrātiō, ōrātiōnis (*f.*)   speech
    sacerdōs, sacerdōtis (*m./f.*)   priest, priestess
  4th
    affectus, -ūs (*m.*)   mood, feeling

Grammatica
    appellātīvum, -ī (*nōmen*)   common noun
    cāsus, -ūs (*m.*)   fall, case
    causālis (*coniūnctiō*) (*f.*)   causal conjunction
    comparātiō, comparātiōnis (*f.*)   a comparison
    coniugātiō, coniugātiōnis (*f.*)   conjugation
    coniūnctiō, coniūnctiōnis (*f.*)   conjunction
    cōpulātīva (*coniūnctiō*) (*f.*)   copulative conjunction
    disiūnctīva (*coniūnctiō*) (*f.*)   disjunctive conjunction
    explētīva (*coniūnctiō*) (*f.*)   exclamatory conjunction
    interiectiō, interiectiōnis (*f.*)   interjection
    optātīvus (*modus*)   optative (wishing) mood
    positīvus (*gradus*)   positive degree[1]
    proprium, -ī (*nōmen*)   proper noun
    quālitās, quālitātis (*f.*)   quality
    quantitās, quantitātis (*f.*)   quantity
    ratiōnālis (*coniūnctiō*) (*f.*)   conjunction showing the train
                                                    of thought
    significātiō, significātiōnis (*f.*)   meaning, sense

---

1. Of an adjective or adverb.

speciēs, -ēī	appearance, aspect, sort
synōnymum, -ī	synonym

Verba
  -āre (1)
(explānō) explānāre, -āvisse, -ātum	make intelligible, explain
(luctor) luctārī, luctātum	wrestle
(ōrdinō) ōrdināre, -āvisse, -ātum	put in order

  -ere (3)
(adnectō) adnectere, -nexuisse, -nexum	bind, tie
(dēmō) dēmere, dēmpsisse, dēmptum	take away
(īnflectō) īnflectere, -flexisse, -xum	bend, curve, inflect[2]
mentiōnem facere	mention

Adiectīva
  1st/2nd (-us/er, -a, -um)
| inconditus, -a, -um | unpolished, rough |
  3rd
| similis, -e | similar |

Adverbia
dumtaxat	only, just
forsitan	maybe, perhaps
proptereā	therefore
quāpropter	why
quidnī	why not
sīquidem	seeing that, since
tantundem	just as much

Praepositiōnēs
| adversus/-um (*prp. +acc.*) | toward, against |
| cis (*prp. +acc.*) | on this side of |

Interiectiōnēs
attat	exclamation of joy, pain, wonder, fright
eia	exclamation of joy, pleased surprise; also "come on," "hurry up"
ēn	presents something important and/or unexpected
euax	exclamation of joy
papae	exclamation of wonder and joy

---

2. Inflect: To form the pattern of a word, decline a noun or conjugate a verb.

Grammatica Latina

The Parts of Speech

The **parts of speech**, or word classes, are:

- **Noun** (or **substantive**), e.g. *Mārcus, Rōma, puer, oppidum leō, aqua, color, pugna, mors,* etc.
- **Adjective**, e.g. *Rōmānus, bonus, pulcher, brevis,* etc.
- **Pronoun**, e.g. *tū, nōs, is, hic, ille, quis, quī, nēmō,* etc.
- **Verb**, e.g. *amāre, habēre, venīre, emere, īre, esse,* etc.
- **Adverb**, e.g. *bene, rēctē, fortiter, ita, nōn, hīc,* etc.
- **Conjunction**, e.g. *et, neque, sed, aut, quia, dum, sī, ut,* etc.
- **Preposition**, e.g. *in, ab, ad, post, inter, sine, dē,* etc.
- **Interjection**, e.g. *ō, ei, heu, heus, ecce,* etc.
- **Numerals** are nouns and adjectives which denote numbers, e.g. *trēs, tertius, ternī.*
- Adverbs, conjunctions, prepositions and interjections are **indeclinable** words, so-called **particles.**

parts of speech:
nouns (substantives)
adjectives
pronouns
verbs
adverbs
conjunctions
prepositions
interjections

numerals

particles

NOUNS

Gender, number, case

There are three **genders: masculine**, e.g. *servus,* **feminine**, e.g. *ancilla*, and **neuter**, e.g. *oppidum.*

There are two **numbers: singular**, e.g. *servus,* and **plural**, e.g. *servī.* Nouns which have no singular are called **plūrālia tantum.**

There are six **cases: nominative**, e.g. *servus,* **accusative**, e.g. *servum,* **genitive**, e.g. *servī,* **dative**, e.g. *servō,* **ablative**, e.g. *(ā) servō,* and **vocative**, e.g. *serve.*

genders: masc., m.
             fem., f.
             neut., n.

numbers: sing. pl.
cases: nom.
             acc.
             gen.
             dat.
             abl.
             voc.

Stem and ending

The **stem** is the main part of a word, e.g. *serv-, ancill-, oppid-, magn-, brev-,* to which various inflectional **endings** are added, e.g. *-um, -ī, -am, -ae, -ō, -ēs, -ibus.*

In the examples in this book the stem is separated from the ending with a thin vertical stroke [|], e.g. *serv|us, serv|ī.*

stems: *serv-, ancill-, oppid-,* etc.

endings: *-ī, -am, -ae,* etc.

Declensions

There are five **declensions**:

1st declension: gen. sing. -*ae*, e.g. *īnsul|a -ae*.

2nd declension: gen. sing. -*ī*, e.g. *serv|us -ī, oppid|um -ī*.

3rd declension: gen. sing. -*is*, e.g. *sōl sōl|is, urb|s -is*.

4th declension: gen. sing. -*ūs*, e.g. *man|us -ūs*.

5th declension: gen. sing. -*ēī/-eī*, e.g. *di|ēs -ēī, r|ēs -eī*.

First Declension

Genitive: sing. -*ae*, pl. -*ārum*.

Example: *īnsul|a -ae* f.

	sing.	pl.
nom.	*īnsul|a*	*īnsul|ae*
acc.	*īnsul|am*	*īnsul|ās*
gen.	*īnsul|ae*	*īnsul|ārum*
dat.	*īnsul|ae*	*īnsul|īs*
abl.	*īnsul|ā*	*īnsul|īs*

Masculine (male persons): *nauta, agricola, aurīga, pīrāta, poēta*, etc.

Second Declension

Genitive: sing. -*ī*, pl. -*ōrum*.

1. Masculine.

Examples: ***equ|us -ī, liber libr|ī, puer puer|ī.***

	sing.	pl.	sing.	pl.	sing.	pl.
nom.	*equ|us*	*equ|ī*	*liber*	*libr|ī*	*puer*	*puer|ī*
acc.	*equ|um*	*equ|ōs*	*libr|um*	*libr|ōs*	*puer|um*	*puer|ōs*
gen.	*equ|ī*	*equ|ōrum*	*libr|ī*	*libr|ōrum*| *puer|ī*	*puer|ōrum*
dat.	*equ|ō*	*equ|īs*	*libr|ō*	*libr|īs*	*puer|ō*	*puer|īs*
abl.	*equ|ō*	*equ|īs*	*libr|ō*	*libr|īs*	*puer|ō*	*puer|īs*
voc.	*equ|e*					

A few are feminine, e.g. *hum|us -ī, papyr|us -ī, Aegypt|us -ī, Rhod|us -ī.*

Nom. sing. -*ius*, voc. -*ī*: *Iūlius, Iūlī! fīlius, fīlī!*

2. Neuter.

Example: ***verb|um -ī.***

	sing.	pl.
nom.	*verb|um*	*verb|a*
acc.	*verb|um*	*verb|a*
gen.	*verb|ī*	*verb|ōrum*
dat.	*verb|ō*	*verb|īs*
abl.	*verb|ō*	*verb|īs*

declension (decl.)
1st decl.: gen. -*ae*
2nd decl.: gen. -*ī*
3rd decl.: gen. -*is*
4th decl.: gen. -*ūs*
5th decl.: gen. -*ēī/-eī*

-*a*	-*ae*
-*am*	-*ās*
-*ae*	-*ārum*
-*ae*	-*īs*
-*ā*	-*īs*

-*us/-*	-*ī*
-*um*	-*ōs*
-*ī*	-*ōrum*
-*ō*	-*īs*
-*ō*	-*īs*
-*e*	

-*um*	-*a*
-*um*	-*a*
-*ī*	-*ōrum*
-*ō*	-*īs*
-*ō*	-*īs*

Third Declension

Genitive: sing. *-is*, pl. *-um/-ium*.

[A] Genitive plural: *-um*.

1. Masculine and feminine.

Examples: ***sōl*** *sōl|is* m., ***leō*** *leōn|is* m., ***vōx*** *vōc|is* f.

	sing.	pl.	sing.	pl.	sing.	pl.			
nom.	*sōl*	*sōl|ēs*	*leō*	*leōn|ēs*	*vōx*	*vōc|ēs*		*-/-s*	*-ēs*
acc.	*sōl|em*	*sōl|ēs*	*leōn|em*	*leōn|ēs*	*vōc|em*	*vōc|ēs*		*-em*	*-ēs*
gen.	*sōl|is*	*sōl|um*	*leōn|is*	*leōn|um*	*vōc|is*	*vōc|um*		*-is*	*-um*
dat.	*sōl|ī*	*sōl|ibus*	*leōn|ī*	*leōn|ibus*	*vōc|ī*	*vōc|ibus*		*-ī*	*-ibus*
abl.	*sōl|e*	*sōl|ibus*	*leōn|e*	*leōn|ibus*	*vōc|e*	*vōc|ibus*		*-e*	*-ibus*

[1] Nom. *-er*, gen. *-r|is*: *pater patr|is* m., *māter mātr|is* f.   *-er -r|is*

[2] Nom. *-or*, gen. *-ōr|is*: *pāstor -ōr|is* m.   *-or -ōr|is*

[3] Nom. *-ōs*, gen. *-ōr|is*: *flōs flōr|is* m.   *-ōs -ōr|is*

[4] Nom. *-ō*, gen. *-in|is*: *virgō -in|is* f., *homō -in|is* m.   *-ō -in|is*

[5] Nom. *-x*, gen. *-g|is*: *lēx lēg|is* f., *rēx rēg|is* m.   *-x -g|is*

[6] Nom. *-ex*, gen. *-ic|is*: *index -ic|is* m.   *-ex -ic|is-s -t|is*

[7] Nom. *-s*, gen. *-t|is*: *aetās -āt|is* f., *mīles -it|is* m.   *-s -d|is*

[8] Nom. *-s*, gen. *-d|is*: *laus laud|is* f., *pēs ped|is* m.

[9] Irregular nouns: *sanguis -in|is* m.; *coniūnx -iug|is* m./f.; *senex sen|is* m.; *bōs bov|is* m./f., pl. *bov|ēs boum*, dat./abl. *bōbus/būbus*.

2. Neuter

Examples: *ōs ōr|is*, ***corpus*** *corpor|is*, ***opus*** *-er|is*, ***nōmen*** *nōmin|is*.

	sing.	pl.	sing.	pl.			
nom.	*ōs*	*ōr|a*	*corpus*	*corpor|a*		*-*	*-a*
acc.	*ōs*	*ōr|a*	*corpus*	*corpor|a*		*-*	*-a*
gen.	*ōr|is*	*ōr|um*	*corpor|is*	*corpor|um*		*-is*	*-um*
dat.	*ōr|ī*	*ōr|ibus*	*corpor|ī*	*corpor|ibus*		*-ī*	*-ibus*
abl.	*ōr|e*	*ōr|ibus*	*corpor|e*	*corpor|ibus*		*-e*	*-ibus*
nom.	*opus*	*oper|a*	*nōmen*	*nōmin|a*			
acc.	*opus*	*oper|a*	*nōmen*	*nōmin|a*			
gen.	*oper|is*	*oper|um*	*nōmin|is*	*nōmin|um*			
dat.	*oper|ī*	*oper|ibus*	*nōmin|ī*	*nōmin|ibus*			
abl.	*oper|e*	*oper|ibus*	*nōmin|e*	*nōmin|ibus*			

Irregular nouns: *cor cord|is*; *caput capit|is*; *lac lact|is*; *os oss|is* (gen. pl. *-ium*); *mel mell|is*; *iter itiner|is*; *vās vās|is*, pl. *vās|a -ōrum* (2nd decl.); *thema -at|is*.   *-ma -mat|is*

[B] Genitive plural: *-ium.*

1. Masculine and feminine.

Examples: *nāv|is -is* f., **urb|s** *-is* f., **mōns** *mont|is* m.

	sing.	pl.	sing.	pl.	sing.	pl.
nom.	*nāv|is*	*nāv|ēs*	*urb|s*	*urb|ēs*	*mōns*	*mont|ēs*
acc.	*nāv|em*	*nāv|ēs*	*urb|em*	*urb|ēs*	*mont|em*	*mont|ēs*
gen.	*nāv|is*	*nāv|ium*	*urb|is*	*urb|ium*	*mont|is*	*mont|ium*
dat.	*nāv|ī*	*nāv|ibus*	*urb|ī*	*urb|ibus*	*mont|ī*	*mont|ibus*
abl.	*nāv|e*	*nāv|ibus*	*urb|e*	*urb|ibus*	*mont|e*	*mont|ibus*

margin:
-(i)s   -ēs
-em   -ēs
-is   -ium
-ī   -ibus
-e   -ibus

[1] Nom. *-is*, acc. *-im* (pl. *-īs*), abl. *-ī: pupp|is -is* f., *Tiber|is -is* m.

margin: -is, acc. -im, abl. -ī

[2] Nom. *-ēs*, gen. *-is: nūb|ēs -is* f.

margin: -ēs -is

[3] Nom. *-x*, gen. *-c|is: falx falc|is* f.

margin: -x -c|is

[4] Irregular nouns: *nox noct|is* f.; *nix niv|is* f.; *carō carn|is* f.; *as ass|is* m.; *vīs*, acc. *vim*, abl. *vī*, pl. *vīr|ēs -ium* f.

2. Neuter

Examples: *mar|e -is*, **animal** *-āl|is.*

	sing.	pl.	sing.	pl.
nom.	*mar|e*	*mar|ia*	*animal*	*animāl|ia*
acc.	*mar|e*	*mar|ia*	*animal*	*animāl|ia*
gen.	*mar|is*	*mar|ium*	*animāl|is*	*animāl|ium*
dat.	*mar|ī*	*mar|ibus*	*animāl|ī*	*animāl|ibus*
abl.	*mar|ī*	*mar|ibus*	*animāl|ī*	*animāl|ibus*

margin:
-e/-   -ia
-e/-   -ia
-is   -ium
-ī   -ibus
-ī   -ibus

Fourth Declension

Genitive: sing. *-ūs*, pl. *-uum.*

Examples: **port|us** *-ūs* m., **corn|ū** *-ūs* n.

	sing.	pl.	sing.	pl.
nom.	*port|us*	*port|ūs*	*corn|ū*	*corn|ua*
acc.	*port|um*	*port|ūs*	*corn|ū*	*corn|ua*
gen.	*port|ūs*	*port|uum*	*corn|ūs*	*corn|uum*
dat.	*port|uī*	*port|ibus*	*corn|ū*	*corn|ibus*
abl.	*port|ū*	*port|ibus*	*corn|ū*	*corn|ibus*

margin:
-us -ūs   -ū -ua
-um -ūs   -ū -ua
-ūs -uum   -ūs -uum
-uī -ibus   -ū -ibus
-ū -ibus   -ū -ibus

dom|us -ūs f., abl. *-ō*, pl. *dom|ūs -ōrum* (*-uum*), acc. *-ōs.*

Fifth Declension

Genitive: sing. *-ēī/-eī*, pl. *-ērum.*

Examples: **di|ēs** *-ēī* m. (f.), **rēs** *reī* f.

	sing.	pl.	sing.	pl.
nom.	*di|ēs*	*di|ēs*	*rēs*	*rēs*
acc.	*di|em*	*di|ēs*	*rem*	*rēs*
gen.	*di|ēī*	*di|ērum*	*reī*	*rērum*
dat.	*di|ēī*	*di|ēbus*	*reī*	*rēbus*
abl.	*di|ē*	*di|ēbus*	*rē*	*rēbus*

margin:
-ēs   -ēs
-em   -ēs
-ēī/-eī   -ērum
-ēī/-eī   -ēbus
-ē   -ēbus

ADJECTIVES

First and Second Declensions

[A] Genitive singular -ī -ae -ī.

Example: **bon|us** -a -um.

	sing. masc.	fem.	neut.	pl. masc.	fem.	neut.			
nom.	bon|us	bon|a	bon|um	bon|ī	bon|ae	bon|a	-us	-a	-um
acc.	bon|um	bon|am	bon|um	bon|ōs	bon|ās	bon|a	-um	-am	-um
gen.	bon|ī	bon|ae	bon|ī	bon|ōrum	bon|ārum	bon|ōrum	-ī	-ae	-ī
dat.	bon|ō	bon|ae	bon|ō	bon|īs	bon|īs	bon|īs	-ō	-ae	-ō
abl.	bon|ō	bon|ā	bon|ō	bon|īs	bon|īs	bon|īs	-ō	-ā	-ō
voc.	bon|e						-ī	-ae	-a
							-ōs	-ās	-a
							-ōrum	-ārum	-ōrum
							-īs	-īs	-īs
							-īs	-īs	-īs
							-er	-(e)r|a	-(e)r|um

Examples: **niger** -gr|a -gr|um, **līber** -er|a -er|um.

	sing. masc.	fem.	neut.	masc.	fem.	neut.
nom.	niger	nigr|a	nigr|um	līber	līber|a	līber|um
acc.	nigr|um	nigr|am	nigr|um	līber|um	līber|am	līber|um

etc. (as above, but voc. = nom. -er)

[B] Genitive singular -īus.

Example: **sōl|us** -a -um, gen. -īus, dat. -ī.

		masc.	fem.	neut.			
sing.	nom.	sōl|us	sōl|a	sōl|um	pl. (as bon|ī -ae -a)	-us	-a	-um
	acc.	sōl|um	sōl|am	sōl|um		-um	-am	-um
	gen.	sōl|īus	sōl|īus	sōl|īus		-īus	-īus	-īus
	dat.	sōl|ī	sōl|ī	sōl|ī		-ī	-ī	-ī
	abl.	sōl|ō	sōl|ā	sōl|ō		-ō	-ā	-ō

Third Declension

[A] Genitive plural -ium (abl. sing. -ī).
Example: **brev|is** -e.

	sing. masc./fem.	neut.	pl. masc./fem.	neut.				
nom.	brev|is	brev|e	brev|ēs	brev|ia	-is	-e	-ēs	-ia
acc.	brev|em	brev|e	brev|ēs	brev|ia	-em	-e	-ēs	-ia
gen.	brev|is	brev|is	brev|ium	brev|ium	-is	-is	-ium	-ium
dat.	brev|ī	brev|ī	brev|ibus	brev|ibus	-ī	-ī	-ibus	-ibus
abl.	brev|ī	brev|ī	brev|ibus	brev|ibus	-ī	-ī	-ibus	-ibus

Examples: **ācer** ācr|is ācr|e, **celer** -er|is -er|e.

	sing. masc.	fem.	neut.	masc.	fem.	neut.		
nom.	ācer	ācr|is	ācr|e	celer	celer|is	celer|e	-er -(e)r|is	-(e)r|e
acc.	ācr|em		ācr|e	celer|em		celer|e	-(e)r|em	-(e)r|e

etc. (as above) etc. (as above)

Examples: **fēlīx**, gen. -īc|is; **ingēns**, gen. -ent|is (-x < -c|s, -ns < -nt|s)

		masc./fem.	neut.	masc./fem.	neut.		
sing.	nom.	fēlīx	fēlīx	ingēns	ingēns	-s	-s
	acc.	fēlīc|em	fēlīx	ingent|em	ingēns	-em	-s
	gen.	fēlīc|is	fēlīc|is	ingent|is	ingent|is	-is	-is

etc. (as above) etc. (as above)

[B] Genitive plural -*um* (abl. sing. -*e*).

Examples: **prior** *prius,* gen. *priōr|is;* **vetus,** gen. *veter|is.*

<table>
<thead>
<tr><th></th><th></th><th>masc./fem.</th><th>neut.</th><th>masc./fem.</th><th>neut.</th></tr>
</thead>
<tbody>
<tr><td>sing.</td><td>nom.</td><td>*prior*</td><td>*prius*</td><td>*vetus*</td><td>*vetus*</td></tr>
<tr><td></td><td>acc.</td><td>*priōr|em*</td><td>*prius*</td><td>*veter|em*</td><td>*vetus*</td></tr>
<tr><td></td><td>gen.</td><td>*priōr|is*</td><td>*priōr|is*</td><td>*veter|is*</td><td>*veter|is*</td></tr>
<tr><td></td><td>dat.</td><td>*priōr|ī*</td><td>*priōr|ī*</td><td>*veter|ī*</td><td>*veter|ī*</td></tr>
<tr><td></td><td>abl.</td><td>*priōr|e*</td><td>*priōr|e*</td><td>*veter|e*</td><td>*veter|e*</td></tr>
<tr><td>pl.</td><td>nom.</td><td>*priōr|ēs*</td><td>*priōr|a*</td><td>*veter|ēs*</td><td>*veter|a*</td></tr>
<tr><td></td><td>acc.</td><td>*priōr|ēs*</td><td>*priōr|a*</td><td>*veter|ēs*</td><td>*veter|a*</td></tr>
<tr><td></td><td>gen.</td><td>*priōr|um*</td><td>*priōr|um*</td><td>*veter|um*</td><td>*veter|um*</td></tr>
<tr><td></td><td>dat.</td><td>*priōr|ibus*</td><td>*priōr|ibus*</td><td>*veter|ibus*</td><td>*veter|ibus*</td></tr>
<tr><td></td><td>abl.</td><td>*priōr|ibus*</td><td>*priōr|ibus*</td><td>*veter|ibus*</td><td>*veter|ibus*</td></tr>
</tbody>
</table>

So *pauper* (m./f.), gen. -*er|is; dīves,* gen. *dīvit|is.*

Comparison

There are three **degrees: positive,** e.g. *longus,* **comparative,** e.g. *longior,* and **superlative,** e.g. *longissimus.*

The comparative ends in -*ior* and is declined like *prior.* The superlative ends in -*issim|us* (-*im|us*) and is declined like *bon|us.*

[A] Superlative -*issim|us.*

pos.   *long|us -a -um*   *brev|is -e*   *fēlīx -īc|is*
comp. *long|ior -ius -iōr|is*   *brev|ior -ius -iōr|is*   *fēlīc|ior -ius -iōr|is*
sup.   *long|issim|us-a -um*   *brev|issim|us -a -um*   *fēlīc|issim|us -a -um*

[B] Superlative -*rim|us,* -*lim|us.*

pos.   *piger -gr|a -gr|um*   *celer -er|is -er|e*   *facil|is -e*
comp. *pigr|ior -ius -iōr|is*   *celer|ior -ius -iōr|is*   *facil|ior -ius -iōr|is*
sup.   *piger|rim|us -a -um*   *celer|rim|us -a -um*   *facil|lim|us -a -um*

[C] Irregular comparison

positive	comparative	superlative
bon|us -a -um	*melior -ius -iōr|is*	*optim|us -a -um*
mal|us -a -um	*pēior -ius -iōr|is*	*pessim|us -a -um*
magn|us -a -um	*māior -ius -iōr|is*	*māxim|us -a -um*
parv|us -a -um	*minor minus -ōr|is*	*minim|us -a -um*
mult|um -ī	*plūs plūr|is*	*plūrim|um -ī*
mult|ī -ae -a	*plūr|ēs -a -ium*	*plūrim|ī -ae -a*
(*īnfrā*) *īnfer|us*	*īnferior -ius -iōr|is*	*īnfim|us/īm|us -a -um*
(*suprā*) *super|us*	*superior -ius -iōr|is*	*suprēm|us/summ|us -a -um*
(*intrā*)	*interior -ius -iōr|is*	*intim|us -a -um*
(*extrā*)	*exterior -ius -iōr|is*	*extrēm|us -a -um*
(*citrā*)	*citerior -ius -iōr|is*	*citim|us -a -um*
(*ultrā*)	*ulterior -ius -iōr|is*	*ultim|us -a -um*
(*prae*)	*prior -ius -iōr|is*	*prīm|us -a -um*
(*post*)	*posterior -ius -iōr|is*	*postrēm|us -a -um*
(*prope*)	*propior -ius -iōr|is*	*proxim|us -a -um*
vetus -er|is	*vetustior -ius -iōr|is*	*veterrim|us -a -um*

Margin notes:

-      -
-em   -
-is   -is
-ī   -ī
-e   -e
-ēs   -a
-ēs   -a
-ium   -ium
-ibus   -ibus
-ibus   -ibus

degrees:
positive (pos.)
comparative (comp.)
superlative (sup.)

-us -a -um/-(i)s (-e)
-ior -ius -iōr|is
-issim|us -a -um

-er   -il|is
-(e)rior   -ilior
-errim|us   -illim|us

ADJECTIVES AND ADVERBS

Adjectīves of the 1st/2nd declension form adverbs in -ē, e.g. *rēct|us > rēct|ē*.

Adjectives of the 3rd declension form adverbs in -*iter*, e.g. *fort|is > fort|iter*.

The comparative of the adverbs ends in -*ius* (= neuter of the adjective), e.g. *rēct|ius*, the superlative ends in -*issimē* (-*imē*), e.g. *rēct|issimē*.

Adjective declension		Adverb positive	comparative	superlative
1st/2nd	*rēct|us -a -um*	*rēctē*	*rēctius*	*rēctissimē*
	pulcher -chr|a -um	*pulchrē*	*pulchrius*	*pulcherrimē*
	miser -er|a -er|um	*miserē*	*miserius*	*miserrimē*
3rd	*fort|is -e*	*fortiter*	*fortius*	*fortissimē*
	ācer ācr|is ācr|e	*ācriter*	*ācrius*	*ācerrimē*
	celer -er|is -er|e	*celeriter*	*celerius*	*celerrimē*
	fēlīx	*fēlīciter*	*fēlīcius*	*fēlīcissimē*

Nom. sing. -*ns*, adverb -*nter*: *prūdēns -ent|is*, adv. *prūdenter*.

Some adjectives of the 1st/2nd declension form adverbs in -*ō*, e.g. *certō, falsō, necessāriō, rārō, subitō, tūtō, prīmō, postrēmō* (adjectives: *cert|us, fals|us, necessāri|us*, etc.).

Irregular adverbs: *bene < bon|us, male < mal|us, valdē < valid|us, facile < facil|is, difficulter < difficil|is, audācter < audāx*.

NUMERALS

Roman	Arabic
I	1
II	2
III	3
IV	4
V	5
VI	6
VII	7
VIII	8
IX	9
X	10
XI	11
XII	12
XIII	13
XIV	14
XV	15
XVI	16
XVII	17
XVIII	18
XIX	19
XX	20
XXI	21
XXX	30
XL	40
L	50
LX	60
LXX	70
LXXX	80
XC	90
C	100
CC	200
CCC	300
CCCC	400
D	500
DC	600
DCC	700
DCCC	800
DCCCC	900
M	1000
MM	2000

Cardinal numbers	Ordinal numbers	Distributive numbers
ūn|us -a -um	prīm|us -a -um	singul|ī -ae -a (ūn|ī)
du|o -ae -o	secund|us	bīn|ī
tr|ēs -ia	terti|us	tern|ī (trīn|ī)
quattuor	quārt|us	quatern|ī
quīnque	quīnt|us	quīn|ī
sex	sext|us	sēn|ī
septem	septim|us	septēn|ī
octō	octāv|us	octōn|ī
novem	nōn|us	novēn|ī
decem	decim|us	dēn|ī
ūn-decim	ūn-decim|us	ūn-dēn|ī
duo-decim	duo-decim|us	duo-dēn|ī
trē-decim	terti|us decim|us	tern|ī dēn|ī
quattuor-decim	quārt|us decim|us	quatern|ī dēn|ī
quīn-decim	quīnt|us decim|us	quīn|ī dēn|ī
sē-decim	sext|us decim|us	sēn|ī dēn|ī
septen-decim	septim|us decim|us	septēn|ī dēn|ī
duo-dē-vīgintī	duo-dē-vīcēsim|us	duo-dē-vīcēn|ī
ūn-dē-vīgintī	ūn-dē-vīcēsim|us	ūn-dē-vīcēn|ī
vīgintī	vīcēsim|us	vīcēn|ī
vīgintī ūn|us /ūn|us et vīgintī	vīcēsim|us prīm|us /ūn|us et vīcēsim|us	vīcēn|ī singul|ī /singul|ī et vīcēn|ī
trīgintā	trīcēsim|us	trīcēn|ī
quadrāgintā	quadrāgēsim|us	quadrāgēn|ī
quīnquāgintā	quīnquāgēsim|us	quīnquāgēn|ī
sexāgintā	sexāgēsim|us	sexāgēn|ī
septuāgintā	septuāgēsim|us	septuāgēn|ī
octōgintā	octōgēsim|us	octōgēn|ī
nōnāgintā	nōnāgēsim|us	nōnāgēn|ī
centum	centēsim|us	centēn|ī
ducent|ī -ae -a	ducentēsim|us	ducēn|ī
trecent|ī	trecentēsim|us	trecēn|ī
quadringent|ī	quadringentēsim|us	quadringēn|ī
quīngent|ī	quīngentēsim|us	quīngēn|ī
sescent|ī	sescentēsim|us	sescēn|ī
septingent|ī	septingentēsim|us	septingēn|ī
octingent|ī	octingentēsim|us	octingēn|ī
nōngent|ī	nōngentēsim|us	nōngēn|ī
mīlle	mīllēsim|us	singula mīlia
duo mīlia	bis mīllēsim|us	bīna mīlia

[1] ūn\|us -a -um is declined like sōl\|us: gen. -īus, dat. -ī.

[2] du\|o -ae -o and tr\|ēs -ia:

	masc.	fem.	neut.	masc./fem.	neut.
nom.	du|o	du|ae	du|o	tr|ēs	tr|ia
acc.	du|ōs/o	du|ās	du|o	tr|ēs	tr|ia
gen.	du|ōrum	du|ārum	du|ōrum	tr|ium	tr|ium
dat.	du|ōbus	du|ābus	du|ōbus	tr|ibus	tr|ibus
abl.	du|ōbus	du|ābus	du|ōbus	tr|ibus	tr|ibus

[3] mīl\|ia -ium (n. pl.) is declined like mar\|ia (3rd decl.).

Numeral adverbs

1× semel	6× sexiēs	11× ūndeciēs	40× quadrāgiēs	90× nōnāgiēs
2× bis	7× septiēs	12× duodeciēs	50× quīnquāgiēs	100× centiēs
3× ter	8× octiēs	13× ter deciēs	60× sexāgiēs	200× ducentiēs
4× quater	9× noviēs	20× vīciēs	70× septuāgiēs	300× trecentiēs
5× quīnquiēs	10× deciēs	30× trīciēs	80× octōgiēs	1000× mīliēs

PRONOUNS

Personal Pronouns

	1st person		2nd person	
	sing.	pl.	sing.	pl.
nom.	*ego*	*nōs*	*tū*	*vōs*
acc.	*mē*	*nōs*	*tē*	*vōs*
gen.	*meī*	*nostrī/nostrum*	*tuī*	*vestrī/vestrum*
dat.	*mihi*	*nōbīs*	*tibi*	*vōbīs*
abl.	*mē*	*nōbīs*	*tē*	*vōbīs*

objective gen.:
nostrī, vestrīi

partitive gen.:
nostrum, vestrum

mī = mihi

- 3rd person and demonstrative pronoun

	sing.			pl.			reflexive
	masc.	fem.	neut.	masc.	fem.	neut.	pronoun
nom.	*i|s*	*e|a*	*i|d*	*i|ī*	*e|ae*	*e|a*	
acc.	*e|um*	*e|am*	*i|d*	*e|ōs*	*e|ās*	*e|a*	*sē*
gen.	*e|ius*	*e|ius*	*e|ius*	*e|ōrum*	*e|ārum*	*e|ōrum*	
dat.	*e|ī*	*e|ī*	*e|ī*	*i|īs*	*i|īs*	*i|īs*	*sibi*
abl.	*e|ō*	*e|ā*	*e|ō*	*i|īs*	*i|īs*	*i|īs*	*sē*

nom. pl. *e\|ī = i\|ī*

sēsē = sē

e\|īs = i\|īs

Possessive Pronouns

	sing.	pl.
1st pers.	*me|us -a -um*	*noster -tr|a -tr|um*
2nd pers.	*tu|us -a -um*	*vester -tr|a -tr|um*
3rd pers.	*su|us -a -um* (reflexive)	

eius, eōrum, eārum (gen. of *is ea id*)

me\|us, voc. sing. *mī*.

Demonstrative Pronouns

		sing.			pl.		
[1]		masc.	fem.	neut.	masc.	fem.	neut.
	nom.	*hic*	*haec*	*hoc*	*hī*	*hae*	*haec*
	acc.	*hunc*	*hanc*	*hoc*	*hōs*	*hās*	*haec*
	gen.	*huius*	*huius*	*huius*	*hōrum*	*hārum*	*hōrum*
	dat.	*huic*	*huic*	*huic*	*hīs*	*hīs*	*hīs*
	abl.	*hōc*	*hāc*	*hōc*	*hīs*	*hīs*	*hīs*
[2]	nom.	*ill|e*	*ill|a*	*ill|ud*	*ill|ī*	*ill|ae*	*ill|a*
	acc.	*ill|um*	*ill|am*	*ill|ud*	*ill|ōs*	*ill|ās*	*ill|a*
	gen.	*ill|īus*	*ill|īus*	*ill|īus*	*ill|ōrum*	*ill|ārum*	*ill|ōrum*
	dat.	*ill|ī*	*ill|ī*	*ill|ī*	*ill|īs*	*ill|īs*	*ill|īs*
	abl.	*ill|ō*	*ill|ā*	*ill|ō*	*ill|īs*	*ill|īs*	*ill|īs*

[3] *ist\|e -a -ud* is declined like *ill\|e -a -ud*.

[4] *ips\|e -a -um* is declined like *ill\|e* except neut. sing. *ips\|um*.

[5] *is ea id*, demonstrative and personal: see above.

[6] *ī-dem ea-dem idem* (< *is ea id* + *-dem*):

	sing.			pl.		
	masc.	fem.	neut.	masc.	fem.	neut.
nom.	*īdem*	*eadem*	*idem*	*iidem*	*eaedem*	*eadem*
acc.	*eundem*	*eandem*	*idem*	*eōsdem*	*eāsdem*	*eadem*
gen.	*eiusdem*	*eiusdem*	*eiusdem*	*eōrundem*	*eārundem*	*eōrundem*
dat.	*eīdem*	*eīdem*	*eīdem*	*iīsdem*	*iīsdem*	*iīsdem*
abl.	*eōdem*	*eādem*	*eōdem*	*iīsdem*	*iīsdem*	*iīsdem*

īdem < is-dem

-n-dem < -m-dem

nom. pl. *eīdem = iīdem*

eīsdem = iīsdem

Interrogative Pronouns

[1] *quis quae quid* (subst.); *quī/quis… quae… quod…* (adj.).

	sing.			pl.		
	masc.	fem.	neut.	masc.	fem.	neut.
nom.	*quis/quī*	*quae*	*quid/quod*	*quī*	*quae*	*quae*
acc.	*quem*	*quam*	*quid/quod*	*quōs*	*quās*	*quae*
gen.	*cuius*	*cuius*	*cuius*	*quōrum*	*quārum*	*quōrum*
dat.	*cui*	*cui*	*cui*	*quibus*	*quibus*	*quibus*
abl.	*quō*	*quā*	*quō*	*quibus*	*quibus*	*quibus*

[2] *uter utr|a utr|um*, gen. *utr|īus*, dat. *utr|ī* (like *sōl|us*, but nom. m. sing. *ut<u>er</u>*).

Relative Pronoun

[1] *quī quae quod*

	sing.			pl.		
	masc.	fem.	neut.	masc.	fem.	neut.
nom.	*quī*	*quae*	*quod*	*quī*	*quae*	*quae*
acc.	*quem*	*quam*	*quod*	*quōs*	*quās*	*quae*
gen.	*cuius*	*cuius*	*cuius*	*quōrum*	*quārum*	*quōrum*
dat.	*cui*	*cui*	*cui*	*quibus*	*quibus*	*quibus*
abl.	*quō*	*quā*	*quō*	*quibus*	*quibus*	*quibus*

[2] *quī- quae- quod-cumque* (indefinite relative) = *quis-quis quid-quid/quic-quid* (indecl. subst.).

Indefinite Pronouns

nēmō < ne- + homō

[1] *nēmō*, acc. *nēmin|em*, dat. *nēmin|ī*.

nīl = nihil

[2] *nihil*, neuter (indecl.).

[3] *ūll|us -a -um* and *nūll|us -a -um* are declined like *sōl|us*.

neuter < ne- + uter

[4] *neuter -tr|a -tr|um* and *uter-que utr|a-que utr|um-que* are declined like *uter*: gen. *neutr|īus*, *utr|īus-que*.

[5] *alter -er|a -er|um*, gen. *-er|īus*, dat. *-er|ī*.

[6] *ali|us -a -ud*, dat. *ali|ī* (gen. *alter|īus*).

The following pronouns are declined like *quis/quī*:

n. pl. *(ali-)qua*

[7] *ali-quis/-quī -qu<u>a</u> -quid/-quod* and (*sī, nisi, nē, num*) *quis/quī qu<u>a</u> quid/quod*.

[8] *quis-quam quid-quam/quic-quam*.

-n-dam < -m-dam

[9] *quī-dam quae-dam quid-dam/quod-dam*, acc. sing. m. *que<u>n</u>-dam*, f. *qua<u>n</u>-dam*, gen. pl. m./n. *quōru<u>n</u>-dam*, f. *quāru<u>n</u>-dam*.

[10] *quis-que quae-que quid-que/quod-que*.

[11] *quī- quae- quid-/quod-vīs* = *quī- quae- quid-/quod-libet*.

VERBS
Voice and Mood

The **voice** of the verb is either **active**, e.g. *amat*, or **passive**, e.g. *amātur*. Verbs which have no active voice (except participles and gerund), e.g. *cōnārī, loquī*, are called **deponent** verbs.

The **moods** of the verb are: **infinitive**, e.g. *amāre*, **imperative**, e.g. *amā*, **indicative**, e.g. *amat*, and **subjunctive**, e.g. *amet*.

Tense, Number, Person

The **tenses** of the verb are: **present**, e.g. *amat*, **future**, e.g. *amābit*, **imperfect**, e.g. *amābat*, **perfect**, e.g. *amāvit*, **pluperfect**, e.g. *amāverat*, and **future perfect**, e.g. *amāverit*.

The **numbers** of the verb are: **singular**, e.g. *amat*, and **plural**, e.g. *amant*.

The **persons** of the verb are: **1st person**, e.g. *amō*, **2nd person**, e.g. *amās*, and **3rd person**, e.g. *amat*. Verbs which have no 1st and 2nd persons, e.g. *licēre* and *pudēre,* are called **impersonal**.

Conjugations

There are four **conjugations**:

[1] **1st conjugation**: inf. *-āre, -ārī* e.g. *amāre, cōnārī*.

[2] **2nd conjugation**: inf. *-ēre, -ērī* e.g. *monēre, verērī*.

[3] **3rd conjugation**: inf. *-ere, -ī* e.g. *legere, ūtī*.

[4] **4th conjugation**: inf. *-īre, -īrī* e.g. *audīre, partīrī*.

Stem

Verbal stems:

The **present stem**, e.g. *amā-, monē-, leg-, audī-*.

The **perfect stem**, e.g. *amāv-, monu-, lēg-, audīv-*.

The **supine stem**, e.g. *amāt-, monit-, lēct-, audīt-*.

Personal endings

[1]	Active		Passive	
	sing.	pl.	sing.	pl.
pers. 1	*-m/-ō*	*-mus*	*-r/-or*	*-mur*
pers. 2	*-s*	*-tis*	*-ris*	*-minī*
pers. 3	*-t*	*-nt*	*-tur*	*-ntur*

[2] Endings of the perfect indicative active:

	sing.	pl.
pers. 1	~ī	~imus
pers. 2	~istī	~istis
pers. 3	~it	~ērunt (~ēre)

Side notes:

voice: act. pass.

mood: inf. ind. imp. subj.

tense: pres. perf. imperf. fut. fut. perf.
pluperf.
number: sing. pl.

person: 1 2 3

conjugations:
[1] *-āre/-ārī*
[2] *-ēre/-ērī*
[3] *-ere/-ī*
[4] *-īre/-īrī*

verbal stems:
present stem [–]
perfect stem [~]
supine stem [≈]

after a consonant:
-ō -imus -or -imur
-is -itis -eris -iminī
-it -unt -itur -untur

Conjugation

[A] Active

Infinitive

present

[1] *amā|re*   [2] *monē|re*   [3] *leg|ere*   [4] *audī|re*

perfect

amāv|isse   *monu|isse*   *lēg|isse*   *audīv|isse*

future

amāt|ūr|um esse   *monit|ūr|um esse*   *lēct|ūr|um esse*   *audīt|ūr|um esse*

Indicative

present

		[1]	[2]	[3]	[4]
sing.	1	*am|ō*	*mone|ō*	*leg|ō*	*audi|ō*
	2	*amā|s*	*monē|s*	*leg|is*	*audī|s*
	3	*ama|t*	*mone|t*	*leg|it*	*audi|t*
pl.	1	*amā|mus*	*monē|mus*	*leg|imus*	*audī|mus*
	2	*amā|tis*	*monē|tis*	*leg|itis*	*audī|itis*
	3	*ama|nt*	*mone|nt*	*leg|unt*	*audi|unt*

imperfect

sing.	1	*amā|ba|m*	*monē|ba|m*	*leg|ēba|m*	*audi|ēba|m*
	2	*amā|bā|s*	*monē|bā|s*	*leg|ēbā|s*	*audi|ēbā|s*
	3	*amā|ba|t*	*monē|ba|t*	*leg|ēba|t*	*audi|ēba|t*
pl.	1	*amā|bā|mus*	*monē|bā|mus*	*leg|ēbā|mus*	*audi|ēbā|mus*
	2	*amā|bā|tis*	*monē|bā|tis*	*leg|ēbā|tis*	*audi|ēbā|tis*
	3	*amā|ba|nt*	*monē|ba|nt*	*leg|ēba|nt*	*audi|ēba|nt*

future

sing.	1	*amā|b|ō*	*monē|b|ō*	*leg|a|m*	*audi|a|m*
	2	*amā|b|is*	*monē|b|is*	*leg|ē|s*	*audi|ē|s*
	3	*amā|b|it*	*monē|b|it*	*leg|e|t*	*audi|e|t*
pl.	1	*amā|b|imus*	*monē|b|imus*	*leg|ē|mus*	*audi|ē|mus*
	2	*amā|b|itis*	*monē|b|itis*	*leg|ē|tis*	*audi|ē|tis*
	3	*amā|b|unt*	*monē|b|unt*	*leg|e|nt*	*audi|e|nt*

perfect

sing.	1	*amāv|ī*	*monu|ī*	*lēg|ī*	*audīv|ī*
	2	*amāv|istī*	*monu|istī*	*lēg|istī*	*audīv|istī*
	3	*amāv|it*	*monu|it*	*lēg|it*	*audīv|it*
pl.	1	*amāv|imus*	*monu|imus*	*lēg|imus*	*audīv|imus*
	2	*amāv|istis*	*monu|istis*	*lēg|istis*	*audīv|istis*
	3	*amāv|ērunt*	*monu|ērunt*	*lēg|ērunt*	*audīv|ērunt*

pluperfect

sing.	1	*amāv|era|m*	*monu|era|m*	*lēg|era|m*	*audīv|era|m*
	2	*amāv|erā|s*	*monu|erā|s*	*lēg|erā|s*	*audīv|erā|s*
	3	*amāv|era|t*	*monu|era|t*	*lēg|era|t*	*audīv|era|t*
pl.	1	*amāv|erā|mus*	*monu|erā|mus*	*lēg|erā|mus*	*audīv|erā|mus*
	2	*amāv|erā|tis*	*monu|erā|tis*	*lēg|erā|tis*	*audīv|erā|tis*
	3	*amāv|era|nt*	*monu|era|nt*	*lēg|era|nt*	*audīv|era|nt*

future perfect

sing.	1	*amāv|er|ō*	*monu|er|ō*	*lēg|er|ō*	*audīv|er|ō*
	2	*amāv|eri|s*	*monu|eri|s*	*lēg|eri|s*	*audīv|eri|s*
	3	*amāv|eri|t*	*monu|eri|t*	*lēg|eri|t*	*audīv|eri|t*
pl.	1	*amāv|eri|mus*	*monu|eri|mus*	*lēg|eri|mus*	*audīv|eri|mus*
	2	*amāv|eri|tis*	*monu|eri|tis*	*lēg|eri|tis*	*audīv|eri|tis*
	3	*amāv|eri|nt*	*monu|eri|nt*	*lēg|eri|nt*	*audīv|eri|nt*

Left margin endings:

[1, 2, 4]   [3]
−*re*   −*ere*

~*isse*

≈*ūr\|us -a -um esse*

[1, 2, 4]   [3]
−*ō*   −*ō*
−*s*   −*is*
−*t*   −*it*
−*mus*   −*imus*
−*tis*   −*itis*
−*(u)nt*   −*unt*

[1, 2]   [3, 4]
−*ba\|m*   −*ēba\|m*
−*bā\|s*   −*ēbā\|s*
−*ba\|t*   −*ēba\|t*
−*bā\|mus*   −*ēbā\|mus*
−*bā\|tis*   −*ēbā\|tis*
−*ba\|nt*   −*ēba\|nt*

[1, 2]   [3, 4]
−*b\|ō*   −*a\|m*
−*b\|is*   −*ē\|s*
−*b\|it*   −*e\|t*
−*b\|imus*   −*ē\|mus*
−*b\|itis*   −*ē\|tis*
−*b\|unt*   −*e\|nt*

~*ī*
~*istī*
~*it*
~*imus*
~*istis*
~*ērunt*

~*era\|m*
~*erā\|s*
~*era\|t*
~*erā\|mus*
~*erā\|tis*
~*era\|nt*

~*er\|ō*
~*eri\|s*
~*eri\|t*
~*eri\|mus*
~*eri\|tis*
~*eri\|nt*

Subjunctive

present

					[1]	[2, 3, 4]
sing.1	am|e|m	mone|a|m	leg|a|m	audi|a|m	(-)e|m	–a|m
2	am|ē|s	mone|ā|s	leg|ā|s	audi|ā|s	(-)ē|s	–ā|s
3	am|e|t	mone|a|t	leg|a|t	audi|a|t	(-)e|t	–a|t
pl.1	am|ē|mus	mone|ā|mus	leg|ā|mus	audi|ā|mus	(-)ē|mus	–ā|mus
2	am|ē|tis	mone|ā|tis	leg|ā|tis	audi|ā|tis	(-)ē|tis	–ā|tis
3	am|e|nt	mone|a|nt	leg|a|nt	audi|a|nt	(-)e|nt	–a|nt

imperfect

					[1, 2, 4]	[3]
sing.1	amā|re|m	monē|re|m	leg|ere|m	audī|re|m	–re|m	–ere|m
2	amā|rē|s	monē|rē|s	leg|erē|s	audī|rē|s	–rē|s	–erē|s
3	amā|re|t	monē|re|t	leg|ere|t	audī|re|t	–re|t	–ere|t
pl.1	amā|rē|mus	monē|rē|mus	leg|erē|mus	audī|rē|mus	–rē|mus	–erē|mus
2	amā|rē|tis	monē|rē|tis	leg|erē|tis	audī|rē|tis	–rē|tis	–erē|tis
3	amā|re|nt	monē|re|nt	leg|ere|nt	audī|re|nt	–re|nt	–ere|nt

perfect

sing.1	amāv|eri|m	monu|eri|m	lēg|eri|m	audīv|eri|m	≈eri|m
2	amāv|eri|s	monu|eri|s	lēg|eri|s	audīv|eri|s	≈eri|s
3	amāv|eri|t	monu|eri|t	lēg|eri|t	audīv|eri|t	≈eri|t
pl.1	amāv|eri|mus	monu|eri|mus	lēg|eri|tis	audīv|eri|mus	≈eri|mus
2	amāv|eri|tis	monu|eri|tis	lēg|eri|tis	audīv|eri|tis	≈eri|tis
3	amāv|eri|nt	monu|eri|nt	lēg|eri|nt	audīv|eri|nt	≈eri|nt

pluperfect

sing.1	amāv|isse|m	monu|isse|m	lēg|isse|m	audīv|isse|m	≈isse|m
2	amāv|issē|s	monu|issē|s	lēg|issē|s	audīv|issē|s	≈issē|s
3	amāv|isse|t	monu|isse|t	lēg|isse|t	audīv|isse|t	≈isse|t
pl.1	amāv|issē|mus	monu|issē|mus	lēg|issē|mus	audīv|issē|mus	≈issē|mus
2	amāv|issē|tis	monu|issē|tis	lēg|issē|tis	audīv|issē|tis	≈issē|tis
3	amāv|isse|nt	monu|isse|nt	lēg|isse|nt	audīv|isse|nt	≈isse|nt

Imperative

present

					[1, 2, 4]	[3]
sing.	amā	monē	leg|e	audī	–	–e
pl.	amā|te	monē|te	leg|ite	audī|te	–te	–ite

future

sing.	amā|tō	monē|tō	leg|itō	audī|tō	–tō	–itō
pl.	amā|tōte	monē|tōte	leg|itōte	audī|tōte	–tōte	–itōte

Participle

present

				[1, 2]	[3, 4]
	amā|ns -ant|is	monē|ns -ent|is	leg|ēns -ent|is	–ns	–ēns
				–nt|is	–ent|is

future

	amāt|ūr|us -a -um	monit|ūr|us -a -um	lēct|ūr|us -a -um	audīt|ūr|us -a -um	≈ūr|us -a -um

Supine

I	amāt|um	monit|um	lēct|um	audīt|um	≈um
II	amāt|ū	monit|ū	lēct|ū	audīt|ū	≈ū

Gerund

					[1, 2]	[3, 4]
acc.	ama|nd|um	mone|nd|um	leg|end|um	audi|end|um	–nd|um	–end|um
gen.	ama|nd|ī	mone|nd|ī	leg|end|ī	audi|end|ī	–nd|ī	–end|ī
abl.	ama|nd|ō	mone|nd|ō	leg|end|ō	audi|end|ō	–nd|ō	–end|ō

[B] Passive

Infinitive

Left-margin endings:

[1, 2, 4]	[3]
–rī	–ī

≈us -a -um esse

≈um īrī

present

[1] amā|rī	[2] monē|rī	[3] leg|ī	[4] audī|rī

perfect

amāt|um esse	monit|um esse	lēct|um esse	audīt|um esse

future

amāt|um īrī	monit|um īrī	lēct|um īrī	audīt|um īrī

Indicative

Left-margin endings:

[1, 2, 4]	[3]
–or	–or
–ris	–eris
–tur	–itur
–mur	–imur
–minī	–iminī
–(u)ntur	–untur

[1, 2]	[3, 4]
–ba|r	–ēba|r
–bā|ris	–ēbā|ris
–bā|tur	–ēbā|tur
–bā|mur	–ēbā|mur
–bā|minī	–ēbā|minī
–ba|ntur	–ēba|ntur

[1, 2]	[3, 4]
–b|or	–a|r
–b|eris	–ē|ris
–b|itur	–ē|tur
–b|imur	–ē|mur
–b|iminī	–ē|minī
–b|untur	–e|ntur

present

		[1]	[2]	[3]	[4]
sing.	1	am|or	mone|or	leg|or	audi|or
	2	amā|ris	monē|ris	leg|eris	audī|ris
	3	amā|tur	monē|tur	leg|itur	audī|tur
pl.	1	amā|mur	monē|mur	leg|imur	audī|mur
	2	amā|minī	monē|minī	leg|iminī	audī|minī
	3	ama|ntur	mone|ntur	leg|untur	audi|untur

imperfect

sing.	1	amā|ba|r	monē|ba|r	leg|ēba|r	audi|ēba|r
	2	amā|bā|ris	monē|bā|ris	leg|ēbā|ris	audi|ēbā|ris
	3	amā|bā|tur	monē|bā|tur	leg|ēbā|tur	audi|ēbā|tur
pl.	1	amā|bā|mur	monē|bā|mur	leg|ēbā|mur	audi|ēbā|mur
	2	amā|bā|minī	monē|bā|minī	leg|ēbā|minī	audi|ēbā|minī
	3	amā|ba|ntur	monē|ba|ntur	leg|ēba|ntur	audi|ēba|ntur

future

sing.	1	amā|b|or	monē|b|or	leg|a|r	audi|a|r
	2	amā|b|eris	monē|b|eris	leg|ē|ris	audi|ē|ris
	3	amā|b|itur	monē|b|itur	leg|ē|tur	audi|ē|tur
pl.	1	amā|b|imur	monē|b|imur	leg|ē|mur	audi|ē|mur
	2	amā|b|iminī	monē|b|iminī	leg|ē|minī	audi|ē|minī
	3	amā|b|untur	monē|b|untur	leg|e|ntur	audi|e|ntur

Left-margin:

≈us -a (-um)
sum
es
est
≈ī -ae (-a)
sumus
estis
sunt

perfect

		[1]	[2]	[3]	[4]
		amāt|us	monit|us	lēct|us	audīt|us
sing.	1	sum	sum	sum	sum
	2	es	es	es	es
	3	est	est	est	est
		amāt|ī	monit|ī	lēct|ī	audīt|ī
pl.	1	sumus	sumus	sumus	sumus
	2	estis	estis	estis	estis
	3	sunt	sunt	sunt	sunt

Left-margin:

≈us -a (-um)
eram
erās
erat
≈ī -ae (-a)
erāmus
erātis
erant

pluperfect

		[1]	[2]	[3]	[4]
		amāt|us	monit|us	lēct|us	audīt|us
sing.	1	eram	eram	eram	eram
	2	erās	erās	erās	erās
	3	erat	erat	erat	erat
		amāt|ī	monit|ī	lēct|ī	audīt|ī
pl.	1	erāmus	erāmus	erāmus	erāmus
	2	erātis	erātis	erātis	erātis
	3	erant	erant	erant	erant

future perfect

	amāt|us	monit|us	lēct|us	audīt|us	≈us -a (-um)	
sing.1	erō	erō	erō	erō	erō	
2	eris	eris	eris	eris	eris	
3	erit	erit	erit	erit	erit	
	amāt|ī	monit|ī	lēct|ī	audīt|ī	≈ī -ae (-a)	
pl.1	erimus	erimus	erimus	erimus	erimus	
2	eritis	eritis	eritis	eritis	eritis	
3	erunt	erunt	erunt	erunt	erunt	

Subjunctive
Present

	amāt	monit	lēct	audīt	[1]	[2, 3, 4]
sing.1	am|e|r	mone|a|r	leg|a|r	audi|a|r	(-)e|r	–a|r
2	am|ē|ris	mone|ā|ris	leg|ā|ris	audi|ā|ris	(-)ē|ris	–ā|ris
3	am|ē|tur	mone|ā|tur	leg|ā|tur	audi|ā|tur	(-)ē|tur	–ā|tur
pl.1	am|ē|mur	mone|ā|mur	leg|ā|mur	audi|ā|mur	(-)ē|mur	–ā|mur
2	am|ē|minī	mone|ā|minī	leg|ā|minī	audi|ā|minī	(-)ē|minī	–ā|minī
3	am|e|ntur	mone|a|ntur	leg|a|ntur	audi|a|ntur	(-)e|ntur	–a|ntur

Imperfect

					[1, 2, 4]	[3]
sing.1	amā|re|r	monē|re|r	leg|ere|r	audī|re|r	–re|r	–ere|r
2	amā|rē|ris	monē|rē|ris	leg|erē|ris	audī|rē|ris	–rē|ris	–erē|ris
3	amā|rē|tur	monē|rē|tur	leg|erē|tur	audī|rē|tur	–rē|tur	–erē|tur
pl.1	amā|rē|mur	monē|rē|mur	leg|erē|mur	audī|rē|mur	–rē|mur	–erē|mur
2	amā|rē|minī	monē|rē|minī	leg|erē|minī	audī|rē|minī	–rē|minī	–erē|minī
3	amā|re|ntur	monē|re|ntur	leg|ere|ntur	audī|re|ntur	–re|ntur	–ere|ntur

Perfect

	amāt|us	monit|us	lēct|us	audīt|us	≈us -a (-um)	
sing.1	sim	sim	sim	sim	sim	
2	sīs	sīs	sīs	sīs	sīs	
3	sit	sit	sit	sit	sit	
	amāt|ī	monit|ī	lēct|ī	audīt|ī	≈ī -ae (-a)	
pl.1	sīmus	sīmus	sīmus	sīmus	sīmus	
2	sītis	sītis	sītis	sītis	sītis	
3	sint	sint	sint	sint	sint	

Pluperfect

	amāt|us	monit|us	lēct|us	audīt|us	≈us -a (-um)	
sing.1	essem	essem	essem	essem	essem	
2	essēs	essēs	essēs	essēs	essēs	
3	esset	esset	esset	esset	esset	
	amāt|ī	monit|ī	lēct|ī	audīt|ī	≈ī -ae (-a)	
pl.1	essēmus	essēmus	essēmus	essēmus	essēmus	
2	essētis	essētis	essētis	essētis	essētis	
3	essent	essent	essent	essent	essent	

Participle
Perfect

amāt|us	monit|us	lēct|us	audīt|us	≈us -a -um
-a -um	-a -um	-a -um	-a -um	

Gerundive

ama|nd|us	mone|nd|us	leg|end|us	audi|end|us	[1, 2]	[3, 4]
-a -um	-a -um	-a -um	-a -um	–nd|us -a	–end|us -a
				-um	-um

Deponent verbs

Infinitive

pres.	*cōnā|rī*	*verē|rī*	*ūt|ī*	*partī|rī*
perf.	*cōnāt|um esse*	*verit|um esse*	*ūs|um esse*	*partīt|um esse*
fut.	*cōnāt|ūr|um esse*	*verit|ūr|um esse*	*ūs|ūr|um esse*	*partīt|ūr|um esse*

[1, 2, 4]   **[3]**
–rī   *–ī*
≈*us -a -um esse*
≈*ūr\|us -a -um esse*

Indicative

pres.	*cōnā|tur*	*verē|tur*	*ūt|itur*	*partī|tur*
imperf.	*cōnā|bā|tur*	*verē|bā|tur*	*ūt|ēbā|tur*	*parti|ēbā|tur*
fut.	*cōnā|b|itur*	*verē|b|itur*	*ūt|ē|tur*	*parti|ē|tur*
perf.	*cōnāt|us est*	*verit|us est*	*ūs|us est*	*partīt|us est*
pluperf.	*cōnāt|us erat*	*verit|us erat*	*ūs|us erat*	*partīt|us erat*
fut. perf.	*cōnāt|us erit*	*verit|us erit*	*ūs|us erit*	*partīt|us erit*

3rd pers. sing.
≈*(i)tur*
≈*(ē)bā\|tur*
–b\|itur   *–ē\|tur*
≈*us -a -um est*
≈*us -a -um erat*
≈*us -a -um erit*

Subjunctive

pres.	*cōn|ē|tur*	*vere|ā|tur*	*ūt|ā|tur*	*parti|ā|tur*
imperf.	*cōnā|rē|tur*	*verē|rē|tur*	*ūt|erē|tur*	*parti|rē|tur*
perf.	*cōnāt|us sit*	*verit|us sit*	*ūs|us sit*	*partīt|us sit*
pluperf.	*cōnāt|us esset*	*verit|us esset*	*ūs|us esset*	*partīt|us esset*

(–)ē\|tur   *–ā\|tur*
≈*(e)rē\|tur*
≈*us -a -um sit*
≈*us -a -um esset*

Imperative

sing.	*cōnā|re*	*verē|re*	*ūt|ere*	*partī|re*
pl.	*cōnā|minī*	*verē|minī*	*ūt|iminī*	*partī|minī*

[1, 2, 4]   **[3]**
–re   *–ere*
–minī   *–iminī*

Participle

pres.	*cōnā|ns*	*verē|ns*	*ūt|ēns*	*parti|ēns*
perf.	*cōnāt|us*	*verit|us*	*ūs|us*	*partīt|us*
fut.	*cōnāt|ūr|us*	*verit|ūr|us*	*ūs|ūr|us*	*partīt|ūr|us*

[1, 2]   **[3, 4]**
–ns   *–ēns*
≈*us -a -um*
≈*ūr\|us -a -um*
–um   *–ū*

Supine	*cōnāt|um -ū*	*verit|um -ū*	*ūs|um -ū*	*partīt|um -ū*

Gerund

	cōna|nd|um	*vere|nd|um*	*ūt|end|um*	*parti|end|um*

[1, 2]   **[3, 4]**
–nd\|um   *–end\|um*

Gerundive

	cōna|nd|us	*vere|nd|us*	*ūt|end|us*	*parti|end|us*

–nd\|us -a   *–end\|us -a*
    -um   *-um*

Third conjugation: present stem *-i*

Examples: ***capere, patī*** (present stem: *capi-, pati-*)

Infinitive	act.	pass.	dep.
present	*cape|re*	*cap|ī*	*pat|ī*

Indicative

present

i > e before r

cape\|re < *capi\|re
capī < *capi\|ī
patī < *pati\|ī

cape\|ris < *capi\|ris
pate\|ris < *pati\|ris

		act.	pass.	dep.
sing.	1	*capi|ō*	*capi|or*	*pati|or*
	2	*capi|s*	*cape|ris*	*pate|ris*
	3	*capi|t*	*capi|tur*	*pati|tur*
pl.	1	*capi|mus*	*capi|mur*	*pati|mur*
	2	*capi|tis*	*capi|minī*	*pati|minī*
	3	*capi|unt*	*capi|untur*	*pati|untur*

imperfect

		act.	pass.	dep.
sing.	1	*capi|ēba|m*	*capi|ēba|r*	*pati|ēba|r*
	2	*capi|ēbā|s*	*capi|ēbā|ris*	*pati|ēbā|ris*
	3	*capi|ēba|t*	*capi|ēbā|tur*	*pati|ēbā|tur*
pl.	1	*capi|ēbā|mus*	*capi|ēbā|mur*	*pati|ēbā|mur*
	2	*capi|ēbā|tis*	*capi|ēbā|minī*	*pati|ēbā|minī*
	3	*capi|ēba|nt*	*capi|ēba|ntur*	*pati|ēba|ntur*

future
sing.	1	capi|a|m	capi|a|r	pati|a|r
	2	capi|ē|s	capi|ē|ris	pati|ē|ris
	3	capi|e|t	capi|ē|tur	pati|ē|tur
pl.	1	capi|ē|mus	capi|ē|mur	pati|ē|mur
	2	capi|ē|tis	capi|ē|minī	pati|ē|minī
	3	capi|e|nt	capi|e|ntur	pati|e|ntur

Subjunctive
present
sing.	1	capi|a|m	capi|a|r	pati|a|r
	2	capi|ā|s	capi|ā|ris	pati|ā|ris
	3	capi|a|t	capi|ā|tur	pati|ā|tur
pl.	1	capi|ā|mus	capi|ā|mur	pati|ā|mur
	2	capi|ā|tis	capi|ā|minī	pati|ā|minī
	3	capi|a|nt	capi|a|ntur	pati|a|ntur

imperfect
sing.	1	cape|re|m	cape|re|r	pate|re|r
	2	cape|rē|s	cape|rē|ris	pate|rē|ris
	3	cape|re|t	cape|rē|tur	pate|rē|tur
pl.	1	cape|rē|mus	cape|rē|mur	pate|rē|mur
	2	cape|rē|tis	cape|rē|minī	pate|rē|minī
	3	cape|re|nt	cape|re|ntur	pate|re|ntur

cape\|rem < *capi\|rem

Imperative
| sing. | cape | | pate\|re |
| pl. | capi\|te | | pati\|minī |

cape < *capi

Participle
| present | capi\|ēns -ent\|is | | pati\|ēns -ent\|is |

Gerund capi\|end\|um   pati\|end\|um

Gerundive   capi\|end\|us   pati\|end\|us

Irregular verbs I: present stem

1. Infinitive **es\|se** (stem *es-, er-, s-*)

er- ante vōcālem

Indicative
pres.	imperf.	fut.
s|um	er|a|m	er|ō
es	er|ā|s	er|is
es|t	er|a|t	er|it
s|umus	er|ā|mus	er|imus
es|tis	er|ā|tis	er|itis
s|unt	er|a|nt	er|unt

Subjunctive
pres.	imperf.
s|i|m	es|se|m
s|ī|s	es|sē|s
s|i|t	es|se|t
s|ī|mus	es|sē|mus
s|ī|tis	es|sē|tis
s|i|nt	es|se|nt

Imperative
pres.	fut.
es	es|tō
es|te	es|tōte

in composite verbs:
ab- ad- de- in- inter- prae-
prōd- super-esse
prōd-est prō-sunt
 prōd-e... prō-s...
de-est dē-sunt
in-est in-sunt

2. Infinitive **posse**

Indicative
pres.	imperf.	fut.
pos-sum	pot-eram	pot-erō
pot-es	pot-erās	pot-eris
pot-est	pot-erat	pot-erit
pos-sumus	pot-erāmus	pot-erimus
pot-estis	pot-erātis	pot-eritis
pot-sunt	pot-erant	pot-erunt

Subjunctive
pres.	imperf.
pos-sim	possem
pos-sīs	possēs
pos-sit	posset
pos-sīmus	possēmus
pos-sītis	possētis
pos-sint	possent

pot-e...
pos-s...

nōlle < ne- + velle

mālle < magis + velle

3. Infinitive *velle, nōlle, mālle*

Indicative

pres.	vol|ō	nōl|ō	māl|ō
	vīs	nōn vīs	māvīs
	vul|t	nōn vult	māvult
	vol|umus	nōl|umus	māl|umus
	vul|tis	nōn vultis	māvultis
	vol|unt	nōl|unt	māl|unt
imperf.	vol|ēba|m	nōl|ēba|m	māl|ēba|m
	vol|ēbā|s	nōl|ēbā|s	māl|ēbā|s
fut.	vol|a|m	nōl|a|m	māl|a|m
	vol|ē|s	nōl|ē|s	māl|ē|s

Subjunctive

pres.	vel|i|m	nōl|i|m	māl|i|m
	vel|ī|s	nōl|ī|s	māl|ī|s
	vel|i|t	nōl|i|t	māl|i|t
	vel|ī|mus	nōl|ī|mus	māl|ī|mus
	vel|ī|tis	nōl|ī|tis	māl|ī|tis
	vel|i|nt	nōl|i|nt	māl|i|nt
imperf.	velle|m	nōlle|m	mālle|m
	vellē|s	nōllē|s	māllē|s
	velle|t	nōlle|t	mālle|t
	vellē|mus	nōllē|mus	māllē|mus
	vellē|tis	nōllē|tis	māllē|tis
	velle|nt	nōlle|nt	mālle|nt

Participle

pres.	vol|ēns	nōl|ēns

Imperative

nōl\|ī -īte + inf.

sing.		nōl|ī
pl.		nōl|īte

4. Infinitive *ī\|re*

passive (impersonal)

ī\|rī

ī\|tur ī\|bā\|tur ī\|b\|itur

e\|ā\|tur ī\|rē\|tur

gerundive:

e\|und\|um (est)

Indicative			Subjunctive		Imperative	
pres.	imperf.	fut.	pres.	imperf.	pres.	fut.
e|ō	ī|ba|m	ī|b|ō	e|a|m	ī|re|m	ī	ī|tō
ī|s	ī|bā|s	ī|b|is	e|ā|s	ī|rē|s	ī|te	ī|tōte
i|t	ī|ba|t	ī|b|it	e|a|t	ī|re|t	Participium	
ī|mus	ī|bā|mus	ī|b|imus	e|ā|mus	ī|rē|mus	i|ēns e|unt|is	
ī|tis	ī|bā|tis	ī|b|itis	e|ā|tis	ī|rē|tis	Gerundium	
e|unt	ī|ba|nt	ī|b|unt	e|a|nt	ī|re|nt	e|und|um	

5. Infinitive *fi\|erī*

Indicative				Subjunctive	
pres.	imperf.	fut.	pres.	imperf.	
fi|ō	fi|ēba|m	fi|a|m	fi|a|m	fi|ere|m	
fi|s	fi|ēbā|s	fi|ē|s	fi|ā|s	fi|erē|s	
fi|t	fi|ēba|t	fi|e|t	fi|a|t	fi|ere|t	
fi|mus	fi|ēbā|mus	fi|ē|mus	fi|ā|mus	fi|erē|mus	
fi|tis	fi|ēbā|tis	fi|ē|tis	fi|ā|tis	fi|erē|tis	
fi|unt	fi|ēba|nt	fi|e|nt	fi|a|nt	fi|ere|nt	

6. Infinitive: active *fer|re*, passive *fer|rī*

Indicative

		act.	pass.			act.	pass.
pres.		*fer|ō*	*fer|or*	imperf.		*fer|ēba|m*	*fer|ēba|r*
		fer|s	*fer|ris*			*fer|ēbā|s*	*fer|ēbā|ris*
		fer|t	*fer|tur*				
		fer|imus	*fer|imur*	fut.		*fer|a|m*	*fer|a|r*
		fer|tis	*fer|iminī*			*fer|ē|s*	*fer|ē|ris*
		fer|unt	*fer|untur*			*fer|e|t*	*fer|ē|tur*

Subjunctive

		act.	pass.			act.	pass.
pres.		*fer|a|m*	*fer|a|r*	imperf.		*fer|re|m*	*fer|re|r*
		fer|ā|s	*fer|ā|ris*			*fer|rē|s*	*fer|rē|ris*
		fer|a|t	*fer|ā|tur*			*fer|re|t*	*fer|rē|tur*
		fer|ā|mus	*fer|ā|mur*			*fer|rē|mus*	*fer|rē|mur*
		fer|ā|tis	*fer|ā|minī*			*fer|rē|tis*	*fer|rē|minī*
		fer|a|nt	*fer|a|ntur*			*fer|re|nt*	*fer|re|ntur*

Imperative		Participle	Gerund	Gerundive
pres.	*fer fer|te*	*fer|ēns*	*fer|end|um*	*fer|end|us*
fut.	*fer|tō -tōte*			

7. Infinitive: act. *ēs|se*, pass. *ed|ī*

Indicative

pres.	imperf.	fut.	Subjunctive pres.	imperf.
ed|ō	*ed|ēba|m*	*ed|a|m*	*ed|i|m (-a|m)*	*ēs|se|m*
ēs	*ed|ēbā|s*	*ed|ē|s*	*ed|ī|s (-ā|s)*	*ēs|sē|s*
ēs|t	*ed|ēba|t*	*ed|e|t*	*ed|i|t (-a|t)*	*ēs|se|t*
ed|imus	*ed|ēbā|mus*	*ed|ē|mus*	*ed|ī|mus (-ā|mus)*	*ēs|sē|mus*
ēs|tis	*ed|ēbā|tis*	*ed|ē|tis*	*ed|ī|tis (-ā|tis)*	*ēs|sē|tis*
ed|unt	*ed|ēba|nt*	*ed|e|nt*	*ed|i|nt (-a|nt)*	*ēs|se|nt*

Imperative		Participle	Gerund	Gerundive
pres.	*ēs ēs|te*	*ed|ēns*	*ed|end|um*	*ed|end|us*
fut.	*ēs|tō -tōte*			

8. Infinitive *da|re*

Present stem *da-* (short *a*): *da|re*, *da|mus*, *da|ba|m*, *da|b|ō*, *da|re|m*, etc., except *dā* (imp.), *dā|s* (ind. pres. 2 sing.), *dā|ns* (pres. part.).

Defective verbs

9. *ait*

Indicative

pres.			imperf.	
āi|ō	--		*āi|ēba|m*	*āi|ēbā|mus*
ai|s	--		*āi|ēbā|s*	*āi|ēbā|tis*
ai|t	*āi|unt*		*āi|ēba|t*	*āi|ēba|nt*

10. *inquit*

Indicative

pres.		fut.	
inquam	--	--	
inquis	--	*inquiēs*	
inquit	*inquiunt*	*inquiet*	

pass. ind. pres. 3rd pers.
ēs|tur ed|untur

ain'? = ais-ne?

11. Verbs without present stem:

memin|isse (imperative: *memen|tō -tōte*)
ōd|isse

Irregular verbs II: perfect and supine stems
First conjugation

		pres. inf.	perf. inf.	perf. part./sup.
ac-cubāre	1.	*cubā|re*	*cubu|isse*	*cubit|um*
	2.	*vetā|re*	*vetu|isse*	*vetit|um*
ex-plicāre	3.	*im-plicā|re*	*-plicu|isse*	*-plicit|um*
	4.	*secā|re*	*secu|isse*	*sect|um*
ad-iuvāre	5.	*iuvā|re*	*iūv|isse*	*iūt|um*
	6.	*lavā|re*	*lāv|isse*	*laut|um/lavāt|um*
	7.	*stā|re*	*stet|isse*	
prae-stāre	8.	*cōn-stā|re*	*-stit|isse*	
circum-dare	9.	*da|re*	*ded|isse*	*dat|um*

Second conjugation

		pres. inf.	perf. inf.	perf. part./sup.
	10.	*docē|re*	*docu|isse*	*doct|um*
	11.	*miscē|re*	*miscu|isse*	*mixt|um*
	12.	*tenē|re*	*tenu|isse*	*tent|um*
abs- re- sus-tinēre	13.	*con-tinē|re*	*-tinu|isse*	*-tent|um*
	14.	*cēnsē|re*	*cēnsu|isse*	*cēns|um*
	15.	*dēlē|re*	*dēlēv|isse*	*dēlēt|um*
	16.	*flē|re*	*flēv|isse*	*flēt|um*
com- ex-plēre	17.	*im-plē|re*	*-plēv|isse*	*-plēt|um*
	18.	*cavē|re*	*cāv|isse*	*caut|um*
	19.	*favē|re*	*fāv|isse*	*faut|um*
per- re-movēre	20.	*movē|re*	*mōv|isse*	*mōt|um*
	21.	*sedē|re*	*sēd|isse*	*sess|um*
	22.	*possidē|re*	*possēd|isse*	*possess|um*
in-vidēre	23.	*vidē|re*	*vīd|isse*	*vīs|um*
	24.	*augē|re*	*aux|isse*	*auct|um*
	25.	*lūcē|re*	*lūx|isse*	
	26.	*lūgē|re*	*lūx|isse*	
	27.	*iubē|re*	*iuss|isse*	*iuss|um*
dē-rīdēre	28.	*rīdē|re*	*rīs|isse*	*rīs|um*
dis- per-suādēre	29.	*suādē|re*	*suās|isse*	*suās|um*
dē-tergēre	30.	*tergē|re*	*ters|isse*	*ters|um*
re-manēre	31.	*manē|re*	*māns|isse*	*māns|um*
	32.	*re-spondē|re*	*-spond|isse*	*-spōns|um*
	33.	*mordē|re*	*momord|isse*	*mors|um*
	34.	*fatē|rī*	*fass|um esse*	
	35.	*cōn-fitē|rī*	*-fess|um esse*	
	36.	*solē|re*	*solit|um esse*	
	37.	*audē|re*	*aus|um esse*	
	38.	*gaudē|re*	*gavīs|um esse*	

Third conjugation

39. *leg|ere*	*lēg|isse*	*lēct|um*	
40. *ē-lig|ere*	*-lēg|isse*	*-lēct|um*	
41. *em|ere*	*ēm|isse*	*ēmpt|um*	
42. *red-im|ere*	*-ēm|isse*	*-ēmpt|um*	
43. *cōn-sīd|ere*	*-sēd|isse*		
44. *ēs|se ed|ō*	*ēd|isse*	*ēs|um*	
45. *ag|ere*	*ēg|isse*	*āct|um*	
46. *cōg|ere*	*co-ēg|isse*	*co-āct|um*	
47. *cap|ere -iō*	*cēp|isse*	*capt|um*	
48. *ac-cip|ere -iō*	*-cēp|isse*	*-cept|um*	*re-cipere*
49. *fac|ere -iō*	*fēc|isse*	*fact|um*	*imp. fac!*
50. *af-fic|ere -iō*	*-fēc|isse*	*-fect|um*	*cōn- ef- inter- per- ficere*
51. *iac|ere -iō*	*iēc|isse*	*iact|um*	
52. *ab-ic|ere -iō*	*-iēc|isse*	*-iect|um*	*ad- ē- prō-icere*
53. *fug|ere -iō*	*fūg|isse*		*au- ef-fugere*
54. *vinc|ere*	*vīc|isse*	*vict|um*	
55. *fund|ere*	*fūd|isse*	*fūs|um*	*ef-fundere*
56. *re-linqu|ere*	*-līqu|isse*	*-lict|um*	
57. *rump|ere*	*rūp|isse*	*rupt|um*	*ē-rumpere*
58. *frang|ere*	*frēg|isse*	*frāct|um*	
59. *carp|ere*	*carps|isse*	*carpt|um*	
60. *dīc|ere*	*dīx|isse*	*dict|um*	*imp. dīc! dūc!*
61. *dūc|ere*	*dūx|isse*	*duct|um*	*ab- ē- re-dūcere*
62. *scrīb|ere*	*scrīps|isse*	*scrīpt|um*	*īn-scribere*
63. *nūb|ere*	*nūps|isse*	*nupt|um*	
64. *a-spic|ere -iō*	*-spex|isse*	*-spect|um*	*cōn- dē- prō- re- su-spicere*
65. *al-lic|ere -iō*	*-lēx|isse*	*-lect|um*	
66. *reg|ere*	*rēx|isse*	*rēct|um*	
67. *cor-rig|ere*	*-rēx|isse*	*-rēct|um*	
68. *perg|ere*	*per-rēx|isse*		
69. *surg|ere*	*sur-rēx|isse*		
70. *dīlig|ere*	*dīlēx|isse*	*dīlēct|um*	
71. *intelleg|ere*	*intellēx|isse*	*intellēct|um*	
72. *negleg|ere*	*neglēx|isse*	*neglēct|um*	
73. *cing|ere*	*cīnx|isse*	*cīnct|um*	
74. *iung|ere*	*iūnx|isse*	*iūnct|um*	*ad- con- dis-iungere*
75. *coqu|ere*	*cox|isse*	*coct|um*	
76. *trah|ere*	*trāx|isse*	*tract|um*	*con- dē- re-trahere*
77. *veh|ere*	*vēx|isse*	*vect|um*	*ad- in-vehere*
78. *īn-stru|ere*	*-strūx|isse*	*-strūct|um*	
79. *flu|ere*	*flūx|isse*		*īn-fluere*
80. *vīv|ere*	*vīx|isse*		*part. fut. vīct|ūr|us*
81. *sūm|ere*	*sūmps|isse*	*sūmpt|um*	*cōn-sūmere*
82. *prōm|ere*	*prōmps|isse*	*prōmpt|um*	
83. *dēm|ere*	*dēmps|isse*	*dēmpt|um*	

	84.	*ger|ere*	*gess|isse*	*gest|um*
	85.	*ūr|ere*	*uss|isse*	*ust|um*
	86.	*fīg|ere*	*fīx|isse*	*fīx|um*
īn-flectere	87.	*flect|ere*	*flex|isse*	*flex|um*
ac- dis- prō- re- cēdere	88.	*cēd|ere*	*cess|isse*	*cess|um*
	89.	*claud|ere*	*claus|isse*	*claus|um*
	90.	*in-clūd|ere*	*-clūs|isse*	*-clūs|um*
	91.	*dīvid|ere*	*dīvīs|isse*	*dīvīs|um*
	92.	*lūd|ere*	*lūs|isse*	*lūs|um*
	93.	*laed|ere*	*laes|isse*	*laes|um*
	94.	*ē-līd|ere*	*-līs|isse*	*-līs|um*
	95.	*plaud|ere*	*plaus|isse*	*plaus|um*
ā- ad- dī- per- prō- re-mittere	96.	*mitt|ere*	*mīs|isse*	*miss|um*
	97.	*quat|ere -iō*	--	*quass|um*
	98.	*per-cut|ere -iō*	*-cuss|isse*	*-cuss|um*
sub-mergere	99.	*merg|ere*	*mers|isse*	*mers|um*
	100.	*sparg|ere*	*spars|isse*	*spars|um*
	101.	*a-sperg|ere*	*-spers|isse*	*-spers|um*
	102.	*prem|ere*	*press|isse*	*press|um*
	103.	*im-prim|ere*	*-press|isse*	*-press|um*
	104.	*contemn|ere*	*contēmps|isse*	*contēmpt|um*
	105.	*stern|ere*	*strāv|isse*	*strāt|um*
	106.	*cern|ere*	*crēv|isse*	*crēt|um*
	107.	*ser|ere*	*sēv|isse*	*sat|um*
	108.	*arcess|ere*	*arcessīv|isse*	*arcessīt|um*
	109.	*cup|ere -iō*	*cupīv|isse*	*cupīt|um*
	110.	*sap|ere -iō*	*sapi|isse*	
	111.	*pet|ere*	*petīv|isse*	*petīt|um*
	112.	*quaer|ere*	*quaesīv|isse*	*quaesīt|um*
	113.	*re-quīr|ere*	*-quīsīv|isse*	*-quīsīt|um*
	114.	*sin|ere*	*sīv|isse*	*sit|um*
	115.	*dēsin|ere*	*dēsi|isse*	*dēsit|um*
ap- dē- ex- im- prae- re-pōnere	116.	*pōn|ere*	*posu|isse*	*posit|um*
	117.	*al|ere*	*alu|isse*	*alt|um*
in-colere	118.	*col|ere*	*colu|isse*	*cult|um*
	119.	*dēser|ere*	*dēseru|isse*	*dēsert|um*
	120.	*rap|ere -iō*	*rapu|isse*	*rapt|um*
sur-ripere	121.	*ē-rip|ere -iō*	*-ripu|isse*	*-rept|um*
	122.	*trem|ere*	*tremu|isse*	
	123.	*frem|ere*	*fremu|isse*	
re-cumbere	124.	*ac-cumb|ere*	*-cubu|isse*	
	125.	*tang|ere*	*tetig|isse*	*tāct|um*
	126.	*cad|ere*	*cecid|isse*	
oc-cidere	127.	*ac-cid|ere*	*-cid|isse*	
	128.	*caed|ere*	*cecīd|isse*	*caes|um*
	129.	*oc-cīd|ere*	*-cīd|isse*	*-cīs|um*

130.	curr|ere	cucurr|isse	curs|um
131.	ac-curr|ere	-curr|isse	-curs|um	ex- oc- per- prō-currere
132.	par|ere -iō	peper|isse	part|um
133.	pell|ere	pepul|isse	puls|um
134.	parc|ere	peperc|isse	
135.	can|ere	cecin|isse	
136.	fall|ere	fefell|isse		per- red- trā-dere
137.	ad-d|ere	-did|isse	-dit|um
138.	crēd|ere	crēdid|isse	crēdit|um
139.	vēnd|ere	vēndid|isse		dē- re-sistere
140.	cōn-sist|ere	-stit|isse	
141.	scind|ere	scid|isse	sciss|um
142.	bib|ere	bib|isse	
143.	dēfend|ere	dēfend|isse	dēfēns|um	ap- re-prehendere
144.	prehend|ere	prehend|isse	prehēns|um	cōn- dē-scendere
145.	a-scend|ere	-scend|isse	-scēns|um
146.	ac-cend|ere	-cend|isse	-cēns|um
147.	ostend|ere	ostend|isse	ostent|um	ā- con-vertere
148.	vert|ere	vert|isse	vers|um
149.	minu|ere	minu|isse	minūt|um
150.	statu|ere	statu|isse	statūt|um
151.	cōn-stitu|ere	-stitu|isse	-stitūt|um
152.	indu|ere	indu|isse	indūt|um
153.	metu|ere	metu|isse	
154.	solv|ere	solv|isse	solūt|um	ē-volvere
155.	volv|ere	volv|isse	volūt|um	re-quiēscere
156.	quiēsc|ere	quiēv|isse	
157.	crēsc|ere	crēv|isse	
158.	ērubēsc|ere	ērubu|isse	
159.	nōsc|ere	nōv|isse	
160.	ignōsc|ere	ignōv|isse	ignōt|um
161.	cognōsc|ere	cognōv|isse	cognitum
162.	pāsc|ere	pāv|isse	pāstum
163.	posc|ere	poposc|isse	
164.	disc|ere	didic|isse	
165.	fer|re	tul|isse	lāt|um
166.	af-fer|re	at-tul|isse	ad|lātum
167.	au-fer|re	abs-tul|isse	ab|lātum
168.	ef-fer|re	ex-tul|isse	ē-lāt|um
169.	of-fer|re	ob-tul|isse	ob-lāt|um
170.	re-fer|re	rettul|isse	re-lāt|um	per- prae- prō- trāns- ferre
171.	toll|ere	sustul|isse	sublāt|um
172.	in-cip|ere -iō	coep|isse	coept|um
173.	fīd|ere	fīs|um esse		cōn-fīdere
174.	revert|ī	revert|isse	revers|um
175.	loqu|ī	locūt|um esse		col-loquī

cōn- per-sequī	176. *sequ|ī*	*secūt|um esse*
	177. *quer|ī*	*quest|um esse*
	178. *mor|ī -ior*	*mortu|um esse*
	179. *pat|ī -ior*	*pass|um esse*
prō-gredī	180. *ē-gred|ī -ior*	*-gress|um esse*
	181. *ūt|ī*	*ūs|um esse*
	182. *complect|ī*	*complex|um esse*
	183. *lāb|ī*	*lāps|um esse*
	184. *nāsc|ī*	*nāt|um esse*
	185. *proficīsc|ī*	*profect|um esse*
	186. *oblīvīsc|ī*	*oblīt|um esse*

Fourth conjugation

	187. *aperī|re*	*aperu|isse*	*apert|um*
	188. *operī|re*	*operu|isse*	*opert|um*
	189. *salī|re*	*salu|isse*	
circum- prō-silīre	190. *dē-silī|re*	*-silu|isse*	
ex-haurīre	191. *haurī|re*	*haus|isse*	*haust|um*
	192. *vincī|re*	*vīnx|isse*	*vīnct|um*
	193. *sentī|re*	*sēns|isse*	*sēns|um*
ad- con- in- per- re- venīre	194. *venī|re*	*vēn|isse*	*vent|um*
	195. *reperī|re*	*repper|isse*	*repert|um*
ab- ad- ex- per- red- sub- trāns-īre	196. *ī|re e|ō*	*i|isse*	*it|um*
	197. *opperī|rī*	*oppert|um esse*	
pres. stem orī-/ori-	198. *orī|rī ori|tur*	*ort|um esse*	

Irregular verbs III

	pres. inf.		perf. inf.
	199. *vel|le vol|ō*		*volu|isse*
	200. *nōl|le*		*nōlu|isse*
inter- prae- super- esse	201. *māl|le*		*mālu|isse*
	202. *es|se sum*		*fu|isse*
fut. part. *futūr|us*	203. *posse pos-sum*		*potu|isse*
fut. inf. *futūr|um esse, fore*	204. *ab-esse*		*ā-fu|isse*
	205. *ad-esse ad-/as-sum*		*af-fu|isse*
	206. *de-esse dē-sum*		*dē-fu|isse*
	207. *prōd-esse prō-sum*	*prō-fu|isse*	
	208. *fi|erī fī|ō*		*fact|um esse*

Alphabetical List of Irregular Verbs

(Numbers refer to the lists of irregular verbs by conjugation that begin on page 349.)

A
abdūcere 61
abesse 204
abicere 52
abīre 196
abstinēre 13
accēdere 88
accendere 146
accidere 127
accipere 48
accubāre 1
accumbere 124
accurrere 131
addere 137
adesse 205
adicere 52
adīre 196
adiungere 74
adiuvāre 5
admittere 96
advehere 77
advenīre 194
afferre 166
afficere 50
agere 45
alere 117
allicere 65
āmittere 96
aperīre 187
appōnere 116
apprehendere 144
arcessere 108
ascendere 145
aspergere 101
aspicere 64
audēre 37
auferre 167
aufugere 53
augēre 24
āvertere 148

B
bibere 142

C
cadere 126
caedere 128
canere 135

capere 47
carpere 59
cavēre 18
cēdere 88
cēnsēre 14
cernere 106
cingere 73
circumdare 9
circumsilīre 190
claudere 89
cōgere 46
cognōscere 161
colere 118
colloquī 175
complectī 182
complēre 17
cōnficere 50
cōnfīdere 173
cōnfitērī 35
coniungere 74
cōnscendere 145
cōnsequī 176
cōnsīdere 43
cōnsistere 140
cōnspicere 64
cōnstāre 8
cōnstituere 151
cōnsūmere 81
contemnere 104
continēre 13
contrahere 76
convenīre 194
convertere 148
coquere 75
corrigere 67
crēdere 138
crēscere 157
cubāre 1
cupere 109
currere 130

D
dare 9
dēesse 206
dēfendere 143
dēlēre 15
dēmere 83

dēpōnere 116
dērīdēre 28
dēscendere 145
dēserere 119
dēsilīre 190
dēsinere 115
dēsistere 140
dēspicere 64
dētergēre 30
dētrahere 76
dīcere 60
dīligere 70
dīmittere 96
discēdere 88
discere 164
disiungere 74
dissuādēre 29
dīvidere 91
docēre 10
dūcere 61

E
ēdūcere 61
efferre 168
efficere 50
effugere 53
effundere 55
ēgredī 180
ēicere 52
ēlīdere 94
ēligere 40
emere 41
ēripere 121
ērubēscere 158
ērumpere 57
esse 202
ēsse 44
ēvolvere 155
excurrere 131
exhaurīre 191
exīre 196
explēre 17
expōnere 116

F
facere 49
fallere 136
fatērī 34

favēre 19
ferre 165
fīdere 173
fierī 208
fīgere 86
flectere 87
flēre 16
fluere 79
frangere 58
fremere 123
fugere 53
fundere 55

G
gaudēre 38
gerere 84

H
haurīre 191

I
iacere 51
ignōscere 160
implēre 17
implicāre 3
impōnere 116
imprimere 103
incipere 172
inclūdere 90
incolere 118
induere 152
īnflectere 87
īnfluere 79
īnscrībere 62
īnstruere 78
intellegere 71
interesse 202
interficere 50
invehere 77
invenīre 194
invidēre 23
īre 196
iubēre 27
iungere 74
iuvāre 5

L
lābī 183
laedere 93

lavāre 6
legere 39
loquī 175
lūcēre 25
lūdere 92
lūgēre 26

M
mālle 201
manēre 31
mergere 99
metuere 153
minuere 149
miscēre 11
mittere 96
mordēre 33
morī 178
movēre 20

N
nāscī 184
neglegere 72
nōlle 200
nōscere 159
nūbere 63

O
oblīvīscī 186
occidere 127
occīdere 129
occurrere 131
offerre 169
operīre 188
opperīrī 197
orīrī 198
ostendere 147

P
parcere 134
parere 132
pāscere 162
patī 179
pellere 133

percurrere 131
percutere 98
perdere 137
perferre 165
perficere 50
pergere 68
perīre 196
permittere 96
permovēre 20
persequī 176
persuādēre 29
pervenīre 194
petere 111
plaudere 95
pōnere 116
poscere 163
posse 203
possidēre 22
praeesse 202
praeferre 165
praepōnere 116
praestāre 8
prehendere 144
premere 102
prōcēdere 88
prōcurrere 131
prōdesse 207
prōferre 165
proficīscī 185
prōgredī 180
prōicere 52
prōmere 82
prōmittere 96
prōsilīre 190
prōspicere 64

Q
quaerere 112
quatere 97
querī 177
quiēscere 156

R
rapere 120
recēdere 88
recipere 48
recumbere 124
reddere 137
redimere 42
redīre 196
redūcere 61
referre 170
regere 66
relinquere 56
remanēre 31
remittere 96
removēre 20
reperīre 195
repōnere 116
reprehendere 144
requiēscere 156
requīrere 113
resistere 140
respondēre 32
retinēre 13
retrahere 76
revenīre 194
revertī 174
rīdēre 28
rumpere 57

S
salīre 189
sapere 110
scindere 141
scrībere 62
secāre 4
sedēre 21
sentīre 193
sequī 176
serere 107
sinere 114
solēre 36

solvere 154
spargere 100
stāre 7
statuere 150
sternere 105
suādēre 29
subīre 196
submergere 99
sūmere 81
superesse 202
surgere 69
surripere 121
suspicere 64
sustinēre 13

T
tangere 125
tenēre 12
tergēre 30
tollere 171
trādere 137
trahere 76
trānsferre 165
trānsīre 196
tremere 122

U
ūrere 85
ūtī 181

V
vehere 77
velle 199
vēndere 139
venīre 194
vertere 148
vetāre 2
vidēre 23
vincere 54
vincīre 192
vīvere 80
volvere 155

Index of Nouns, Adjectives and Verbs

Nouns

1st Declension

Gen. sing. *-ae*, pl. *-ārum*

Feminine

āla	fenestra	littera	puella
amīca	fera	lucerna	pugna
amīcitia	fīlia	lūna	rēgula
ancilla	fōrma	mamma	rīpa
anima	fortūna	margarīta	rosa
aqua	fossa	māteria	sagitta
aquila	fuga	mātrōna	scaena
arānea	gemma	memoria	sella
audācia	gena	mēnsa	sententia
bēstia	glōria	mora	silva
catēna	grammatica	Mūsa	stēlla
cauda	grātia	nātūra	syllaba
causa	hasta	nāvicula	tabella
cēna	herba	nota	tabula
cēra	hōra	opera	terra
charta	iactūra	ōra	toga
columna	iānua	paenīnsula	tunica
cōmoedia	iniūria	pāgina	turba
cōpia	inopia	palma	umbra
culīna	īnsula	patientia	ūva
cūra	invidia	patria	vēna
dea	īra	pecūnia	via
domina	lacrima	penna	victōria
epistula	laetitia	persōna	vigilia
fābula	lāna	pila	vīlla
fāma	lectīca	poena	vīnea
familia	līnea	porta	virga
fēmina	lingua	prōvincia	vīta

(pl.)

cūnae	dīvitiae	nōnae	tenebrae
dēliciae	kalendae	nūgae	tībiae

Masculine (/feminine)

agricola	convīva	nauta	poēta
aurīga	incola	parricīda	pīrāta

2nd Declension

Gen. sing. *-ī*, pl. *-ōrum*
1. Nom. sing. *-us* (*-r*)
Masculīne

agnus	deus	locus	pugnus
amīcus	digitus	lūdus	pullus
animus	discipulus	lupus	rāmus
annus	dominus	marītus	rēmus
ānulus	equus	medicus	rīvus
asinus	erus	modus	sacculus
avunculus	fīlius	mundus	saccus
barbarus	fluvius	mūrus	servus
cachinnus	fundus	nāsus	sēstertius
calamus	gallus	nīdus	somnus
calceus	gladius	numerus	sonus
campus	hortus	nummus	stilus
capillus	inimīcus	nūntius	tabernārius
cibus	labyrinthus	ōceanus	taurus
circus	lacertus	ocellus	titulus
cocus	lectus	oculus	tyrannus
colōnus	lēgātus	ōstiārius	umerus
delphīnus	libellus	petasus	ventus
dēnārius	lībertīnus	populus	zephyrus

(nom. sing. *-er*)

ager agrī	faber -brī	magister -trī	puer -erī
culter -trī	liber -brī	minister -trī	vesper -erī

(pl.)
līberī

Feminine

humus	papyrus	Aegyptus	Rhodus

2. Nom. sing. *-um*, plur *-a*
Neuter

aedificium	exemplum	mōnstrum	scamnum
aequinoctium	factum	negōtium	scūtum
arātrum	fātum	odium	saeculum
argentum	ferrum	officium	saxum
ātrium	fīlum	oppidum	scalpellum
aurum	folium	ōrnāmentum	signum
auxilium	forum	ōsculum	silentium
baculum	fretum	ōstium	solum
balneum	frūmentum	ōtium	speculum
bāsium	fūrtum	ōvum	stipendium
bellum	gaudium	pābulum	studium
beneficium	gremium	pallium	supplicium
bonum	imperium	pecūlium	talentum
bracchium	impluvium	pēnsum	tēctum
caelum	ingenium	perīculum	templum
capitulum	initium	peristylum	tergum
cerebrum	īnstrūmentum	pīlum	theātrum
colloquium	labrum	pirum	triclīnium
collum	lignum	pōculum	vāllum
cōnsilium	līlium	praedium	vēlum
convīvium	lucrum	praemium	verbum
cubiculum	maleficium	pretium	vestīgium
dictum	malum	prīncipium	vestīmentum
dōnum	mālum	prōmissum	vīnum
dorsum	mendum	respōnsum	vocābulum

(pl.)

arma -ōrum	castra -ōrum	loca -ōrum	vāsa -ōrum

3rd Declension

Gen. sing. *-is*
1. Gen. pl. *-um*

Masculine

āēr āeris	*gladiātor -ōris*	*piscātor -ōris*
amor -ōris	*grex -egis*	*praedō -ōnis*
arātor -ōris	*gubernātor -ōris*	*prīnceps -ipis*
bōs bovis	*homō -inis*	*pudor -ōris*
calor -ōris	*hospes -itis*	*pulmō -ōnis*
carcer -eris	*iānitor -ōris*	*rēx rēgis*
cardō -inis	*imperātor -ōris*	*rūmor -ōris*
clāmor -ōris	*iuvenis -is*	*sacerdōs -ōtis*
color -ōris	*labor -ōris*	*sāl salis*
comes -itis	*leō -ōnis*	*sanguis -inis*
coniūnx -iugis	*mercātor -ōris*	*senex senis*
cruor -ōris	*mīles -itis*	*sermō -ōnis*
dolor -ōris	*mōs mōris*	*sōl sōlis*
dux ducis	*ōrdō -inis*	*spectātor -ōris*
eques -itis	*passer -eris*	*tībīcen -inis*
fidicen -inis	*pāstor -ōris*	*timor -ōris*
flōs -ōris	*pater -tris*	*victor -ōris*
frāter -tris	*pedes -itis*	
fūr fūris	*pēs pedis*	

(pl.)

parentēs -um   *septentriōnēs -um*

Feminine

aestās -ātis	*māter -tris*	*quālitās -ātis*
aetās -ātis	*mentiō -ōnis*	*ratiō -ōnis*
arbor -oris	*mercēs -ēdis*	*salūs -ūtis*
condiciō -ōnis	*mulier -eris*	*servitūs -ūtis*
crux -ucis	*multitūdō -inis*	*significātiō -ōnis*
cupiditās -ātis	*nārrātiō -ōnis*	*soror -ōris*
expugnātiō -ōnis	*nāvigātiō -ōnis*	*tempestās -ātis*
fēlīcitās -ātis	*nex necis*	*tranquillitās -ātis*
hiems -mis	*nūtrīx -īcis*	*uxor -ōris*
imāgō -inis	*nux nucis*	*valētūdō -inis*
laus laudis	*ōrātiō -ōnis*	*virgō -inis*
legiō -ōnis	*pāx pācis*	*virtūs -ūtis*
lēx lēgis	*potestās -ātis*	*voluntās -ātis*
lībertās -ātis	*pōtiō -ōnis*	*vorāgō -inis*
lūx lūcis	*pulchritūdō -inis*	*vōx vōcis*

(pl.)

frūgēs -um   *opēs -um*   *precēs -um*

Neuter (pl. nom. /acc. *-a*)

agmen -inis	*holus -eris*	*pectus -oris*
caput -itis	*iecur -oris*	*pecus -oris*
carmen -inis	*iter itineris*	*phantasma -atis*
certāmen -inis	*iūs iūris*	*praenōmen -inis*
cognōmen -inis	*lac lactis*	*rūs rūris*
cor cordis	*latus -eris*	*scelus -eris*
corpus -oris	*līmen -inis*	*sēmen -inis*
crūs -ūris	*lītus -oris*	*tempus -oris*
epigramma -atis	*mel mellis*	*thema -atis*
flūmen -inis	*mūnus -eris*	*vās vāsis*
frīgus -oris	*nōmen -inis*	*vēr vēris*
fulgur -uris	*opus -eris*	*vulnus -eris*
genus -eris	*ōs ōris*	

(pl.)

verbera -um   *viscera -um*

2. Gen. pl. *-ium*

Masculine

amnis	hostis	oriēns -entis
as assis	ignis	orbis
cīvis	imber -bris	pānis
collis	īnfāns -antis	piscis
dēns dentis	mēnsis	pōns pontis
ēnsis	mōns montis	testis
fīnis	occidēns -entis	venter -tris

Feminine

apis	famēs -is	ovis
ars artis	foris	pars partis
auris	frōns -ontis	puppis
avis	gēns gentis	ratis
caedēs -is	mēns mentis	sitis
carō carnis	merx -rcis	urbs -bis
classis	mors -rtis	vallis
clāvis	nāvis	vestis
cohors -rtis	nix nivis	vītis
cōnsonāns -antis	nox noctis	vōcālis
falx -cis	nūbēs -is	

(pl.)

fidēs -ium	sordēs -ium	vīrēs -ium

Neuter

animal -ālis	mare -is	rēte -is

(pl.)

mīlia -ium	moenia -ium

4th Declension

Gen. sing. *-ūs*, pl. *-uum*

Masculine

affectus	cursus	impetus	sinus
arcus	equitātus	lacus	strepitus
cantus	exercitus	metus	tonitrus
cāsus	exitus	passus	tumultus
cōnspectus	flūctus	portus	versus
currus	gradus	rīsus	vultus

Feminine

anus	domus	manus

(pl.)
īdūs -uum

Neuter

cornū	genū

5th Declension

Gen. sing. *-ēī/-eī* (pl. *-ērum*)

Feminine

aciēs -ēī	glaciēs -ēī	fidēs -eī	spēs -eī
faciēs -ēī	speciēs -ēī	rēs reī	

Masculine

diēs -ēī	merīdiēs -ēī

Adjectives

1st/2nd Declension

Nom. sing. m. *-us*, f. *-a*, n. *-um*

acerbus	ferus	mellītus	rēctus
acūtus	fessus	mercātōrius	reliquus
adversus	fīdus	merus	rīdiculus
aegrōtus	foedus	meus	Rōmānus
aequus	fōrmōsus	minimus	rūsticus
albus	frīgidus	mīrus	saevus
aliēnus	fugitīvus	misellus	salvus
altus	futūrus	molestus	sānus
amīcus	gemmātus	mortuus	scaenicus
amoenus	gladiātōrius	mundus	scelestus
angustus	glōriōsus	mūtus	secundus
antīquus	grātus	mūtuus	septimus
apertus	gravidus	necessārius	serēnus
arduus	horrendus	nimius	sērius
argenteus	ignārus	niveus	sevērus
armātus	ignōtus	nōnus	sextus
asinīnus	immātūrus	nōtus	siccus
attentus	improbus	novus	situs
aureus	īmus	nūbilus	sordidus
avārus	incertus	nūdus	studiōsus
barbarus	inconditus	obscūrus	stultus
beātus	indignus	octāvus	summus
bellus	indoctus	optimus	superbus
bonus	industrius	ōtiōsus	superus
caecus	īnferus	pallidus	surdus
calidus	īnfēstus	parātus	suus
candidus	īnfīdus	parvulus	tacitus
cārus	īnfimus	parvus	tantus
cautus	inhūmānus	pecūniōsus	tardus
celsus	inimīcus	perīculōsus	temerārius
centēsimus	iniūstus	perpetuus	tenebricōsus
certus	internus	perterritus	timidus
cēterus	invalidus	pessimus	tertius
clārus	iocōsus	plānus	togātus
claudus	īrātus	plēnus	tranquillus
clausus	iūcundus	poēticus	turbidus
contrārius	iūstus	postrēmus	turgidus
crassus	laetus	praeteritus	tūtus
cruentus	laevus	prāvus	tuus
cūnctus	largus	pretiōsus	ultimus
cupidus	Latīnus	prīmus	ūmidus
decimus	lātus	prīvātus	ūniversus
dignus	legiōnārius	propinquus	urbānus
dīmidius	ligneus	proprius	vacuus
dīrus	longus	proximus	validus
doctus	maestus	pūblicus	varius
dubius	magnificus	pūrus	venustus
dūrus	magnus	quantus	vērus
ēbrius	malus	quārtus	vīvus
ēgregius	maritimus	quiētus	-issimus
exiguus	mātūrus	quīntus	sup.
falsus	māximus	rapidus	-ēsimus
ferreus	medius	rārus	num.

(pl.)

cēterī	paucī	singulī	ducentī
multī	plērī-que	bīnī	trecentī
nōnnūllī	plūrimī	cēt.	cēt.

Nom. sing. *-er -(e)ra -(e)rum*

aeger -gra -grum	niger -gra -grum	ruber -bra -brum
āter -tra -trum	noster -tra -trum	sinister -tra -trum
dexter -tra -trum	piger -gra -grum	vester -tra -trum
impiger -gra -grum	pulcher -chra	līber -era -erum
integer -gra -grum	-chrum	miser -era -erum

3rd Declension

Nom. sing. m./f. *-is,* n. *-e*

brevis	fertilis	levis	rudis
circēnsis	fortis	mīlitāris	similis
commūnis	gracilis	mīrābilis	tālis
crūdēlis	gravis	mollis	tenuis
dēbilis	humilis	mortālis	terribilis
difficilis	immortālis	nōbilis	trīstis
dulcis	incolumis	omnis	turpis
facilis	inermis	quālis	vīlis

Nom. sing. m./f./n. *-ns,* gen. *-ntis*

absēns	dēpōnēns	ingēns	prūdēns
amāns	dīligēns	neglegēns	sapiēns
clēmēns	frequēns	patiēns	-ns part.
cōnstāns	impatiēns	praesēns	pres.

Nom. sing. m./f./n. *-x,* gen. *-cis*

audāx	fēlīx	īnfēlīx
fallāx	ferōx	vēlōx

Nom. sing. m. *-er,* f. *-(e)ris,* n. *-(e)re*

ācer ācris	celer -eris	September -bris
Octōber -bris	November -bris	December -bris

Verbs

1st Conjugation
Inf. pres. act. -āre, pass. -ārī

aberrāre	dare	iuvāre	properāre
accubāre	dēlectāre	labōrāre	pugnāre
accūsāre	dēmōnstrāre	lacrimāre	pulsāre
adiuvāre	dēsīderāre	lātrāre	putāre
adōrāre	dēspērāre	laudāre	recitāre
aedificāre	dēvorāre	lavāre	rēgnāre
aegrōtāre	dictāre	levāre	rēmigāre
aestimāre	dōnāre	līberāre	repugnāre
affirmāre	dubitāre	memorāre	revocāre
amāre	ēducāre	mīlitāre	rigāre
ambulāre	errāre	mōnstrāre	rogāre
appellāre	ēvolāre	mūtāre	rogitāre
apportāre	excitāre	nārrāre	salūtāre
appropin-	exclāmāre	natāre	salvāre
quāre	excōgitāre	nāvigāre	sānāre
arāre	excruciāre	necāre	secāre
armāre	excūsāre	negāre	servāre
bālāre	exīstimāre	nōmināre	signāre
cantāre	exōrnāre	numerāre	significāre
cēnāre	explānāre	nūntiāre	spectāre
certāre	expugnāre	occultāre	spērāre
cessāre	exspectāre	oppugnāre	spīrāre
circumdare	fatīgāre	optāre	stāre
clāmāre	flāre	ōrāre	suscitāre
cōgitāre	gubernāre	ōrdināre	turbāre
commemo-	gustāre	ōrnāre	ululāre
rāre	habitāre	ōscitāre	verberāre
comparāre	iactāre	palpitāre	vetāre
computāre	ignōrāre	parāre	vigilāre
cōnstāre	illūstrāre	perturbāre	vītāre
conturbāre	imperāre	pīpiāre	vocāre
convocāre	implicāre	plōrāre	volāre
cōpulāre	interpellāre	portāre	vorāre
cruciāre	interrogāre	postulāre	vulnerāre
cubāre	intrāre	pōtāre	
cūrāre	invocāre	praestāre	

Deponent verbs

admīrārī	fārī	luctārī	tumultuārī
arbitrārī	hortārī	minārī	versārī
comitārī	fābulārī	mīrārī	
cōnārī	imitārī	ōsculārī	
cōnsōlārī	laetārī	precārī	

2nd Conjugation

Inf. pres. act. *-ēre*, pass. *-ērī*

abstinēre	favēre	merēre	retinēre
appārēre	flēre	miscēre	rīdēre
audēre	frīgēre	monēre	rubēre
augēre	gaudēre	mordēre	salvēre
carēre	habēre	movēre	sedēre
cavēre	horrēre	nocēre	silēre
cēnsēre	iacēre	oportēre	solēre
complēre	impendēre	pallēre	studēre
continēre	implēre	pārēre	stupēre
dēbēre	invidēre	patēre	suādēre
decēre	iubēre	permovēre	sustinēre
dēlēre	latēre	persuādēre	tacēre
dērīdēre	libēre	placēre	tenēre
dētergēre	licēre	possidēre	tergēre
dēterrēre	lūcēre	pudēre	terrēre
dissuādēre	lūgēre	remanēre	timēre
docēre	maerēre	removēre	valēre
dolēre	manēre	respondēre	vidēre

Deponent verbs

cōnfitērī	intuērī	verērī
fatērī	tuērī	

3rd Conjugation
Inf. pres. act. -ere, pass. -ī
1. Ind. pres. pers. 1 sing. -ō, -or

abdūcere	coquere	inclūdere	quaerere
accēdere	corrigere	incolere	quiēscere
accendere	crēdere	induere	recēdere
accidere	crēscere	īnflectere	recognōscere
accumbere	currere	īnfluere	recumbere
accurrere	dēfendere	īnscrībere	reddere
addere	dēmere	īnstruere	redimere
adiungere	dēscendere	intellegere	redūcere
admittere	dēserere	invehere	regere
adnectere	dēsinere	iungere	relinquere
advehere	dēsistere	laedere	remittere
agere	dētrahere	legere	repōnere
alere	dīcere	lūdere	reprehendere
animadvertere	dīligere	mergere	requiēscere
āmittere	dīmittere	metere	requīrere
appōnere	discēdere	metuere	resistere
apprehendere	discere	minuere	retrahere
arcessere	disiungere	mittere	rumpere
ascendere	dīvidere	neglegere	scindere
aspergere	dūcere	nōscere	scrībere
āvertere	ēdūcere	nūbere	serere
bibere	effundere	occidere	sinere
cadere	ēlīdere	occīdere	solvere
caedere	ēligere	occurrere	spargere
canere	emere	ostendere	statuere
carpere	ērubēscere	parcere	sternere
cēdere	ērumpere	pāscere	submergere
cernere	ēvolvere	pellere	sūmere
cingere	excurrere	percurrere	surgere
claudere	expōnere	perdere	tangere
cōgere	extendere	pergere	tollere
cognōscere	fallere	permittere	trādere
colere	fīdere	petere	trahere
cōnfīdere	fīgere	plaudere	tremere
coniungere	flectere	pōnere	ūrere
cōnscendere	fluere	poscere	vehere
cōnsīdere	frangere	praepōnere	vēndere
cōnsistere	fremere	prehendere	vertere
cōnstituere	fundere	premere	vincere
cōnsūmere	gerere	prōcēdere	vīsere
contemnere	ignōscere	prōcurrere	vīvere
contrahere	impōnere	prōmere	
convertere	imprimere	prōmittere	

Deponent verbs

colloquī	lābī	persequī	revertī
complectī	loquī	proficīscī	sequī
cōnsequī	nāscī	querī	ūtī
fruī	oblīvīscī	reminīscī	

2. Ind. pres. pers. 1 sing. *-iō, -ior*

abicere	*cōnspicere*	*iacere*	*rapere*
accipere	*cupere*	*incipere*	*recipere*
adicere	*dēspicere*	*interficere*	*sapere*
afficere	*efficere*	*parere*	*surripere*
allicere	*effugere*	*percutere*	*suscipere*
aspicere	*ēicere*	*perficere*	*suspicere*
aufugere	*ēripere*	*prōicere*	
capere	*facere*	*prōspicere*	
cōnficere	*fugere*	*quatere*	

Deponent verbs

ēgredī	*morī*	*patī*	*prōgredī*

4th Conjugation

Inf. pres. act. *-īre*, pass. *-īrī*

advenīre	*exaudīre*	*oboedīre*	*scīre*
aperīre	*exhaurīre*	*operīre*	*sentīre*
audīre	*fīnīre*	*pervenīre*	*servīre*
circumsilīre	*haurīre*	*prōsilīre*	*vāgīre*
convenīre	*invenīre*	*pūnīre*	*venīre*
cūstōdīre	*mollīre*	*reperīre*	*vestīre*
dēsilīre	*mūnīre*	*revenīre*	*vincīre*
dormīre	*nescīre*	*salīre*	

Deponent vebs

largīrī	*opperīrī*	*mentīrī*	*orīrī*
partīrī			

Vocabulary by Chapter

I. Imperium Romanum
nōmina
fluvius
imperium
īnsula
ōceanus
oppidum
prōvincia
verba grammatica
capitulum
exemplum
grammatica
littera
numerus
singulāris
pēnsum
plūrālis
syllaba
vocābulum
adiectīva
duo
Graecus
Latīnus
magnus
mīlle
multī
parvus
paucī
prīmus
Rōmānus
secundus
sex
tertius
trēs
ūnus
verba
est
sunt
praepositiō
in
coniunctiōnes
et

sed
quoque
adverba
nōn
vocābula interrogātīva
-ne?
ubi?
num?
quid?

II. Familia Romana
Nōmina
ancilla
domina
dominus
familia
fēmina
fīlia
fīlius
liber
līberī
māter
pāgina
pater
puella
puer
servus
titulus
vir
verba grammatica
fēminīnum
genetīvus
masculīnum
neutrum
adiectīva
antīquus
centum
cēterī
duae
meus
novus
tria
tuus

coniunctiōnes
-que
vocābula interrogātīva
cuius?
quae?
quī?
quis?
quot?

III. Puer Improbus
nomina
mamma
persōna
scaena
verba grammatica
accūsātīvus
nōminātīvus
verbum
adiectīva
improbus
īrātus
laetus
probus
verba
audit
cantat
dormit
interrogat
plōrat
pulsat
respondet
rīdet
venit
verberat
videt
vocat
pronomina
eam
eum
hīc
mē
quae
quam

quem
qui
tē
adverbia
iam
vocābula interrogātīva
cūr?
coniunctiōnes
neque
quia
alia
ō!

IV. Dominus et Servi
nōmina
baculum
mēnsa
nummus
pecūnia
sacculus
verba grammatica
indicātīvus
vocātīvus
adiectīva
bonus
decem
novem
nūllus
octō
quattuor
quīnque
septem
suus
vacuus
verba
abest
accūsat
adest
discēdit
habet
imperat
numerat
pāret
pōnit
salūtat
sūmit
tacet
pronōmina
eius
is
adverbia
rūrsus
tantum
alia
salvē

V. Villa et Hortus
nōmina
aqua
ātrium
cubiculum
fenestra
hortus
impluvium
līlium
nāsus
ōstium
peristÿlum
rosa
vīlla
verba grammatica
ablātīvus
adiectīva
foedus
pulcher
sōlus
verba
agit
amat
carpit
dēlectat
habitat
pronōmina
is, ea, id
adverbium
etiam
praepositiōnes
ab
cum
ex
sine

VI. Via Latina
nōmina
amīca
amīcus
equus
inimīcus
lectīca
mūrus
porta
saccus
umerus
via
verba grammatica
praepositiō
locātīvus
āctīvum
passīvum
adiectīva
duodecim

fessus
longus
malus
verba
ambulat
intrat
it/eunt
portat
timet
vehit
adverbia
ante
autem
itaque
nam
quam
tam
praepositiōnes
ā
ad
ante
apud
circum
inter
per
post
procul ab
prope
vocābula interrogātīva
unde?
quō?

VII. Puella et Rosa
nōmina
lacrima
mālum
oculus
ōsculum
ōstiārius
pirum
speculum
verba grammatica
datīvus
adiectīva
fōrmōsus
plēnus
verba
adit
advenit
aperit
claudit
currit
dat
es
exit

exspectat
inest
lacrimat
tenet
terget
vertit
pronōmina
cui
eī
haec
hic
hoc
iīs
illīc
sē
adverbia
immō
non...sōlum
praepositiō
ē
coniunctiō
et...et
neque...neque
alia
nōnne?

VIII. Taberna Romana
nōmina
ānulus
collum
digitus
gemma
līnea
margarīta
ōrnāmentum
pretium
prōnōmen
sēstertius
taberna
tabernārius
adiectīva
alius
gemmātus
medius
nōnāginta
octōgintā
pecūniōsus
quantus
quārtus
tantus
vīgintī
verba
abit
accipit
aspicit

clāmat
cōnsistit
cōnstat
convenit
emit
mōnstrat
ōrnat
ostendit
vēndit
pronōmina
ille
adverbia
nimis
satis
coniunctiō
aut

IX. Pastor et Oves
nōmina
arbor
caelum
campus
canis
cibus
clāmor
collis
dēclīnātiō
dēns
herba
lupus
modus
mōns
nūbēs
ovis
pānis
pāstor
rīvus
silva
sōl
terra
timor
umbra
vallis
vestīgium
verba grammatica
dēclīnātiō
adiectīva
albus
niger
ūndēcentum
verba
accurrit
bālat
bibit
dēclīnat

dūcit
errat
ēst edunt
iacet
impōnit
lātrat
lūcet
petit
quaerit
relinquit
reperit
ululat
pronōmina
ipse
adverbia
procul
praepositiō
sub
suprā
coniūnctiōnēs
dum
ut

X. Bestiae et Homines
nōmina
āēr
āla
anima
animal
aquila
asinus
avis
bēstia
cauda
deus
fera
flūmen
folium
homo
lectus
leō
mare
mercātor
nīdus
nūntius
ōvum
pēs
petasus
pila
piscis
pullus
pulmō
rāmus
vōx
verba grammatica

īnfīnītīvus
adiectīva
crassus
ferus
mortuus
perterritus
tenuis
vīvus
verba
ascendere
audēre
cadere
canere
capere
facere
lūdere
movēre
natāre
necesse est
occultāre
parere
potest possunt
spīrāre
sustinēre
vīvere
volāre
vult volunt
pronōmina
nēmō
adverbia
ergō
coniunctiōnes
quod
cum
enim

XI. Corpus Humanum
nōmina
auris
bracchium
capillus
caput
cerebrum
color
cor
corpus
crūs
culter
frons
gena
iecur
labrum
manus
medicus
membrum

ōs
pectus
pōculum
sanguis
vēna
venter
viscera
adiectīva
aeger
hūmānus
noster
ruber
sānus
stultus
verba
aegrōtāre
appōnere
arcessere
dētergēre
dīcere
dolēre
fluere
gaudēre
horrēre
iubēre
palpitāre
posse
putāre
revenīre
sānāre
sedēre
sentīre
spectāre
stāre
tangere
adverbia
bene
male
modo
praepositiōnes
dē
īnfrā
super
coniunctiōnes
atque
nec

XII. Miles Romanus
Nōmina
arcus
arma
avunculus
bellum
castra
cognōmen

dux
eques
equitātus
exercitus
fīnis
fossa
frāter
gladius
hasta
hostis
impetus
lātus
metus
mīles
mīlia
nōmen
pars
passus
patria
pedes
pīlum
praenōmen
pugnus
sagitta
scūtum
soror
vāllum
versus
verba grammatica
adiectīvum
comparātīvus
adiectīva
altus
armātus
barbarus
brevis
fortis
gravis
levis
trīstis
vester
verba
dēfendere
dīvidere
expugnāre
ferre
fugere
iacere
incolere
metuere
mīlitāre
oppugnāre
pugnāre
coniunctiō
ac

praepositiō
contrā

XIII. Annus et Menses
nōmina
aequinoctium
aestās
annus
autumnus
diēs
faciēs
fōrma
glaciēs
hiems
hōra
īdūs
imber
initium
kalendae
lacus
lūna
lūx
māne
mēnsis
merīdiēs
nix
nōnae
nox
saeculum
stēlla
tempus
urbs
vēr
vesper
verba grammatica
indēclīnābilis
superlātīvus
adiectīva
aequus
calidus
clārus
decimus
dīmidius
ducentī
duodecimus
exiguus
frīgidus
nōnus
obscūrus
octāvus
postrēmus
quīntus
septimus
sexāgintā
sextus
tōtus

trecentī
trīgintā
ūndecim
ūndecimus
verba
erat, erant
illūstrāre
incipere
nōmināre
operīre
velle
adverbia
item
māne
nunc
quandō
tunc
coniunctiōnes
igitur
vel

XIV. Novus Dies
nōmina
calceus
gallus
nihil (also *adv.*)
parentēs
rēgula
rēs
stilus
tabula
toga
tunica
vestīmentum
verba grammatica
participium
adiectīva
alter
apertus
clausus
dexter
neuter
nūdus
omnis
pūrus
sinister
sordidus
togātus
uter
uterque
verba
afferre
cubāre
excitāre
frīgēre
gerere

induere
inquit
lavāre
mergere
poscere
solēre
surgere
valēre
vestīre
vigilāre
pronōmina
mēcum
mihi
sēcum
tēcum
tibi
adverbia
adhūc
deinde
hodiē
nihil (also noun)
prīmum
quōmodo
praepositiō
praeter
coniunctiō
an
interrogatīva
uter?
alia
valē

XV. Magister et Discipuli
nōmina
discipulus
domī
iānua
lectulus
lūdus
magister
sella
tergum
virga
adiectīva
īnferior
malus
posterior
prior
sevērus
tacitus
vērus
verba
cōnsīdere
dēsinere
es
estis

exclāmāre
licēre
pūnīre
recitāre
reddere
redīre
sum
sumus
prōnomina
ego
nōs
tū
vōs
adverbia
quid?
nōndum
statim
tum
praepositiō
antequam
coniunctiōnēs
at
nisi
sī
vērum

XVI. Tempestas
nōmina
altum
flūctus
fulgur
gubernātor
merx
nauta
nāvis
occidēns
oriēns
portus
locus
ōra
puppis
septentriōnēs
tempestās
tonitrus
vēlum
ventus
verba grammatica
dēpōnēns
adiectīva
āter
contrārius
īnferus
maritimus
serēnus
situs

superus
tranquillus
turbidus
verba
appellāre
cernere
complectī
cōnārī
cōnscendere
cōnsōlārī
ēgredī
fierī fit fiunt
flāre
gubernāre
haurīre
iactāre
implēre
īnfluere
interesse
intuērī
invocāre
lābī
laetārī
loquī
nāvigāre
occidere
opperīrī
orīrī
proficīscī
sequī
servāre
turbāre
verērī
adverbia
iterum
paulum
praetereā
semper
simul
vērō
vix
coniunctiō
sīve
praepositiō
propter

XVII. Numerī Difficiles
nōmina
as
dēnārius
respōnsum
adiectīva
absēns
centēsimus
certus

difficilis
doctus
duodēvīgintī
facilis
incertus
indoctus
industrius
largus
nōngentī
octingentī
piger
prāvus
prūdēns
quadrāgintā
quadringentī
quattuordecim
quīndecim
quīngentī
quīnquāgintā
rēctus
sēdecim
septendecim
septingentī
septuāgintā
sescentī
trēdecim
ūndēvīgintī
verba
cōgitāre
computāre
dēmōnstrāre
discere
docēre
interpellāre
largīrī
laudāre
nescīre
oportēre
partīrī
prōmere
repōnere
reprehendere
scīre
tollere
pronōmina
quisque
adverbia
aequē
numquam
postrēmō
prāvē
quārē
rēctē
saepe
tot

ūsque
coniunctiōnes
quamquam

XVIII. Litterae Latinae
nōmina
apis
calamus
cēra
charta
epistula
erus
ferrum
māteria
mendum
mercēs
papȳrus
zephyrus
verba grammatica
adverbium
cōnsonāns
sententia
vōcālis
adiectīva
dūrus
frequēns
impiger
mollis
quālis
rārus
tālis
turpis
varius
verba
addere
animadvertere
comparāre
coniungere
corrigere
deesse
dēlēre
dictāre
efficere
exaudīre
imprimere
intellegere
iungere
legere
premere
scrībere
signāre
significāre
superesse
pronōmina
īdem, eadem, idem

quisque, quaeque, quodque
adverbia
bis
deciēs
ita
quater
quīnquiēs
quotiēs
semel
sexiēs
sīc
ter
totiēs

XIX. Maritus et Uxor
nōmina
adulēscēns
amor
columna
coniūnx
dea
domus
dōnum
flōs
forum
marītus
mātrōna
pulchritūdō
signum
tēctum
templum
uxor
virgō
Verba grammatica
praesēns
praeteritum
adiectīva
beātus
dignus
dīves
gracilis
magnificus
māior
māximus
melior
minimus
minor
miser
optimus
pauper
pēior
pessimus
plūrēs
plūrimī
verba

augēre
convenīre
minuere
mittere
opus esse
ōsculārī
possidēre
remittere
pronōmina
mī
ūllus
praepositōnēs
ergā
adverbia
cotīdiē
minus
plūs
tamen

XX. Parentes
nōmina
colloquium
cūnae
domō
fīliola
fīliolus
gradus
īnfāns
lac
mulier
nūtrīx
officium
sermō
silentium
somnus
verba grammatica
adiectīva
aliēnus
futūrus
necessārius
parvulus
ūmidus
verba
advehere
alere
carēre
colloquī
cūrāre
dēbēre
decēre
dīligere
fārī
manēre
nōlle
occurrere

pergere
postulāre
revertī
silēre
vāgīre
adverbia
crās
magis
mox
rārō

XXI. Pugna Discipulorum
nōmina
bōs
causa
cornū
cruor
genū
humī
humus
porcus
pugna
solum
sordēs
tabella
vestis
verba grammatica
imperfectum
perfectum
adiectīva
angustus
candidus
falsus
indignus
mundus
validus
verba
āiō
cognōscere
cōnspicere
crēdere
dubitāre
excūsāre
fallere
fuisse
mentīrī
mūtāre
nārrāre
vincere
pronōmina
aliquid
aliquis
adverbia
interim

coniunctiōnes
postquam

XXII. Cave Canem
nōmina
aurum
cardō
catēna
faber
foris
iānitor
imāgō
lignum
līmen
pallium
tabellārius
verba grammatica
supīnum
adiectīva
aureus
ferōx
ferreus
ligneus
verba
accēdere
admittere
arbitrārī
cavēre
cēdere
cūstōdīre
dērīdēre
fremere
monēre
mordēre
pellere
prehendere
prōcēdere
recēdere
removēre
resistere
retinēre
rogitāre
rumpere
salīre
scindere
sinere
solvere
terrēre
tremere
vincīre
pronōmina
iste, ista, istud
adverbia
anteā
forās

forīs
nuper
posteā
prius
quīn
scīlicet
sīcut
tandem

XXIII. Epistula Magistrī
nōmina
clāvis
comes
factum
laus
litterae
prōmissum
pudor
signum
verbera
vultus
adiectīva
integer
pallidus
plānus
superior
verba
āvertere
comitārī
continēre
dēbēre
dīmittere
fatērī
inclūdere
īnscrībere
merēre
negāre
pallēre
perdere
prōmittere
pudēre
rubēre
salūtem dīcere
solvere
trādere
pronōmina
quidnam?
quisnam?
adverbia
antehāc
fortasse
herī
hinc
illinc
posthāc

umquam
praepositiō
ob

XXIV. Puer Aegrōtus
nōmina
dolor
latus
os
sonus
strepitus
tumultus
verba grammatica
plūsquam perfectum
adiectīva
aegrōtus
cruentus
impār
laevus
pār
subitus
verba
convertere
cupere
flēre
frangere
ignōrāre
mīrārī
nōscere
patī
percutere
recumbere
coniunctiōnes
etsī
praepositiōnes
iūxtā
adverbia
aliter
certō
cēterum
continuō
dēnuō
intus
prīmō
subitō
valdē

XXV. Theseus et Minotaur
nōmina
aedificium
agnus
auxilium
cīvis
cōnspectus
cupiditās

currus
exitus
expugnātiō
fābula
fīlum
glōria
labyrinthus
lītus
moenia
mōnstrum
mora
mors
nārrātiō
nex
rēx
saxum
taurus
adiectīva
complūrēs
cupidus
humilis
mīrābilis
parātus
saevus
terribilis
timidus
verba
aedificāre
coepisse
cōnstituere
dēscendere
dēserere
interficere
maerēre
necāre
oblīvīscī
occīdere
patēre
pollicērī
prōspicere
regere
trahere
vorāre
adverbia
brevī
forte
hūc
ibi
illūc
ōlim
quotannīs

XXVI. Daedalus et Icarus
nōmina
ars

carcer
cōnsilium
fuga
ignis
lacertus
lībertās
multitūdō
nātūra
opus
orbis
paenīnsula
penna
verba grammatica
cāsus
gerundium
adiectīva
audāx
cautus
celer
īnfimus
ingēns
līber
propinquus
reliquus
studiōsus
summus
temerārius
verba
aberrāre
accidere
cōnficere
cōnsequī
cōnsūmere
dēspicere
effugere
ēvolāre
excōgitāre
figere
imitārī
invenīre
iuvāre
levāre
mollīre
perficere
persequī
quatere
revocāre
suspicere
ūrere
vidērī
pronōmina
quisquam
coniunctiōnes
sīn
praepositiōnes
trans

adverbia
deorsum
haud
paene
quidem
quoniam
sūrsum
tamquam
vērum

XXVII. Rēs Rūsticae
nōmina
ager
agricola
arātrum
calor
colōnus
cōpia
cūra
falx
frīgus
frūgēs
frūmentum
grex
īnstrūmentum
labor
lāna
negōtium
ōtium
pābulum
patientia
pecus
praedium
precēs
regiō
rūs
sēmen
ūva
vīnea
vīnum
vītis
adiectīva
amoenus
fertilis
gravidus
immātūrus
inhūmānus
mātūrus
neglegēns
nēquam
patiēns
rudis
rūsticus
siccus
suburbānus
trīcēsimus

urbānus
verba
arāre
cēnsēre
cingere
colere
crēscere
exīstimāre
invehere
labōrāre
metere
neglegere
nocēre
ōrāre
pāscere
prōdesse
prohibēre
prōicere
quiēscere
rapere
rigāre
serere
spargere
ūtī
pronōmina
quīdam
praepositiōnēs
abs
circā
prae
prō
coniunctiōnēs
nē
-ve
adverbia
dēnique
parum
tantum

XXVIII. Pericula Maris
nōmina
animus
dictum
fāma
fretum
libellus
mundus
nāvicula
pecūlium
perīculum
phantasma
potestās
praedō
prīnceps
tībīcen
tranquillitās

turba
vigilia
vorāgō
adiectīva
attentus
caecus
claudus
cōnstāns
immortālis
mortālis
mūtus
perīculōsus
quadrāgēsimus
salvus
surdus
tūtus
ūniversus
verba
admīrārī
adōrāre
apprehendere
cessāre
disiungere
ēicere
ēvolvere
extendere
habērī
impendēre
mālle
memorāre
morī
nāscī
oboedīre
perīre
persuādēre
pervenīre
rēgnāre
rogāre
salvāre
servīre
spērāre
suscitāre
tumultuārī
versārī
vītāre
coniunctiōnēs
velut
adverbia
potius
utrum

XXIX. Nāvigāre Necesse Est
nōmina
beneficium

cantus
carmen
delphīnus
dīvitiae
dorsum
fēlīcitās
fidēs
fidicen
fortūna
fundus
fūr
fūrtum
iactūra
invidia
laetitia
lucrum
maleficium
nāvigātiō
piscātor
rēmus
salūs
spēs
trīstitia
tyrannus
vīta
adiectīva
celsus
fallāx
fēlīx
ignārus
ignōtus
maestus
mīrus
nōbilis
nōtus
pretiōsus
rapidus
vēlōx
verba
abicere
abstinēre
adicere
aestimāre
afficere
allicere
āmittere
appārēre
appropinquāre
cōnfitērī
dēsilīre
dēspērāre
dēterrēre
dētrahere
dōnāre
ēripere

expōnere
fīnīre
invidēre
parcere
permittere
permovēre
perturbāre
precārī
querī
recognōscere
redūcere
remanēre
secāre
stupēre
suādēre
subīre
surripere
pronōmina
nōnnūllī
sēsē
adverbia
frūstrā
inde
nōnnumquam
prōtinus
quasi
repente

XXX. Convīvium
nōmina
argentum
balneum
bonum
calida
carō
cēna
cocus
convīva
convīvium
culīna
famēs
genus
holus
hospes
iter
lībertīnus
medium
mel
merum
minister
nux
sāl
sitis
triclīnium
vās

adiectīva
acerbus
acūtus
argenteus
bīnī
dīligēns
dulcis
glōriōsus
īmus
inexspectātus
iūcundus
merus
molestus
singulī
tardus
ternī
verba
accubāre
accumbere
apportāre
aspergere
cēnāre
complēre
contrahere
coquere
ēligere
exhaurīre
exōrnāre
fruī
fundere
gustāre
līberāre
miscēre
nūntiāre
parāre
perferre
placēre
pōtāre
praeesse
prōferre
recipere
requiēscere
salvēre iubēre
sternere
vīsere
praepositiōnēs
circiter
adverbia
dēmum
diū
equidem
paulisper
prīdem
sānē

XXXI. Inter Pōcula
nōmina
crux
fidēs
iniūria
iūs
iuvenis
lēx
memoria
mōs
mūnus
nūgae
parricīda
poena
pōtiō
praemium
rūmor
scelus
senex
supplicium
adiectīva
asinīnus
avārus
clēmēns
crūdēlis
dēbilis
ēbrius
fīdus
fugitīvus
impatiēns
īnfēlix
īnfidus
iniūstus
invalidus
iūstus
nōnāgēsimus
praesēns
sapiēns
scelestus
vetus
verba
abdūcere
auferre
aufugere
cōnfīdere
cruciāre
ēducāre
fābulārī
fīdere
ignōscere
interpellāre
latēre
ōdisse
optāre
retrahere

statuere
vetāre
pronōmina
quidquid
quisquis
praepositiōnēs
cōram
super
adverbia
aliquantum
funditus
ideō
namque
nimium/nimis
priusquam
quamobrem
quantum

XXXII. Classis Rōmāna
nōmina
amīcitia
amphitheātrum
audācia
classis
condiciō
cursus
gēns
grātia
incola
inopia
pīrāta
poēta
populus
servitūs
talentum
victor
victōria
vīrēs
vīs
voluntās
adiectīva
adversus
cārus
commūnis
cūnctus
ēgregius
grātus
inermis
īnfēstus
internus
mercātōrius
mūtuus
nūbilus
proximus
superbus

vīlis
verba
adiuvāre
armāre
contemnere
dēsistere
dissuādēre
ēdūcere
flectere
meminisse
minārī
offerre
percurrere
praeferre
praepōnere
redimere
referre
rēmigāre
reminīscī
repugnāre
submergere
tuērī
coniunctiōnēs
neu
seu
adverbia
aliquandō
aliquot
dōnec
etiamnunc
intereā
ubīque
utinam

XXXIII. Exercitus Rōmānus
nōmina
aciēs
aetās
agmen
amnis
caedēs
cohors
ēnsis
gaudium
imperātor
lēgātus
legiō
legiōnārius
ōrdō
pāx
proelium
ratis
rīpa
stipendium

studium
valētūdō
virtūs
vulnus
adiectīva
arduus
citerior
dēnī
dīrus
horrendus
idōneus
incolumis
mīlitāris
ōtiōsus
posterus
prīvātus
pūblicus
quaternī
quīnī
rīdiculus
sēnī
trīnī
ulterior
ūnī
verba
adiungere
caedere
circumdare
cōgere
commemorāre
convocāre
cōpulāre
dēsīderāre
effundere
ērumpere
excurrere
fatīgāre
fore
hortārī
īnstruere
mūnīre
praestāre
prōcurrere
prōgredī
properāre
studēre
trānsferre
trānsīre
vulnerāre
pronōmina
plērīque
praepositiōnēs
citrā
secundum
ultrā

adverbia
diūtius
etenim
ferē
praecipuē
prīdiē
quamdiū
tamdiū
ultrā

XXXIV. De Arte Poëticā
nōmina
anus
arānea
aurīga
bāsium
cachinnus
certāmen
circus
cōmoedia
dēliciae
fātum
gladiātor
gremium
ingenium
lucerna
lūdus
mēns
nīl
nota
ocellus
odium
opera
opēs
palma
passer
prīncipium
ratiō
rēte
rīsus
scalpellum
sinus
spectātor
tenebrae
testis
theātrum
verba grammatica
dactylus
dipthongus
epigramma
hendecasyllabus
hexameter
iambus
pentameter
spondēus
trochaeus

versiculus
adiectīva
ācer
bellus
circēnsis
dubius
geminus
gladiātōrius
iocōsus
mellītus
misellus
niveus
perpetuus
poēticus
scaenicus
sērius
tenebricōsus
turgidus
ultimus
venustus
verba
accendere
affirmāre
certāre
circumsilīre
conturbāre
dēvorāre
ēlīdere
ērubēscere
excruciāre
favēre
implicāre
laedere
libenter
libēre
lūgēre
nūbere
ōscitāre
pīpiāre
plaudere
prōsilīre
requīrere
sapere
adverbia
dein
interdum
plērumque
coniunctiō
dummodo

XXXV. Ars Grammatica
nōmina
admīrātiō
affectus
īra
mūsa

ōrātiō
sacerdōs
scamnum
verba grammatica
appellātīvum (nōmen)
cāsus
causālis (coniūnctiō)
comparātiō
coniugātiō
coniūnctiō
cōpulātīvus (coniūnctiō)
disiūnctīvus (coniūnctiō)
explētīvus (coniūnctiō)
īnflectere
interiectiō
optātīvus (modus)
positīvus (gradus)

proprium (nōmen)
quālitās
quantitās
ratiōnālis (coniūnctiō)
significātiō
speciēs
synōnymum
adiectīva
inconditus
similis
verba
adnectere
dēmere
explānāre
luctārī
mentiōnem facere
ōrdināre

adverbia
dumtaxat
forsitan
proptereā
quāpropter
quidnī
sīquidem
tantundem
praepositiōnēs
adversum
cis
interiectiōnēs
attat
eia
ēn
euax
papae

Latin–English Vocabulary

A

ā/ab/abs *prp* +*abl* from, of, since, by

ab-dūcere take away, carry off

ab-errāre wander away, stray

ab-esse ā-fuisse be absent/ away/distant

ab-icere throw away

ab-īre -eō -iisse go away

abs *v.* ā/ab/abs

absēns -entis *adi* absent

abs-tinēre keep off

ac *v.* atque/ac

ac-cēdere approach, come near

accendere -disse -ēnsum light, inflame

ac-cidere -disse happen, occur

ac-cipere receive

ac-cubāre recline at table

ac-cumbere -cubuisse lie down at table

ac-currere -rrisse come running

accūsāre accuse

ācer -cris -cre keen, active, fierce

acerbus -a -um sour, bitter

aciēs -ēī *f* line of battle

acūtus -a -um sharp

ad *prp* +*acc* to, toward, by, at, till

ad-dere -didisse -ditum add

ad-esse af-fuisse (+*dat*) be present, stand by

ad-hūc so far, till now, still

ad-icere add

ad-īre -eō -iisse -itum go to, approach

ad-iungere join to, add

ad-iuvāre help

ad-mīrārī admire, wonder at

admīrātiō -ōnis *f* wonder, admiration

ad-mittere let in, admit

ad-nectere -xuisse -xum attach, connect

ad-ōrāre worship, adore

adulēscēns -entis *m* young man

ad-vehere carry, convey (to)

ad-venīre arrive

adversus/-um *prp* +*acc* toward, against

adversus -a -um contrary, unfavorable

aedificāre build

aedificium -ī *n* building

aeger -gra -grum sick, ill

aegrōtāre be ill

aegrōtus -a -um sick

aequē equally

aequinoctium -ī *n* equinox

aequus -a -um equal, calm

āēr -eris *m* air

aestās -ātis *f* summer

aestimāre value, estimate

aetās -ātis *f* age

affectus -ūs *m* mood, feeling

af-ferre at-tulisse al-lātum bring (to, forward, about)

af-ficere affect, stir

af-firmāre assert, affirm

age -ite +*imp* come on! well, now

ager -grī *m* field

agere ēgisse āctum drive, do, perform

agmen -inis *n* army on the march, file

agnus -ī *m* lamb

agricola -ae *m* farmer, peasant

ain' you don't say? really?

āiō ais ait āiunt say

āla -ae *f* wing

albus -a -um white

alere -uisse altum feed

aliēnus -a -um someone else's

ali-quandō sometimes

ali-quantum a good deal

ali-quī -qua -quod some

ali-quis -quid someone, something

ali-quot *indēcl* some, several

aliter otherwise

alius -a -ud another, other

aliī…aliī some…others

allicere -iō -ēxisse -ectum attract

alter -era -erum one, the other, second

altum -ī *n* the open sea

altus -a -um high, tall, deep

amāns -antis *m* lover

amāre love

ambulāre walk

amīca -ae *f* girlfriend

amīcitia -ae *f* friendship

amīcus -ī *m* friend

amīcus -a -um friendly

ā-mittere lose

amnis -is *m* river

amoenus -a -um lovely, pleasant

amor -ōris *m* love

amphitheātrum -ī *n* amphitheater

an or

ancilla -ae *f* female slave, servant

angustus -a -um narrow

anima -ae *f* breath, life, soul
anim-ad-vertere notice
animal -ālis *n* animal, living
   being
animus -ī *m* mind, soul
annus -ī *m* year
ante *prp +acc, adv* in front
   of, before
anteā before, formerly
ante-hāc formerly
ante-quam before
antīquus -a -um old,
   ancient, former
ānulus -ī *m* ring
anus -ūs *f* old woman
aperīre -uisse -rtum open,
   disclose
apertus -a -um open
apis -is *f* bee
ap-pārēre appear
appellāre call, address
ap-pōnere place (on), serve
ap-portāre bring
ap-prehendere seize
ap-propinquāre
   (*+dat*) approach, come
   near
Aprīlis -is (mēnsis) April
apud *prp +acc* beside, near,
   by
aqua -ae *f* water
aquila -ae *f* eagle
arānea -ae *f* spider, cobweb
arāre plow
arātor -ōris *m* plowman
arātrum -ī *n* plow
arbitrārī think, believe
arbor -oris *f* tree
arcessere -īvisse -ītum send
   for, fetch
arcus -ūs *m* bow
arduus -a -um steep
argenteus -a -um silver, of
   silver
argentum -ī *n* silver
arma -ōrum *n pl* arms
armāre arm, equip
armātus -a -um armed
ars artis *f* art, skill
as assis *m* as (copper coin)
a-scendere -disse climb, go
   up, mount
asinīnus -a -um ass's
asinus -ī *m* ass, donkey

a-spergere -sisse -sum
   sprinkle, scatter (on)
a-spicere look at, look
   at but
āter -tra -trum black, dark
atque/ac and, as, than
ātrium -ī *n* main room, hall
attentus -a -um attentive
audācia -ae *f* boldness,
   audacity
audāx -ācis *adi* bold,
   audacious
audēre ausum esse dare,
   venture
audīre hear, listen
au-ferre abs-tulisse
   ablātum carry off, take
   away
au-fugere run away, escape
augēre -xisse -ctum
   increase
Augustus -ī
   (mēnsis) August
aureus -a -um gold-, *m* gold
   piece
aurīga -ae *m* charioteer,
   driver
auris -is *f* ear
aurum -ī *n* gold
aut or
aut…aut either…or
autem but, however
autumnus -ī *m* autumn
auxilium -ī *n* help,
   assistance
auxilia -ōrum *n pl* auxiliary
   forces
avārus -a -um greedy,
   avaricious
ā-vertere turn aside, avert
avis -is *f* bird
avunculus -ī *m* (maternal)
   uncle

B

baculum -ī *n* stick
bālāre bleat
balneum -ī *n* bath,
   bathroom
barbarus -a -um foreign,
   barbarian
bāsium -ī *n* kiss
beātus -a -um happy
bellum -ī *n* war
bellus -a -um lovely, pretty

bene well
beneficium -ī *n* benefit,
   favor
bēstia -ae *f* beast, animal
bēstiola -ae *f* small animal,
   insect
bibere -bisse drink
bīnī -ae -a two (each)
bis twice
bonum -ī *n* good, blessing
bonus -a -um good
bōs bovis *m/f* ox
bracchium -ī *n* arm
brevī *adv* soon
brevis -e short

C

cachinnus -ī *m* laugh,
   guffaw
cadere cecidisse fall
caecus -a -um blind
caedere cecīdisse
   caesum beat, fell, kill
caedēs -is *f* killing,
   slaughter
caelum -ī *n* sky, heaven
calamus -ī *m* reed, pen
calceus -ī *m* shoe
calidus -a -um warm, hot, *f*
   hot water
calor -ōris *m* warmth, heat
campus -ī *m* plain
candidus -a -um white,
   bright
canere cecinisse sing (of),
   crow, play
canis -is *m/f* dog
cantāre sing
cantus -ūs *m* singing, music
capere -iō cēpisse
   captum take, catch,
   capture
capillus -ī *m* hair
capitulum -ī *n* chapter
caput -itis *n* head, chief,
   capital
carcer -eris *m* prison
cardō -inis *m* door pivot,
   hinge
carēre *+abl* be without, lack
carmen -inis *n* song, poem
carō carnis *f* flesh, meat
carpere -psisse-
   ptum gather, pick, crop
cārus -a -um dear

castra -ōrum *n pl* camp
cāsus -ūs *m* fall, case
catēna -ae *f* chain
cauda -ae *f* tail
causa -ae *f* cause, reason
gen (/meā) +causā for the sake of
cautus -a -um cautious
cavēre cāvisse cautum beware (of)
cēdere cessisse go, withdraw
celer -eris -ere swift, quick
celsus -a -um tall
cēna -ae *f* dinner
cēnāre dine, have dinner
cēnsēre -uisse -sum think
centēsimus -a -um hundredth
centum a hundred
cēra -ae *f* wax
cerebrum -ī *n* brain
cernere crēvisse discern, perceive
certāmen -inis *n* contest, fight
certāre contend, fight
certē certainly, at any rate
certō *adv* for certain
certus -a -um certain, sure
cessāre leave off, cease
cēterī -ae -a the other(s), the rest
cēterum *adv* besides, however
cēterus -a -um remaining
charta -ae *f* paper
cibus -ī *m* food
cingere cīnxisse cīnctum surround
-cipere -iō -cēpisse -ceptum
circā *prp* +acc round
circēnsēs -ium *m pl* games in the circus
circēnsis -e of the circus
circiter about
circum *prp* +acc round
circum-dare surround
circum-silīre hop about
circus -ī *m* circle, orbit, circus
cis *prp* +acc on this side of
citerior -ius *comp* nearer
citrā *prp* +acc on this side of
cīvis -is *m/f* citizen, countryman

clāmāre shout
clāmor -ōris *m* shout, shouting
clārus -a -um bright, clear, loud
classis -is *f* fleet
claudere -sisse -sum shut, close
claudus -a -um lame
clausus -a -um closed, shut
clāvis -is *f* key
clēmēns -entis *adi* mild, lenient
cocus -ī *m* cook
coep- *v.* incipere
cōgere co-ēgisse -āctum compel, force
cōgitāre think
cognōmen -inis *n* surname
cognōscere -ōvisse -itum get to know, recognize
cohors -rtis *f* cohort
colere -uisse cultum cultivate
collis -is *m* hill
col-loquī talk, converse
colloquium -ī *n* conversation
collum -ī *n* neck
colōnus -ī *m* (tenant-) farmer
color -ōris *m* color
columna -ae *f* column
comes -itis *m* companion
comitārī accompany
com-memorāre mention
commūnis -e common
cōmoedia -ae *f* comedy
com-parāre compare
com-plectī -exum embrace
com-plēre -ēvisse -ētum fill, complete
com-plūrēs -a several
com-putāre calculate, reckon
cōnārī attempt, try
condiciō -ōnis *f* condition
cōn-ficere make, accomplish
cōn-fīdere +dat trust
cōn-fitērī -fessum confess
con-iungere join, connect
coniūnx -iugis *m/f* consort, wife

cōn-scendere -disse mount, board
cōn-sequī follow, overtake
cōn-sīdere -sēdisse sit down
cōnsilium -ī *n* advice, decision, intention, plan
cōn-sistere -stitisse stop, halt
cōn-sōlārī comfort, console
cōnsonāns -antis *f* consonant
cōnspectus -ūs *m* sight, view
cōn-spicere catch sight of, see
cōnstāns -antis *adi* steady, firm
cōn-stāre -stitisse be fixed, cost
cōnstāre ex consist of
cōn-stituere -uisse -ūtum fix, decide
cōn-sūmere spend, consume
con-temnere -mpsisse -mptum despise, scorn
con-tinēre -uisse -tentum contain
continuō *adv* immediately
contrā *prp* +acc against
con-trahere draw together, wrinkle
contrārius -a -um opposite, contrary
con-turbāre mix up, confound
con-venīre come together, meet
convenīre (ad/+dat) fit, be fitting
con-vertere turn
convīva -ae *m/f* guest
convīvium -ī *n* dinner-party
con-vocāre call together
cōpia -ae *f* abundance, lot
cōpulāre join, connect
coquere -xisse -ctum cook
cor cordis *n* heart
cōram *prp* +abl in the presence of
cornū -ūs *n* horn
corpus -oris *n* body

cor-rigere -rēxisse -rēctum correct
cotīdiē every day
crās tomorrow
crassus -a -um thick, fat
crēdere -didisse +*dat* believe, trust, entrust
crēscere -ēvisse grow
cruciāre torture, torment
crūdēlis -e cruel
cruentus -a -um blood-stained, bloody
cruor -ōris *m* blood-stained, bloody
crūs -ūris *n* leg
crux -ucis *f* cross
cubāre -uisse -itum lie (in bed)
cubiculum -ī *n* bedroom
culīna -ae *f* kitchen
culter -trī *m* knife
cum *prp* +*abl* with
cum *coniūnctiō* when, as
cum prīmum +*perf* as soon as
cūnae -ārum *f pl* cradle
cūnctus -a -um whole, *pl* all
cupere -iō -īvisse desire
cupiditās -ātis *f* desire
cupidus -a -um (+*gen*) desirous (of), eager (for)
cūr why
cūra -ae *f* care, anxiety
cūrāre care for, look after, take care
currere cucurrisse run
currus -ūs *m* chariot
cursus -ūs *m* race, journey, course
cūstōdīre guard

D
dare dedisse datum give
dē *prp* +*abl* (down) from, of, about
dea -ae *f* goddess
dēbēre owe, be obliged
dēbilis -e weak
decem ten
December -bris (mēnsis) December
decēre be fitting, become
deciēs ten times

decimus -a -um tenth
dēclīnāre decline, inflect
de-esse dē-fuisse (+*dat*) be missing, fail
dē-fendere -disse -ēnsum defend
de-inde/dein afterward, then
dēlectāre delight, please
dēlēre -ēvisse -ētum delete, efface
dēliciae -ārum *f pl* delight, pet
delphīnus -ī *m* dolphin
dēmere -mpsisse -mptum remove
dē-mōnstrāre point out, show
dēmum *adv* at last, only
dēnārius -ī *m* denarius (silver coin)
dēnī -ae -a ten (each)
dēnique finally, at last
dēns dentis *m* tooth
dē-nuō anew, again
deorsum *adv* down
dē-rīdēre laugh at, make fun of
dē-scendere -disse go down, descend
dē-serere -uisse -rtum leave, desert
dēsīderāre long for, miss
dē-silīre -uisse jump down
dē-sinere -siisse finish, stop, end
dē-sistere -stitisse leave off, cease
dē-spērāre lose hope, despair (of)
dē-spicere look down (on), despise
dē-tergēre wipe off
dē-terrēre deter
dē-trahere pull off
deus -ī *m*, *pl* deī/diī/dī god
dē-vorāre swallow up, devour
dexter -tra -trum right, *f* the right (hand)
dīcere -xisse dictum say, call, speak
dictāre dictate
dictum -ī *n* saying, words
diēs -ēī *m* (*f*) day, date

dif-ficilis -e, *sup* -illimus difficult, hard
digitus -ī *m* finger
dignus -a -um worthy
dīligēns -entis *adi* careful, diligent
dīligere -ēxisse -ēctum love, be fond of
dīmidius -a -um half
dī-mittere send away, dismiss
dīrus -a -um dreadful
dis-cēdere go away, depart
discere didicisse learn
discipulus -ī *m* pupil, disciple
dis-iungere separate
dis-suādēre advise not to
diū, *comp* diūtius long
dīves -itis *adi* rich, wealthy
dīvidere -īsisse -īsum separate, divide
dīvitiae -ārum *f pl* riches
docēre -uisse doctum teach, instruct
doctus -a -um learned, skilled
dolēre hurt, feel pain, grieve
dolor -ōris *m* pain, grief
domī *loc* at home
domina -ae *f* mistress
dominus -ī *m* master
domum *adv* home
domus -ūs *f*, *abl* -ō house, home
dōnāre give, present with
dōnec as long as
dōnum -ī *n* gift, present
dormīre sleep
dorsum -ī *n* back
dubitāre doubt
dubius -a -um undecided, doubtful
du-centī -ae -a two hundred
dūcere -xisse ductum guide, lead, draw, trace
uxōrem dūcere marry
dulcis -e sweet
dum while, as long as, till
dum-modo provided that, if only
dumtaxat only, just
duo -ae -o two

duo-decim twelve
duo-decimus -a -um twelfth
duo-dē-trīgintā twenty-eight
duo-dē-vīgintī eighteen
dūrus -a -um hard
dux ducis *m* leader, chief, general

E
ē *v.* ex/ē
ēbrius -a -um drunk
ecce see, look, here is
ēducāre bring up
ē-dūcere bring out, draw out
ef-ficere make, effect, cause
ef-fugere escape, run away
ef-fundere pour out, shed
ego mē mihi/mī I, me, myself
ē-gredī -ior -gressum go out
ēgregius -a -um outstanding, excellent
ē-icere throw out
ē-līdere -sisse -sum omit, elide
ē-ligere -lēgisse -lēctum choose, select
emere ēmisse ēmptum buy
ēn look, here is
enim for
ēnsis -is *m* sword
eō *adv* to that place, there
epigramma -atis *n* epigram
epistula -ae *f* letter
eques -itis *m* horseman
equidem indeed, for my part
equitātus -ūs *m* cavalry
equus -ī *m* horse
ergā *prp +acc* toward
ergō therefore, so
ē-ripere -iō -uisse -reptum snatch away, deprive of
errāre wander, stray
ē-rubēscere -buisse blush
ē-rumpere break out
erus -ī *m* master

esse sum fuisse futūrum esse/fore be
ēsse edō ēdisse ēsum eat
et and, also
et...et both...and
et-enim and indeed, for
etiam also, even, yet
etiam atque etiam again and again
etiam-nunc still
et-sī even if, although
ē-volāre fly out
ē-volvere -visse -lūtum unroll
ex/ē *prp +abl* out of, from, of, since
ex-audīre hear
ex-citāre wake up, arouse
ex-clāmāre cry out, exclaim
ex-cōgitāre think out, devise
ex-cruciāre torture, torment
ex-currere -rrisse -rsum run out, rush out
ex-cūsāre excuse
exemplum -ī *n* example, model
exercitus -ūs *m* army
ex-haurīre drain, empty
exiguus -a -um small, scanty
ex-īre -eō -iisse -itum go out
ex-īstimāre consider, think
exitus -ūs *m* exit, way out, end
ex-ōrnāre adorn, decorate
ex-plānāre explain
ex-pōnere put out/ashore, expose
ex-pugnāre conquer
ex-pugnātiō -ōnis *f* conquest
ex-spectāre wait (for), expect
ex-tendere -disse -tum stretch out, extend
extrā *prp +acc* outside

F
faber -brī *m* artisan, smith
fābula -ae *f* story, fable, play
fābulārī talk, chat

facere -iō fēcisse factum make, do, cause
faciēs -ēī *f* face
facile *adv* easily
facilis -e, *sup* -illimus easy
factum -ī *n* deed, act
fallāx -ācis *adi* deceitful
fallere fefellisse falsum deceive
falsus -a -um false
falx -cis *f* sickle
fāma -ae *f* rumor, reputation
famēs -is *f* hunger, famine
familia -ae *f* domestic staff, family
fārī speak
fatērī fassum admit, confess
fatīgāre tire out, weary
fātum -ī *n* fate, destiny, death
favēre fāvisse +*dat* favor, support
Februārius -ī (mēnsis) February
fēlīcitās -ātis *f* good fortune, luck
fēlīx -īcis *adi* fortunate, lucky
fēmina -ae *f* woman
fenestra -ae *f* window
fera -ae *f* wild animal
ferē about, almost
ferōx -ōcis *adi* fierce, ferocious
ferre tulisse lātum carry, bring, bear
ferreus -a -um of iron, iron
ferrum -ī *n* iron, steel
fertilis -e fertile
ferus -a -um wild
fessus -a -um tired, weary
-ficere -iō -fēcisse -fectum
fīdere fīsum esse +*dat* trust, rely on
fidēs -eī *f* trust, faith, loyalty
fidēs -ium *f pl* lyre
fidicen -inis *m* lyre-player
fīdus -a -um faithful, reliable
fierī factum esse be made, be done, become, happen

fīgere -xisse -xum fix,
    fasten
fīlia -ae *f* daughter
fīliola -ae *f* little daughter
fīliolus -ī *m* little son
fīlius -ī *m* son
fīlum -ī *n* thread
fīnīre limit, finish
fīnis -is *m* boundary, limit,
    end
flāre blow
flectere -xisse -xum bend,
    turn
flēre -ēvisse cry, weep (for)
flōs -ōris *m* flower
flūctus -ūs *m* wave
fluere -ūxisse flow
flūmen -inis *n* river
fluvius -ī *m* river
foedus -a -um ugly, hideous
folium -ī *n* leaf
forās *adv* out
foris -is *f* leaf of a door,
    door
forīs *adv* outside, out of
    doors
fōrma -ae *f* form, shape,
    figure
fōrmōsus -a -um beautiful
forsitan perhaps, maybe
fortasse perhaps, maybe
forte *adv* by chance
fortis -e strong, brave
fortūna -ae *f* fortune
forum -ī *n* square
fossa -ae *f* ditch, trench
frangere frēgisse
    frāctum break, shatter
frāter -tris *m* brother
fremere -uisse growl
frequēns -entis
    adi numerous, frequent
fretum -ī *n* strait
frīgēre be cold
frīgidus -a -um cold, chilly,
    cool
frīgus -oris *n* cold
frōns -ontis *f* forehead
frūgēs -um *f pl* fruit, crops
fruī +*abl* enjoy
frūmentum -ī *n* corn, grain
frūstrā in vain
fuga -ae *f* flight
fugere -iō fūgisse run away,
    flee

fugitīvus -a -um runaway
fulgur -uris *n* flash of
    lightning
fundere fūdisse
    fūsum pour, shed
funditus *adv* to the bottom,
    utterly
fundus -ī *m* bottom
fūr -is *m* thief
fūrtum -ī *n* theft
futūrus -a -um (*v.* esse)
    future
tempus futūrum future

G
gallus -ī *m* cock, rooster
gaudēre gavīsum esse be
    glad, be pleased
gaudium -ī *n* joy, delight
geminus -a -um twin
gemma -ae *f* precious stone,
    jewel
gemmātus -a -um set with
    a jewel
gena -ae *f* cheek
gēns gentis *f* nation, people
genū -ūs *n* knee
genus -eris *n* kind, sort
gerere gessisse
    gestum carry, wear, carry
    on, do
glaciēs -ēī *f* ice
gladiātor -ōris *m* gladiator
gladiātōrius -a -um
    gladiatorial
gladius -ī *m* sword
glōria -ae *f* glory
glōriōsus -a -um glorious,
    boastful
gracilis -e slender
gradus -ūs *m* step, degree
Graecus -a -um Greek
grammatica -ae *f* grammar
grātia -ae *f* favor, gratitude
gen (/meā) + grātiā for the
    sake of
grātiam habēre be grateful
grātiās agere thank
grātus -a -um pleasing,
    grateful
gravida *adi f* pregnant
gravis -e heavy, severe,
    grave
gremium -ī *n* lap

grex -egis *m* flock, herd,
    band
gubernāre steer, govern
gubernātor -ōris
    m steersman
gustāre taste

H
habēre have, hold, consider
habitāre dwell, live
hasta -ae *f* lance
haud not
haurīre -sisse -stum draw
    (water), bail
herba -ae *f* grass, herb
herī yesterday
heu o! alas!
heus hey! hello!
hic haec hoc this
hīc here
hiems -mis *f* winter
hinc from here, hence
hodiē today
holus -eris *n* vegetable
homō -inis *m* human being,
    person
hōra -ae *f* hour
horrendus -a -um dreadful
horrēre bristle, stand on
    end, shudder (at)
hortārī encourage, urge
hortus -ī *m* garden
hospes -itis *m* guest, guest-
    friend
hostis -is *m* enemy
hūc here, to this place
hūmānus -a -um human
humī *loc* on the ground
humilis -e low
humus -ī *f* ground

I
iacere -iō iēcisse
    iactum throw, hurl
iacēre lie
iactāre throw, toss about
iactūra -ae *f* throwing away,
    loss
iam now, already
iānitor -ōris *m* doorkeeper
iānua -ae *f* door
Iānuārius -ī
    (mēnsis) January
ibi there
-icere -iō -iēcisse -iectum

īdem eadem idem the same
id-eō for that reason
idōneus -a -um fit, suitable
īdūs -uum *f pl* 13th/15th (of the month)
iecur -oris *n* liver
igitur therefore, then, so
ignārus -a -um ignorant, unaware
ignis -is *m* fire
ignōrāre not know
ignōscere -ōvisse +*dat* forgive
ignōtus -a -um unknown
ille -a -ud that, the one, he
illīc there
illinc from there
illūc there, thither
illūstrāre illuminate, make clear
imāgō -inis *f* picture
imber -bris *m* rain, shower
imitārī imitate
im-mātūrus -a -um unripe
immō no, on the contrary
im-mortālis -e immortal
im-pār -aris *adi* unequal
im-patiēns -entis *adi* impatient
im-pendēre +*dat* threaten
imperāre +*dat* command, order, rule
imperātor -ōris *m* (commanding) general
imperium -ī *n* command, empire
impetus -ūs *m* attack, charge
im-piger -gra -grum active, industrious
im-plēre -ēvisse -ētum fill, complete
im-plicāre -uisse -itum enfold
impluvium -ī *n* water basin
im-pōnere place (in/on), put
im-primere -pressisse -pressum press (into)
im-probus -a -um bad, wicked
īmus -a -um *sup* lowest
in *prp* +*abl* in, on, at
prp +*acc* into, to, against
in-certus -a -um uncertain

in-cipere -iō coepisse coeptum begin
in-clūdere -sisse -sum shut up
incola -ae *m/f* inhabitant
in-colere inhabit
incolumis -e unharmed, safe
inconditus -a -um unpolished, rough
inde from there, thence
index -icis *m* list, catalogue
in-dignus -a -um unworthy, shameful
in-doctus -a -um ignorant
induere -uisse -ūtum put on (clothes)
indūtus +*abl* dressed in
industrius -a -um industrious
in-ermis -e unarmed
in-esse be (in)
in-exspectātus -a -um unexpected
īnfāns -antis *m/f* little child, baby
īn-fēlīx -īcis *adi* unlucky, unfortunate
īnferior -ius *comp* lower, inferior
īnferus -a -um lower
Īnferī -ōrum *m pl* the underworld
īnfēstus -a -um unsafe, infested
īn-fīdus -a -um faithless
īnfimus -a -um *sup* lowest
īn-fluere flow into
īnfrā *prp* +*acc* below
ingenium -ī *n* nature, character
ingēns -entis *adi* huge, vast
in-hūmānus -a -um inhuman
in-imīcus -ī *m* (personal) enemy
in-inimīcus -a -um unfriendly
initium -ī *n* beginning
iniūria -ae *f* injustice, wrong
in-iūstus -a -um unjust, unfair
inopia -ae *f* lack, scarcity

inquit -iunt (he/she) says/ said
inquam I say
īn-scrībere write on, inscribe
īnscrīptiō -ōnis *f* inscription
īn-struere -ūxisse -ūctum draw up, arrange
īnstrūmentum -ī *n* tool, instrument
īnsula -ae *f* island
integer -gra -grum undamaged, intact
intellegere -ēxisse -ēctum understand, realize
inter *prp* +*acc* between, among, during
inter sē (with) one another
inter-dum now and then
inter-eā meanwhile
inter-esse be between
inter-ficere kill
interim meanwhile
internus -a -um inner, internal
inter-pellāre interrupt
inter-rogāre ask, question
intrā *prp* +*acc* inside, within
intrāre enter
intuērī look at, watch
intus *adv* inside
in-validus -a -um infirm, weak
in-vehere import
in-venīre find
in-vidēre +*dat* envy, grudge
invidia -ae *f* envy
in-vocāre call upon, invoke
iocōsus -a -um humorous, funny
ipse -a -um himself
īra -ae *f* anger
īrātus -a -um angry
īre eō iisse itum go
is ea id he, she, it, that
iste -a -ud this, that (of yours)
ita so, in such a way
ita-que therefore
item likewise, also
iter itineris *n* journey, march, way
iterum again, a second time

iubēre iussisse
    iussum order, tell
iūcundus -a -um pleasant,
    delightful
Iūlius -ī (mēnsis) July
iungere iūnxisse
    iūnctum join, combine
Iūnius -ī (mēnsis) June
iūs iūris *n* right, justice
iūre justly, rightly
iūstus -a -um just, fair
iuvāre iūvisse iūtum help,
    delight
iuvenis -is *m* young man
iūxtā *prp +acc* next to, beside

K
kalendae -ārum *f pl* the 1st
    (of the month)
kalendārium -ī *n* calendar

L
lābī lāpsum slip, drop, fall
labor -ōris *m* work, toil
labōrāre toil, work, take
    trouble
labrum -ī *n* lip
labyrinthus -ī *m* labyrinth
lac lactis *n* milk
lacertus -ī *m* (upper) arm
lacrima -ae *f* tear
lacrimāre shed tears, weep
lacus -ūs *m* lake
laedere -sisse -sum injure,
    hurt
laetārī rejoice, be glad
laetitia -ae *f* joy
laetus -a -um glad, happy
laevus -a -um left
lāna -ae *f* wool
largīrī give generously
largus -a -um generous
latēre be hidden, hide
Latīnus -a -um Latin
lātrāre bark
latus -eris *n* side, flank
lātus -a -um broad, wide
laudāre praise
laus laudis *f* praise
lavāre lāvisse lautum wash,
    bathe
lectīca -ae *f* litter, sedan
lectulus -ī *m* (little) bed
lectus -ī *m* bed, couch
lēgātus -ī *m* envoy, delegate

legere lēgisse lēctum read
legiō -ōnis *f* legion
legiōnārius -a -um
    legionary
leō -ōnis *m* lion
levāre lift, raise
levis -e light, slight
lēx lēgis *f* law
libellus -ī *m* little book
libenter with pleasure,
    gladly
liber -brī *m* book
līber -era -erum free
līberāre free, set free
libēre: libet +*dat* it pleases
līberī -ōrum *m pl* children
lībertās -ātis *f* freedom,
    liberty
lībertīnus -ī *m* freedman
licēre: licet +*dat* it is
    allowed, one may
ligneus -a -um wooden
lignum -ī *n* wood
līlium -ī *n* lily
līmen -inis *n* threshold
līnea -ae *f* string, line
lingua -ae *f* tongue,
    language
littera -ae *f* letter
lītus -oris *n* beach, shore
locus -ī *m* place
loca -ōrum *n pl* regions,
    parts
longē far, by far
longus -a -um long
loquī locūtum speak, talk
lūcēre lūxisse shine
lucerna -ae *f* lamp
lucrum -ī *n* profit, gain
luctārī wrestle
lūdere -sisse -sum play
lūdus -ī *m* play, game,
    school
lūgēre -xisse mourn
lūna -ae *f* moon
lupus -ī *m* wolf
lūx lūcis *f* light, daylight

M
maerēre grieve
maestus -a -um sad,
    sorrowful
magis more
magister -trī
    m schoolmaster, teacher

magnificus -a -um
    magnificent, splendid
magnus -a -um big, large,
    great
māior -ius *comp* bigger,
    older
Māius -ī (mēnsis) May
male *adv* badly, ill
maleficium -ī *n* evil deed,
    crime
mālle māluisse prefer
malum -ī *n* evil, trouble,
    harm
mālum -ī *n* apple
malus -a -um bad, wicked,
    evil
mamma -ae *f* mummy
māne *indēcl n*,
    adv morning, in the
    morning
manēre mānsisse remain,
    stay
manus -ūs *f* hand
mare -is *n* sea
margarīta -ae *f* pearl
maritimus -a -um sea,
    coastal
marītus -ī *m* husband
Mārtius -ī (mēnsis) March
māter -tris *f* mother
māteria -ae *f* material,
    substance
mātrōna -ae *f* married
    woman
mātūrus -a -um ripe
māximē most, especially
māximus -a -um biggest,
    greatest, oldest
medicus -ī *m* physician,
    doctor
medium -ī *n* middle, center
medius -a -um mid, middle
mel mellis *n* honey
melior -ius *comp* better
mellītus -a -um sweet
membrum -ī *n* limb
meminisse +*gen*/
    acc remember, recollect
memorāre mention
memoria -ae *f* memory
mendum -ī *n* mistake,
    error
mēns mentis *f* mind
mēnsa -ae *f* table
mēnsa secunda dessert

mēnsis -is *m* month
mentiō -ōnis *f* mention
mentīrī lie
mercātor -ōris *m* merchant
mercātōrius -a -um
  merchant-
mercēs -ēdis *f* wage, fee,
  rent
merēre earn, deserve
mergere -sisse -sum dip,
  plunge, sink
merīdiēs -ēī *m* midday,
  noon, south
merum -ī *n* neat wine
merus -a -um pure, neat,
  undiluted
merx -rcis *f* commodity, *pl*
  goods
metere reap, harvest
metuere -uisse fear
metus -ūs *m* fear
meus -a -um, *voc* mī my,
  mine
mīles -itis *m* soldier
mīlitāre serve as a soldier
mīlitāris -e military
mīlle, *pl* mīlia -ium
  n thousand
minārī +*dat* threaten
minimē by no means, not
  at all
minimus -a -um
  sup smallest, youngest
minister -trī *m* servant
minor -us *comp* smaller,
  younger
minuere -uisse -ūtum
  diminish, reduce
minus -ōris *n, adv* less
mīrābilis -e marvelous,
  wonderful
mīrārī wonder (at), be
  surprised
mīrus -a -um surprising,
  strange
miscēre -uisse mixtum mix
misellus -a -um poor,
  wretched
miser -era -erum unhappy,
  miserable
mittere mīsisse
  missum send, throw
modo only, just
modo…modo now…now
modus -ī *m* manner, way

nūllō modō by no means
moenia -ium *n pl* walls
molestus -a -um
  troublesome
mollīre make soft, soften
mollis -e soft
monēre remind, advise,
  warn
mōns montis *m* mountain
mōnstrāre point out, show
mōnstrum -ī *n* monster
mora -ae *f* delay
mordēre momordisse -sum
  bite
morī mortuum die
mors mortis *f* death
mortālis -e mortal
mortuus -a -um (< morī)
  dead
mōs mōris *m* custom, usage
movēre mōvisse
  mōtum move, stir
mox soon
mulier -eris *f* woman
multī -ae -a many, a great
  many
multitūdō -inis *f* large
  number, multitude
multō +*comp* much, by far
multum -ī *n, adv* much
mundus -ī *m* world,
  universe
mundus -a -um clean, neat
mūnīre fortify
mūnus -eris *n* gift
mūrus -ī *m* wall
Mūsa -ae *f* Muse
mūtāre change, exchange
mūtus -a -um dumb
mūtuus -a -um on loan
mūtuum dare/sūmere lend/
  borrow

N
nam for
-nam …ever?
namque for
nārrāre relate, tell
nārrātiō -ōnis *f* narrative
nāscī nātum be born
nāsus -ī *m* nose
natāre swim
nātūra -ae *f* nature
nātus -a -um (< nāscī)
  born

XX annōs nātus 20 years
  old
nauta -ae *m* sailor
nāvicula -ae *f* boat
nāvigāre sail
nāvigātiō -ōnis *f* sailing,
  voyage
nāvis -is *f* ship
-ne …? if, whether
nē that not, lest, that
nē…quidem not even
nec *v.* ne-que/nec
necāre kill
necessārius -a -um
  necessary
necesse est it is necessary
negāre deny, say that…not
neglegēns -entis
  adi careless
neglegere -ēxisse -ēctum
  neglect
negōtium -ī *n* business,
  activity
nēmō -inem -inī no one,
  nobody
nēquam *adi indēcl, sup*
  nēquissimus worthless,
  bad
ne-que/nec and/but not,
  nor, not
n…n. neither…nor
ne-scīre not know
neu *v.* nē-ve/neu
neuter -tra -trum neither
nē-ve/neu and (that) not,
  nor
nex necis *f* killing, murder
nīdus -ī *m* nest
niger -gra -grum black
nihil/nīl nothing
nimis too, too much
nimium too much
nimius -a -um too big
nisi if not, except, but
niveus -a -um snow-white
nix nivis *f* snow
nōbilis -e well known,
  famous
nocēre +*dat* harm, hurt
nōlī -īte +*īnf* don't…!
nōlle nōluisse be unwilling,
  not want
nōmen -inis *n* name
nōmināre name, call
nōn not

nōnae -ārum *f pl* 5th/7th (of the month)
nōnāgēsimus -a -um ninetieth
nōnāgintā ninety
nōn-dum not yet
nōn-gentī -ae -a nine hundred
nōn-ne not?
nōn-nūllī -ae -a some, several
nōn-numquam sometimes
nōnus -a -um ninth
nōs nōbīs we, us, ourselves
nōscere nōvisse get to know, *perf* know
noster -tra -trum our, ours
nostrum *gen* of us
nota -ae *f* mark, sign
nōtus -a -um known
novem nine
November -bris (mēnsis) November
nōvisse (< nōscere) know
novus -a -um new
nox noctis *f* night
nūbere -psisse +*dat* marry
nūbēs -is *f* cloud
nūbilus -a -um cloudy
nūdus -a -um naked
nūgae -ārum *f pl* idle talk, rubbish
nūllus -a -um no
num …? if, whether
numerāre count
numerus -ī *m* number
nummus -ī *m* coin, sesterce
numquam never
nunc now
nūntiāre announce, report
nūntius -ī *m* messenger, message
nūper recently
nūtrīx -īcis *f* nurse
nux nucis *f* nut

O
ō o!
ob *prp* +*acc* on account of
oblīvīscī -lītum +*gen*/ *acc* forget
ob-oedīre +*dat* obey
obscūrus -a -um dark
occidēns -entis *m* west

oc-cidere -disse fall, sink, set
oc-cīdere - disse -sum kill
occultāre hide
oc-currere -rrisse +*dat* meet
ōceanus -ī *m* ocean
ocellus -ī *m* (little) eye
octāvus -a -um eighth
octin-gentī -ae -a eight hundred
octō eight
Octōber -bris (mēnsis) October
octōgintā eighty
oculus -ī *m* eye
ōdisse hate
odium -ī *n* hatred
of-ferre ob-tulisse oblātum offer
officium -ī *n* duty, task
ōlim once, long ago
omnis -e all, every
opera -ae *f* effort, pains
operīre -uisse -ertum cover
opēs -um *f pl* resources, wealth
oportēre: oportet it is right, you should
opperīrī -ertum wait (for), await
oppidum -ī *n* town
op-pugnāre attack
optāre wish
optimus -a -um *sup* best, very good
opus -eris *n* work
opus est it is needed
ōra -ae *f* border, coast
ōrāre pray, beg
ōrātiō -ōnis *f* speech
orbis -is *m* circle, orbit
orbis terrārum the world
ōrdināre arrange, regulate
ōrdō -inis *m* row, rank, order
oriēns -entis *m* east
orīrī ortum rise, appear
ōrnāmentum -ī *n* ornament, jewel
ōrnāre equip, adorn
os ossis *n* bone
ōs ōris *n* mouth
ōscitāre gape, yawn
ōsculārī kiss

ōsculum -ī *n* kiss
ostendere -disse show
ōstiārius -ī *m* door-keeper, porter
ōstium -ī *n* door, entrance
ōtiōsus -a -um leisured, idle
ōtium -ī *n* leisure
ovis -is *f* sheep
ōvum -ī *n* egg

P
pābulum -ī *n* fodder
paene nearly, almost
paen-īnsula -ae *f* peninsula
pāgina -ae *f* page
pallēre be pale
pallidus -a -um pale
pallium -ī *n* cloak, mantle
palma -ae *f* palm
palpitāre beat, throb
pānis -is *m* bread, loaf
papyrus -ī *f* papyrus
pār paris *adi* equal
parāre prepare, make ready
parātus -a -um ready
parcere pepercisse +*dat* spare
parentēs -um *m pl* parents
parere -iō peperisse give birth to, lay
pārēre (+*dat*) obey
parricīda -ae *m* parricide
pars -rtis *f* part, direction
partīrī share, divide
parum too little, not quite
parvulus -a -um little, tiny
parvus -a -um little, small
pāscere pāvisse pāstum pasture, feed, feast
passer -eris *m* sparrow
passus -ūs *m* pace (1.48 m)
pāstor -ōris *m* shepherd
pater -tris *m* father
patēre be open
patī passum suffer, undergo, bear
patiēns -entis *adi* patient
patientia -ae *f* forbearance, patience
patria -ae *f* native country/ town
paucī -ae -a few, a few
paulisper for a short time

paulō +*comp, ante/post* a little
paulum a little, little
pauper -eris *adi* poor
pāx pācis *f* peace
pectus -oris *n* breast
pecūlium -ī *n* money given to slaves
pecūnia -ae *f* money
pecūniōsus -a -um wealthy
pecus -oris *n* livestock, sheep, cattle
pedes -itis *m* foot-soldier
pēior -ius *comp* worse
pellere pepulisse pulsum push, drive (off)
penna -ae *f* feather
pēnsum -ī *n* task
per *prp* +*acc* through, by, during
per-currere -rrisse -rsum run over, pass over
per-cutere -iō -cussisse -cussum strike, hit
per-dere -didisse -ditum destroy, ruin, waste
per-ferre carry, endure
per-ficere complete, accomplish
pergere -rexi, -rectum proceed, go on
perīculōsus -a -um dangerous, perilous
perīculum -ī *n* danger, peril
per-īre -eō -iisse perish, be lost
peristylum -ī *n* peristyle
per-mittere allow, permit
per-movēre move deeply
perpetuus -a -um continuous, permanent
per-sequī follow, pursue
persōna -ae *f* character, person
per-suādēre -sisse +*dat* persuade, convince
per-territus -a -um terrified
per-turbāre upset
per-venīre get to, reach
pēs pedis *m* foot
pessimus -a -um *sup* worst
petasus -ī *m* hat
petere -īvisse -ītum make for, aim at, attack, seek, ask for, request

phantasma -atis *n* ghost, apparition
piger -gra -grum lazy
pila -ae *f* ball
pīlum -ī *n* spear, javelin
pīpiāre chirp
pīrāta -ae *m* pirate
pirum -ī *n* pear
piscātor -ōris *m* fisherman
piscis -is *m* fish
placēre +*dat* please
plānē plainly, clearly
plānus -a -um plain, clear
plaudere -sisse (+*dat*) clap, applaud
plēnus -a -um (+*gen/abl*) full (of)
plērī-que plērae- plēra- most, most people
plērumque mostly
plōrāre cry
plūrēs -a *comp* more
plūrimī -ae -a *sup* most, a great many
plūs plūris *n, adv* more
pōculum -ī *n* cup, glass
poena -ae *f* punishment, penalty
poēta -ae *m/f* poet
poēticus -a -um poetical
pollicērī promise
pōnere posuisse positum place, put, lay down
populus -ī *m* people, nation
porcus -ī *m* pig
porta -ae *f* gate
portāre carry
portus -ūs *m* harbor
poscere poposcisse demand, call for
posse potuisse be able
possidēre -sēdisse possess, own
post *prp* +*acc, adv* behind, after, later
post-eā afterward, later
posterior -ius *comp* back-, hind-, later
posterus -a -um next, following
posthāc from now on, hereafter
post-quam after, since
postrēmō *adv* finally
postrēmus -a -um *sup* last

postulāre demand, require
pōtāre drink
potestās -ātis *f* power
pōtiō -ōnis *f* drinking, drink
potius rather
prae *prp* +*abl* before, for
praecipuē especially, above all
praedium -ī *n* estate
praedō -ōnis *m* robber, pirate
prae-esse (+*dat*) be in charge (of)
prae-ferre prefer
praemium -ī *n* reward, prize
prae-nōmen -inis *n* first name
prae-pōnere +*dat* put before/in charge of
praesēns -entis *adi* present
prae-stāre -stitisse furnish, fulfill
praeter *prp* +*acc* past, besides, except
praeter-eā besides
praeteritus -a -um past
prāvus -a -um faulty, wrong
precārī pray
precēs -um *f pl* prayers
prehendere -disse -ēnsum grasp, seize
premere pressisse pressum press
pretiōsus -a -um precious
pretium -ī *n* price, value
prīdem long ago
prī-diē the day before
prīmō *adv* at first
prīmum *adv* first
prīmus -a -um first
prīnceps -ipis *m* chief, leader
prīncipium -ī *n* beginning
prior -ius first, former, front-
prius *adv* before
prius-quam before
prīvātus -a -um private
prō *prp* +*abl* for, instead of
probus -a -um good, honest, proper
prō-cēdere go forward, advance
procul far (from), far away

prō-currere -rrisse -rsum
    run forward, charge
prōd-esse prō-fuisse
    +*dat* be useful, do good
proelium -ī *n* battle
profectō indeed, certainly
prō-ferre bring forth,
    produce
proficīscī -fectum set out,
    depart
prō-gredī -ior -gressum go
    forward, advance
pro-hibēre keep off,
    prevent
prō-icere throw (forward)
prōmere -mpsisse -mptum
    take out
prōmissum -ī *n* promise
prō-mittere promise
prope *prp* +*acc, adv* near,
    nearly
properāre hurry
propinquus -a -um near,
    close
proprius -a -um own,
    proper
propter *prp* +*acc* because of
propter-eā therefore
prō-silīre -uisse spring
    forth
prō-spicere look out, look
    ahead
prōtinus at once
prōvincia -ae *f* province
proximus -a -um *sup*
    nearest
prūdēns -entis *adi* prudent,
    clever
pūblicus -a -um public,
    State-
pudēre: pudet mē (+*gen*) I
    am ashamed (of)
pudor -ōris *m* (sense of)
    shame
puella -ae *f* girl
puer -erī *m* boy
pugna -ae *f* fight
pugnāre fight
pugnus -ī *m* fist
pulcher -chra -chrum
    beautiful, fine
pulchritūdō -inis *f* beauty
pullus -ī *m* young (of an
    animal)
pulmō -ōnis *m* lung

pulsāre strike, hit, knock
    (at)
pūnīre punish
puppis -is *f* stern, poop
pūrus -a -um clean, pure
putāre think, suppose

Q
quadrāgēsimus -a -um
    fortieth
quadrāgintā forty
quadrin-gentī -ae -a four
    hundred
quaerere -sīvisse -sītum
    look for, seek, ask (for)
quālis -e what sort of,
    (such) as
quālitās -ātis *f* quality
quam how, as, than
quam +*sup* as...as possible
quam-diū how long, (as
    long) as
quam-ob-rem why
quamquam although
quandō when, as
quantitās -ātis *f* quantity,
    size
quantum -ī *n* how much,
    (as much) as
quantus -a -um how large,
    (as large) as
quā-propter why
quā-rē why
quārtus -a -um fourth
quārta pars fourth, quarter
quasi as, like, as if
quater four times
quatere -iō shake
quaternī -ae -a four (each)
quattuor four
quattuor-decim fourteen
-que and
querī questum complain,
    grumble
quī quae quod who, which,
    he who
quī quae quod (...?) what,
    which
quia because
quid *n* (*v.* quis) what,
    anything
quid *adv* why
quī-dam quae- quod- a
    certain, some
quidem indeed, certainly

nē quidem not even
quidnī why not
quid-quam anything
neque/nec quidquam and
    nothing
quid-quid whatever,
    anything that
quiēscere -ēvisse rest
quiētus -a -um quiet
quīn why not, do...!
quīn-decim fifteen
quīn-gentī -ae -a five
    hundred
quīnī -ae -a five (each)
quīnquāgintā fifty
quīnque five
quīnquiēs five times
Quīntīlis -is (mēnsis) July
quīntus -a -um fifth
quis quae quid who, what
quis quid (sī/num/
    nē...) anyone, anything
quis-nam quid-nam who/
    what ever?
quis-quam anyone
neque/nec quisquam and
    no one
quis-que quae- quod- each
quis-quis whoever, anyone
    who
quō *adv* where (to)
quod (= quia) because, that
quod *n* (*v.* quī) what, which,
    that which
quō-modo how
quoniam as, since
quoque also, too
quot *indēcl* how many, (as
    many) as
quot-annīs every year
quotiēs how many times

R
rāmus -ī *m* branch, bough
rapere -iō -uisse -ptum tear
    away, carry off
rapidus -a -um rushing,
    rapid
rārō *adv* rarely, seldom
rārus -a -um rare
ratiō -ōnis *f* reason
ratis -is *f* raft
re-cēdere go back, retire
re-cipere receive, admit
recitāre read aloud

re-**cognōscere** recognize

rēctus -a -um straight,
  correct

rēctā (viā) straight

re-**cumbere** -cubuisse lie
  down

red-**dere** -didisse -ditum
  give back, give

red-**imere** -ēmisse -ēmptum
  ransom

red-**īre** -eō -iisse -itum go
  back, return

re-**dūcere** lead back, bring
  back

re-**ferre** rettulisse bring
  back, return

regere rēxisse
  rēctum direct, guide,
  govern

regiō -ōnis *f* region, district

rēgnāre reign, rule

rēgula -ae *f* ruler

re-**linquere** -līquisse -lictum
  leave

reliquus -a -um remaining,
  left

re-**manēre** remain, stay
  behind

rēmigāre row

re-**mīniscī** +*gen/
  acc* recollect

re-**mittere** send back

re-**movēre** remove

rēmus -ī *m* oar

repente suddenly

reperīre repperisse
  repertum find

re-**pōnere** put back

re-**prehendere** blame,
  censure

re-**pugnāre** fight back,
  resist

re-**quiēscere** rest

re-**quīrere** -sīvisse -sītum
  seek, ask

rēs reī *f* thing, matter, affair

re-**sistere** -stitisse +*dat* halt,
  resist

re-**spondēre** -disse -sum
  answer

respōnsum -ī *n* answer

rēte -is *n* net

re-**tinēre** -uisse -tentum
  hold back

re-**trahere** pull back, bring
  back

re-**venīre** come back

revertī -tisse -sum return,
  come back

re-**vocāre** call back, revoke

rēx rēgis *m* king

rīdēre -sisse -sum laugh,
  make fun of

rīdiculus -a -um ridiculous

rigāre irrigate

rīpa -ae *f* bank

rīsus -ūs *m* laughter, laugh

rīvus -ī *m* brook

rogāre ask, ask for

rogitāre ask (repeatedly)

Rōmānus -a -um Roman

rosa -ae *f* rose

ruber -bra -brum red

rubēre be red, blush

rudis -e crude, rude

rūmor -ōris *m* rumor

rumpere rūpisse
  ruptum break

rūrī *loc* in the country

rūrsus again

rūs rūris *n* the country

rūsticus -a -um rural, rustic,
  farm-

S

sacculus -ī *m* purse

saccus -ī *m* sack

sacerdōs -ōtis *m/f* priest,
  priestess

saeculum -ī *n* century

saepe often

saevus -a -um fierce, cruel

sagitta -ae *f* arrow

sāl salis *m* salt, wit

salīre -uisse jump

salūs -ūtis *f* safety, well-
  being

salūtem dīcere +*dat* greet

salūtāre greet

salvāre save

salvē -ēte hallo, good
  morning

salvēre iubēre greet

salvus -a -um safe,
  unharmed

sānāre heal, cure

sānē certainly, quite

sanguis -inis *m* blood

sānus -a -um healthy, well

sapere -iō -iisse be wise,
  have sense

sapiēns -entis *adi* wise

satis enough, rather

saxum -ī *n* rock

scaena -ae *f* scene, stage

scaenicus -a -um theatrical

scalpellum -ī *n* scalpel,
  surgical knife

scamnum -ī *n* stool

scelestus -a -um criminal,
  wicked

scelus -eris *n* crime

scīlicet of course

scindere scidisse
  scissum tear, tear up

scīre know

scrībere -psisse -ptum write

scūtum -ī *n* shield

sē sibi himself

secāre -uisse -ctum cut

secundum *prp* +*acc* along

secundus -a -um second,
  favorable

sed but

sē-decim sixteen

sedēre sēdisse sit

sella -ae *f* stool, chair

semel once

sēmen -inis *n* seed

semper always

senex senis *m* old man

sēnī -ae -a six (each)

sententia -ae *f* opinion,
  sentence

sentīre sēnsisse
  sēnsum feel, sense, think

septem seven

September -bris (mēnsis)
  September

septen-decim seventeen

septentriōnēs -um *m
  pl* north

septimus -a -um seventh

septin-gentī -ae -a seven
  hundred

septuāgintā seventy

sequī secūtum follow

serēnus -a -um clear,
  cloudless

serere sēvisse satum sow,
  plant

sērius -a -um serious

sermō -ōnis *m* talk,
  conversation

servāre preserve, save

servīre +*dat* be a slave,
  serve

servitūs -ūtis *f* slavery

servus -ī *m* slave, servant
ses-centī -ae -a six hundred
sēsē himself
sēstertius -ī *m* sesterce
(coin)
seu *v.* sī-ve/seu
sevērus -a -um stern, severe
sex six
sexāgintā sixty
sexiēs six times
Sextīlis -is (mēnsis) August
sextus -a -um sixth
sī if
sīc in this way, so, thus
siccus -a -um dry
sīc-ut just as, as
signāre mark, seal
significāre indicate, mean
significātiō -ōnis
f meaning, sense
signum -ī *n* sign, seal,
statue
silentium -ī *n* silence
silēre be silent
silva -ae *f* wood, forest
similis -e similar, like
simul together, at the same
time
simul atque +*perf* as soon as
sīn but if
sine *prp* +*abl* without
sinere sīvisse situm let,
allow
singulī -ae -a one (each),
each
sinister -tra -trum left, *f* the
left (hand)
sinus -ūs *m* fold (of toga)
sī-quidem seeing that, since
sitis -is *f* thirst
situs -a -um situated
sī-ve/seu or, or if
s. ... s. whether...or
sōl -is *m* sun
solēre -itum esse be
accustomed
solum -ī *n* soil, ground,
floor
sōlum *adv* only
sōlus -a -um alone, lonely
solvere -visse
solūtum untie, discharge,
pay
nāvem solvere cast off, set
sail

somnus -ī *m* sleep
sonus -ī *m* sound, noise
sordēs -ium *f pl* dirt
sordidus -a -um dirty,
mean, base
soror -ōris *f* sister
spargere -sisse -sum scatter
speciēs -ēī *f* appearance,
aspect, sort
spectāre watch, look at
spectātor -ōris *m* spectator
speculum -ī *n* mirror
spērāre hope (for)
spēs -eī *f* hope
-spicere -iō -spexisse
-spectum
spīrāre breathe
stāre stetisse stand
statim at once
statuere -uisse -ūtum fix,
determine
stēlla -ae *f* star
sternere strāvisse
strātum spread
stilus -ī *m* stylus
stipendium -ī *n* soldier's
pay, service
strepitus -ūs *m* noise, din
studēre +*dat* devote oneself
to
studiōsus -a -um
(+*gen*) interested (in)
studium -ī *n* interest, study
stultus -a -um stupid,
foolish
stupēre be aghast
suādēre -sisse +*dat* advise
sub *prp* +*abl/acc* under,
near
sub-īre -eō -iisse go under,
undergo
subitō *adv* suddenly
subitus -a -um sudden
sub-mergere sink
sub-urbānus -a -um near
the city
sūmere -mpsisse -mptum
take
summus -a -um *sup* highest,
greatest
super *prp* +*acc* on (top of),
above
prp +*abl* on, about
superbus -a -um haughty,
proud

super-esse be left, be in
excess
superior -ius *comp* higher,
upper, superior
superus -a -um upper
supplicium -ī *n* (capital)
punishment
suprā *prp* +*acc, adv* above
surdus -a -um deaf
surgere sur-rēxisse rise,
get up
sur-ripere -iō -uisse
-reptum steal
sūrsum up, upward
suscitāre wake up, rouse
su-spicere look up (at)
sus-tinēre support, sustain,
endure
suus -a -um his/her/their
(own)
syllaba -ae *f* syllable

T
tabella -ae *f* writing-tablet
tabellārius -ī *m* letter-
carrier
taberna -ae *f* shop, stall
tabernārius -ī
m shopkeeper
tabula -ae *f* writing-tablet
tacēre be silent
tacitus -a -um silent
talentum -ī *n* talent
tālis -e such
tam so, as
tam-diū so long, as long
tamen nevertheless, yet
tam-quam as, like
tandem at length, at last
tangere tetigisse
tāctum touch
tantum -ī *n* so much
alterum tantum twice as
much
tantum *adv* so much, only
tantun-dem just as much
tantus -a -um so big, so
great
tardus -a -um slow, late
tata -ae *m* daddy
taurus -ī *m* bull
tēctum -ī *n* roof
temerārius -a -um reckless
tempestās -ātis *f* storm
templum -ī *n* temple

tempus -oris *n* time
tenebrae -ārum *f pl* darkness
tenebricōsus -a -um dark
tenēre -uisse -ntum hold, keep (back)
tenuis -e thin
ter three times
tergēre -sisse -sum wipe
tergum -ī *n* back
ternī -ae -a three (each)
terra -ae *f* earth, ground, country
terrēre frighten
terribilis -e terrible
tertius -a -um third
testis -is *m/f* witness
theātrum -ī *n* theater
tībiae -ārum *f pl* flute
tībīcen -inis *m* flute-player
timēre fear, be afraid (of)
timidus -a -um fearful, timid
timor -ōris *m* fear
titulus -ī *m* title
toga -ae *f* toga
togātus -a -um wearing the toga
tollere sus-tulisse sublātum raise, lift, pick up, remove, take away
tonitrus -ūs *m* thunder
tot *indēcl* so many
totiēs so many times
tōtus -a -um the whole of, all
trā-dere -didisse -ditum hand over, deliver
trahere -āxisse -actum drag, pull
tranquillitās -ātis *f* calmness
tranquillus -a -um calm, still
trāns *prp +acc* across, over
trāns-ferre transfer, transport
trāns-īre -eō -iisse -itum cross, pass
tre-centī -ae -a three hundred
trē-decim thirteen
tremere -uisse tremble
trēs tria three
trīcēsimus -a -um thirtieth

triclīnium -ī *n* dining-room
trīgintā thirty
trīnī -ae -a three
trīstis -e sad
trīstitia -ae *f* sadness
tū tē tibi you, yourself
tuērī tūtum guard, protect
tum then
tumultuārī make an uproar
tumultus -ūs *m* uproar
tunc then
tunica -ae *f* tunic
turba -ae *f* throng, crowd
turbāre stir up, agitate
turbidus -a -um agitated, stormy
turgid(ul)us -a -um swollen
turpis -e ugly, foul
tūtus -a -um safe
tuus -a -um your, yours
tyrannus -ī *m* tyrant

U
ubi where
ubi prīmum *+perf* as soon as
ubī-que everywhere
ūllus -a -um any
nec/neque ūllus and no
ulterior -ius *comp* farther, more distant
ultimus -a -um *sup* most distant, last
ultrā *prp +acc* beyond
ululāre howl
umbra -a *f* shade, shadow
umerus -ī *m* shoulder
ūmidus -a -um wet, moist
umquam ever
nec/neque umquam and never
ūnā *adv* together
unde from where
ūn-dē-centum ninety-nine
ūn-decim eleven
ūndecimus -a -um eleventh
ūn-dē-trīgintā twenty-nine
ūn-dē-vīgintī nineteen
ūnī -ae -a one
ūniversus -a -um the whole of, entire
ūnus -a -um one, only
urbānus -a -um of the city, urban
urbs -bis *f* city

ūrere ussisse ustum burn
ūsque up (to), all the time
ut like, as
ut *+ coni* that, in order that, to
uter utra utrum which (of the two)
uter-que utra- utrum- each of the two, both
ūtī ūsum *+abl* use, enjoy
utinam I wish that, if only…!
utrum…an …or…? whether…or
ūva -ae *f* grape
uxor -ōris *f* wife

V
vacuus -a -um empty
vāgīre wail, squall
valdē strongly, very (much)
valē -ēte farewell, goodbye
valēre be strong, be well
valētūdō -inis *f* health
validus -a -um strong
vallis -is *f* valley
vāllum -ī *n* rampart
varius -a -um varied, different
vās vāsis *n, pl* -a -ōrum vessel, bowl
-ve or
vehere vēxisse vectum carry, convey, *pass* ride, sail, travel
vel or
velle volō voluisse want, be willing
vēlōx -ōcis *adi* swift, rapid
vēlum -ī *n* sail
vel-ut like, as
vēna -ae *f* vein
vēn-dere -didisse sell
venīre vēnisse ventum come
venter -tris *m* belly, stomach
ventus -ī *m* wind
venustus -a -um charming
vēr vēris *n* spring
verbera -um *n pl* lashes, flogging
verberāre beat, flog
verbum -ī *n* word, verb
verērī fear

vērō really, however, but
neque/nec vērō but not
versārī move about, be
present
versiculus -ī *m* short verse
versus -ūs *m* line, verse
versus: ad...versus toward
vertere -tisse -sum turn
vērum but
vērus -a -um true, *n* truth
vesper -erī *m* evening
vesperī *adv* in the evening
vester -tra -trum your,
yours
vestīgium -ī *n* footprint,
trace
vestīmentum -ī *n* garment,
clothing
vestīre dress
vestis -is *f* clothes, cloth
vestrum *gen* of you
vetāre forbid
vetus -eris *adi* old
via -ae *f* road, way, street
vīcēsimus -a -um twentieth
victor -ōris *m,*
adi conqueror, victorious

victōria -ae *f* victory
vidēre vīdisse vīsum see,
pass seem
vigilāre be awake
vigilia -ae *f* night watch
(I-IV)
vīgintī twenty
vīlis -e cheap
vīlla -ae *f* country house,
villa
vincere vīcisse
victum defeat, overcome,
win
vincīre -nxisse -nctum tie
vīnea -ae *f* vinyard
vīnum -ī *n* wine
vir -ī *m* man, husband
vīrēs -ium *f pl* strength
virga -ae *f* rod
virgō -inis *f* maiden, young
girl
virtūs -ūtis *f* valor, courage
vīs, *acc* vim, *abl* vī force,
violence, power
viscera -um *n pl* internal
organs

vīsere -sisse go and see,
visit
vīta -ae *f* life
vītāre avoid
vītis -is *f* vine
vīvere vīxisse live, be alive
vīvus -a -um living, alive
vix hardly
vocābulum -ī *n* word
vōcālis -is *f* vowel
vocāre call, invite
volāre fly
voluntās -ātis *f* will
vorāgō -inis *f* abyss,
whirlpool
vorāre swallow, devour
vōs vōbīs you, yourselves
vōx vōcis *f* voice
vulnerāre wound
vulnus -eris *n* wound
vultus -ūs *m* countenance,
face

Z
zephyrus -ī *m* west wind

Grammatical Terms

LATIN	ABBREVIATIONS	ENGLISH
ablātīvus (cāsus)	*abl*	**ablative**
accūsātīvus (cāsus)	*acc*	**accusative**
āctīvum (genus)	*āct*	**active**
adiectīvum (nōmen)	*adi*	**adjective**
adverbium -ī *n*	*adv*	**adverb**
appellātīvum (nōmen)		**appellative**
cāsus -ūs *m*		**case**
comparātiō -ōnis *f*		**comparison**
comparātīvus (gradus)	*comp*	**comparative**
coniugātiō -ōnis *f*		**conjugation**
coniūnctiō -ōnis *f*	*coni*	**conjunction**
coniūnctīvus (modus)	*coni*	**subjunctive**
datīvus (cāsus)	*dat*	**dative**
dēclīnātiō -ōnis *f*	*dēcl*	**declension**
dēmōnstrātīvum (prōnōmen)		**demonstrative**
dēpōnentia (verba)	*dēp*	**deponent**

LATIN	ABBREVIATIONS	ENGLISH
fēminīnum (genus)	*f, fēm*	feminine
futūrum (tempus)	*fut*	future
futūrum perfectum (tempus)	*fut perf*	future perfect
genetīvus (cāsus)	*gen*	genitive
genus (nōminis/verbī)		gender/voice
gerundium -ī *n* gerundīvum -ī *n*		gerund/gerundive
imperātīvus (modus)	*imp, imper*	imperative
imperfectum (tempus praeteritum)	*imperf*	imperfect
indēclīnābile (vocābulum)	*indēcl*	indeclinable
indēfīnītum (prōnōmen)		indefinite
indicātīvus (modus)	*ind*	indicative
īnfīnītīvus (modus)	*īnf*	infinitive
interiectiō -ōnis *f*		interjection
interrogātīvum (prōnōmen)		interrogative
locātīvus (cāsus)	*loc*	locative
masculīnum (genus)	*m, masc*	masculine
modus (verbī)		mode
neutrum (genus)	*n, neutr*	neuter
nōminātīvus (cāsus)	*nōm*	nominative
optātīvus (modus)		optative
pars ōrātiōnis		part of speech
participium -ī *n*	*part*	participle
passīvum (genus)	*pass*	passive
perfectum (tempus praeteritum)	*perf*	perfect
persōna -ae *f*	*pers*	person
persōnāle (prōnōmen)		personal
plūrālis (numerus)	*pl, plūr*	plural
plūsquamperfectum (tempus praet.)	*plūsqu*	pluperfect
positīvus (gradus)	*pos*	positive
possessīvum (prōnōmen)		possessive
praepositiō -ōnis *f*	*prp, praep*	preposition
praesēns (tempus)	*praes*	present
praeteritum (tempus)	*praet*	preterite, past tense
prōnōmen -inis *n*	*prōn*	pronoun
proprium (nōmen)		proper name
relātīvum (prōnōmen)	*rel*	relative
singulāris (numerus)	*sg, sing*	singular
superlātīvus (gradus)	*sup*	superlative
supīnum		supine
tempus (verbī)		tense
verbum	*vb*	verb
vocātīvus (cāsus)	*voc*	vocative

Index

ablative. *See also* preposition
  of agent, 47
  absolute (*ablātīvus absolūtus*) (*see* participle)
  expressions of time 110, 114, 179
  of attendant circumstances, 122, 140
  of comparison, 218
  of degree of difference, 142, 171
  of description, 297
  with *locus*, 163
  of manner, 84, 229
  of means/instrument, 47, 59, 247
  of price (*ablātīvus pretiī*), 63
  of respect 92, 171, 197, 228, 312
  of separation, 45, 139, 178, 251, 297
  of time when (*ablātīvus temporis*), 110, 113
  review: 3rd declension sing. in -*ī* and -*e*, 103; expressions of time and space, 114
accusative. *See also* preposition
  acc. and inf. construction, 83, 91
  double, 113
  expressions of time, 111, 114, 179
  of exclamation, 130
  of extent of space, 130
  review: expressions of time and space, 114
adjective
  and substantive, 4, 189
  2nd declension, 4; in -*er*, 37, 158
  3rd declension: adjectives of two terminations, 98; adjectives of one termination, 170; adjectives of

three terminations, 239; summary of 3rd declension forms, 239
  as substantive, 4, 189
  comparison, 100, 112, 160, 166, 218
  interrogative (*see under* interrogative)
  irregular, 166
  nūllus, ūllus, tōtus, solus, 167
  numerical, 148
  participle as an adjective: perfect, 188; present, 122
  possessive, 29, 51, 93
  vs. pronouns, review, 30 158
  reflexive possessive, 29
  review: adjectives and pronouns, 23; comparison with adverbs, 160
  superlative, 112; + partitive genitive, 167; absolute, 167; in -*er*, 158; irregular, 158; *quisque* +, 291
  uter, neuter, alter, uterque, 120
adverb
  comparative degree, 159
  correlative, 44
  forās, forīs, 201
  from 1st/2nd declension adjectives, 150, 159
  from 3rd declension adjectives, 159
  in -*ō*, 217
  interrogative, 12, 21, 43
  nihil, 127n2
  numerical, 161
  of place, 227
  minus, magis 177
  parum, 251

positive degree, 159
review, 233; comparison with
    adjectives, 158, 160
superlative degree, 160
āēr, 240
antonym, 3
apposition. *See* points of style: idioms
assimilation, 73

cardinal directions, 138. See also *locus*
cognōmen. See *tria nōmina*
comparative
    of adjectives (Caps. XII, XIII, XXIV)
    of adverbs (Cap. XVIII)
    summary of adjective comparison, 218
conditions
    with indicative, 312
    with subjunctive, 309, 312
    summary, 312
conjunction, 11, 21, 72, 79, 92, 113, 157,
    218, 250, 269
    temporal, 73, 79
convenit, 133. *See also* Points of Style
correlative
    tam/quam, 44
    tantus/quantus, 62
    talis/qualis (Cap. XVIII)
cum. See conjunction; preposition
    review, 282
    subordinate clauses, 269

dative, 52
    of indirect object, xvii, 63
    of interest, 82, 121
    of possession, 96
    with intransitive verbs, xxiv, 100,
        189, 250
declension, 11, 15, 69, 72, 74, 90, 99,
    109, 110, 334
decline, 15, 69
deliberative questions, 268
domus, 170, 177

ecce, 14
enclitic, 5, 11, 15

esse
    perfect stem, 187
    subjunctive present, 253
    subjunctive imperfect, 263
    summary, 179
ēst/edunt, 71
expressions of time and space.
    See ablative; accusative

facere/fierī, 143
fear clauses, 301
ferre
    imperatives, 98
    review, 299
fruī, 279

gender, xxi, 10
genitive, 11
    archaic, 167
    objective/subjective, 230
    of quality/description, 168
    of the charge, 272
    of value, 269
    partitive, 101, 142, 272; with *mīlia*,
        103; with *plēnus*, 43; with *sēster-
        tium*, 300; with superlatives, 167
gerund, 237
    uses and cases of, 238
gerundive, 290
    attraction, 309
glides. *See* semi-vowels

imperative, xxii, 28, 38
    future, 241, 312
    of *agere*, 39
    of *esse*, 52
    of *salvēre*, 53
    irregular, 98
implied subject, 21
impersonal verbs. *See* verbs:
    impersonal
indeclinable adjective, 5, 31, 103
indefinite pronouns. *See* pronouns:
    indefinite
indicative, xxii, 28, 32

indirect commands (*verba postulandī*),
249
    vs. indirect statement, 262
indirect questions, 270, 300
indirect statement. *See also* accusative:
    acc. and inf. construction; infinitive:
    acc. and inf. construction
        vs. *verba postulandī*, 262
        reflexive pronoun in, 132
infinitive, xxii
    acc. and inf. construction, 83, 91, 209
    construed with: *audēre*, 83; *dīcitur* +
        nom. and inf., 114; *iubēre*, 91, 230;
        necesse est + the inf. and dat. of
        interest, 67; *oportēre*, 151; *velle*,
        83, 228
    deponent, 140
    tenses of:
    —future: active, 209; passive, 209;
        summary, 210
    —perfect: active, 187; passive, 188
    —present: active, 80; in *-se*, 81;
        passive, 81
    relative time of, 196, 201
    review, 210
inquit, 124
interrogative, 2, 4, 55
    adjective, 60
    adverb, 12, 21, 44
    pronoun, 12, 21
    review: pronoun vs. adjective, 60
intervocalic -s-, 81
īre, 44, 142
    present participle, 212
ita...ut/ut...ita. See Points of Style:
    idioms

lexical entry, 24, 79
licet, 134
locative, 45, 170, 178, 185, 229
    summary 247
locus, 139, 247

mālle, 263, 308. See also *velle*
māne, 110

meter, 321
    hendecasyllables, 322
    hexameter, 322
    metric feet, 321
    pentameter, 322
    syllabic division, 321
    syllabic quantity, 321
mīlle/mīlia, 102
mood (*modī*), 28, 31, 248, 343

-ne. See interrogative
nēmō, 83
neuter, xxi, 10
nōlle, 177, 263, 308. See also *velle*
nominative
    dīcitur + nom. and inf., 114
    predicate nom./adj. xxiii
nostrum/nostri vs. *vestrum/vestri*, 272
noun
    1st declension, summary of endings,
        53
    2nd declension, summary of endings,
        53; in *-er*, 14
    3rd declension, 69; ablative in, 103;
        i-stems, 71, 90; masculine and
        feminine, 71, 78; neuter, 82, 89;
        pure *i*-stems, 139
    4th declension, 99
    5th declension, 109
    vocative, 30; for nouns in *-īus*, 170
nūllus, 124, 167
num. See interrogative
number
    cardinal, 31, 103, 111, 148
    distributive, 280, 307
    fractions, 111
    numerical adverbs, 161
    ordinals, 111, 149

orthography, xvi

participle
    ablative absolute (*ablātīvus
        absolūtus*), 140, 200
    future, 208; summary, 210

perfect, 184, 188; as adjective, 188;
    vs. the supine, 197
present (*participium praesēns*), 122,
    relative time of, 201
review, 206; participles and infini-
    tives, 210, 223
vs. supine, 197
parts of speech, xxi
perfect. *See* verbs
place constructions, 45, 229
pluperfect. *See* verbs
points of style
    alius…alius, cauda movet/movētur,
        84
    bene/male velle, 231
    concision, 5
    convenit, 63
    enumerations, 13
    et…et/neque….neque/nōn sōlum…
        sed etiam, 54
    hyperbaton, 221
    idiom, to marry, 324
    idiom *suum ciuque,* 158
    idioms, 171
    participles, 241
    posse, 221
    quī = et is, 231
    quid agis, 221
    relative sentences, 22
    sē hābēre, 124
    word order, 143
posse, 80, 93, 133, 157, 221
possessive. *See* adjective; pronoun
praenōmen. See tria nōmina
predicate, xxiii
    nom./adj., xxiii
preposition, xxiii
    with compound verbs, 273
principal parts, 195
pronoun, xxi, 20
    demonstrative, 54; *hic, haec, hoc,*
        54; *īdem, eadem, idem,* 156; *ille,*
        illa, illud, 61; *ipse, ipsa, ipsum,* 73;
        is, ea, id, 53; *iste, ista, istud,* 200;
        review, 65, 200

indefinite: *aliquis, aliquid,* 187, 199;
    quīdam, quaedam, quoddam, 302;
    quisquis, quidquid, 289; *quisquam,*
    quidquam, 240; *quisque, quaeque,*
    quodque, 147, 156
indefinite relative, 288
interrogative, 21,
nūllus, ūllus, tōtus, solus, 167
personal: review, 273
possessive: adjective vs. pronoun,
    29, 30
reflexive, 50, 218, 261
relative, 21; *quī = is quī,* 59, 231
uter, neuter, alter, uterque, 120
vs. possessive adjectives, review, 134
pronunciation, xvi
pudēre, 207
purpose and result. *See* subjunctive

qu- words, 302
quam. See points of style: idioms;
    correlative
    with *tam,* 44
    in exclamations, 62
    review, 62, 171
quantus. See correlative
    with *tantus,* 62
quid. See interrogative
quis, quid. See pronoun: indefinite;
    interrogative
quod. See conjunction; pronoun:
    relative; interrogative: adjective

reflexive. *See* pronoun
relative. *See* pronoun
    sentences (*see* points of style)
relative time of participles and infini-
    tives, 201
Roman calendar (Julian calendar),
    108
    divisions/names of the months, 113

salvē/salvēte. See Imperative
semi-vowels (glides), viii
sōlus, 167

subject, xviii, 19, 23. *See also* noun
  implied, 21, 23
subjunctive, 248
  contrafactual, 309, 311
  posse: with indicative, 221; with *cum*,
    269, 283
  deliberative questions, 268
  fear clauses, 301
  horatatory, 281, 291
  imperfect, 258; *esse*, 263; *velle, nōlle,*
    malle, 308
  indirect questions, 270, 300
  jussive, 291
  optative, 291, 301, 311
  pluperfect in subordinate clauses,
    239
  prohibitions, 300
  purpose, 262
  result, 261
  review, 211
  signals of the subjunctive, 313
  subordinate clauses, 263, 299, 310;
    indicative vs. subjunctive, 273
  summary, 272
  tenses of:
  —perfect, 298
  —pluperfect, 310
  —present, 248; *esse*, 253; *īre,* 203;
    velle, nōlle, malle, 308
  —sequence of tenses, 261, 300, 311
  verba postulandī, 249
  verba curandī, 252
  wishes, 308
superlative, 112, 158, 160
  absolute, 160, 167
  with partitive genitive, 167
  with *quam*, 253
  with *quisque*, 291
supine Stem, 196. *See also* verbs:
  supine

tam, 44. *See also* correlative
tantus, 62. *See also* correlative
tantum (adv.), 62
totus, 167
time, expressions of, 110

transitive. *See* verbs
tria nōmina, 104

ut, 250
ūllus, 167
ūtor, 247

verbs
  compound, 54, 273
  deponent (*verba dēpōnentia*), 139,
    218; imperative, 232; perfect
    participle, 230; semi-deponent,
    292
  impersonal: *convenit,* 133; *decet,* 181;
    licet, 134; *necesse est,* 82; *oportet,*
    151; *opus est,* 171; with ablative,
    297
  inquit, 124
  intransitive, xxvi, 20; sative with, 100;
    passive of, 310
  irregular, 352; alphabetical List, 357;
    ūtor, 247
  of remembering and forgetting, 297;
    meminisse, 297; *oblīvīscī,* 232;
    reminīscī, 297; *ōdisse,* 223
  passive voice, 46, 150; indicative, 219;
    subjunctive, 307
  principal parts, or the three verbal
    stems, 195,
  supine, 196; ablative, 197; accusative,
    196; vs. the perfect passive
    participle, 197
  tenses of:
  —imperfect (*preterite*), 87, 111; of
    all conjugations, active & passive,
    168
  —future, 175; imperative, 241, 312;
    infinitive, 209
  —future perfect, 280
  —perfect (*tempus praeteritum*
    perfectum), 141, 143; infinitive
    active, 145; infinitive passive, 146;
    passive, 142, 148; reduplicated
    perfects, 166; root perfects, 166;
    stem, 143, 150; summary, 189
  —pluperfect, 170

—transitive/intransitive, 15; *velle*, 83,
    177, 263; + acc. and inf., 228;
    bene/male, 231; *mālle,* 263, 308;
    nōlle, 177, 263, 308
—subjunctive: present subjunctive,
    298; imperfect subjunctive, 308
vel, 113. *See also* conjunction
velle, 177, 263, 308

verba cūrandī, (verbs of effecting),
    252
verba postulandi, (indirect commands),
    249
    complements in, 250
    vs. indirect statement, 262
vidērī, 241
vocative, 30, 32, 130, 170, 399